Challenging US Foreign Policy

Challenging US Foreign Policy

America and the World in the Long Twentieth Century

Edited By

Bevan Sewell
Lecturer in American History, School of American & Canadian Studies, University of Nottingham, UK

and

Scott Lucas
Professor in American Studies, Department of American and Canadian Studies, University of Birmingham, UK

Editorial matter, selection and introduction © Bevan Sewell and Scott Lucas 2011
All remaining chapters © their respective authors 2011
All rights reserved. No reproduction, copy or transmission of this publication may be made without written permission.

No portion of this publication may be reproduced, copied or transmitted save with written permission or in accordance with the provisions of the Copyright, Designs and Patents Act 1988, or under the terms of any licence permitting limited copying issued by the Copyright Licensing Agency, Saffron House, 6–10 Kirby Street, London EC1N 8TS.

Any person who does any unauthorized act in relation to this publication may be liable to criminal prosecution and civil claims for damages.

The authors have asserted their rights to be identified as the authors of this work in accordance with the Copyright, Designs and Patents Act 1988.

First published 2011 by
PALGRAVE MACMILLAN

Palgrave Macmillan in the UK is an imprint of Macmillan Publishers Limited, registered in England, company number 785998, of Houndmills, Basingstoke, Hampshire RG21 6XS.

Palgrave Macmillan in the US is a division of St Martin's Press LLC, 175 Fifth Avenue, New York, NY 10010.

Palgrave Macmillan is the global academic imprint of the above companies and has companies and representatives throughout the world.

Palgrave® and Macmillan® are registered trademarks in the United States, the United Kingdom, Europe and other countries

ISBN 978-0-230-24989-9

This book is printed on paper suitable for recycling and made from fully managed and sustained forest sources. Logging, pulping and manufacturing processes are expected to conform to the environmental regulations of the country of origin.

A catalogue record for this book is available from the British Library.

A catalogue record for this book is available from the Library of Congress.

10 9 8 7 6 5 4 3 2 1
20 19 18 17 16 15 14 13 12 11

Printed and bound in Great Britain by
CPI Antony Rowe, Chippenham and Eastbourne

For Helen & Leo
And for Lesley.
For all their love and support.

Contents

Acknowledgements		ix
Notes on the Contributors		x
Introduction Bevan Sewell and Scott Lucas		1
1	Reflex Actions: Colonialism, Corruption and the Politics of Technocracy in the Early Twentieth Century United States Paul Kramer	14
2	Ambassador W. Averell Harriman and the Shift in US Policy toward Moscow after Roosevelt's Death Frank Costigliola	36
3	The Kennan Diaries David Milne	56
4	Ideology, Race and Nonalignment in US Cold War Foreign Relations: or, How the Cold War Racialized Neutralism Without Neutralizing Race Jason Parker	75
5	America's Great Game: The CIA and the Middle East, 1947–67 Hugh Wilford	99
6	The Perfect and Sustainable Road to Economic Development?: The Eisenhower Administration and Latin America Bevan Sewell	113
7	The Defeat of Ernest Lefever's Nomination: Keeping Human Rights on the United States Foreign Policy Agenda Sarah Snyder	136
8	Areas of Concern: Area Studies and the New American Studies John Carlos Rowe	162

9	*Libertas* or *Fri*? On US Liberty, Decline, Freedom and Pluralism *David Ryan*	183
10	The United States and the United Nations: Hegemony, Unilateralism and the Limits of Internationalism *Andrew Johnstone*	205
11	The US War in Iraq: Confronting the Vietnam Analogy *Andrew Priest*	225
12	Domesticating Katrina: Eliding the International Coordinates of a 'Natural' Disaster *Anna Hartnell*	244
13	American Foreign Policy and Women's Rights *Helen Laville*	260
Conclusion *Scott Lucas*		281
Index		297

Acknowledgements

In our addition to our gratitude to all the authors in this volume and to the staff at Palgrave Macmillan, our thanks go to our colleagues at the Universities of Birmingham and Nottingham. Scott Lucas would also like to acknowledge his colleagues and readers at EA WorldView, a news and analysis website which was launched as this book was being developed.

And our thanks to all those who, in discussion and written exchanges, have shown us that the question of power is one which never reaches a final answer.

Notes on the Contributors

John Carlos Rowe is University of South Carolina Associates' Professor of the Humanities and Chair of the Department of American Studies and Ethnicity at the University of Southern California. He is the author of *Henry Adams and Henry James: The Emergence of a Modern Consciousness* (1976), *Through the Custom-House: Nineteenth-Century American Fiction and Modern Theory* (1982), *The Theoretical Dimensions of Henry James* (1984), *At Emerson's Tomb: The Politics of Classic American Literature* (1997), *The Other Henry James* (1998), *Literary Culture and U.S. Imperialism: From the Revolution to World War II* (2000), *The New American Studies* (2002), *Afterlives of Modernism: Liberalism, Transnationalism, and Political Critique* (2011), and *The Cultural Politics of the New American Studies* (2011), as well as over 150 scholarly essays and critical reviews.

Frank Costigliola is Professor in History at the University of Connecticut. He is the author of *Awkward Dominion: American Political, Economic, and Cultural Relations with Europe, 1919–1933* (1984) and *France and the United States: The Cold Alliance Since World War II* (1992). He is currently writing a book on the impact of emotions and of perceived cultural differences in the shaping of US, British, and Soviet foreign policy during and immediately after World War II. The book is entitled *Lost Alliances: How Personal Politics Helped Win World War II and Form the Early Cold War*.

Anna Hartnell is a Lecturer in Contemporary Literature at Birkbeck, University of London. Her research interests centre on representations of race, nation and religion in American culture, and much of her recent work has focused on post-Katrina New Orleans. Her forthcoming book, *Rewriting Exodus: American Futures from Du Bois to Obama*, is to be published in 2011.

Andrew Johnstone is a Lecturer in American History at the University of Leicester. He received his PhD from the University of Birmingham, and is the author of *Dilemmas of Internationalism: The American Association for the United Nations and US Foreign Policy, 1941–1948* (2009). He is also the co-editor (with Helen Laville) of *The US Public and American Foreign*

Policy (2010), and his articles have appeared in *Diplomatic History*, the *Journal of American Studies*, and the *Journal of Transatlantic Studies*. His current project is on internationalism, ideology, and US entry into World War II.

Paul Kramer is an Associate Professor of History at Vanderbilt University. His first book *The Blood of Government: Race, Empire, the United States and the Philippines* explored the imperial politics of race-making between US and Philippine societies in the late nineteenth and early twentieth centuries. The book was awarded the Organization of American Historians' James A. Rawley Prize and the Society for Historians of American Foreign Relations' Stuart L. Bernath Book Prize. He is currently at work on a manuscript on the US imperial politics of race between the 1860s and 1960s.

Helen Laville is a Senior Lecturer in the Department of American and Canadian Studies at the University of Birmingham. She gained her Doctorate in 1998 from the University of Nottingham. Her first book was *Cold War Women* published in 2002 by Manchester University Press. She has published articles on gender and foreign policy, and on the relationship between the US government and private groups. She has co-edited two books which explore the relationship of private groups and public opinion to foreign policy. She is currently researching and writing a monograph on the role of white women's organizations in the implementation of civil rights legislation.

Scott Lucas is Professor of American Studies at the University of Birmingham, UK, and has held posts at University College Dublin, Ireland, American University Beirut, Lebanon, and Theran University, Iran. He is the author of nine books and more than 40 major articles on US and British foreign policy since 1945, intelligence series, public diplomacy, and media. He is also the founder of EA Worldview, a leading web-based provider of news and analysis on international affairs.

David Milne is Senior Lecturer in Political History at the University of East Anglia. His first monograph, *America's Rasputin: Walt Rostow and the Vietnam War* was published in 2008. His work has appeared in the *Journal of Military History, International Affairs, Review of International Studies*, and the *International Journal*. He is currently writing a book provisionally titled *A Universe Still in Progress: Intellectualism in American Diplomacy*.

Jason Parker is an Associate Professor of History at Texas A&M University. His research centres on the interplay of the Cold War and decolonization in US relations with the 'Third World'. He is the author of *Brother's Keeper: The United States, Race, and Empire in the British Caribbean, 1937–1962* (2008). His current projects are a history of US Cold War public diplomacy in the Third World, and a comparative study of postwar federations in the decolonizing European empires.

Andrew Priest is a Lecturer in International Politics at Aberystwyth University. He is the author of *Kennedy, Johnson and NATO: Britain, America and the Dynamics of Alliance, 1962–68* (2006) and several articles and chapters on US foreign policy. He is currently writing a book about the United States and its views of European empires during its rise to power.

David Ryan works in the School of History and is Associate Dean, The Gradate School, University College Cork, Ireland. He is the author and editor of numerous books and articles including *US-Sandinista Diplomatic Relations* (1995), *US Foreign Policy in World History* (2000), *The United States and Europe* (2003), and *Frustrated Empire* 2007). He is the co-editor of *The United States and Decolonization* (2000), *Vietnam in Iraq* (2007), *and America and Iraq* (2009). He is currently completing a book on US Collective Memory and Intervention since 1969.

Bevan Sewell is a Lecturer in American History at the University of Nottingham. He has published articles in *Diplomatic History, The English Historical Review* and *Intelligence and National Security*, and is currently working on a book on US-Latin American relations in the long 1950s.

Sarah B. Snyder is a Lecturer in International History at University College London and specializes in the Cold War, human rights activism, and United States human rights policy. She previously served as postdoctoral fellow at Yale University. She is the author of *Human Rights Activism and the End of the Cold War: A Transnational History of the Helsinki Network*. She has also published in *Cold War History, Diplomacy and Statecraft, Journal of Transatlantic Studies*, and *Journal of American Studies*. She received her PhD from Georgetown University.

Hugh Wilford is Professor of United States History at California State University, Long Beach. He is the author of several books on Cold War American culture and foreign relations, including most recently *The Mighty Wurlitzer: How the CIA Played America* (2008). He is currently writing a book about the CIA and the Middle East.

Introduction

Bevan Sewell and Scott Lucas

Following the terrorist attacks on the US in September, 2001, and the subsequent response of military incursions into Afghanistan and Iraq, much of the discourse about America and its role in the world focused on the issue of Empire. 'Americans overwhelmingly interpreted their government's response to the terrorist attacks on the World Trade Center and the Pentagon,' Richard Immerman writes, 'according to their beliefs about the American empire (it was not one) and liberty (America was its bastion).'[1] This compulsion, with debates about the essence of America and the wider world recurrent in the media and across American society, was structured around an implicit understanding about the notion of American power. Just what kind of power America was and what drove its intellectual identity might be up for debate, but America's capacity to shape a one-way relationship between a dominant US and a pliant world remained unquestioned.[2] American power was not, it seemed, negotiable. Arguably, this has translated into a doubled-edged phenomenon – not only is there a two-dimensional vision of the implementation of US foreign policy, but spheres of discussion are constrained through being tied to this notion of Empire by proponents and critics alike. From Noam Chomsky to Niall Ferguson, from Andrew Bacevich to Max Boot, the recurrent discourse of 'Empire' has set the limits for interrogations of US foreign policy; for policymakers, meanwhile, it has also served as the predominant frame, not as a concept to be engaged but as a legitimizing force underpinning their approach to the wider world. Both George W. Bush and, at the time of writing, Barack Obama have pursued policies born – at least conceptually – out of a mindset that promotes notions of US supremacy and centrality.

The nature of this debate has led to two important simplifications. Firstly, and perhaps most importantly, it has returned contemporary foreign policy debates about the very essence of the US relationship with the wider world to an early Cold War incarnation, one which saw American strength as being posited against an irrational 'other' and which portrayed US pre-eminence and its capacity to project power where it saw fit as a necessary counter-measure. Whether that was an 'Empire by Invitation' or a less harmonious relationship, the idea defined studies of US foreign policy, principally with respect to the start of the Cold War, in a very particular way. Notions of Empire were not set in stone – they could be challenged or disputed – but that they *had* to be is the essential point. Our understanding of American power in the post-1945 era, therefore, has stemmed from these very particular constructions. We understand US power and its role in the world by framing it within the context of the Cold War; similarly, we understand US power and its role in the world since 9/11 by framing it within the context of the War on Terror or the discourse of Empire.[3] Set against such monolithic backdrops, our perceptions of American power make sense. We examine and perceive of it in a two-dimensional way because that is how it has been presented to us.

In the same way that 'Empire' has too often been seen as omnipresent, so the Cold War was deployed to permeate every aspect of post-World War Two foreign affairs. The two debates reinforced each other: the overwhelming dominance of the Cold War context made assumptions about US power – and the nature of that power – understandable. Whether you viewed US power as benevolent or expansionist, the discourse of Empire served as an explanatory framework as the Cold War dominated international history, US policy and the way that US officials perceived that policy.

The need to challenge monolithic constructions of the Cold War, and its central role in US policy, is now being addressed by some scholars who, rather than viewing the Cold War as *the* event of the twentieth century, are arguing that it now needs to be seen as just one event of many during this era.[4] This re-conception would alter our understanding about the basis and nature of American power and American foreign relations during this era. Robbed of previously dominant contexts, scholars would be challenged to examine US foreign policy away from neat categorizations and, instead, consider the history of the twentieth century afresh. In particular, this re-assessment suggests a need to consider in more detail just how the US has interacted with the world, and how its ideas about itself and its role have developed across the period that we might label as 'America as a world power' (1900–2010). As Paul Kramer has argued, once we recognize the fluid nature of US power and its place in the world across this era we can begin to forge a fuller understanding of America's global position.[5] And if these fundamental features of the Cold War can be deconstructed so, in an intellectual sense, can the post-9/11 epoch.

If this framing has been both caused, and supported, by the notion of Empire, so has the second consequence of this construction: the over-simplification of global anti-American sentiments. The post-9/11 context of 'you are either with us or with the terrorists' stymied our understanding of anti-Americanism, sublimated to the idea of an irrational hatred of America, its institutions, and beliefs. They hate us, so the argument went, because we are so good. Many scholars have tried to address this misrepresentation, focusing on the propositions that, first, anti-Americanism is a reaction to US policies rather than an entrenched hatred of the US and, second, that it is possible for this antipathy to exist alongside an abiding sense of kinship between the world and America. Opposition to US actions might well be widespread and tangible, but that does not necessarily sully all that the world believes to be best about America or undermine its hope of an improvement.[6]

Slowly, these works are beginning to redress the balance, presenting anti-Americanism as a fluid, changeable concept that cannot be characterized by simple slogans or formulations. 'What is indisputable,' notes Juan Cole in appraising the field, 'is that the sentiments are not generated by a clash over basic values. It's the foreign policy, stupid.'[7] Other scholars, meanwhile, have taken issue with the idea of the 'anti' in 'anti-Americanism'. Greg Grandin explains, 'What is often taken for anti-Americanism in Latin America is, in fact, a competing version of Americanism.'[8] Greater understanding of 'Americanism' can help in the critique of notions of American power; however, in having to expend so much time on disproving reductionist formulations of anti-Americanism, interrogations of US power have become sidelined. Even the rebuttal of the consequences of the discourse of Empire has reinforced rather than taken down this overarching context. Hence, the assumption that America – for better or worse – possesses the capacity and the will to aggressively project its ideas and interests outward has too often remained unchallenged.[9]

Not only has this discourse framed US power against the weakness or receptiveness of others, it has also rejected any acknowledgment that the US can be constrained and influenced; the idea that 'America' can learn from other nations has been too often pushed to the sidelines. Even now, with the world in the midst of a severe global economic downturn and contrary to much evidence of a reduction in American power, the nature of the debate has not altered. It has, rather, changed tack. Empire, it is now suggested, might be a bit strong as a label; decline is the new buzzword for analysts of US foreign relations.[10] Nevertheless, as the work of scholars like Ian Tyrell demonstrates, the US has been influenced, both positively and negatively, by 'others' throughout its history. Indeed, the very essence of US power – and the way that America interacts with the world – is born out of a much more fluid conception than is often allowed for.[11]

The history of a nation, of course, is often written backwards – starting with the endpoint and framing what comes before as a progression toward that historical terminus.[12] Thus, American Empire and rumors, exaggerated or otherwise, of its potential collapse have come to dominate our understanding of America's history. From the Declaration of Independence, through the westward push toward the Pacific, the Spanish-American War, the Cold War, and the post-1989 re-ordering of the world, the tale of US foreign policy has focused upon explaining how a nation founded on anti-imperial sentiments could become an Empire itself; upon explaining how, and why, America has become so powerful. But what if this is an overstatement? What if the tale of American history is less one of an emerging empire, and more one of a fluid global situation that has consistently seen America exerting its influence on, but also being affected and influenced by, other nations? Analysts may perceive the US to have acted like an Empire at times, but how have US officials viewed power and how have their conceptions of themselves and the world been shaped? Is the process as straightforward as the Empire – and attendant decline, Cold War and War on Terror – discourses suggests?

Admittedly, it is difficult to measure and explain the fluidity of multilateralism and globalization, where borders are porous and the nature of state-to-state relations is permeated by fluctuating interests and ideas that do not always complement each other. Still, this argues for rather than against a re-conceptualization of America's place in the world, one that could work in numerous directions rather than the one-dimensional model of America projecting itself outwards. Moreover, in doing so we connect the American present with emerging works on the American past. Historical studies of American foreign policy have changed dramatically in the last thirty years. No longer concerned solely with the question of who said what to whom, and what happened in certain battles or meetings, the field of diplomatic history has broadened its horizons. Race, gender, religion, and ideology are all now common explanatory frameworks for the course of US foreign relations; the influence that other nations have been able to exert over the US, meanwhile, is now an irrefutable part of the historical tale.[13] However, while this shift has enhanced what we know about US foreign policy there is a gap: while we have come to understand much more about the way that the US has perceived and evaluated other nations, and in particular as to how they have exerted their influence over the policy process, it is less clear that we have advanced as far on the equally important question of how the US perceives itself and its own power.

Traditional models for assessing power, of course, support the idea of American predominance: from World War II onwards, the US has without question been the world's strongest economic, military and cultural force. America produces more, spends more, can destroy more, and projects its interests and ideals more than any other nation. This was true in 1945, and it remains true today. Yet, if the US has been the world's pre-eminent force for the last sixty five years, this has very rarely translated into a foreign policy of unbridled, unilateral supremacy. Even in the wake of 9/11, when US power was arguably at its greatest, the window of unipolar foreign policy was noticeably brief. Wars in Afghanistan and Iraq might have begun under the auspices of American pre-eminence (though in both cases this is arguable), but this soon evaporated as events in both conflicts served to restrain American might. By 2005, in fact, the aggressive parameters of the Bush Doctrine had been replaced by a necessary retrenchment in US thinking. In earlier times, there are a series of examples of limits on US power: Vietnam, of course, is the obvious case study, but it could also be suggested that in both world wars and the Cold War that the US was less an Empire and more of a participant in a fluid international system. America might be a powerful nation; the shape of US power, though, is not born solely from the homeland, and it is certainly influenced by international factors and events.

It must be noted that this is not, perhaps, a phenomenon of which Americans – both in government and in the wider public – have always been aware. At times, such as the aftermath of the Vietnam War, the lessons learnt from other nations and the limits on American power have been obvious; however, on other occasions, the influence of others has been much less evident as US policymakers have become imbued with the hubris so redolent of those who have an innate faith in the power of their nation.[14] To fully appreciate this dynamic, America would need not just to consider its role in the world outside of categorizations like Empire or Cold War; it would also need to re-consider some of its most fundamental principles and ideals, for much of the weight behind

American power stems from the perennial nature of its ideals. Exceptionalism and Manifest Destiny, for example, have exerted a monumental influence over the essence of American identity. The outward projection of the US – and, more importantly, the way we as scholars have understood that process – has been primarily shaped by these constructs. Empire happens because of Manifest Destiny; the Cold War, in some narratives, is an inevitable consequence of American Exceptionalism.[15] As George Herring writes: 'A set of assumed ideas and shared values have determined the way Americans viewed themselves and others and how they dealt with other peoples and responded to and sought to shape events abroad.'[16] These ideals, as Herring suggests, have fostered a collective sense of myopia, blinding America to the beliefs and principles of other nations, and consistently measuring them and appraising them by their own imagined standard.

Inevitably, this has led to an endemic failure by US officials over the last one hundred and twenty years to negotiate the difference between American ideals and interests and those of other nations. Even during a moment when discussions and negotiations were the event, such as an international conference or a summit, the US standpoint has often been rigidly defined and ideological. Some give and take might be necessary; but core American ideals and interests would remain unshakeable. In day-to-day diplomacy, this disparity has only widened as America's sense of itself governed the way it acted toward other nations. To be clear: this has not prevented other nations from influencing the US, but it has created a dichotomy between the theory of how the US sees its role in the world and the reality of the actual international system.

This leaves us, then, with a dialectical tension. On the one hand, the US has clearly been influenced by, drawn lessons from and reacted to other nation-states and their role in the world. It has sought to influence others, we might argue, because it recognizes the influence that other nations have had upon it. On the other hand, and in a somewhat illogical sense, this has not necessarily influenced the way the US conceives of itself and its policies. Its actions might well be affected by other countries; the US vision of the world system, though, is not. The core ideologies underpinning US foreign policy have remained unaltered. Of course, this raises a seemingly irreconcilable problem: how can we explain this gap between 'reality' and 'ideas'? To solve it, we need to accept that ideology – though undoubtedly a major force in shaping US views – is not the sole determinant of US foreign policy. It undoubtedly exerts a significant influence and shapes the way that US policymakers have viewed themselves and the world. Even so, events, the nature of international relations, and rational interests of nation-states can predominate over ideology. The US may well conceive of itself as a power without equal, either in moral or in political, economic, and cultural measurements; that does not mean it could, and now can, act like one.

The essays in this collection, seek to reconsider the role of US foreign policy in light of this argument – eschewing easy categorizations such as Empire, Globalization and Cold War, in order to demonstrate the more fluid state of American foreign affairs. They do not seek to offer a 'new' categorization; instead, they examine US policies in their actual settings and outside of the constraints of reductionist frameworks. Doing so, they also avoid labels such as primacy, decline and dominance; US policy, the essays contained here argue, should not necessarily be viewed as being ascendant or in decline. On the one hand, the power of American exceptionalism remains undiminished and continues to guide the way that the US has presented itself with respect to the world. On the other hand, the US has clearly drawn lessons from other nations, has been constrained by the practicalities of the world system and the expectations of others, and has generally adopted a more pliant stance toward the wider world than the imperial discourse suggests.

This collection will depict instances of US foreign policy within this context. They will chart an important theme in our understanding of America's diplomatic history: that US power – and, indeed, our understanding of that term – is driven by an amalgamation of domestic and international factors. In that sense, therefore, this is a book not about America *in* the World, but America *and* the World.

To do this, the book is split into two sections – the first considering historical case studies of US power, the second adopting a more contemporary standpoint. In the opening chapter, Paul Kramer charts the evolution of a debate within the US about the possible benefits and dangers of American imperialism in the late nineteenth/early twentieth century. This debate, he argues, was carried out by two differing sides: those who argued that an American Empire in the Philippines could serve as a valuable training ground for American bureaucrats and provide powerful lessons for the US governmental system vs. those who argued that the dangers of Empire would corrupt American conceptions of governance and civil service.

Following from this, Frank Costigliola examines the effect that government service in Moscow during World War Two had on a number of key officials, most notably Averell Harriman. Costigliola suggests that Harriman's animosity toward the Soviets, a key factor in Harry Truman's ramping up of US-Soviet tensions, was the result of his experiences in Moscow. First-hand experience of Soviet unfriendliness, coupled with anecdotal evidence of myriad other examples, persuaded Harriman that US-Soviet cooperation in the future was impossible.

Building on this approach, David Milne's chapter examines the diaries of George Kennan – one of the foremost architects of America's Cold War, but a man whose role as an intellectual has all too often been overlooked. Milne argues that the recently opened diaries demonstrate Kennan's perceptiveness of the global situation after 1945 and his views on the dynamics of key relationships during the Cold War. His assessments of others in the world – the Soviets, obviously, but also those in the developing world – provide a compelling insight into the American mindset.

The next three chapters all examine these issues in different regions of the world. Firstly, Jason Parker studies the role of the non-aligned movement (NAM) (or neutralist) in the Cold War, and argues that it needs to be evaluated afresh. Too often, he contends, the NAM has been viewed as being racially distinct, that is, non-white. But, he continues, this was not always the case: initially, US fears about nonalignment in the Cold War stemmed not from its racial connotations but from the fear that it might take root in Europe. It was only in the mid-1950s, and following the Bandung Conference of 1955, that NAM assumed a racial identity to match its ideological one, and that was an identity forged by the NAM itself rather than imposed by policymakers in Washington.

Secondly, Hugh Wilford challenges notions about the CIA, in particular, its role in the Middle East. The Agency, Wilford notes, has often been seen in a one-dimensional sense – seeking to undermine undesirable regimes and conspiring in the Middle East against a succession of Arab States. Yet this was not always so. In the CIA's early years, Wilford's chapter demonstrates, the CIA formulated an effective network in the Arab states, peopled by Middle Eastern specialists and founded on a deep sensitivity toward the region; the CIA in this period had an uncommon degree of cooperation with Arab states.

Thirdly, Bevan Sewell examines the Eisenhower administration's economic policies toward Latin America. Rather than being wholly subsumed by fighting the Cold War or quelling Latin American economic nationalism, he suggests that Eisenhower's approach toward the region can instead be characterized by an ideology of development that remained fixed throughout the President's two terms. Though this was rarely the sole motivating factor in determining the administration's approach, it cast a significant shadow over inter-American relations and explains why no major changes to economic policy were forthcoming in this period.

Finally in this section, Sarah Snyder's chapter examines the role that perceptions of human rights in foreign policy have played on American politics. During the early years of the Reagan administration, the nomination of Ernest Lefever as head of the State Department's Bureau of Human Rights and Humanitarian Affairs led to a substantial debate about how important human rights was to America's image of itself. The nomination of an avowed opponent of human rights to a key position led to a rapid mobilization of Congressional opposition, deeply concerned about the picture of America that would be projected abroad.

The second section begins with John Carlos Rowe's chapter on the relationship between US national identity and American Studies as an academic discipline. Previously American Studies scholarship had been criticized for buying into notions about American exceptionalism, but this has mutated in recent years to a thinly veiled attack on the subject for being anti-American in the way it challenges conceptions of American identity. Consequently, American Studies as a discipline – and the critiques it has recently faced – cut to the heart of how we understand American power and its role in the world.

This is followed by David Ryan, who examines the way that the rise of neo-conservatism in the 1970s – some of which, of course, fed into the Bush era mentioned above – was constructed on foundations of a particular definition of 'liberty' that, contrary to its intentions, accelerated the decline it was intended to prevent. Visions of America and its place in the world, Ryan argues, distorted the reality of the situation they faced, leading to unforeseen consequences.

Andrew Johnstone, meanwhile, explores the evolving relationship that the US has had with the United Nations. Oftentimes, he argues, the US stance toward the UN has been one of 'unilateralism' – of effectively acting irrespective of the position taken by the UN itself. But, he continues, this has been matched by a retreat to multilateralism – and, indeed, engagement with the US – when the ever-apparent limits of American primacy have been recognized.

The next chapter is Andrew Priest's examination of analogies between the wars in Vietnam and Iraq. Rather than contrast the two wars in search of similarities, he critiques the discourse that has surrounded Vietnam-Iraq comparisons. Public intellectuals on both the right and left, he argues, have consistently been constrained in their views on Iraq by their views on Vietnam, and the perpetual back-and-forth as to whether Vietnam was a good or bad war has shaped the discourse over Iraq. The inevitable outcome, he suggests, has been a severe restriction of the ways in which the two wars are understood and the application of lessons from the past to the present.

The final two chapters of the book deal with very different manifestations and discourses on US power in the contemporary era. Anna Hartnell deals with the image of America, and American power, in a domestic context. Her chapter looks at the aftermath of Hurricane Katrina in 2005, with efforts to 'contain' the narrative of the hurricane to stymie debates about the state of the nation. The innate resonance of this local situation on a global scale, she argues, depicts the inherent problems of a globalized world. America is judged, she suggests, not just by what it does abroad but also by what it does at home. American power – and, importantly, the way it is received – can be undermined by the shocking spectacle that came out of New Orleans after Katrina. How can America shape the world, Hartnell asks, if it cannot look after its own citizens?

Finally, Helen Laville tackles the role of women's rights in American foreign policy. Like the issue of human rights, the desire to portray America as a firm supporter of universal female equality has been a resonant theme in US policy. This has led to a complex relationship – one that simultaneously sees the US government appropriating women's rights for its own ends and, on the other hand, women's rights groups trying to use the relationship with the state to pursue their own goals and objectives.

Ultimately, the chapters in this collection point to a complicated relationship between the US and the wider world that needs to be considered outside of sweeping terms such as Empire, War on Terror and Decline. Instead, it points to much more fluid, less easily categorized understandings of America and the world. As John Thompson has argued in examining the reach of Wilsonianism – another oft-invoked and sweeping term – there is a perpetual tension at play in US thinking, between how the nation appears abroad and how it appears at home. 'The tensions implicit in what has become known as Wilsonianism,' Thompson writes, 'do highlight a persistent dilemma facing American policy-makers. They have all been fated to wrestle with the same fundamental problem that confronted – and eventually defeated – Woodrow Wilson: how to reconcile the external reality of a diverse, conflict-strewn world with the internal reality of American opinion.'[17] It is that problem, as Thompson terms it, that is at the heart of US foreign policy discussions and which has been throughout the era of America as a great power. It is the same problem, moreover, that has confronted Barack Obama since he took office in 2009. Indeed, it was apparent within his inaugural address, which, in attempting to fuse the portrayal of engagement and idealism abroad with they type of strength required for a domestic audience, merely reconfirmed the presence of this abiding tension.

> As for our common defense, we reject as false the choice between our safety and our ideals. Our Founding Fathers, faced with perils that we can scarcely imagine, drafted a charter to assure the rule of law and the rights of man, a charter expanded by the blood of generations. Those ideals still light the world, and we will not give them up for expedience's sake. And so to all the other peoples and governments who are watching today, from the grandest capitals to the small village where my father was born, know that America is a friend of each nation and every man, woman, and child who seeks a future of peace and dignity, and we are ready to lead once more… guided by these principles once more, we can meet those new threats that demand even greater effort, even greater cooperation and understanding between nations. We will begin to responsibly leave Iraq to its people and forge a hard-earned peace in Afghanistan. With old friends and former foes, we will work tirelessly to lessen the nuclear threat and roll back the specter of a warming planet. We will not apologize for our way of life, nor will we waver in its defense. And for those who seek to advance their aims by inducing terror and slaughtering innocents, we say to you now that our spirit is stronger and cannot be broken. You cannot outlast us, and we will defeat you.[18]

Notes

1 Richard Immerman, *Empire for Liberty: A History of American Imperialism from Benjamin Franklin to Paul Wolfowitz* (Princeton, New Jersey: Princeton University Press, 2010), 234.
2 On this, see Andrew Bacevich, *The Limits of Power: The End of American Exceptionalism* (New York: Henry Holt, 2009).
3 Melvyn Leffler, *A Preponderance of Power: National Security, the Truman Administration, and the Cold War* (Stanford, CA: Stanford University Press, 1991); John Lewis Gaddis, *Strategies of Containment: A Critical Appraisal of American National Security Policy during the Cold War*, Revised Edition (New York: Oxford University Press, 2005); Andrew Bacevich, *American Empire: The Realities and Consequences of US Diplomacy* (Cambridge, Mass.: Harvard University Press, 2004); Timothy Lynch and Rob Singh, *After Bush: The Case for Continuity*

12 *Introduction*

   in American Foreign Policy (Cambridge, UK: Cambridge University Press, 2008).
4 Odd Arne Westad, 'The Cold War and the International History of the Twentieth Century', in Melvyn Leffler and Odd Arne Westad, eds., *The Cambridge History of the Cold War*, Vol. I (Cambridge, UK: Cambridge University Press, 2010), 1–8; Niall Ferguson, Charles Maier, Erez Manela and Daniel Sargent, eds., *The Shock of the Global: The 1970s in Perspective* (Cambridge, Mass.: Harvard University Press, 2010); Matthew Connolly, *Fatal Misconception: The Struggle to Control World Population* (Cambridge, Mass.: Belknap Press of Harvard University Press, 2008).
5 Paul Kramer, 'Is the World Our Campus? International Students and US Global Power in the Long Twentieth Century', *Diplomatic History*, Vol. 33, No. 5 (November 2009), 775–807; Jason Parker, '"Made-in-America Revolutions"?: The "Black University" and the American Role in the Decolonization of the Black Atlantic', *Journal of American History*, Vol. 96, No. 3 (December 2009), 727–51.
6 See, for example, Max Paul Friedman, 'Anti-Americanism and U.S. Foreign Relations', *Diplomatic History*, Vol. 32, No. 4 (September 2008), 497–514.
7 Juan Cole, 'Anti-Americanism: It's the Policies', *American Historical Review* Vol. 111, No. 4 (October 2006), 1120–9; John Esposito, 'It's the Policy, Stupid: Political Islam and US Foreign Policy', *Harvard International Review*. Accessed at: http://hir.harvard.edu/index.php?page=article&id=1453 May 6 2010.
8 Greg Grandin, 'Your Americanism and Mine: Americanism and Anti-Americanism in the Americas', *American Historical Review*, Vol. 111, No. 4 (October 2006), 1047; Alan McPherson, 'Americanism Against American Empire', in Michael Kazin and Joseph McMartin, eds., *Americanism: New Perspectives on the History of an Ideal* (Chapel Hill: University of North Carolina Press, 2006), 169–91.
9 Niall Ferguson, *Colossus: The Rise and Fall of the American Empire* (London: Penguin, 2004); David Ryan, *Frustrated Empire: US Foreign Policy since 9/11* (London: Pluto Books, 2008); Lloyd Gardner and Marilyn Young, *The New American Empire: A 21st Century Teach-In on US Foreign Policy* (New York: The New Press, 2005); Lloyd Gardner, *The Long Road to Baghdad: A History of US Foreign Policy from the 1970s to the Present* (New York: The New Press, 2008); Immerman, *Empire of Liberty*; Bacevich, *American Empire*.
10 Niall Ferguson, 'Complexity and Collapse: Empires on the Edge of Chaos', *Foreign Affairs*, Vol. 89, No. 2 (March/April 2010), 18–32; Paul Kennedy, *The Rise and Fall of the Great Powers: Economic Change and Military Conflict, 1500–2000* (London: Fontana Press, 1989).
11 Ian Tyrell, *Transnational Nation: United States History in Global Perspective since 1789* (London: Palgrave, 2007).
12 David Reynolds, *Empire of Liberty: America, A New History* (London: Penguin, 2008).
13 Joel Isaac, 'The Human Sciences in Cold War America', *The Historical Journal*, Vol. 50, No. 3 (2007), 725–46; Thomas Zeiler, 'A Diplomatic History Bandwagon', *Journal of American History*, Vol. 95, No. 4 (March 2008), 1053–73.
14 See, for example, Jeremi Suri, 'Henry Kissinger and American Grand Strategy', in Fredrik Logevall and Andrew Preston, eds., *Nixon in the World: American*

Foreign Relations, 1969–1977 (New York: Oxford University Press, 2008), 67–85; for a time when limits on US power were less recognized, at least in the minds of US officials, Michael Latham, *Modernization as Ideology: American Social Science and 'Nation Building' in the Kennedy Era* (Chapel Hill: University of North Carolina Press, 2000); Seth Jacobs, *America's Miracle Man in Vietnam: Ngo Dinh Diem, Religion, Race, and US Intervention in Southeast Asia* (Durham, NC: Duke University Press, 2004).
15. There are swathes of work on these topics. But for excellent introductions: Anders Stephanson, *Manifest Destiny: American Expansion and the Empire of Right* (New York: Hill and Wang, 1995); Michael Hunt, *Ideology and US Foreign Policy* (New Haven, Connecticut: Yale University Press, 1987).
16. George Herring, *From Colony to Superpower: US Foreign Relations since 1776* (New York: Oxford University Press, 2008), 2.
17. John Thompson, 'Wilsonianism: The Dynamics of a Conflicted Concept', *International Affairs*, Vol. 86, Issue 1 (January 2010), 47; on the nexus between international affairs and domestic interests, Campbell Craig and Fredrik Logevall, *America's Cold War: The Politics of Insecurity* (Cambridge, Mass.: Belknapp Press of Harvard University Press, 2010); Robert Dallek, *The American Style of Foreign Policy: Cultural Politics and Foreign Affairs* (New York: Knopf, 1983).
18. Inaugural Address by President Barack Obama, January 20 2009, *Public Papers of the Presidents of the United States 2009*. Accessed at: http://www.presidency.ucsb.edu/ws/index ob May 8 2010.

1
Reflex Actions: Colonialism, Corruption and the Politics of Technocracy in the Early Twentieth Century United States

Paul Kramer

In August 1898, a forty-two year old political scientist at Princeton University, a conservative Southern Presbyterian with a somewhat provincial air, was brought suddenly to the edge of an intellectual and political crisis. Woodrow Wilson had tracked events of the previous months closely as the United States defeated Spain in Cuba and at Manila Bay, and found himself perplexed. He took out his memorandum pad and at the top of a page wrote: 'What Ought We to Do?' Beneath, he unspooled a meditation on the recent war and its potential impact on American life. 'A brief season of war has deeply changed our thought,' he reflected, 'and has altered, it may be permanently, the conditions of our national life.' With the armistice with Spain on the horizon, and the United States moving towards the control of a far-flung colonial empire in the Caribbean and Pacific, Wilson noted to himself: 'We cannot return to the point whence we set out. The scenes, the stage upon which we act, are changed. We have left the continent which has hitherto been our only field of action and have gone out upon the seas, where the nations are rivals and we cannot live or act apart.' Before too long, Wilson had gathered a confident sense that this wider 'field of action' meant good things for American political institutions, but in mid-1898, he found himself at a puzzling crossroads.[1]

Wilson was not alone in his uneasiness about what colonial rule might mean for American politics, as a rich historiography of US anti-colonialism has made clear.[2] This essay explores the ways this debate on the United States' global role played out among a group of reformers usually associated exclusively with 'domestic' politics: civil service reformers who, like Wilson (who counted himself among their number) sought to construct a new administrative state that could insulate American governance from what they saw as the corrupting influence of political parties and private interests. In the years after 1898, these reformers asked probing questions about US colonial empire that were also, both incidentally and self-consciously, questions about the ways that 'domestic' US institutions interacted with the global environment. Would colonial empire distract or magnify reform impulses? Would new colonial governments magnetize the very malefactors that reformers had hoped to banish from political institutions, or would the massing of state power that accompanied colonial rule allow reformers to paint, on a canvas (in theory) emptied of institutional competitors, hopes of expert-led governance that might, in turn, propel domestic reform?

The political stakes were high, for at least two reasons. First was the ideological fragility of overseas colonialism and the depth of contestation over its advent. While traditionally reduced to a 'great aberration' or what might be called splendid littleness, 1898 and its aftermath, to the contrary, prompted one of the most sustained and contentious debates Americans have ever had about the ends and means of US participation in global affairs, and one that many observers at the time experienced as one of ragged urgency: Wilson at his memo pad.[3] Colonialism's advocates did not, at least initially, hold the upper hand. It was true that narratives of 'Manifest Destiny' had marked out a universal, global ambit which could, in both theory and practice, contain and legitimate novel colonial undertakings.[4] But, as the ideologies of a settler-colonial republic, they were simultaneously tethered to contiguous territory, not built to cross oceans. One of the key signs of the territorial underpinnings of nineteenth century imperial ideology was the fact that it was 1898, rather than the North American territorializing project itself, that had raised the anxious specter of 'imperialism': as 'anti-imperialist' critics passionately asserted, overseas projections of military and colonial power threatened 'militarism' and declining liberty at 'home.' In light of these challenges, colonialists were compelled to develop new, amphibious arguments that could bridge territorial and transoceanic empires historically, politically and morally. In the short term, colonialists won most of the key battles, but only by addressing and neutralizing many of their opponents' demands, and the struggle's outcome was far from foreordained.

Second was the centrality of corruption discourse to US politics at the turn of the twentieth century. While reformers debated its root and resolution, something stank in modernizing America: while fear of 'corruption' was a long-standing element of republican discourse, late-nineteenth century reformers developed and relied upon 'corruption' in making sense of urban-industrial society, and new configurations of corporate power and mass, party-based politics: among other advantages, 'corruption' channeled moral thunder while externalizing injustice and exploitation from the proper workings of industrial capitalist society. For civil service reformers, anti-corruption meant the insulation of state institutions from what they saw as the nefarious influence of party politics through the 'merit system' of examination and promotion. Civil service reform crossed over loosely into elite and middle-class literary and academic public opinion, particularly on the East Coast, where it participated in strong transatlantic and Anglo-American networks. Reformers would be ridiculed for elitism, snobbery and effeminacy – as 'snivel service' advocates unsuited to the rigors of 'manly' rough and tumble of party politics – but they also commanded wide authority in the public sphere, occupying prominent positions in the academic, literary and journalistic worlds.[5] Their take on US colonialism mattered far beyond their numbers, particularly given their status as self-conscious conservatives confronted with what was widely regarded as a 'revolution' in the United States' relationship to the wider world: for reformers and those who heeded their cautions, the moral measure of colonialism itself would be whether it enlarged and deepened, or staunched or reversed, the 'corruption' at the heart of American politics.

If the stakes of this struggle were high for historical actors, what is in it for historians? This essay pursues a number of distinct historiographic goals. It tracks a political-institutional thread of the 'imperialism' debate that has been relatively unexplored relative to questions of exceptionalism, race and history.[6] It reveals an imperial dimension to the transatlantic crossings of reform ideas discussed by Daniel Rodgers: in discussing how best to administer the colonies, colonialist reformers turned to British imperial history, in ways not dissimilar to the ways Rodgers' social-democratic reformers drew inspiration and models from contemporary European reform experiments.[7] It helps explain in a preliminary way the origins of the administrative architecture of the colonial states themselves: the building of civil service regimes in both the Philippines and Puerto Rico, the direct result of these reformers' actions, had long-term implications for both societies' politics.[8] Finally, this history can be seen as an opening and defining round in a century-long debate Americans conducted about where exactly the boundary stood between the 'outsides' and 'insides' of US politics, and about how political change flowed across it, debates that only intensified with the growth of US global power in the twentieth century. How did a national polity navigate through a world in which it could no longer 'live or act apart'? Did stepping out onto a global 'stage,' as Wilson had put it, come with the power to dictate stage directions, or did it mean being subject to the dictates of others?

On one level, what was surprising was that many civil service reformers had qualms about overseas colonialism after 1898. If empire was defined in terms of the top-down exercise of unaccountable power, this was not something that, in and of itself, many reformers had a problem with. Indeed, there was a strong elective affinity between imperial and civil service ways of thinking about politics, whether it came to governance by elites, the insulation of power from lower orders or the narration of success through racialized languages of hygiene and 'purity.' In both instances, the disenfranchisement of ignorant, irresponsible and disorderly subjects – racialized differently in both metropolitan and colonial instances – was required to protect them and the larger social order they jeopardized.

Empire had, in fact, long played a key role in the imaginations of US civil reformers. Alongside the strong resonance between imperial and civil service political verticality, there were two principal reasons for this. First, US civil service reformers were connected through dense, transatlantic ties to British counterparts who moved within a self-consciously 'imperial' state with global reach.[9] Second, whether they called it an 'empire' or not, US reformers themselves operated within a sprawling and growing continental and overseas empire whose extension raised thorny problems: how to guarantee the 'purity' of a state that continued to burst the bounds of scrutiny and regulation? It was for both these reasons that Britain's Indian Civil Service was turned to by American reformers as exemplary of civil service governance in general. Take, for example, the two chapters dedicated to the Indian colonial state in Dorman B. Eaton's 1880 *Civil Service in Great Britain*, a foundational text for the US movement. For Eaton, British rule under the East India Company had been one of 'pillage and spoils'; its aristocratic patronage politics meant the appointment of incompetent favorites. Reform had come in the shape of the 36th and 37th clauses of the 1853 India Act, which required open competition between candidates and two years' special training for Indian service. The resulting system was 'unsurpassed in justice and purity' not merely 'among all instances of foreign domination' but 'even as compared with the domestic administration of the leading States.' For Eaton, India's civil service had played a critical role in securing social and political control. The earlier patronage system had failed to 'command the respect of the more intelligent portion of the people of India' and to 'overawe the unruly classes,' leading to 'a hotbed of abuses' that had ultimately sparked the Indian uprising of 1857. Post-1857 imperial order vindicated the service, explaining how 'a little band of a few thousand, scattered over a vast empire' had succeeded in 'holding in obedience nearly one hundred and ninety millions of people of different races, castes and religions.' It had been responsible for 'the safety of an empire'; upon it depended 'the prosperity and safety of England and India alike.'[10]

Understood in this way, civil service politics was not only congruent with but fully realized in colonial settings. And if an empire's measure was, in part, how well it ran its civil service, a state's measure was, in part, how 'clean' its empire was. The problem was that, run in either direction, the Americans fared badly. American reformers repeatedly contrasted Britain's Indian service with the corrupt, ineffectual governance of their own imperial fringes, where politicians parceled out to their incompetent cronies either consular positions or Indian agencies, the latter identified as 'the Rock of Ages for ship-wrecked politicians' by reformer Hebert Welsh.[11] Senator George F. Hoar (later the leading Senate anti-colonialist) lamented that England had managed to train a 'race of gentlemen to govern well her three hundred and fifty millions of subjects,' while the United States had not governed Alaska, with its 'two hundred and fifty thousand Indian dependents even decently.'[12] Some projected these failures onto a hypothetical US colonial state overseas. Were the United States to acquire 'dependencies,' James Bryce warned in 1888, administrative posts there would 'certainly be jobbed, and the dependent country itself probably maladministered'; the government's work 'of this kind' had already been 'badly done' and had 'given rise to scandals.'[13]

One way to think about reformers' sharp, mutually distorting contrasts between British and US imperial administration is in spatial terms, as ideological, comparative maps of metropole and periphery. The Americans, reformers widely agreed, let their empire outrun reform efforts: even as 'good government' consolidated, borderlands of failed statehood proliferated just beyond its edges, threatening the whole. By contrast, it was a commonplace among reformers that Britons had tried and tested their civil service experiment first in India, and then imported it to the metropole: empire was the space where reform was forged, not dissipated. The 'first example of its kind,' wrote Eaton, the reform of the Indian civil service had involved a 'clearing of the way for the introduction of the merit system, pure and simple, into civil administration in the home government.'[14] The United States dumped corruption abroad, in other words; Britain reformed itself inward.

This narrative of mid-nineteenth century British imperial reform from the 'outside' in, encapsulated in the phrase 'reflex action' (or 'reflex influence') proved to be a stalwart of US colonialist argument after 1898.[15] Its proponents, among them many civil service reformers, implicitly called on their audiences to share two spatio-political assumptions. One was that peripheries pushed back: that rather than simply representing the latest place that the metropole had transplanted itself (for better or worse) empire's edges remade the whole. The question of what difference a society's edges made was not, as such, so new: in one sense, Frederick Jackson Turner's frontier thesis was 'reflex action' thinking *par excellence*. But a second, newer sense suggested that borderlands could be remade into spaces of exceptional order precisely because they were beyond the pressures and constraints (understood as corruptions and contaminations) of metropolitan politics. Both spatial frameworks raised the question of whether you commanded your peripheries, or were commanded by them, and to what end.

These questions were raised sharply by the US invasions of Cuba, Puerto Rico and Manila in the middle months of 1898, events which prompted bewildered responses among scholars, observers and reformers of American politics. Constitutional historian Francis Newton Thorpe called the developments 'novel, sudden, tempting, and also disturbing.' Stanford University President David Starr Jordan, speaking of a 'great world crisis,' inquired of 'the reflex effect of great victories, suddenly realized strength, the patronizing applause, the ill-concealed envy of great nations, the conquest of strange territories, the raising of our flag beyond the seas.' Such experiences were 'new to us... un-American [and] contrary to our traditions'; they were also 'delicious' and 'intoxicating.'[16]

For civil service reformers, a great deal of discomfort attached to the sense that colonial empire had yanked the United States' fragmentary civil service, suddenly and unwillingly, into a global spotlight. They imagined world politics as a kind of test before European examiners – perhaps not so different from a civil service exam – in which powerful empires established the criteria for membership, authority and power, and rising ones studied dutifully, competed and won promotion. Success or failure in the making of a colonial civil service was a key element in the recognition of a nation's 'fitness.' The US's notorious state and municipal governments – conveyed most famously in Bryce's *American Commonwealth* – were bad enough, but corruption at an 'imperial' level, under national jurisdiction, would bring international discredit to the United States as a whole. It did not help that the Philippines, for example, was not situated in 'a remote corner of the earth like Alaska,' as Edward Bourne put it, where 'failure would be hidden or unnoticed' but lay 'at the very meeting place of nations,' where US policy would be 'under a white light of publicity'; Europe's 'most energetic and ambitious powers' would be 'our neighbors and critics.'[17] Some commentators welcomed this new, nervous self-awareness. An editorial in the *Atlantic Monthly* saw this 'consciousness of world influence' as the Spanish-Cuban-American War's 'best result.' Where earlier civil service reform had been 'inconspicuous,' the fact that officials must now be chosen for 'important posts, upon which the eyes of the whole world will rest,' would attract greater 'public attention' to the issue.[18]

There was also unease in the fact that the civil service leadership split messily over the colonial question. Colonialists counted among their ranks Theodore Roosevelt, the crusading anti-machine Governor of New York and later Vice-President and President, Massachusetts Senator Henry Cabot Lodge, and Indiana reformer William Dudley Foulke. The anti-colonialists included Carl Schurz, President of the National Civil-Service Reform League (NCSRL), lawyer Moorfield Storey, Indian policy reformer Herbert Welsh, Massachusetts Senator George Frisbee Hoar and Baltimore-based reformer Charles Bonaparte. Between these two poles were many who were uncertain of how reform and colonial empire intersected with each other. Political tensions were evident in the annual meetings of the NCSRL; in Schurz's annual Presidential address in December 1898, the same month as the signing of the Treaty of Paris ceding Spain's colonies to the United States, for example, he cautiously asserted (even as discussion raged among reformers), that it was 'not the [moment] for discussing the question of whether it is desirable or not for this Republic to possess colonial dependencies.' Schurz, an anti-colonialist, praised Roosevelt as a 'champion of civil service reform,' bracketing 'whatever other respects some of us may differ with him.'[19] Forced in 1900 to choose between McKinley, who had embarked on a colonial policy and failed to live up to his civil service promises, and Bryan, an anti-colonialist and opponent of the merit system, Schurz supported Bryan, then stepped down from the NCSRL presidency to prevent the movement from dividing on the 'imperial' question.

Finally, as reformers attempted to make sense of colonialism's meaning for their effort, it did not help that the Secretary of War had, beginning in early May 1898, proposed the suspension of civil service rules for wartime employees, resulting in the passage of a clause in war legislation which authorized War Department officials to appoint clerks and subordinates, as the NCSRL organ *Good Government* put it, 'without examination of any sort and for whatever reasons they chose'; according to the journal, five hundred appointments had been made in the Department's Washington offices, and several thousand outside of it. These 'temporary' or 'emergency' appointments aroused the scrutiny and political pressure of civil service reformers, and may have played a role in associating colonial imperatives and the evasion of civil service regulations, for at least some.[20]

The abrupt exposure of an incomplete system, a divided leadership, an early sense that politicians might end-run civil service regulations during imperial 'emergencies': all these prompted a wide-ranging debate about colonial empire among civil service reformers, and a colonialist/anti-colonialist debate about governance, in American reform, academic and literary circles during the first years of the twentieth century. The Civic Federation called a special conference in Saratoga Springs, New York in August 1898, on 'The Foreign Policy of the United States.' Arguments appeared in elite periodicals such as the *Atlantic* and *North American Review*, in academic publications like the *Political Science Quarterly*, and in social-political venues like the meetings of the Academy of American Political and Social Sciences, whose 1900 conference centered on US foreign policy. Scholars and government agencies published detailed comparative surveys of colonial government, and colonial civil services specifically.[21] In these settings, questions of colonial rule became fundamentally interwoven with the struggle for 'pure,' efficient administration. And as the debate unfolded, two overlapping and competing senses of 'corruption' emerged and, with them, very different ways of imagining the relationship between corruption and 'empire.' One, a republican sense, defined corruption philosophically and historically: as the tragic end-stage in the cyclical rise and fall of civic virtue to which republics, particularly over-extended ones, fell prey. A second, technocratic sense – at the center of civil service politics – defined corruption institutionally, as illegitimate influence and control over and profit from state agencies, such as the preferential granting of licenses and contracts or the abuse of government for private gain. The post-1898 struggle would be about the merits of US colonialism with respect to reform, but it would also, inseparably, be about the relative authority of republican and technocratic modes of understanding for making sense of the United States' role in the world.

Colonialism's opponents and skeptics turned to both republican and technocratic arguments about corruption in making their case. Republican political languages, beaten back on many fronts by the turn of the century, came roaring back in the mouths of anti-colonialists. Senator Henry M. Teller of Colorado, for example, expressed his faith that

Americans would not adopt a policy 'that threatens the death of the Republic or even great danger to it.'[22] Senator Hoar feared empire's venom: 'what poison is to the human frame the abandonment of our great doctrine of liberty will be to the Republic.'[23] Corruption was crucial to these republican arguments: militarized governance and overseas conquests translated into the erosion and contamination of Americans' defining freedoms, and moral-political rot. For Carl Schurz, democratic empire was a paradox that 'cannot fail to breed corruption and decay.'[24] While a monarchy's arbitrary treatment of subjects was 'suited to its nature,' a democracy could not exercise this type of power 'without doing a thing utterly incompatible with the fundamental reason of its own being...'. South Dakota Senator Richard Pettigrew, a Silver Republican, enlisted a 'reflex action' narrative for anti-colonial purposes. 'I believe the reflex action upon our people of the conquest of other peoples and their government, against their will,' he wrote, 'has undermined the free institutions of this country, and has already resulted in the destruction of the republic.'[25]

For some anti-colonialists, the toll empire took on reform was one of attention: it distracted public opinion away from pressing questions of domestic reform. Speaking in 1899, William Lloyd Garrison, Jr. condemned what he called the 'stampede of the reformers' towards war, which necessarily blinded them to 'the high-handed doings of the politicians who rule New York.' David Starr Jordan agreed. 'The glory of war turns our attention from civil affairs,' he wrote; the 'true patriotism' that always undergirded reform declined as 'war spirit' rose. Until this 'war fever' passed, there was 'no use of talking of better financial methods, of fairer adjustments of taxes, of wiser administration of affairs...'. Distraction from reform was the by-product of war, but it could also be a strategy. A self-conscious politics of diversion had been used successfully in ancient Rome, where the 'pomp of imperialism' had been deployed to 'put off the day of final reckoning.'[26]

Many critics in the civil service reform movement expressed their fears of corruption in technocratic terms: colonial states would provide refuge to the very forces the reformers had sought to banish. Speaking in December 1898 before the NCSRL, Eaton darkly prophesied that the unchecked forces of corruption would rush hungrily out to the new colonies and return home engorged and in magnified form. Politicians of all parties – from the great bosses to 'every little Blarneyville and Patronageville' – would 'hustle and bribe to secure the offices and spoils of these dependencies... wrangling and clamoring over the appointments.' Meanwhile, '[u]nscrupulous corporations' would attempt 'to purchase plantations, to monopolize docks, to acquire mines, to make and manage railroads, [and] to get control of the forests and fisheries.' These corporate forces, strengthened by colonial franchises, would 'bitterly oppose an honest, stable and competent Civil Service,' as it would 'interfere with their schemes and their illegitimate gains.' Presenting 'abundant nominees of their own for every office,' they would soon become 'a mighty power in Congress and at the White House.'[27]

Others feared the consequences of political corruption for the United States' new subjects. Charles Bonaparte, for example, imagined the United States 'holding by the sword a vast vassal empire peopled by dumb, helpless millions of the East,' while 'placing over them as rulers... the creatures of our "Bosses" and the satellites of our "Rings."' He cited two instances in which the United States had 'failed to deal worthily' with a 'burden imposed on us by Providence' which he believed 'bear some measure of analogy' to the present crisis. The first was Reconstruction, when the South had been preyed upon by professional politicians and carpet-baggers; the second was Indian policy, which had turned Native Americans over to 'those people who in our country make office hunting a profession, under the name of "politics."' It was not, therefore, unreasonable to fear that 'we may see again what we have too often seen already,' with corrupt US agents able to 'fatten leech-like upon hapless folk beyond the seas.' What he called 'the carpet-bagger proconsul' of 'our future subject province' were about to discover a 'veritable land of promise for his ends.'[28]

Colonialists advanced their own versions of republican argument, ones whose sense of popular political self-activity was well-suited to an era of mass, racialized and class disenfranchisement: the United States would spread the 'capacity' for 'self-government' to its colonies through a long-term, disciplinary education in political rationality and, in doing so, would escape the traditional, republican association of empire with corruption.[29] But the 'corruption' they seized on most consistently was technocratic and, against the claims of anti-colonialists, colonial empire would be its solvent: reforms that Americans had found impossible to accomplish on domestic terrain would first be realized on an imperial one; they would then find their way back to the metropole by 'reflex action.' If the costs and benefits of colonialism were frighteningly uncertain to many, the language of 'reflex' rang with a comforting determinism, the automatic and predictable connection of cause and effect.[30] 'To induce the American people to establish an empire beyond the seas,' noted J.W. Martin, skeptically, 'it is strongly alleged that various political advantages would follow in the States themselves.'

Indeed, the argument had 'been repeated with the monotony of a Music Hall chorus.'[31]

It was a foregone conclusion that the British Empire, its history and institutions were the chorus' principal, recurring themes, between Britain's sheer geopolitical pre-eminence, Anglo-American diplomatic rapprochement, and an Anglo-Saxonist racial exceptionalism that linked British and US histories through ties of blood, language and history.[32] There was also the fact of the Anglo-centered 'reflex actions' narrative itself, a piece of reformers' folklore at least two decades old by 1898: it gave a fledging US overseas colonialism a triumphant pre-history in somebody else's empire.[33] 'Advocates of [U. S.] expansion are very laudatory of the British Civil Service,' noted Martin, 'and suppose that its excellences are due to the expansiveness of Britain.'[34] Stanford University historian George Elliott Howard concurred. 'The argument... that wider responsibility will prove a great moral stimulant in the regeneration of our domestic civil service,' he wrote, 'with appeal to the alleged example of Great Britain, has become a favorite one among American expansionists.'[35]

If 'reflex action' was a music hall chorus, it had five recognizable verses or themes, in all of which the British Empire hovered near the center.[36] The first held that colonialism would enlarge Americans' political outlook and provide them the kinds of solidarity and collective will required to undertake domestic reforms. As University of Pennsylvania professor Leo S. Rowe put it, 'expansion' would unify Americans, allowing them to experience an 'energizing civic force' in rallying around a truly national effort, while breeding idealism and determination. 'Foreign adventure,' would breed a lasting intolerance for domestic failure. 'A nation that has once placed itself in the service of a great cause,' he wrote, 'will not permit corruption and inefficiency to sap the strength of its institutions.' Rowe's model was England, where demonstrations of 'national power and influence' abroad had awakened 'intense civic activity' at home and 'guard[ed] against the more extreme forms of class-antagonism.'[37] A second verse suggested that colonialism would attract the 'best men' into politics, cleansing the state of political corruption in the process. For Marion Couthouy Smith of the New York Civil Service Reform Association's Women's Auxiliary, 'the increase of national responsibility' was 'a strong force in favor of reform.' When England had discovered that 'a sound system was absolutely essential in her colonial governments,' she noted, 'the clearest and most powerful minds in the United Kingdom were brought to bear upon a problem so imperative.'[38]

Perhaps more thrilling was a third verse, in which colonial governance made men out of those who entered its service. Male reformers had always been vulnerable (as would anti-colonialists after 1898) to charges of effeminacy, closely tied to their education and elite positions in society; they countered that the colonial civil service was both manly and masculinizing.[39] Theodore Roosevelt noted in 'The Strenuous Life' that 'England's rule in India and Egypt has been of great benefit to England, for it has trained up generations of men accustomed to look at the larger and loftier side of public life.'[40] Julian Hawthorne wrote of the otherwise dissolute, effeminate American aristocrats who 'if the chance were offered them, might become the peers of the Rhodeses and Lawrences of our kin across the sea…'. These men, masculinized by colonial rule, would be the means of 'introducing into our national life a fresh and most welcome element,' he wrote, 'an element of unselfishness, of conscientiousness, of dignified and earnest manhood, which has been but sparingly represented of late.'[41]

A fourth verse held that overseas colonies would promote the beneficial concentration of executive power and the corresponding development of executive leadership. One of its chief soloists was Woodrow Wilson who, after his initial ambivalence, affirmed the annexation of the Philippines publically and energetically. In a 1900 essay in the *Atlantic Monthly*, Wilson argued that colonial empire would teach the United States crucial lessons in unified leadership. 'As long as we have only domestic subjects we have no real leaders,' he wrote. 'May it not be that the way to perfection lies along these new paths of struggle, or discipline, and of achievement?' he asked rhetorically.

> What will the reaction of new duty be? What self-revelations will it afford; what lessons of unified will, of simplified method, of clarified purpose; what disclosures of the fundamental principles of right action, the efficient means of just achievement, if we but keep our ideals and our character?

Not only might the United States learn from its new 'duties'; it must reform abroad in order to legitimate reform domestically. '[W]e shall not realize these ideals at home,' he wrote, 'if we suffer them to be hopelessly discredited amongst the peoples who have yet to see liberty and the peaceable days of order and comfortable progress.' Furthermore, empire would help the nation wean itself from disorderly democracy. 'We have been governed in all things by mass meetings,' he continued, a method that would 'serve very awkwardly, if at all, for action in international affairs or in the government of distant dependencies.' Empire would teach the domestic United States by reflex that leadership must be 'single, open, responsible and of the whole.'[42]

The fifth and final verse, widespread even among anti-colonialists, told of how the colonial civil services would (or should) provide domestic models. David Starr Jordan noted with some ambivalence that through the concentration of executive power in colonial administrations, 'we may be able to make of Havana and Manila clean and orderly cities. Shall we not by similar means, sooner or later, purify San Francisco and New York? If martial government is good for Luzon, or for Santiago, why not for Washington, or even for Boston?'[43] For Senator Albert Beveridge, colonial governance would 'have its effect upon us here in America…'. It was 'not true' that 'perfect government must be achieved at home before administering it abroad'; rather its exercise abroad was 'a suggestion, an example, and a stimulus for the best government at home'; it would be 'as if we projected ourselves upon a living screen' and 'beheld ourselves at work.' Answering the charge that colonialism distracted a polity from domestic reform, he enlisted the British Empire, as had many others, while revealing how heavily freighted transatlantic crossings of social-democratic ideas could be with imperial ones.[44] England's 'administration of Bombay did not divert attention from Glasgow,' which was 'to-day the model for all students of municipal problems'; indeed, the 'sanitary regeneration of filthy Calcutta made it clearer that Birmingham must be regenerated, too.'[45]

In a context of sharply divided opinion, the NCSRL's formal plank on colonialism transmuted the question of ends – emphasized in republican approaches – into a technocratic question of means. It was 'beyond the province of the League to pass upon the rightfulness or wisdom of territorial extension,' read Resolution VII, passed unanimously at its December 1899 annual meeting. But should 'any lands be brought under our dominion,' public office in them must 'be consistently treated as a trust to be administered for the sole benefit of their inhabitants.' To do otherwise – '[t]o abuse the public service of dependent provinces, in the interest of American parties or politicians' – would constitute 'a crime against civilization and humanity, disgraceful to our Republic.' The resolution urged that 'adequate provision be made for a non-partisan [sic] service recruited through open competition and assured of promotion through merit and of continued employment during good behavior and efficiency.'[46] Following that meeting, the NCSRL appointed a special 'Committee on the Civil Service in the Dependencies' consisting of three of its most prominent members, balanced on the colonial question: Bonaparte was a critic, Foulke a proponent, and Richard Henry Dana's position reflected the larger, emerging technocratic compromise: 'much opposed to taking the Philippines,' he believed that 'once taken over,' 'we ought to do our best to train them in self-government...'.[47] The Committee was tasked with lobbying the executive branch on the necessity of civil services for the colonies, investigating the status of the new states' administrative codes and legislative enactments, and reporting back to the League on the relative advance – or non-advance – of civil service principles into the colonies. It was a solution that addressed both colonialism's skeptics and enthusiasts within the civil service movement: while 'a wide difference of opinion exists among patriotic, intelligent and well informed citizens as to the expediency of our recent territorial acquisitions,' the Committee noted, no American 'truly solicitous for the honor and welfare of his country' could 'fail to be profoundly interested in their good government.' The kind of conditional approval it promoted – making civil service reformers' consent for colonial rule contingent on the building of institutions upon which they happened to be 'experts' – may have been more effective in securing them a place at the table than either complete rejection or support for colonialism would have done. Two members of the 'dependencies' committee, Foulke and Dana, would have the chance to meet with President McKinley in April 1901 to press the issue of a civil service for the Philippines and Puerto Rico, among other concerns.[48]

It perhaps goes without saying that civil services in the new US colonies did not emerge according to 'reflex actions' specifications, or their opposites. Space does not permit any more than a very brief discussion of the outcome of the Committee's efforts. By December 1900, it reported with satisfaction the Philippine Commission's passage of an 'admirably drawn' civil service law the previous September, to go into effect in January 1901, although it noted that the Commission had not found it 'practicable' to apply it to all branches of the service.[49] Through coordination with the US Civil Service Commission, a Philippine Civil Service Board was up and running soon afterwards; despite what they perceived as gaps, the Committee reported with satisfaction that their lobbying efforts have been acknowledged in the Commission's prioritization of the civil service code. Reformers were much less satisfied with their efforts in Puerto Rico. By October 1902, they reported that while the Islands' federal officials were being appointed under civil service laws, no laws or regulations had been adopted for insular or municipal government employees. A draft of civil service laws had been rejected by members of the Islands' Executive Council and a majority of the members of an appointed civil service commission, on the grounds that 'civil service regulations ought not to be introduced until after the administrative system of the Island had been fully reorganized'; in any case, reformers had found the bill itself seriously flawed, for allowing promotion through non-competitive examination. They attributed slower progress to two factors: ongoing ambiguity as to Puerto Ricans' formal status within US law, and the larger structures of the Puerto Rican colonial state. Unlike the Philippines, where executive and legislative power was concentrated in a US-appointed Commission, Puerto Rico had an insular legislature that must pass any civil service legislation: 'it is evident that the Federal Administration cannot directly impose a civil service law on the cities of the Island,' one editorial noted. Puerto Rican civil service would remain a major focus on NCSRL attention; the passage of a civil service law for Puerto Rico would only come in 1907. This suggested that the 'reflex actions' narrative, as both history and politics, had things reversed: it was not that colonialism itself 'taught' states how to concentrate executive power into civil services; it was that highly focused executive power – the initially undivided authority of the Philippine Commission, as opposed to Puerto Rico's executive/legislative split – that was required to make possible civil service institutions in a colonial context.[50]

The civil services, even in their embryonic form, came to play a key role in the ideological grounding of US colonial rule, displacing fears that colonial states might become havens of political corruption. Most important in spreading the word was William Foulke's May 1902 article on 'The Civil Service in Our New Dependencies,' published in the *Annals of the American Academy of Political and Social Science*. Foulke was an Indiana-based lawyer and a leader in the national civil service reform movement, with close personal ties to Theodore Roosevelt, who had appointed him to the US Civil Service Commission in 1901. Like Roosevelt, he was an advocate of US colonialism; his celebratory account of the Philippine service, based on exchanges with PCSB chairman Frank Kiggins, used the new civil service to justify US colonial rule in the Islands.[51] 'It may be well doubted whether there can be found in the history of any other nation an example of the government of a dependent people undertaken in as disinterested a spirit,' he wrote. As some had hoped, the Philippines' law was 'much more comprehensive than our own law,' having 'filled up the gaps' and 'provided for as complete a system as is possible at the present time.' Unsurprisingly, Foulke invoked 'reflex actions,' but now the United States' colonial civil service paralleled Britain's Indian civil service as triggers of potential metropolitan reform. 'The reflex action upon our Government at home of the establishment of a complete merit system in the Philippine Islands can hardly fail to be beneficial,' Foulke anticipated. Just as 'this reform came from Calcutta to London,' in the British case, 'it was not impossible nor unreasonable to expect that its perfect consummation may come from Manila to Washington.'[52]

To be sure, there would be many responses to celebratory accounts like Foulke's by American and Filipino critics, responses that emphasized the relatively low intellectual hurdles raised by the service's examinations, the *de facto* racial segregation of US and Filipino civil servants by rank and pay scale, and the fact that American officials appointed on a 'merit' basis had been charged with fraud and embezzlement. But these criticisms quietly reinforced an underlying shift away from republican assessments of colonial rule, and toward technocratic ones. As critics became more deeply invested in the question of how to extend or improve the colonial service, they were drawn away from the republican sense of empire as tyranny: corruption was not inherent in empire, but was symptomatic of an empire that was badly managed; it was not systemic, but exceptional, punishable and preventable. Increasingly, corruption itself was externalized: intrinsic to neither empire nor colonial state-building, it was cast more and more as an essential feature of Filipino political behavior. 'Cacique' politics – an intractable and unchanging system of patron/client relations – emerged as a key racial descriptor, the civil service's defining other, and a leading argument for the semi-permanent retention of the Islands by the United States. It was a sign of the merit system's discursive triumph in the Philippines that the racialization of Filipinos was expressed in a distinctly civil-service idiom.[53]

In the end, was there any truth to the 'reflex action' narrative? What came 'back' from empire? Here historians should proceed with caution. Narratives of unmediated transmission – whether apprehended with biological metaphors of 'reflex' or commercial ones of 'export' and 'import' – can prove as seductive to present-day historians as they were to past reformers. Reconstructing career trajectories, selective invocations of models from elsewhere, their transplant into new settings, and the intellectual and structural limits on this process, will get scholars at least part of the way towards histories of mediated transfer. But to do so, scholars ought to avoid for analytic purposes the sense of automatic transmission conveyed in 'reflex action': a narrative of long-distance change which connects contexts by emptying out one or more of them. Precisely by distancing ourselves from it analytically, 'reflex action' emerges as an actor's category eminently worth investigating, as one attempts to make sense of, and give shape to, a chaotic and unpredictable historical reality.

Ultimately, the most durable legacies of these debates may not be found – although they may be[54] – in the 'return' of civil services practices and institutions, but in the technocratic and spatial frameworks that were implicit and explicit in the 'reflex action' narrative, and which it played a role in constructing. The shift in assessments of the United States' role in the world from a republican towards a technocratic footing resolved colonial empire – or perhaps even empire more generally – from an existential threat to a set of definable and soluble problems. And they recast the ill-defined edges of empire from contaminating spaces of immorality and disorder to containable spaces of purity and control. The assurance that empire would uplift rather than pollute the metropole, and that metropolitan will could determine peripheral outcomes, had a long and embattled path ahead of it.

Notes

1 Woodrow Wilson, 'What Ought We to Do?' Memorandum, c. August 1, 1898, in Arthur Link, ed., *The Papers of Woodrow Wilson*, Vol. 10, pp. 574–6. On Wilson in the context of Princeton University's broader encounter with US colonialism during and after 1898, see Paul A. Kramer, 'Princeton University and the Academic Life of Empire,' *Princeton University Program in Latin American Studies (PLAS) Cuadernos Series*, Vol. 1 (June 1998), 1–23.

2 The literature on 'anti-imperialism' is extensive: see, especially, Richard E. Welch Jr., *Response to Imperialism: The United States and the Philippine-American War, 1899–1902* (Chapel Hill: University of North Carolina Press, 1979); Daniel Schirmer, *Republic or Empire: American Resistance to the Philippine War* (Cambridge, Mass.: Schenkman Pub. Co, 1972); Robert L. Beisner, *Twelve Against Empire: The Anti-Imperialists, 1898–1900* (New York: McGraw Hill, 1968); E. Berkeley Thompkins, *Anti-Imperialism in the United States: The Great Debate, 1890–1920* (Philadelphia: University of Pennsylvania Press, 1970); Jim Zwick, 'The Anti-Imperialist League and the Origins of Filipino-American Oppositional Solidarity,' *Amerasia Journal*, 24 (Summer 1998), 64–85.

3 The phrase 'great aberration' comes from diplomatic historian Samuel Flagg Bemis, *A Diplomatic History of the United States* (New York: H. Holt and Co., 1936); 'splendid little war' was the coinage of John Hay, US ambassador to Great Britain in 1898. For explorations in the historiography of US colonialism see, especially, Joseph A. Fry, 'Imperialism, American Style, 1890–1916,' in Gordon Martel, ed., *American Foreign Relations Reconsidered, 1890–1993* (London: Routledge, 1994), 52–70; Edward P. Crapol, 'Coming to Terms with Empire: The Historiography of Late-Nineteenth Century American

Foreign Relations,' *Diplomatic History*, Vol. 16 (1992), 573–97; Hugh De Santis, 'The Imperialist Impulse and American Innocence, 1865–1900,' in Gerald K. Haines and Samuel K. Walker, eds., *American Foreign Relations: A Historiographical Review* (Westport, CT, 1981); Julian Go, 'Introduction; Global Perspectives on the U.S. Colonial State in the Philippines,' in Julian Go and Anne Foster, eds., *The American Colonial State in the Philippines: Global Perspectives* (Durham: Duke University Press, 2003), 1–42.

4 On Manifest Destiny as ideology, see Anders Stephanson, *Manifest Destiny: American Expansion and the Empire of Right* (New York: Hill and Wang, 1995).

5 On the civil service and state-building in this period, see Stephen Skowronek, *Building a New American State: The Expansion of National Administrative Capacities, 1877–1920* (Cambridge; New York: Cambridge University Press, 1982); Ari Hoogenboom, *Outlawing the Spoils: A History of the Civil Service Reform Movement* (Urbana: University of Illinois Press, 1961); Frank Mann Stewart, *National Civil-Service Reform League: History, Activities, and Problems* (Austin: University of Texas, 1929). On civil service reform and urban politics, see Martin J. Schiesl, *The Politics of Efficiency: Municipal Administration and Reform in America, 1800–1920* (Berkeley: University of California Press, 1977). On the cultural politics of the civil service reformers, often termed 'Mugwumps' by their opponents, see esp. John G. Sproat, *The Best Men: Liberal Reformers in the Gilded Age* (New York: Oxford University Press, 1968). For historiographic interpretations of this community, see Geoffrey Blodgett, 'The Mugwump Reputation, 1870 to the Present,' *Journal of American History*, Vol. 66, No. 4 (1980), 867–87. On gender and civil service politics, see Kevin P. Murphy, *Political Manhood: Red Bloods, Mollycoddles, and the Politics of Progressive Era Reform* (New York: Columbia University Press, 2008).

6 For anti-colonialist arguments, see Philip Foner and Richard C. Winchester, *The Anti-Imperialist Reader: A Documentary History of Anti-Imperialism in the United States* (New York: Holmes and Meier, 1984). On anti-colonialism and race, see Christopher Lasch, 'The Anti-Imperialists, the Philippines, and the Inequality of Man,' *Journal of Southern History*, 24 (Aug. 1958), 319–31; on anti-colonialists, history and exceptionalism, see Fabian Filfrich, 'Falling Back into History: Conflicting Visions of National Decline and Destruction in the Imperialism Debate around the Turn of the Century,' in *The American Nation, National Identity, Nationalism*, ed., Knud Krakau (Münster, 1997), 149–66; Paul A. Kramer, 'Empires, Exceptions and Anglo-Saxons: Race and Rule Between the British and U.S. Empires, 1880–1910,' *Journal of American History*, Vol. 88 (March 2002), 1315–53.

7 Daniel T. Rodgers, *Atlantic Crossings: Social Politics in a Progressive Age* (Cambridge: Harvard University Press, 1998).

8 More work than can be undertaken here needs to be done on the institutional politics of the colonial civil services themselves. For histories of the civil service in the Philippines, see Visitacion R. De la Torre, *History of the Philippine Civil Service* (Quezon City: New Day Publishers, 1986); Onofre D. Corpuz, *The Bureaucracy in the Philippines* (Quezon City: Institute of Public Administration, University of the Philippines, 1957).

9 On Anglo-American reform and intellectual linkages, see Robert Kelley, *The Transatlantic Persuasion: The Liberal-Democratic Mind in the Age of Gladstone* (New York: Knopf, 1969); Kenneth O. Morgan, 'The Future at Work:

Anglo-American Progressivism, 1890–1917,' in *Contrast and Connection: Bicentennial Essays in Anglo-American History*, ed., H.C. Allen and Roger Thompson (London: Bell, 1976), 245–71; Rodgers, *Atlantic Crossings*; Sproat, *The Best Men*.

10 Dorman B. Eaton, *Civil Service in Great Britain* (New York: Harper and Brothers, 1880), 178, 180, 254, 255, 257.

11 On consular reform, see Thomas G. Paterson, 'American Businessmen and Consular Service Reform, 1890s to 1906,' *Business History Review*, Vol. XL, No. 1 (Spring 1966), 77–97; Robert Beisner, *From the Old Diplomacy to the New, 1865–1900* (Arlington Heights, Ill.: Harlan Davidson, 1986). For Welsh's criticism of Indian policy, see *The Murrain of Spoils in the Indian Service: A Paper Read at the Annual Meeting of the National Civil Service Reform League at Baltimore, Md., December 16, 1898* (New York: National Civil Service Reform League, 1898).

12 George F. Hoar, 'Statesmanship in England and the United States,' *The Forum* (August 1897), 721.

13 James Bryce, *American Commonwealth* (New York: Macmillan, 1903 [1888]), Vol. II, p. 531.

14 Eaton, *Civil Service in Great Britain*, 179.

15 The term could be used by proponents and critics of colonialism. For the former see, for example, Mercer Green Johnston, 'The Reflex Value of the Philippines to America,' in *Plain Talk in the Philippines* (Manila: J.R. Edgar and Co., 1907). For the latter see, for example, Adlai E. Stevenson et al., 'Bryan or McKinley? The Present Duty of American Citizens,' *The North American Review*, Vol. 171, No. 527 (Oct. 1900), 433–516: 'We dread the reflex action, the example, the familiarizing of our people with despotic methods,' 445; H.C. Potter, 'National Bigness or Greatness: Which?' *The North American Review*, Vol. 168, No. 509 (April 1899), 433–44, refers to those who 'have to feel the reflex influence of a condition of things in which a vast body of men discharge a responsibility, under conditions so remote and so unobserved by the public eye that it will practically be utterly impossible for us to know what they are doing...,' 436.

16 Francis Newton Thorpe, 'The Civil Service and Colonization,' *Harper's New Monthly Magazine* ([1902]), 860; David Starr Jordan, *Lest We Forget: An Address Delivered Before the Graduating Class of 1898, Leland Stanford University on May 25, 1898*, Leland Stanford University Publications, Published by John J. Valentine, Esq. (Palo Alto, August 10, 1898), 9.

17 Edward Gaylord Bourne, 'A Trained Colonial Civil Service,' *North American Review*, Vol. 169, Issue 515 (October 1899), 529.

18 'A Wholesome Stimulus to Higher Politics,' *Atlantic Monthly*, Vol. LXXXIII (March 1899), 292.

19 Carl Schurz, *A Review of the Year: An Address Delivered at the Annual Meeting of the National Civil Service Reform League at Baltimore, M. D. December 15, 1898 by the President, Hon. Carl Schurz* (New York: National Civil Service Reform League, 1898), 28.

20 'The 'Suspension' of the Rules in the War Department,' *Good Government*, Vol. XVI, No. 9 (Dec. 15, 1898), 122–4; 'The War Emergency Appointments,' *Good Government*, Vol. XVII, No. 1 (July 15, 1899), 7–12; 'The War "Emergency" Appointments,' Good Government, Vol. XVII, No. 1 (August 15, 1899), 25–7.

21 On the study of colonialism within academic and professional social science settings, see Frank Ng, 'Knowledge for Empire: Academics and Universities in the Service of Imperialism,' in Robert David Johnson, ed., *On Cultural Ground: Essays in International History* (Chicago: Imprint Publications, 1994); Gary Marotta, 'The Academic Mind and the Rise of U.S. Imperialism: Historians and Economists as Publicists for Ideas of Colonial Expansion,' *American Journal of Economics and Sociology*, Vol. 42, No. 2 (April 1983), 217–34. For the most extensive study of comparative colonial civil services conducted during this period, see A. Lawrence Lowell, *The Colonial Civil Service* (New York: Macmillan and Co., 1900).
22 Henry M. Teller, 'A Nation's Power,' in William Jennings Bryan et al., *Republic or Empire?: The Philippine Question* (Chicago: Independence Company, 1899), 234.
23 Hoar, 'Our Government As It Was Intended,' in Bryan et al., *Republic or Empire?*, 151.
24 Schurz, 'Thoughts on American Imperialism,' *The Century*, Vol. 56, No. 5 (September 1898), 786.
25 Richard Pettigrew, in James P. Boyd, ed., *Men and Issues of 1900: The Vital Questions of the Day* (n.p., 1900).
26 Jordan, *Lest We Forget*, 10, 12, 34.
27 Dorman B. Eaton, *The Need and Best Means for Providing a Competent and Stable Civil Service for Our New Dependencies: A Paper Read at the Annual Meeting of the National Civil Service Reform League at Baltimore, Md., December 16, 1898* (New York: National Civil Service Reform League, 1898).
28 Charles Bonaparte, *The Spoils System in the Government of Dependencies: A Paper Read at the 19th Annual Meeting of the National Civil Service Reform League, held at Indianapolis, December 15, 1899* (n.p., 1899), 4–6. As early as September 1898, Bonaparte had accommodated himself to colonial rule in the Caribbean, but remained a critic of colonialism in the Philippines, especially on the grounds of political corruption. 'Mr. Bonaparte on Foreign Possessions,' *New York Times*, September 26, 1898, 6.
29 On ideologies of tutelary colonialism in the Philippine context, see Paul A. Kramer, *The Blood of Government: Race, Empire, the United States and the Philippines* (Chapel Hill: University of North Carolina Press, 2006), esp. ch. 3.
30 In his 1881 essay 'Reflex Action and Theism,' William James defined the term 'reflex action' to refer to the fact 'that the acts we perform are always the result of outward discharges from the nervous centres, and that these outward discharges are themselves the result of impressions from the external world, carried in along one or another of our sensory nerves.' He also asserted that '[i]n a general way, all educated people know what reflex action means.' See 'Reflex Action and Theism,' in William James, *The Will to Believe and Other Essays in Popular Philosophy* (New York: Longmans, Green and Co., 1896). My thanks to Caleb McDaniel for identifying this source. In 1887, Brooks Adams defined habit as 'the result of reflex action, or the immediate response of the nerves to a stimulus, with the intervention of consciousness.' It operated most strikingly in armies which 'when well organized, are machines, wherein subjection to command is instinctive, and insubordination, therefore, practically impossible.' See

Brooks Adams, *The Emancipation of Massachusetts: The Dream and the Reality* (Boston: Houghton, Mifflin, 1887).
31 J.W. Martin, *English Lessons on Territorial Expansion* (New York: League for Political Education, 1902).
32 On Anglo-American rapprochement, Anglo-Saxonist racial ideology, and inter-imperial dialogue, see Stuart Anderson, *Race and Rapprochement: Anglo-Saxonism and Anglo-American Relations, 1895–1904* (Rutherford, NJ: Farleigh Dickinson, 1981); Kramer, 'Empires, Exceptions and Anglo-Saxons.' It was over-determined that Spain would form the other, negative pole in a comparative triad: more than one observer attributed Spain's colonial weakness and defeat to political corruption, even as they upheld Britain's civil service as the fount of its imperial success. See, for example, Mrs. Josephine Shaw-Lowell, 'Spain and Civil Service Reform,' *New York Times*, August 8, 1898, 4.
33 Tellingly, the most extensive post-1898 discussion of the relationship between colonialism and civil service politics in the NCSRL journal *Good Government*, was a massive, multi-part article on British imperial and civil service history, which concluded with lessons for the Philippines, by George R. Bishop: 'Outline of the Development of Colonial Civil Service,' *Good Government*, Vol. XIX, No. 5 (April 1902), 78–80; Vol. XIX, No. 6 (June 1902), 91–4; Vol. XIX, No. 7 (July 1902), 110–12; Vol. XIX, No. 7 (August 1902), 125–8; Vol. XIX, No. 10 (Oct. 1902), 158–60; Vol. XIX, No. 11 (Nov. 1902), pp. 172–6; Vol. XIX, No. 12 (Dec. 1902), 187–92.
34 Martin, *English Lessons*, 24.
35 George Elliot Howard, 'British Imperialism and the Reform of the Civil Service,' *Political Science Quarterly*, Vol. 14, No. 2 (Jun. 1899), 241.
36 It is important to note that the account of British-imperial history upon which the 'reflex actions' narrative was built was itself subject to criticism by anti-colonialists. See this exchange: Frank H. Giddings, 'Imperialism?,' *Political Science Quarterly*, Vol. 13, No. 4 (Dec. 1898), 585–605; George Elliot Howard, 'British Imperialism and the Reform of the Civil Service,' *Political Science Quarterly*, Vol. 14, No. 2 (June, 1899), 240–50.
37 L.S. Rowe, 'The Influence of the War Upon Our Public Life,' *The Forum*, Vol. 27 (March 1899), 55, 58–9.
38 Marion Couthouy Smith, 'Civil Service Reform,' *Good Government*, Vol. XVIII, No. 5 (June 15, 1901), 77.
39 On the feminization of the 'Mugwumps,' see Murphy, *Political Manhood*; Richard Hofstadter, *Anti-Intellectualism in American Life* (New York: Knopf, 1963), ch. 7. On the feminization of anti-colonialists, see Kristin Hoganson, *Fighting for American Manhood: How Gender Politics Provoked the Spanish-American and Philippine-American Wars* (New Haven: Yale University Press, 1998).
40 Theodore Roosevelt, 'The Strenuous Life,' in *The Strenuous Life: Essays and Lectures* (New York: The Century Co., 1900), 18–19.
41 Julian Hawthorne, 'A Side Issue of Expansion,' *Forum*, XXVII (June 1899), 443–4.
42 Woodrow Wilson, 'Democracy and Efficiency,' *The Atlantic Monthly*, LXXXVII (March 1901), 289–99, reprinted in Link, ed., *The Papers of Woodrow Wilson*, Vol. 12, pp. 10, 10–11, 17–18, 18.

43 Jordan, 'False Steps by a Nation are Hard to Retrace,' in Bryan et al., *Republic or Empire?*, 279–80.
44 On Euro-American crossings of social-democratic ideas, see Rodgers, *Atlantic Crossings*.
45 Albert Beveridge, *Policy Regarding the Philippines: Speech of Albert J. Beveridge, of Indiana, in the Senate of the United States, Tuesday, January 9, 1900* (Washington?, 1900), 17–18. See also Beveridge, *For the Greater Republic Not for Imperialism: An Address Delivered by Hon. Albert J. Beveridge, at the Union League of Philadelphia, February 15, 1899* (Philadelphia: Union League of Philadelphia, 1899), 7.
46 Resolution VII, 'The Annual Meeting of the League,' *Good Government*, Vol. XVII, No. 3 (March 15, 1900), 33–4.
47 Dana's diary (1899), quoted in Bliss Perry, *Richard Henry Dana, 1851–1931* (Boston, New York: Houghton Mifflin Co., 1933), 192.
48 'Discuss Civil Service: Committee Calls on President to Suggest Extension of the Present Regulations,' *New York Times*, April 5, 1901, 5.
49 'The Philippines Act,' *Good Government*, Vol. XVIII, No. 4 (May 15, 1901), 56.
50 For comparative analyses of the US's colonial states, see Lanny Thompson, 'The Imperial Republic: A Comparison of the Insular Territories Under U.S. Dominion after 1898,' *Pacific Historical Review*, Vol. 71, No. 4 (2002), 535–74; Julian Go, *American Empire and the Politics of Meaning: Elite Political Cultures in the Philippines and Puerto Rico* (Durham: Duke University Press, 2008).
51 Foulke was promoting the virtues of the Philippine civil service as early as April 1901; see 'Civil Service Reform: W.D. Foulke of Indiana Talks of the Merit System Under the Present Administration,' *New York Times*, April 16, 1901.
52 William Dudley Foulke, 'The Civil Service in Our New Dependencies,' *Annals of the American Academy of Political and Social Science* (May 1902), 11, 12, 20.
53 Introducing its civil service act, the Philippine Commission already make clear distinctions between 'corruption' among Filipino officials – the legacy of the Spanish civil service, and a feature of 'all Oriental governments' – and that among Americans, who experienced a 'weakening of moral restraints of home associations' and turned to corruption 'to make so long a trip result successfully in a pecuniary way.' Quoted in *Good Government*, Vol. XIII, No. 4 (May 15, 1901), 60. On the ideological use of the 'cacique' in US colonial governance and social science, see Reynaldo Ileto, 'Orientalism and the Study of Philippine Politics,' *Philippine Political Science Journal*, Vol. 22, No. 45 (2001); Kramer, *The Blood of Government*, ch. 3.
54 For a recent argument on the colonial origins of the US surveillance state, see Alfred McCoy, *Policing America's Empire: The United States, the Philippines, and the Rise of the Surveillance State* (Madison: University of Wisconsin Press, 2009).

2
Ambassador W. Averell Harriman and the Shift in US Policy toward Moscow after Roosevelt's Death*

Frank Costigliola

Thanks to the fierce winter of 1944–45 in Moscow, historians have a written account revealing how dangerous emotions and divisive discourses developed among US and British officials. Spaso House, the huge, drafty American embassy building, was tough to heat. In December 1944, a kerosene stove was rigged up in the top floor room of Robert Meiklejohn, ambassador W. Averell Harriman's secretary. Meiklejohn jotted in his detailed diary, 'My room is very comfortable now,' and it has become 'the usual gathering place in the evening.'[1] Evenings the ambassador, his daughter Kathleen, the Pentagon's liaison to the Red Army General John R. Deane, embassy officials including George F. Kennan, British ambassador Archibald Clark Kerr and Kennan's friend Frank K. Roberts, and liberated American POWs, clustered around the stove to review the day, gossip, and grumble. The Soviets dished out lots to grumble about. An embassy official 'was going nuts here,' Meiklejohn recorded, 'as not a few people appear to do when they stay too long.'[2] Many diplomats and journalists were frustrated with their personal lives. They suffered anger, sadness, and even depression from being deprived of 'normal' contact with Soviet citizens. The moods and cultural assumptions of these diplomats and journalists shaped how they interpreted Soviet policy and intentions. Their recommendations would have enormous influence once President Franklin D. Roosevelt left the scene.

The breakdown of the Grand Alliance and the formation of the Cold War in 1945–46 were not inevitable. Contingent factors of personality and attitude disrupted Big Three diplomacy following the death of Roosevelt and the defeat of Churchill. Neither the leaders who succeeded these giants, nor the 'Soviet experts,' such as Harriman and Kennan, who asserted a more decisive role than they had hitherto been allowed to play, shared Roosevelt's or even Churchill's commitment to

Big Three accord. Josef Stalin and Vyacheslav Molotov had little respect for Harry Truman and disliked Ernest Bevin. In the pivotal weeks after Roosevelt died, Harriman and Deane helped change how US policy and opinion makers talked and thought about the Soviet Union.[3] The attitudes and rhetoric of Harriman and Deane helped create a discourse of distrust and disgust. The Soviets were increasingly depicted not as valued allies but rather as potential enemies, non-humans, barbarians, and irredeemably evil.

In terms of methodology, this chapter aims to shrink the exaggerated divide between those historians who focus more on state power and those historians who focus more on discourses and texts. I use here a discursive analysis of conversations around that stove and in Washington and San Francisco to help explain a pivotal event, the shift in US policy and attitudes toward the Soviet Union immediately following FDR's death.

In March 1945, Richard Rossbach, an ex-POW well connected to the New York elite, told those gathered around the stove about his experiences after liberation by the Red Army. Commenting that he 'had a much better time with the Germans than with our allies,' he described the Red Army as operating under 'primitive and chaotic conditions.... Their men live like animals, forage off the countryside for their food... and fight in a semi-drunken state maintained by a generous ration of vodka.' Soviet officers robbed Americans of their watches at gun point. Living conditions in the Red Army were so stark that many ex-POWs sought out local Poles, who 'always welcomed and cared for our men as best they could.'[4] The cultural and incipiently political lines of division already seemed obvious: affinities between Americans and Poles and even Germans, in contrast to enmity between Americans and Soviets. 'Primitive,' 'chaotic,' and animal-like men, who stole for sustenance and robbed allies, appeared not as postwar partners but as a horde to be contained or fought. Kremlin bosses whose 'generous ration of vodka' fueled soldiers' 'semi-drunken state' seemed themselves bereft of judgment and a sense of limits. Americans and British reacted with understandable disgust as they saw Soviet soldiers raping, looting, and defecating without restraint. Rossbach and others reported that 'rapes are constantly occurring.' Common were 'cases of thirty or forty Soviet soldiers raping one woman and then killing her.'[5] Searing stories habituated embassy officials to referring to the Soviets as 'animal-like people' even when talking about such mundane matters as overcrowded trains.[6]

The Kremlin's policy of isolating foreigners embittered many of the people who shaped how the Soviets were seen in the outside world.

The Russian friends, lovers, and wives of foreigners were subject to arrest, torture, and exile to Siberia. These harsh rules were enforced unevenly, raising both temptation and anxiety. The secret police tended to ease up when relations with the Allies improved and to crack down when they soured.[7] Foreigners could feel played like a yo-yo. Meiklejohn commented that 'when Stalin is mad at you everybody from the doorman to the bus conductor is mad at you.'[8] Soviet citizens sought contact out of curiosity, love, friendship, desire for stockings, or eagerness to talk English. Some started out as informants or began informing once threatened. Sometimes officially conflicting loyalties did not conflict. Llewellyn 'Tommy' Thompson, who decades later would become JFK's ambassador to Moscow, cultivated a 'close wartime liaison with a member of the Moscow ballet,' an aide recalled. The woman and her secret police connection 'provided a pipeline through which [Thompson] could try out and receive suggestions that could not safely have been made officially.'[9] Such coziness remained the exception. 'We are living in a condition of total isolation' that was 'terribly depressing,' Angus Ward, the US consul in Vladivostok, complained to his Soviet counterpart, S. Gjukarev. When Russian guests begged off from his cocktail party, Ward felt 'a slap in the face, which was still burning' a year later. Not just fear of the secret police, however, but also embarrassment at lacking the wherewithal to return the hospitality had kept some guests away. Unsympathetic to what he saw as Ward's 'boredom,' Gjukarev advised the American to attend more concerts and theater.[10] Like Ward, many Americans and Britons returned from Russia soured on cooperation with an alien system whose repression they had personally experienced or had seen up close.

Geoffrey Wilson, a Russian analyst in the British Foreign Office, pointed to the fallout from the 'appalling isolation' of diplomats and journalists. 'In all too many cases' their 'whole attitude toward Russia is determined by the bitterness to which this [isolation] gives rise. Such [bitterness] is quickly sensed by the Russians and greatly resented.' The Russians were to blame for the vicious cycle. Nevertheless, British policy was skewed, Wilson worried, because experts on Russia found it difficult to retain 'their capacity for balanced judgment.'[11] In short, the personal could become the political – with harmful effects on diplomacy.

Though personal, these grievances were not petty because they linked to a key foreign policy objective. The right to associate with local people was the personal side of the Open Door policy. The logic of the Open Door entailed not just the prerogative to develop economic opportunities but also the right of individuals to move around, meet people, and build influence. The Kremlin's restrictions on contact violated emotionally resonant norms of individual opportunity and freedom. Americans and British regarded informal, personal contacts across borders as a means toward security. To the Russian government, however, whether under the czars or the commissars, the free competition of open contact threatened insecurity. Like their czarist predecessors, the Soviets resented uncontrolled contact with foreigners 'as so much grit in the machine of government.'[12] Conducting espionage in the West on a massive scale, the Soviets had a different set of practices for using personal contacts to gain influence in other nations.

For Kennan, Elbridge Durbrow, Bill Bullitt, and 'Chip' Bohlen, the limits on contact were especially tough to take. They remembered the honeymoon of 1933–34, when Stalin, hoping for US aid against Japan, had allowed Americans to associate freely with Kremlin officials, literary lions, and Bolshoi ballerinas. The lost paradise of those pre-purge years would forever haunt these future Cold Warriors. (The memory of such contact also endured on the Moscow street. An extravagant wedding in the diplomatic community sparked the 'persistent rumor that Harriman was marrying a ballerina.')[13] The enforced isolation saddened Kennan, who loved immersing himself in Russian culture.[14] For all the horrors the Nazis perpetrated, they, unlike the Soviets, allowed scope for both private property and private lives. Durbrow later recalled that officials from the US embassies in Moscow and Berlin 'used to get in awful arguments... whether Hitler was the worse dictator or Stalin. The Moscow boys always won.' He added that Stalin 'made Hitler look like a little kindergarten kid.'[15] On the very night that Durbrow left Moscow in 1937, the secret police arrested his longtime girlfriend Vera, an opera singer. In 1945, 'Durby' again met up with Vera when she returned from the labor camp. Interviewed decades later, Durbrow cited Vera's fate as proof of Soviet iniquity. His personal pain colored – not determined but colored – his overall attitude. His anger and contempt informed his work in heading the state department's Eastern European bureau, in encouraging Harriman's hard-line stance in interpreting the Yalta accords on Poland, in spurring Kennan to write the Long Telegram, in replacing Kennan as number two in the Moscow embassy in 1946 and, appropriately enough, in cementing ties to South Vietnam while ambassador there in the 1950s.

Racialized stereotypes also undermined the Grand Alliance. Russia's Mongol heritage and stretch across Asia, the Kremlin's tyranny, Stalin's Georgian birth, and the prominence of supposedly not-quite-European Jews among the early Bolsheviks fed notions of an 'oriental despotism.'

London officials referred to the Soviet ambassador's 'merry Jewish-Mongolian eyes.'[16] Inspecting the embassy in Moscow, a US state department official worried that Kennan, who already suffered 'poor health' and 'moody spells,' might succumb to 'the spell cast by the semi-oriental, semi-savage atmosphere' of Russia.[17] Because Marxist-Leninism could appear as a rejection of normative Euro-American values, Soviet ideology was often seen as 'Asiatic.' 'Othering' the Russians had a long history. But such representations grew more barbed as the Red Army blasted its way toward Berlin. The atrocities of Soviet soldiers avenged earlier German outrages, which the Americans and British had not witnessed and did not take fully into account. The behavior and appearance of soldiers, some of Siberian ethnicities and riding Siberian ponies, led those clustered around the kerosene heater to brand the rollback of Hitler's armies a 'barbarian invasion of Europe.'[18] This was a description whose emotional implications differed radically from FDR's talk of the Four Policemen.

Imperatives of pride also imperiled cooperation.[19] In 1940–42, Axis military triumphs had humiliated in turn the British, Russians, and Americans. Each regarded its subsequent efforts as the key to victory. The British had fought the longest and for a frightful year all alone. The Soviets had suffered the most blood and damage and had waited three years for the second front. The Americans had donated tens of billions in supplies while massing forces in different theaters on opposite sides of the globe. As victory neared even the liberal Robert Sherwood found it 'difficult not to be an eagle-screaming, flag-waving chauvinist.'[20] Molotov pounded his chest exclaiming: 'I am proud, proud, I tell you, to be the foreign minister of this great country!'[21]

Swollen pride impelled each of the Big Three nations to expect from the others overt gratitude and respect. Cultural differences in signaling respect magnified the tendency of each to see the other's strutting as evidence of disrespect and aggression. Alexandra Kollontay – a hero of the Bolshevik Revolution, a feminist theorist, and the Soviet ambassador to Sweden – described her nation's leaders as 'naive, clumsy, and blundering.... They have no idea of when or why they give offense.' Yet they easily took offense. In triumph 'they want the world to feel their strength and to pat them on the back for their success.' To those in London and Washington who feared the Soviets as a rising menace, Kollontay advised: 'They are children, and must be treated as such.' Deep down Kremlin leaders knew 'that they must cooperate.' Until these adolescents outgrew their 'unruliness,' the Allies had to 'practice patience and more patience.'[22]

Roosevelt believed he understood something of Russian psychology. Before setting off for Tehran in 1943, he commented that Stalin's reluctance to travel far meant that he, Roosevelt, would have to journey 6,000 miles. He said, 'Stalin believed that Russia had grown so 'strong, that she can impose her will, & must be treated *at least* as an equal.' Unlike Truman and every other Cold-War President, Roosevelt did not, however, bristle at such arrogance. Instead, he looked deeper, seeing Stalin as 'may be too anxious to prove his point.... Stalin suffered from an inferiority complex.'[23] Roosevelt calculated that addressing the dictator's craving for respect could reap substantive gains. As Harry Hopkins remarked appreciatively at Tehran, FDR 'had spent his life managing men.'[24] Walter Lippmann later explained that 'Roosevelt was a cynical man. What he thought he could do was outwit Stalin.'[25]

Yet playing the game of respect/humiliation could backfire, as actually happened after Roosevelt's death. General Deane interpreted FDR's self-confident gesture to Stalin as humiliating. He declared: 'No single event of the war irritated me more than seeing the President of the United States lifted from wheel chair, to ship, to shore... in order to go halfway around the world as the only possible means of meeting Stalin.'[26] According to Deane's emotional reasoning, in that wheelchair was not just Franklin D. Roosevelt, a man who wielded power quite effectively while sitting down. Rather, the seated man was 'the President of the United States' – symbolically, the United States itself – and it was being humiliated by having to travel so far in such a visibly helpless condition to meet an imperious Stalin. What proved dangerous in such thinking was that Deane and Harriman convinced others that Washington had to respond to the supposed humiliations of the Roosevelt years by getting 'tough' with the Russians.

Before the Cold War polarized nearly everything, even Stalin could acknowledge some lag in Russian culture. When Finns asked about his postwar agenda for the Soviet Union, he replied, 'first to make the people more human and less like beasts by stilling their animal passions, their fears and lusts.'[27] At Potsdam, he volunteered that Soviet generals 'still lack breeding, and their manners are bad. Our people have a long way to go.'[28] Such hints at a more open perspective faded with the alliance. By 1946, Stalin boasted that Soviet culture would soon be 'a hundred times higher and better than any bourgeois system.'[29] Any campaign to make the Soviet people 'more human' had seemingly ended.

In eight separate interviews done late in life, Molotov boasted that he and Stalin had avoided the humiliation of being made 'fools' by the West.[30] (Seven times he detailed how careful he and Stalin had been to stick to territorial 'limits.'[31]) It 'was my main task... to see that we would not be cheated,' Molotov stressed.[32] He repeated: 'It was hard to fool us.'[33] 'Fools' merited not respect, but rather contempt. Fools lacked the intellectual and cultural capital to hold onto what they had earned. Fools, proletarians, and colonials could be exploited by those who manipulated the rules. Molotov worried that sophisticated Westerners could steal at the conference table what Russians had died for on the battlefield. 'Our people don't like being treated like colonial people,' he blurted out to a British diplomat.[34] Adamant about not looking – or being – fooled, cheated, or otherwise disrespected, the Soviets behaved in ways that Americans and British interpreted as arrogant, grasping, and lacking in respect.

Some Soviets worried about reductive stereotyping by Westerners. In March 1945, a group of Soviet editors and foreign ministry officials attended a lunch hosted by the *London Times*. A Soviet editor stressed, 'the last thing the Russians wanted was "exotic" reporting on Russia.' He 'kept on repeating his objections to "exoticism."' By exoticism he seemed to mean exaggerating and making a spectacle out of either the good or the bad in Russia. Groping toward a concept that scholars decades later would term 'orientalism,' the Soviet editors urged 'giv[ing] a picture of Russia as she [really] is.'[35] Similarly, when Stalin was asked what he would advise Americans, he replied: 'Just judge the Soviet Union objectively. Do not either praise us or scold us. Just know us and judge us as we are and base your estimate of us upon facts and not rumors.'[36] It remains unclear to what extent self-deception prevented Stalin from seeing the contradiction between this invitation to 'know us' and the isolation his secret police imposed on foreigners trying to do just that. Highly emotional issues involving Poland undermined such tentative efforts to bridge the cultural gap.

It proved tragic that a mix of *sui generis* issues centered on Poland became the test case for cooperation at the critical juncture between war and peace. Poland hit home for each of the Big Three. Roosevelt needed votes from Polish-Americans. Stalin nursed both old and new grievances against the Poles. He understood that only a Poland yoked to 'friendship' could overlook the Soviets' 1940 massacre of Polish officers in the Katyn forest. Only close ties would close the Polish gate to another invasion. The British had gone to war over Warsaw's independence. Over 100,000 Polish troops reinforced British forces. 'Appeasing' Russia on Poland could cost Churchill the upcoming Parliamentary election. Britain's ambassador to the London Polish government framed the alternatives as 'abetting a murder' by 'selling the corpse of Poland to Russia' or asserting 'moral authority.'[37] Roosevelt cared not so much. 'I am sick and tired of these people,' he muttered in complaining about the Polish ambassador's badgering him about restoring prewar borders. He added, ' I really think the 1941 frontiers are as just as any.'[38]

Raising the stakes was the Warsaw uprising. In August 1944, street fighters attacked the Nazi occupier. Supported by the London Polish government, they sought national independence. Evidence suggests that some of the fighters may have been trained in the US and parachuted in by the British.[39] Resisters wielded whatever weapons they could scrounge. The Germans pounded them for three excruciating months as Americans and Britons looked on with horror. Stalin refused aid until nearly the end. Nor would he agree, despite appeals from Churchill and Roosevelt, to allow relief planes to refuel at the Poltava base in the Ukraine.[40] Kennan later pinpointed this as the moment for a 'political showdown with the Soviet leaders.' Harriman was so 'shattered by the experience' that he suffered what Kathleen Harriman referred to as a near nervous breakdown.[41]

Making Stalin's veto especially frustrating was that Poltava was a hard-won *American* base. That 'little patch of America in the middle of the Ukraine,' as its commander called it, shone as the proudest achievement of Harriman and Deane.[42] Established in June 1944 for shuttle bombing of German targets, Poltava and the smaller facilities at Mirgorod and Piryatin seemed for few months a wedge that just might open the Soviet Union to Far Eastern air bases against Japan, postwar civil air agreements, and other contacts. Deane, watching US bombers land at their base in the Ukraine, felt 'a thrill beyond description.' Kathleen observed that her father had never 'been so thrilled by anything.'[43] Such intensity of feeling perhaps played a role in coining its ultimate code name, FRANTIC. As the original name, BASEBALL, suggested, the project dovetailed with plans for a US-led, postwar global system of air bases and civil air agreements.

In February–March 1945, Poltava figured in another operation that poked at Soviet control while tugging at American hearts: evacuating from Poland some 7,000 US and British ex-POWs. The Red Army regarded all POWs as more likely cowards than heroes. They forced the ex-POWs to hitchhike and forage (i.e., pillage), much as Red Army soldiers often had to do. In contrast, many Poles went all out for these strangers, partly in hope that gratitude in Washington and London might rescue them from Moscow. The Soviets swept the ex-POWs toward the port of Odessa, from which nearly all were evacuated by V-E day.[44] Americans – who have mythicized and ennobled captives since the days of Mary Rowlandson and the Indians – were appalled at Soviet callousness. Harriman and Deane planned for US planes based at Poltava to criss-cross Poland evacuating ex-POWs. Roosevelt urged Stalin to comply. Such rescue flights would give Poltava a new rationale, since German retreats had ended the need for shuttle bombing.

Stalin saw the rescue plan as yet further meddling in his sphere. As he knew or suspected, British Special Operations were already smuggling anti-Soviet agents in and out of Poland disguised as Allied ex-POWs.[45] Harriman and Deane were pressing for a new air base in Soviet-occupied Hungary. Despite his resentment of the Soviets, Admiral Ernest Archer of the British military mission in Moscow was appalled at London's brazenness in getting into Soviet-occupied Poland. His government had 'kept at the Russians for months until eventually permission was given to inspect an acoustic torpedo' from a U-250 boat at Gdynia. He added that 'it came as something of a shock to hear from the [inspection] party that the visit was really only paid for political reasons, as plenty of information had become available from other sources. The same, I imagine, is true of many other desired visits or facilities, such as bomb damage assessment and the like.'[46] Although such intelligence efforts were dwarfed by Soviet operations in Britain and America, a cloak-and-dagger contest was already underway.

Emotional reasoning linked oppression of Poland and oppression of Americans. As Deane's aide put it, 'the Soviet attitude toward liberated American prisoners is the same as the Soviet attitude toward the countries they have liberated. Prisoners are spoils of war... They maybe be robbed, starved, and abused – and no one has the right to question such treatment.'[47] Deane would recall the quashing of the air rescue as 'my darkest days in Russia.'[48] Harriman cabled Roosevelt: 'I am outraged' at the Russians.[49] He warned FDR that when word of the POW story got out 'there will be great and lasting resentment on the part of the American people.'[50] Though angry, the President refused to escalate the dispute. Unlike Harriman, Roosevelt remained committed to pursuing postwar cooperation.

Harriman and his boss disagreed until the latter's death. Roosevelt, seeking to end his spat with Stalin over the Italian surrender negotiations in Berne, cabled the dictator: 'in any event, there must not be mutual distrust, and minor misunderstandings of this character should not arise in the future.'[51] Instead of delivering the telegram, the ambassador, astoundingly, tried to change it. He urged the President to eliminate the word 'minor' because 'the misunderstanding appeared to me to be of a major character.'[52] FDR insisted: 'I do not wish to delete the word "minor" as it is my desire to consider the... misunderstanding a minor incident.'[53] Two aspects here bear emphasis. First, Roosevelt understood that a dispute he considered minor might remain so, and a dispute he considered major would become so. Second, an angry Harriman was so intent on 'toughening' US policy that he risked his ties to the President.

Denied permission to come to Washington, Harriman on 10 April wrote an extraordinary telegram. He made the emotionally explosive, difficult-to-dislodge argument that the policy of cooperating with Stalin had 'been influenced by a sense of fear.' Charging that a policy was influenced by fear was, in effect, deliberately delegitimating that policy. The draft of this telegram offers evidence of how the ambassador tried to smear Roosevelt's policy by describing it as based on cowardly fear even though he had little proof of such fear. At first, he seemed unsure how to argue his far-fetched proposition. Exactly what did the US fear? In the draft, he first wrote that US decisions 'have been influenced by a sense of fear of the Soviet Union.' He evidently then decided, however, that it would be difficult to convince the President that he, Roosevelt, feared the Soviet Union. So Harriman scratched out 'fear of the Soviet Union,' and wrote the vaguer formulation 'fear of it.' Then he crossed that out and settled for the still vaguer, but even harder to refute, formulation that decisions were 'influenced by a sense of fear on our part.' Harriman then repeated the word 'fear' five times by representing policy concerns as cowardly 'fears.'[54] He used the word 'insult' five times in detailing the 'almost daily,' 'outrageous' indignities he was suffering in Moscow.[55]

After Roosevelt died on 12 April, Harriman got permission to brief the new President. Rushing to Washington, his plane knocked seven hours off the previous flight record. In the hubbub, the Soviets neglected to check departure documents. Ever mindful of the personal contact issue, those on board rued the missed chance to smuggle out some Soviet wives.[56] Agitated, the ambassador displayed a nervous tic in his eye. To Durbrow he appeared 'just steaming.'[57] Meiklejohn believed that US policy toward Russia was 'letting a Frankenstein loose upon Europe.... Until that Frankenstein is disposed of, there will be no peace in the world.'[58] Also aboard was British ambassador Clark Kerr, who described Harriman as 'having careened from "high elation" to the deepest melancholia.... His melancholia had turned into something like hate, and he was determined to advise his government to waste no more time on the effort to understand and to cooperate with the Russians.'[59] Once in Washington Harriman hit it off immediately with Truman, himself anxious about whether he measured up to his daunting job.[60]

Arguably it was the anger at the Soviets over the Warsaw uprising, anger over the ex-POWs, over the brutal domination of Poland – anger also building from frustration at the forced isolation and stoked by Soviet arrogance in victory – arguably it was such anger that blinded Harriman and his advisers to the weakness of their negotiating position on implementing the Yalta agreement on Poland. While in the United States in April and May, Harriman would exercise enormous influence with Truman administration officials, legislators, and journalists. With his on-the-scene authority, the ambassador argued that Soviet insistence on the dominance of the pro-Moscow Lublin Poles violated Yalta. The Yalta accord *was* ambiguous.

But three authoritative American and British sources independently agreed that the Soviets had the stronger case in arguing for retaining the Lublin government and merely adding other Polish elements. Clark Kerr confided to Lippmann that following Yalta, London officials had 'overruled' him and 'asked for an interpretation of the Crimean agreement which made the problem insoluble.'[61] Frank Roberts, who had worked with the London Polish government and who would write his own 'long telegram' in 1946, reported on first arriving in Moscow that the Yalta agreement 'was interpreted not only by the Russians but also by… independent and by no means pro-Russian journalists here as being a Russian victory in the sense that we, for the first time, completely ignored the Polish Government in London and went some way towards recognition' of the Lublin government. 'In so far as we want a new deal, and, in fact, the elimination or subordination of the [Lublin] group, we are fighting for something which the Russians… are not prepared to concede.'[62] Finally, Jimmy Byrnes, who was at Yalta, acknowledged in June 1945 'that there was no question as to what the spirit of the agreement was. There was no intent that a new government was to be created independent of the Lublin government. The basis was to be the Lublin government.'[63] Even though many of Roosevelt's March–April cables regarding Poland were drafted by his more hardline advisers, particularly Leahy and Bohlen, they recognized the primacy of the Lublin Poles to a degree that neither Churchill nor Harriman and Truman would accept.[64]

What Clark Kerr characterized as Harriman's 'hate' influenced four discourse-changing conversations in Washington and in San Francisco. First Harriman spoke with Truman alone, thereafter with Truman and other advisers, and then the President confronted Molotov. A week later, America's top 'Soviet expert' briefed journalists at the San Francisco conference. The talks framed an argument that made it seem not just permissible, but also necessary and realistic to regard the Soviets as more foe than friend. Roosevelt almost certainly would have resisted this discursive revolution and the attitudes and policies flowing from it. In tone and language, FDR's report on Yalta had sought to rein in America's appetite for triumphalism, exceptionalism, and railing at an evil 'other.' Harriman and Truman rejected such emotional restraint. By emphasizing America's global power and righteousness, they fed the vicious circle of pride and anxiety that would soon destroy the wartime alliance.

Meeting with the new President on 20 April, Harriman tossed the fear-bomb. He said that FDR's policy had rested on shameful fear. Proud and insecure, Truman quickly interjected that 'he was not in any sense afraid of the Russians.' Harriman then undercut the rationale for the alliance by presenting as a fatal contradiction that which Roosevelt had regarded as a fact of life. During the postwar transition Moscow would seek both cooperation with its allies and dominance over its neighbors. The ambassador made still another alarmist claim: the Soviets lacked any sense of limits. Therefore getting along with Russia would require the United States to endure a humiliating passivity. He concluded with a flatly wrong prediction. Because the Kremlin 'did not wish to break with the United States... we had nothing to lose by standing firm.'[65]

Roosevelt, understanding that cultural differences could doom the alliance, played them down. Harriman played them up. Indeed, he inflated them. To Truman, who liked reading about Genghis Khan, Harriman repeated the kerosene-stove comment that the armies rolling back the Nazis amounted to a 'barbarian invasion of Europe.' Bohlen liked the zing. While his minutes paraphrased the rest of the conversation, this was the only phrase to appear in quotation marks.[66] Deane meanwhile made similar arguments to Pentagon officials.[67]

On 23 April, Truman canvassed advisers before meeting with Molotov. He set the tone by declaring that the Russians 'could go to hell' if they did not attend the San Francisco conference. Harriman and Deane reconceptualized the problem of Poland so as to directly and morally involve the United States. 'The real issue,' he insisted, 'was whether we were to be a party to a program of Soviet domination of Poland.'[68] According to this provocative formulation, unless Washington escalated Poland into a crisis, US leaders themselves would become 'a party' to Moscow's brutal domination – perpetrators rather than bystanders. In other words, Washington had to assume responsibility for freedom up to the very border of its victorious, touchy, and insistent ally. Or else Polish blood would stain American hands. Such dangerous reasoning greased the slide from the Atlantic Charter to the Cold War.

In the meeting with Truman's advisers Deane's insinuation was equally explosive: 'If we were afraid of the Russians, we would get nowhere.' Washington had to act in order to regain Moscow's respect. Charges of being afraid were an effective slur: easy to make, difficult to disprove. Once someone raised the issue of fear, it became harder to argue against confronting the Russians. Even readier to scuttle the alliance was Secretary of the Navy James Forrestal, who argued that if the Russians did not retreat, 'we had better have a show down with them now than later.' Leahy, who had stood at Roosevelt's side at Yalta, informed the group that the agreement on Poland 'was susceptible to two interpretations.' Nevertheless, he also insisted on 'a free and independent Poland.'[69]

In keeping with the customary discourse of official minutes, Bohlen's record flattened the emotional tone of the talk. The meeting was actually, however, quite emotional as a participant soon informed Felix Frankfurter. There was 'much "banging of fists" on the table in arguing that it was "high time" to take a "tough line" with Russia.' Harsh talk was 'the only language the Russians could understand.' Stalin had sent an 'insulting' note to Roosevelt.[70] Such proto-Cold War, masculine-tough-guy renderings implicitly faulted the late president. Almost in caricature they were implying that the wheelchair-bound Roosevelt may have been unwilling or unable to stand up to the Russians, but the new leadership was eager to prove its grit.

Only Secretary of War Henry Stimson and General George Marshall, the Army Chief Staff, sounded caution. Stimson worried that emotional thinking was distorting perceptions of national interest. He had noted in his diary that Harriman and Deane 'have been suffering personally from the Russians' behavior on minor matters.' 'Influenced by their past bad treatment,' they were arguing 'for strong words by [the] President.'[71] Stimson did not see US vital interests as extending deep into Eastern Europe, especially since '25 years ago all of Poland had been Russian.'[72] Truman, however, ignored Stimson's skepticism.

Molotov was meanwhile lunching with Joe Davies. Molotov told him that in the Kremlin the President's death weighed as 'a great loss and an irreparable one.... Stalin and Roosevelt understood each other.' Despite post-Yalta tensions, Stalin had believed that 'any difference could always be adjusted through mutual discussions and tolerance, for there was a will to achieve cooperation.' Davies urged Molotov to 'specifically ask the President' not to commit himself on the Polish government 'until he has heard all the facts and the Soviet point of view.' A poker buddy of Truman, Davies feared 'the principle danger... would come from a "snap judgment."'[73]

In the meeting with Molotov, Truman lectured rather than listened. Echoing Harriman's provocative new formulation, he warned that America 'could not agree to be a party' to Soviet domination of Poland. Molotov tried to make two points on how the Big Three had managed to function. First, despite their differences, 'the three Governments had been able to find a common language and decide questions by agreement.' Second, they 'had dealt as equal parties, and there had been no case where one or two of the three had attempted to impose their will on another.' Truman repeated that the Yalta agreement on Poland was clear cut. He seemed undeterred by Leahy's admission that Yalta was open to two interpretations. He probably did not know, and may not have cared about, the views of Clark Kerr and Roberts. It remains a puzzle precisely what Byrnes did and did not tell Truman about Yalta. In any case, the President told Molotov that Stalin was violating the agreement. Molotov snapped that unlike other allies, the Soviets had stuck by Yalta. Moreover, Poland loomed on their border, and they would not tolerate anti-Russians in Warsaw. Truman interrupted that there was no use discussing that further. When Molotov brought up the Far Eastern war, where the Red Army would be needed, Truman cut him off, saying, 'That will be all, Mr. Molotov.'[74] Durbrow, who observed the Russian leave, would later recall, 'I've never seen a man come out more ashen in my life.'[75] As Davies had feared, his friend had reached a 'snap judgment' after refusing to consider the Russian viewpoint.

Bohlen would recall the conversation as, quite literally, a discursive break: 'probably the first sharp words uttered during the war by an American President to a high Soviet official.'[76] Memories of an exciting event can become indelible. Decades later Bohlen could still exclaim: 'How I enjoyed translating Truman's sentences!' Perhaps on some level he also enjoyed avenging what he and other young American diplomats had lost in the post-1934 purges. Rather than editing the emotions out of his minutes, Bohlen highlighted them. He probably realized that his new boss would fancy a record of himself talking tough. Afterward, Truman bragged: 'I gave it to him straight. I let him have it. It was straight one-two to the jaw.' Yet the champ remained insecure. 'Did I do right?' he asked.[77]

A week later in San Francisco, Harriman invited a dozen top journalists to his apartment. He ominously announced that 'on long range politics there is an irreconcilable difference' between the Soviet Union and the Western allies. He used emotion-evoking words that had circulated around Meiklejohn's stove. Kennan would employ similar rhetoric in his 1946 long telegram and in his 1947 'Mr. X' article. The ambassador blamed everything on the Kremlin's 'Marxian penetration.' The phrase suggested assault that was simultaneously ideological, political, and sexual. The trope caught on. The first question posed by a journalist asked the difference 'between the Russian policy of penetration, as you put it, and Nazi policy.' Repeating the word 'penetrate,' Harriman answered that the Soviets probably did not intend military aggression. Other journalists also picked up on the emotional phrase. While some journalists bought this scare-argument, others grew furious. Lippmann and Raymond Swing, a popular radio announcer, stormed out in protest. When another reported asked 'has our policy changed since Roosevelt?,' Harriman nervously backtracked. The reporter pressed him: 'But it is obvious there IS A CHANGE.'[78] Once back in Moscow, the ambassador continued efforts at 'indoctrinating' visiting Congressmen and Senators, Meiklejohn noted.[79]

Harriman helped establish the long-lasting discursive frame for US Cold War policy. His emotional language amplified the impact of his authority as a Soviet expert. Policy and opinion makers got the message: it was normal and realistic to refer to the Soviets as dangerous aliens with whom there was an 'irreconcilable,' ideological conflict. This discursive attack on the alliance persisted even when political relations warmed, as they did on and off for the remainder of 1945. Truman never made a splashy statement to stem the tide. Fanning fears proved easier than quieting them. Donald Nelson, a wartime production administrator who had found Stalin eager to expand trade, now feared war. Nelson 'put the responsibility chiefly on Averell Harriman.'[80] Assistant Secretary of State Dean Acheson faulted his friend's attitude and tactics. 'Averell is very ferocious about the Rouskis.... He seems in favor of any stick to beat them with.' Nevertheless, Acheson accepted the ambassador's argument that the Russians 'are behaving badly.'[81] Although Harriman and his cohort sought not armed conflict but rather a calibrated policy of containing Russia and building alliances in the West, their pushing for a tougher stance fed public fears of war.

After Harriman's talks in April–May, it became more customary to talk about the Soviets not as fellow world policemen as Roosevelt had often depicted them, but rather as international criminals. Parallel changes were propelled by Churchill and others in London. British military officials, some already branding Russia the enemy, were emboldened by Churchill's request for a contingency plan to attack the Soviet Union in July.[82] Anti-Soviet stalwarts in the state department and other hardliners, such as Forrestal, did not need Harriman to turn them against

FDR's priority of getting along with Moscow. The ambassador had his greatest impact on Truman, particularly in claiming that Roosevelt's policy had reflected cowardly 'fear' of the Soviets. This argument touched a nerve with the insecure new President, anxious to show he feared neither Stalin nor his new job. For all Truman's public praise of Roosevelt, he liked to think that he was in certain respects a better president because he could act decisively. Harriman was not alone in driving the discursive shift. Yet he voiced the authority of firsthand experience in dealing with Stalin.

The Soviets did do terrible things. Harriman and others were justified in their anger and disgust at the isolation, at the rape and pillage by Red Army soldiers, at Stalin's co-responsibility for the crushing of the Warsaw uprising, at the callousness toward the liberated POWs, and at the oppression of Poland. Nevertheless, personally and morally satisfying expressions of anger produced a rhetoric in which measured, judicious strategic thinking was, tragically, blinkered. Despite the egregiousness of Soviet actions, these actions – and the jabs and counter-jabs that followed – did not justify the Cold War. The costs of that conflict proved far higher: deadly proxy wars, the atomic arms race (the full price of which we perhaps have not yet paid), the militarizing of US society, and, probably, the deepening and prolonging of Soviet oppression. It was unfortunate that Roosevelt died and that Harriman, Kennan, and company came to the fore at such a critical juncture between war and peace. Roosevelt had planned for the Big Three jointly to manage the gradual transition to a stable, more multilateral world. Differences that might have been papered over during such a transition instead blew up into an ideologically-fueled, tit-for-tat conflict.

The spring of 1945 was a critical juncture in history – like August 1914, November 1989, or September 2001. At such turning points, the contingency of personalities, feelings, and cultural assumptions can propel massive events with dangerous (or positive) momentum. Once the discursive shift became public, the kind of quiet deals formerly reached by the Big Three became unworkable in the glare of domestic politics. Rhetoric about the Soviet threat and the vicious spiral of fear and disrespect opened the way for far-right anti-communists who within a few years were labeling even Truman an appeaser. The change from Roosevelt to Truman occurred on many levels, not least in a shift from emotional control to a venting and exaggerating of differences that would explode the wartime alliance.

When Kennan arrived in Moscow in 1933 and Harriman in 1943, they were each excited about becoming a key go-between linking America and

Russia. Bitterly disappointed, they became advocates of a tougher policy – but they did so expecting that this pressure would force the Soviets to yield. Ironically, decades before Russia did open up, both Kennan and Harriman had reversed their earlier tough stances and had become voices for re-engaging Moscow. Harriman went so far as to conclude that 'FDR was basically right in thinking he could make progress by personal relations with Stalin.... The Russians were utterly convinced that the change came as a result of the shift from Roosevelt to Truman.'[83] Harriman bore much of the responsibility for that tragic change.

Finally, that stove: the grumbling around the Spaso House hot stove sparked rhetorical incendiaries that burned for decades. As a nation, the United States is still, in effect, grumbling around the stove about a world that it cannot remake in its image.

Notes

*Part of this essay was published in *Diplomatic History* in January 2010.
1. Robert P. Meiklejohn diary, 23–25 February 1945, box 211, W. Averell Harriman papers, Library of Congress, Washington, DC.
2. Meiklejohn diary, 18 August 1945, box 211, Harriman papers.
3. For an account that minimizes the shift between presidents, see Wilson D. Miscamble, *From Roosevelt to Truman* (New York, 2007). Vladimir Pechatnov, *Stalin, Ruzvel't, Trumen* (Moscow, 2006) is based on both Russian and US archival sources. See recent assessments in David B. Woolner, Warren F. Kimball and David Reynolds, eds., *FDR's World: War, Peace, and Legacies* (New York, 2008).
4. Meiklejohn diary, 17 March 1945, box 211, Harriman papers.
5. Meiklejohn diary, 17 March 1945, box 211, Harriman papers.
6. Meiklejohn diary, 25 March 1945, box 211, Harriman papers.
7. See Frank Costigliola, 'The "Invisible Wall": Personal and Cultural Origins of the Cold War,' *The New England Journal of History*, 64 (Fall 2007), 190–213.
8. Meiklejohn diary, 4 October 1945, box 211, Harriman papers.
9. Kemp Tolley, *Caviar and Commissars* (Annapolis, MD, 1983), 64.
10. S. Gjukarev diary, 7 March 1944, AVPRF, f., op. 28, pap. 155, ll. 24–6.
11. Minute by Geoffrey Wilson, 4 August 1944, F.O. 371/43305, National Archives, Kew, United Kingdom.
12. 'Survey of Contact,' 2 July 1944, F.O. 371/43305.
13. Kathleen to Averell, 4 May 1946, box 5, Harriman papers.
14. See Frank Costigliola, '"Unceasing Pressure for Penetration": Gender, Pathology, and Emotion in George Kennan's Formation of the Cold War,' *Journal of American History*, 83 (March 1997), 1309–39.
15. Reminiscences of Elbridge Durbrow (1981), 76, 78, Columbia University Oral History Research Office Collection, New York (hereafter CUOHROC).
16. Clark Kerr to Foreign Office, 6 April 1945, F.O. 371/47881; Roberts to Bevin, 'Report on Leading Personalities in the Soviet Union,' 22 May 1946, F.O. 371/56871.

17 J.K. Huddle, 'Personnel Conditions at the Moscow Embassy,' 17 April 1937, box 102, Inspection Reports on Foreign Service Posts, Record Group 59, National Archives, Washington, DC.
18 Meiklejohn diary, 17 March 1945, box 211, Harriman papers.
19 For an introduction to the theory, see Gabriele Taylor, *Pride, Shame, and Guilt: Emotions of Self-assessment* (Oxford, 1985); William Ian Miller, *Humiliation* (Ithaca, 1993); Robert A. Nye, *Masculinity and Male Codes of Honor in Modern France* (New York, 1993).
20 Robert Sherwood to Hopkins, 4 April 1945, box 4, series III, Harry L. Hopkins papers, Georgetown University, Washington, DC.
21 Clark Kerr to Anthony Eden, 31 August 1944, N5598/183/38, F.O. 371/43336.
22 Clark Kerr to Foreign Office, 6 April 1945, F.O. 371/47881. Harriman alluded to his talk with Kollontay in his unsent telegram of 10 April 1945, box 178, Harriman papers.
23 Geoffrey C. Ward, ed., *Closest Companion* (Boston, 1995), 253 (emphasis in original).
24 Lord Moran, *Churchill at War 1940–45* (New York, 2002), 162.
25 Reminiscences of Walter Lippmann, p. 217, CUOHROC.
26 John R. Deane, *The Strange Alliance* (New York, 1947), 160.
27 Frank Roberts to Foreign Office, 19 October 1945, F.O. 371/47807.
28 A.H. Birse, *Memoirs of an Interpreter* (New York, 1967), 209.
29 Geoffrey Roberts, *Stalin's Wars* (New Haven, 2006), 331, 333.
30 Albert Resis, ed., *Molotov Remembers* (Chicago, 1993), 11, 19, 23, 44, 53, 55, 69, 77.
31 Resis, ed., *Molotov Remembers*, 8, 52, 59, 65, 66, 73, 74.
32 Resis, ed., *Molotov Remembers*, 53.
33 Resis, ed., *Molotov Remembers*, 69.
34 Molotov conversation with John Balfour, 13 December 1943, AVPRF, f. Secretariat V.M. Molotov'a op. 5, pap. 17, ll. 57.
35 Frank Roberts to Christopher F.A. Warner, 14 March 1945, F.O. 371/47934. An article in *Bolshevik* criticized a tendency of the British to describe as a conception of things which will not fit into their conception of things.' D. Zaslavski, cited in minute by George Hill, 18 April 1945, F.O. 371/47853.
36 'Stalin Voices Aim for Amity and Aid of US in the Peace,' *New York Times*, 1 October 1945, copy in box 206, Harriman papers.
37 Owen O'Malley to Eden, 22 January 1944, F.O. 954/20.
38 Lt. Miles, 'The President at Home,' 20 December 1943, F.O. 371/38516, PRO. The visit ended on Tuesday, 2 November 1943.
39 Irina Mukhina, 'New Revelations from the Former Soviet Archives: The Kremlin, the Warsaw Uprising, and the Coming of the Cold War,' *Cold War History*, 6 (August 2006), 405–6, 410.
40 Jonathan Walker, *Poland Alone: Britain, SOE and the Collapse of the Polish Resistance, 1944* (Stroud, Gloucestershire, 2008), 204–61.
41 George F. Kennan, *Memoirs 1925–1950* (Boston, 1967), 210–11; William Larsh, 'W. Averell Harriman and the Polish Question, December 1943–August 1944,' *East European Politics and Societies*, 7 (Fall 1993), 544, 552.
42 Mark J. Conversino, *Fighting with the Soviets* (Lawrence, KS, 1997), 67.

43 Frank Costigliola, 'I Had Come as a Friend': Emotion, Culture, and Ambiguity in the Formation of the Cold War, 1943–45,' *Cold War History*, 1 (August 2000), 116–17.
44 Frank Costigliola, '"Like Animals or Worse": Narratives of Culture and Emotion by US and British POWs and Airmen behind Soviet Lines, 1944–1945,' *Diplomatic History*, 28, 749–80.
45 SOE memorandum, 'Answers to Questions,' [no date but 1945], HS4/211, National Archives, Kew.
46 Archer to Rushbrooke, 16 April 1945, ADM 223/249, National Archives, Kew.
47 Lt. Col. James D. Wilmeth, 'Report on a Visit to Lublin, Poland 27 February–28 March 1945,' box 22, entry 319, RG 334.
48 Deane, *Strange Alliance*, 182.
49 Harriman to the President, 8 March 1945, box 34, Map Room files (hereafter MR), Franklin D. Roosevelt Presidential Library (hereafter FDRL).
50 Harriman to the President, 24 March 1945, box 34, MR, FDRL.
51 *Stalin's Correspondence with Roosevelt and Truman 1941–1945* (New York, 1965), 214.
52 Harriman to the President, 12 April 1945, box 178, Harriman papers.
53 Roosevelt to Harriman, 12 April 1945, box 178, Harriman papers.
54 Harriman to Secretary of State [unsent], 10 April 1945, box 178, Harriman papers.
55 Pentagon generals, however, examined a list of similar complaints from Deane and judged them 'irritating' but 'of relatively minor moment.' Diane Shaver Clemens, 'From War to Cold War: The Role of Harriman, Deane, and the Joint Chiefs of Staff in the Reversal of Cooperation with the Soviet Union, April, 1945,' *The International History Review*, 14 (May 1992), 280.
56 Meiklejohn diary, 15–17 April 1945, box 211, Harriman papers.
57 Reminiscences of Durbrow, 65, CUOHROC.
58 Meiklejohn diary, 9 April 1945, box 211, Harriman papers.
59 Archibald Clark Kerr to Christopher Warner, 21 June 1945, F.O. 371/47862.
60 For Truman's concerns about assuming the presidency and about the connection between height and presidential greatness, see Robert H. Ferrell, ed., *Off the Record: The Private Papers of Harry S. Truman* (New York, 1980), 16; Margaret Truman, ed., *Where the Buck Stops* (New York, 1989), 77–9. On the activities of Harriman and Deane in Washington, see Clemens, 'Reversal of Cooperation,' 293–303.
61 Lippmann to Hans Kohn, 30 May 1945, box 82, Walter Lippmann papers, Yale University, New Haven, Conn.
62 Frank K. Roberts to Christopher F.A. Warner, 14 March 1945, F.O. 371/47934.
63 Joseph E. Davies diary, 6 June 1945, box 17, Joseph E. Davies papers, Library of Congress. Though Davies sympathized with the Soviets, historians have not questioned the veracity of his diary. The entry cited here is an original, not one of the reworked passages that Davies did in the early 1950s.
64 Warren F. Kimball, ed., *Churchill & Roosevelt* (Princeton, 1984), 3, 593–7.
65 *Foreign Relations of the United States* (hereafter FRUS) *1945*, 5, 232.
66 *FRUS 1945*, 5, 232.
67 Clemens, 'Reversal of Cooperation,' 293–303.

68 *FRUS 1945*, 5, 253.
69 *FRUS 1945*, 5, 253–5.
70 Davies conversation with Frankfurter in Davies journal, 13 May 1945, box 16, Davies papers.
71 Stimson diary, 23 April 1945, Stimson papers.
72 *FRUS 1945*, 5, 253–4.
73 Davies journal, 23, 30 April 1945, box 16, Davies papers.
74 Charles E. Bohlen, *Witness to History 1929–1969* (New York, 1973), 213.
75 Reminiscences of Durbrow, 70, CUOHROC.
76 Bohlen, *Witness to History*, 213.
77 Davies journal, 30 April 1945, box 16, Davies papers. The quotation is from Davies' notes after his talk with Truman.
78 Clark Kerr sent a transcript of the exchange to London. Archibald Clark Kerr to Christopher Warner, 21 June 1945, F.O. 371/47862 (capital letters in original).
79 Meiklejohn diary, 10–11 September 1945, box 211, Harriman papers.
80 John Morton Blum, ed., *The Price of Vision* (Boston, 1973), 447.
81 Dean Acheson to Mary Bundy, 12 May 1945, reel 4, Dean Acheson papers, Yale University, New Haven, Conn.
82 Joint Planning Staff, 'Operation "Unthinkable,"' 22 May 1945, Churchill to Ismay, 10 June 1945, CAB 120/691, National Archives, Kew.
83 Andrew Schlesinger and Stephen Schlesinger, eds., *Journals 1952–2000 Arthur M. Schlesinger, Jr.* (New York, 2007), 335–6.

3
The Kennan Diaries

David Milne

George Frost Kennan kept a diary from 1924 to 2004 – a life in writing that most people would happily call a life. These eighty years were amongst the bloodiest in world history and Kennan's career in the diplomatic service allowed him to observe Europe's darkest hours from Prague in 1938, Berlin in 1939, Paris in 1940, and Moscow in 1944. The diary is replete with prescient geopolitical analysis and unsentimental reflections on the human frailties that lead to conflict. Some days Kennan wrote entries that ran to multiple pages; for weeks he would write nothing at all. Some days he wrote poetry that was conventional in form; at other points he painted cityscapes that were almost Joycean in their freeform lyricism. Kennan's diary is a document of sustained literary quality and historical importance. It is neither as indiscreet as Arthur Schlesinger Jr.'s *Journals* nor as unrevealing as many a stock political memoir.[1] It is generous to friends and enemies – Joseph McCarthy and John Foster Dulles excepted – and erudite and candid in content. The processing of the series was complete in 2009 and scholars who travel to the Seeley-Mudd Library in Princeton can now revisit the history of the twentieth century from the viewpoint of one of America's most perceptive thinkers. The experience is both exhilarating and bracing.

Certain sections of Kennan's diaries have been published already. Kennan's Pulitzer-prize winning memoirs contain long verbatim sections from the diary, as does his 1989 collection of travelogues and reminiscences, *Sketches from a Life*.[2] But these sections are drops in the ocean. Some ninety percent of Kennan's diaries have not been published in any form, which makes its release an important event for historians of the twentieth century. Constituting 4.7 linear feet in twelve tightly-packed boxes, the material contained within Kennan's vast diary will likely take years for scholars to fully digest. With that caveat in mind, this chapter will offer some preliminary thoughts on the main significance of the diaries, primarily in respect to the US foreign policy decisions in which Kennan participated and observed. But it also moves beyond diplomatic history to consider Kennan's character itself: both his estimable qualities as a thinker and his failures in imagination, which sprang mainly from a narrow ethnocentrism. George Kennan was in many ways the most intellectually complex of the Cold War's principals. And unlike Henry Kissinger, say, the best way to understand Kennan is to read him at source.[3]

The significance of the series lies in three broad areas. Firstly, through reading the diaries we are permitted a deeper look into Kennan's character and intellectual predispositions. Scholars such as Barton Gellman, Walter Hixson, David Mayers, and Anders Stephanson have all sought to first identify and second make sense of Kennan's geopolitical philosophy, a forlorn task, in many respects, given Kennan's hostility to unifying theories or value-systems. Nonetheless, the diaries reflect Kennan's inner life, and as such give us the best view available of his particular brand of foreign policy realism. Secondly, the diaries add important fresh detail and evidence which in time will enrich the historiography of the Second World War and Cold War. Kennan's embassy postings traversed most of the important European capitals of the 1930s and 1940s, and his diary entries are usually more candid and illuminating than the official cables deposited at the National Archives. More significantly, perhaps, Kennan's private views on US foreign policy from 1950 to the end of the Clinton administration are remarkably acute and illuminating. Finally, the diary is written with a subtlety, insight and eloquence that will enhance Kennan's reputation as one of America's greatest scholars. Reading the diary is as purely enjoyable an experience as the diplomatic historian – generally starved of artistry – might hope to have. It is intellectually rich and pedagogically instructive; such was the wider intention of the author. In bequeathing his diary to Princeton University, Kennan gave to others in death as much of himself as he possibly could.

There is one overarching theme in Kennan's diary that is finally worth emphasizing as it speaks so clearly to a core objective of this volume. Put simply, it is that Kennan's vision for US foreign policy was formed by profoundly cosmopolitan sources, of which some were illuminating and some less edifying. The nations that Kennan truly admired included Victorian Britain, Bismarck's Germany and Kurt Von Schuschnigg's Austria. Conversely, Kennan found little in the American tradition of diplomacy that was worth retaining in the post-1945 world. Alexander Hamilton was a rare voice of geopolitical reason in the early Republic but few American diplomatists since then struck Kennan as particularly perceptive. A northern European in historical empathy and political and cultural tastes, Kennan's scathing views on the entrenched structural impediments that prevented the developing world from experiencing sustained economic growth and political stability was matched in its vehemence only by his belief that the United States had become a materialistic, self-satisfied and philistine nation. A constant refrain through the diary is Kennan's lament that America should refrain from instructing others on the paths to progress and liberty until it creates a society of its own of substantive, enduring value. It is no small irony that America's central Cold War strategy was crafted by a man so contemptuous of American society and political culture.

* * * * *

Distilling Kennan's diplomatic worldview can be a vexing and frustrating experience, and Kennan has attracted the attention of some fierce critics. Dean Acheson believed that Kennan's writing 'had a sort of sad, lyrical beauty about it which drugs the mind,' and that his musings on foreign policy were invariably interspersed with 'flashes of prophetic insight' and suggestions 'of total impracticality.'[4] In a highly critical essay published in the *Yale Law Journal* in 1978, the neoconservative Eugene Rostow described Kennan as 'an impressionist, a poet, not an earthling,' a man whose mind 'has never moved along mathematical lines and never will.'[5] For Rostow, Kennan knew too much of history and literature and complexity; a tendency towards relativism was one of his many failings. His inability to formulate a cohesive foreign policy strategy – a 'grand design' to guide statesmen – seriously undermined Kennan's claim to be a diplomatic thinker of the first rank. On the other end of the political spectrum, Walter Hixson does identify a Kennan grand design but dislikes what he finds: '[Kennan] remained a prisoner of his visceral anticommunism perceptions and periodically lapsed into his Mr. X persona.'[6]

While Kennan has had his critics, there are more scholars who broadly admire his diplomatic career. In *Contending with Kennan* Barton Gellman, a journalist and scholar who has great respect for his subject's acuity, offers a nuanced analysis of Kennan's foreign policy philosophy, drawing out strands of his thought that strike him as particularly salient. He correctly observes that 'Kennan has all his professional life scorned doctrines, formulas, and pretensions to universal truth,' but expends a lot of energy trying to find one all the same.[7] David Mayers strives to this same end, although he succeeds in writing the most diligent Kennan biography in print, portraying Kennan as a 'self-made aristocrat,' and a conservative diplomatic thinker of a Burkean and Gibbonian complexion.[8] Anders Stephanson's *George Kennan and the Art of Foreign Policy* lights a fuse to countless intellectual fireworks; a few fizzle out, but most soar and illuminate. Stephanson quotes Kennan's view presented in 1952 that diplomacy is 'best done not by professional politicians on the glaring stage of partisan rivalry, but by quieter men whose experience of the world has left them with a certain sense of the tragedy of things, of the unaccountability of the historical process, and of the persistent tendency of brave undertakings to have irrelevant and eccentric endings – men, consequently, with a certain detachment toward all movements governed by political passions, including those of [their] own country.' In fine, foreign policy should be made by men rather like George Kennan, who understand that diplomacy is an art not a science. As Stephanson cautions, 'Whatever its merits, such a view was of little relevance to the American situation and hence fell, as he probably realized, within the category of wishful thinking.'[9]

Much of what Kennan wrote did indeed fall into the category of 'wishful thinking,' and his diary entries contain much that is idealized, unrealistic, and at odds with the transparency required in democratic society. On the near certainty that Moscow would assume a dominant role in Eastern Europe following the defeat of Germany, Kennan believed that Franklin Roosevelt's lack of interest in, firstly extracting a *quid pro quo* from Stalin, and secondly, giving serious consideration to how this might affect the global balance of power was a sad reflection of America's wilful detachment from European matters. As Kennan wrote in his diary on August 4, 1944:

> [T]he average American of longer standing, being himself incapable of understanding the Europeans, finds it comforting to wish a plague upon them all and to take refuge in the sense of self-righteousness which is his American birth-right... We persist in placing foreign affairs in the hands of amateurs... We insist that all our cards should be face-up on the table so that the American people – and everybody else – can see them.[10]

Kennan believed that democracies were particularly ill-suited to pursuing a considered foreign policy and made his own predilection for authoritarianism clear through his writings – particularly through the 1930s, when he started, but mercifully did not complete, a book detailing the superiority of enlightened despotism over democracy as an effective system of government. Kennan had been much impressed by the reactionary Austrian regime led by Kurt Von Schusnigg, which he had viewed firsthand from a posting in Vienna in the late-1930s. In a manuscript entitled 'The Prerequisites: Notes on Problems in the United States in 1938,' Kennan lauded Von Schusnigg's success in implementing a comprehensive law unifying medical and financial procedures drafted entirely by 'experts,' a process from which the Austrian parliament had been excluded. Kennan thought that America would do well to learn from this success, and that its fidelity to democracy and transparency were hurting the consistency of its foreign policy and its ability to deal with the acute social problems that had long afflicted the nation. Kennan's belief in government by experts, his abhorrence of the messy business of democracy and interest group activity – particularly those ethnic lobbies that can so distort foreign policy priorities – is presented with particular force in the diaries. Many of the remarks venerating authoritarianism are unedifying. Yet there is much which rings true, particularly in respect to the way in which interest groups can affect US diplomacy. Kennan believed a Croatian Lobby exerted a baleful influence on US policy toward Tito during his tenure, from 1961 to 1963, as US Ambassador to Yugoslavia. Two influential scholars recently made the same claim regarding an Israel Lobby and US policy toward the Middle East.[11]

Kennan's disillusionment with American society, a theme he took up frequently in books in articles, is afforded a great deal of attention in the diary, even at the most unlikely of moments. On March 21, 1940, for example, as Nazi Germany subjugated and terrorized the European continent, Kennan compared European civilization favorably to American primitivism:

> When they [America's forefathers] turned their backs on Europe, they closed their eyes to the lessons of that continent's past; and their backwoodsmen wisdom was not adequate to the building of anything but the most primitive social scene. It is now too late to remedy the situation. The United States is, for better or for worse, a Latin American rather than a European state. Those of us who were given an old-fashioned bringing-up will scarcely ever adapt ourselves to the situation. The best we can do is to try and adapt our children to it.[12]

That these remarks roughly coincided with Europe's historical nadir testifies to Kennan's powerful alienation from American societal and cultural mores. His hostility to the shallow materialism afflicting American society, the anti-intellectualism in American politics, and the parochialism of the average American citizen, recurs in Kennan's diary with frequency and vehemence. Reflecting on the paranoiac force that was McCarthyism, Kennan confided to his diary on April 15, 1951 that 'I am now in the truest sense of the word an expatriate. As an individual, my game is up in this part of the world.'[13] Six years later, he wrote:

> I have... the conviction that there is – outside the walls of this institute – no place for me in this country... One who calls himself an American and does not belong to the local community is really a lost soul – the true rootless cosmopolitan... Why, then, do I want to change my citizenship and become an expatriate? Would I belong to a local community anywhere else? Certainly not. But in England, at any rate, there is a species of community wider than the local one, to which I was civilly and fully admitted, during my period of residence there.[14]

Kennan was an Anglophile, to be sure, but other nations also attracted his ardor. The diaries permit us greater insight into his foreign policy philosophy, primarily in regard to the views Kennan recorded on the merits and demerits of nations other than the United States. Kennan held a great affinity for Russia, mainly in regard to its nineteenth century literature and culture. A gifted linguist, Kennan's spoken Russian was superior to Stalin's – whose enunciation was hampered by his strong Georgian accent – and he began, but this time sadly did not complete, a biography of Anton Chekhov.[15] Yet he also respected the stoic merits of the Russian people, as reflected in a diary entry of July 1, 1944: 'Lunch was served in a little "stolovaya" where they only had one glass, and chairs were scarce; but everyone was goodnatured and helpful about it. How deeply one sympathizes with the Russians when one encounters the realities of the lives of the people and not the propagandistic pretensions of the government.'[16] While Kennan admired much in Russia's history, its foreign policy record, however, was not one from which the United States could learn fruitfully. After all, the nation had been humiliated by Japan in 1905 and by Germany at Brest-Litovsk in 1918.

Germany was another of Kennan's great passions and, again, he was fluent in the language, but again it was the cultural dimension – the land which produced Bach, Beethoven and Goethe – to which he responded most enthusiastically. Habitual overreach in foreign policy was Germany's curse, a hubristic tendency which Kennan clearly did not wish for the United States. For Kennan, Great Britain represented a nation of cultural attainment and reasoned foreign policy that America should emulate above all others. And it was not until 1999 that he formed a definitive conclusion on the matter:

> I have, incidentally, recently come to the conclusion that the English, with all their faults, are really – have been, at least, the greatest of peoples of post 15th century Europe – this at least, in their literary and scholarly upper class. Their civilization was of course erected on great and unfeeling class distinctions. But the members of the upper class were in many instances no less cruel to each other than to those beneath them. And somehow or other, they produced, out of the unfeeling but firmly disciplined society, some of the greatest of world thought and literature. I don't 'like' the English any more than they like us. But I recognize their qualities – am myself an heir to some of them – and am grateful for this inheritance.[17]

Although this entry is not directly focused on diplomacy, it is this admiration for Britain – Kennan himself was proud of his Scottish lineage – which allows us to better understand his views on foreign policy.[18] Kennan believed that the international system was a living organism and that trying to bend the world to America's will was a forlorn task. It was far better for the United States to come to terms with the difficulties that accompany hegemonic status and embrace Lord Palmerston's dictum that 'We have no eternal allies and no permanent enemies. Our interests are eternal, and those interests it is our duty to follow.'[19] Kennan admired the order of British society, which he attributed to the class-system. But more than that, he believed that the United States should abjure Wilsonianiasm, which he famously denigrated as the 'legalist-moralist' mindset, and embrace hard-headed balance of power politics.[20] In this respect, he was much more in tune with Winston Churchill and his infamous percentages deal, as he himself recognized, than Franklin Roosevelt's unrealistic hopes for a postwar condominium of interest with Stalin's Russia. As he wrote in September 18, 1944, two years before the long telegram (in an entry that was reproduced in his memoirs):

> The Soviet government since Munich has never relaxed its determination to have a fairly extensive sphere of influence in certain neighboring areas of Europe and Asia, in which its power would be unchallenged... There is probably no threat or allurement which could cause them to part in good faith and permanently from their

sphere of influence policy... We must find a means to adjust ourselves and our plans to the situation... We must determine in conjunction with the British the limit of our common vital interests on the Continent, i.e., the line beyond which we cannot afford to permit the Russians to exercise unchallenged authority.[21]

Foreign policy for Kennan was a reactive process governed by the situation on the ground at any given time. In 1944 Washington needed to recognize the strength of Moscow's hand and act accordingly and unsentimentally. The worst thing a diplomat or leader could do was approach a problem with a preconceived plan or from a fixed ideological standpoint; the second worst was to be blind-sided by public opinion or absolute notions of morality. That was why effective diplomats had to possess sound instincts above all. And this is the main reason why identifying Kennan's 'grand design' is nigh-on impossible.[22] There was no such thing, just an eloquent entreaty for policymakers to learn from history, and defer to those like Kennan, with fine-tuned diplomatic sensibilities, when making decisions. Kennan's philosophic purpose was similar to that of William James, the father of pragmatism. The intellectual historian Bruce Kuklick's description of James suits Kennan well: 'Although [he] was intrigued with the nuances of argumentation, he was disdainful of metaphysical "logic-chopping" and never wrote a systematic treatise delineating his views.'[23]

* * * * *

It is impossible in a brief chapter to do justice to the wealth of revelations contained in these diaries, so I will settle on discussing four issues that strike me as particularly revealing: Kennan's views on the Middle East in 1948, China in 1950, on John Foster Dulles through the Eisenhower administration, and on Bill Clinton in 1998. On the creation of Israel, firstly, Kennan was deeply concerned about the repercussions of the United States agreeing to serve as Israel's chief supporter, which would inevitably inflame Arab nationalism in the region. This was not a controversial opinion in 1947/48 – indeed Henry Kissinger, a freshman at Harvard at that time, also believed that US interests would be gravely injured by its support for Israel's creation.[24] Yet the Truman White House (if not the State Department) was largely supportive of Israel's path to nationhood, and of America's vital interest in its long-term survival. Kennan, who was unconvinced by this reasoning, had drafted a paper on Palestine for the Office of United Nations Affairs, which cautioned against America taking a strong position on the Arab-Israeli conflict. As Kennan recorded in his diary, it 'came back with a long memorandum attacking it.' Kennan was irritated that contained in this critical reply 'was no hint of criticism of the Zionists, who were apparently blameless... The solution toward which the memorandum pointed were all ones which would have put further strain on our relations with Britain and the Arabs, and on the relations between Britain and the Arabs. Such a policy could proceed only at the expense of our major political and strategic interests in the Middle East.' For Kennan, supporting Israel was likely to be costly to American resources and to its interests in the region. Sentimentality did not enter his analysis at any point. He believed it was best for Washington to step back and allow events to take their natural Darwinian course, irrespective of outcome:

> unless the inhabitants of Palestine, both Jew and Arab, and the international elements which stand behind them, are finally compelled to face each other eye to eye, without outside interference, and weigh, with a sense of immediate and direct responsibility, the consequences of agreement or disagreement, I think they will continue to react irresponsibly... We Americans must realize that we cannot be the keepers and moral guardians of all the peoples in this world. We must become more modest, and recognize the necessary limits to the responsibility we can assume.[25]

These final two sentences neatly distil Kennan's worldview. It was America's obligation, as the world's single-most powerful nation, to protect Western Europe – the sum total of Western Civilization – from the Soviet Union, an abhorrent regime. This was an essentially moral duty. Beyond that, Washington should learn from history's other great Empires and resist the temptation to assume burdens in potentially volatile regions that outstrip its finite resources. America had no moral duty to support the creation of Israel. Zionist attempts to found a nation in the Middle East should live or die by Jewish resources alone.

A second example of Kennan's lack of sentimentality and opposition to ideologically-charged foreign policy is provided by Kennan's diary entry of July 17, 1950 – written just a few weeks after the onset of hostilities in Korea – that records his support for Communist China's entry into the United Nations:

> As far as I can see, it makes not the slightest difference whether or not the Chinese communists come into the U.N.; and the fact that they might come in would be no reason, in my opinion, why we

should feel obliged to have diplomatic relations with them. I hate to see what seems to me a minor issue, on which we should never have allowed ourselves to get hooked, become something which the Russians can use to our advantage in the Korean affair.

Unsurprisingly, Kennan was 'shouted down on this,' describing the hostile reaction to his proposal as yet another 'instance of the damage done to the conduct of our foreign policy by the irresponsible and bigoted interference of the Chinese Lobby and its friend in Congress.'[26] Again, Kennan's scorn for the lobbies that paid the Congressional piper is abundantly clear. Kennan's views on the People's Republic of China were too far ahead of his time. His was a lonely and brave voice in an era dominated by Senator Joe McCarthy, and the increasingly Manichean dimensions that the Cold War came to assume in the American imagination.

One of Kennan's chief tormentor's on China, as on other issues, was the man who famously later refused to shake Zhou Enlai's hand: John Foster Dulles. Kennan's diaries are generally written with a great generosity of spirit – Paul Nitze is garlanded with praise, for example – but his scathing views on Dulles are a rare exception. In March 1953, Kennan had told Allen Dulles that he did not 'want to be kept in Washington as an adviser without power, just far enough from the administration so that my advice could be ignored with impunity and near enough to it that I would be inhibited from participating in public discussions of any policy questions.' Kennan instead asked that Dulles relay to his brother, the Secretary of State, that 'I would prefer another mission in the field, and did not feel that it ought to necessarily be one of the big Embassies.' No offer was forthcoming. It soon became clear to Kennan that 'the president and John Foster Dulles were apparently not interested either in discussing with me my future or that of the Soviet position, nor were they interested in my views about the Soviet Union or US-Soviet relations.' Kennan was devastated by this realization; it was one of his lowest points through the Cold War. For Kennan, the Eisenhower administration's disinterest in his views means they 'would be of no use to anyone anywhere.'[27]

Kennan's rancor at the Eisenhower administration's slight was forcibly expressed in a diary entry of April 21, 1959 – written as John Foster Dulles lay dying of cancer in Walter Reed hospital – which offers a withering assessment of Dulles personally, and the Eisenhower administration and US public opinion generally:

> I have to struggle to avoid a certain bitterness to which I am constantly prompted (as I am sure are Acheson and others) by

Mr. Dulles' latter-day acceptance in western opinion as a statesman of titanic dimensions. I cannot help but compare with my own powerlessness and obscurity the eulogies heaped on this dying man, with whose physical sufferings we all have the greatest sympathy but who, I cannot forget, secured his position with the Congress at the price of demoralization of the Foreign Service and by sacrificing some of its most deserving members, as well as by mouthing inflammatory slogans ('liberation,' 'massive retaliation,' etc) to which he had no intention of adhering in practice, and who in his years of office had taken no political leadership of any sort, has relied entirely on a negative and defensive military policy as an answer to the Soviet political challenge, and has permitted the division of Europe to congeal – has in fact connived in its congealing – to a point where the eastern half of the continent must now be considered as added in permanence to the Russian empire. What is to be done, one tends to ask oneself, with a public which mistakes this for statesmanship? Is there any use in attempting to appeal to its powers of discrimination?[28]

This bracing critique is atypical in its vehemence, but dovetails with Kennan's other speeches and writings of that time – especially his 1957 Reith lectures – which expressed his alienation from Eisenhower-era Cold War orthodoxy. This feeling of being unloved and out-of-step with the foreign policy establishment was constant throughout the remainder of his career. On January 2, 1961, having received no contact from the incoming Kennedy administration, Kennan wrote in his diary that 'I have failed as a public servant. That I was not wanted in government by Foster Dulles was no proof of this. That I am not wanted by my friends makes it unmistakably clear... Never, I think, has there been a man so wholly alone as I have been at this time. There is literally no-one who could help me – also no-one who seriously cares.' Kennan's tendency toward excessive self-recrimination is amply on display here, and a few weeks later President Kennedy did offer him a job that he duly accepted: the US Ambassadorship to Yugoslavia. But there is something to Kennan's remark that he had failed as a public servant; or rather, that the median foreign policy position in United States government had become considerably more confrontational than Kennan himself deemed wise. A life at odds with the mainstream defined the stances Kennan adopted from 1950, or thereabouts, until the end of his life.

During the Clinton administration, for example, Kennan vigorously opposed the enlargement of NATO into Eastern Europe, deeming this a senseless provocation to Moscow. Kennan wrote a high-profile op-ed piece in the *New York Times* in 1997 which expressed strong reservations about the wisdom of kicking Russia while it was clearly down: 'Expanding NATO would be the most fateful error of the entire post-cold war era.'[29] The article created a lot of noise at the time and Kennan's views were quickly criticized by certain members of the Clinton administration as belonging to a very different age. Deputy Secretary of State Strobe Talbott, for example, cautioned Kennan that 'The NATO we are steering through its transformation is already very different from the one that you and your generation created.'[30] But the 2008 war in Georgia was a stark reminder of how firmly attached Moscow was (and is) to its natural sphere of influence; that certain geopolitical truisms remain historically constant.

A year later, concerned that US diplomacy was losing focus in the febrile political environment created by President Clinton's affair with Monica Lewinsky, Kennan recorded on his dairy that 'the President, having assured himself of a comprehensive pardon, should retire – whether now or after the pending elections, it makes no difference. He presumably won't do this – will, one day or another, stick it out. But much of his effectiveness, even if not impeached, will have been lost; and the country – even in a sense the world – will be the sufferer for it.'[31] Here, Kennan's proposed solution is logical and honorable if, as he conceded, politically unrealistic. It was also highly prescient, for Clinton falling on his sword in 1998 might have spared the world a great many problems. Had Al Gore assumed the presidency in 1998 it is more than likely that he would have prevailed against Bush two years later, boosted by the advantages of incumbency and having proved beyond doubt that he was his own man (and without the need to select Joe Lieberman as Vice President to make the point.) And Gore surely would have resisted the temptation to force a settlement at Camp David in 2000 that Yasser Arafat was incapable of delivering.

Kennan was right on this issue, as on many others, but from a hopelessly peripheral position that was easy to dismiss as antediluvian. As a shaper of US foreign policy he was constantly frustrated, with the exception of the period 1946–1948, when his views and those of his political masters converged briefly on their path to divergence. As an analyst of US foreign policy and of the foibles of politicians, however, he was exceptionally gifted, and history will likely view Kennan's post-1950 record as a public intellectual as far-sighted on a great many counts. And this is in spite of the fact that his ethnocentrism – his veneration of Anglo-Saxons and Nordic virtues and contempt for most others – led to his failure to recognize that some of the world's fastest growing economies, and hence diplomatic forces, would be found in the extra-European world. As Kennan wrote to Walt Rostow, then chair of the State Department's Policy Planning Staff, in 1962, the ability to harmonize 'various elements of the political life of the state is peculiar to peoples who have had their origins on or near to the shores of the North Sea.'[32] Kennan was astute on a great many issues, but his notion of racial hierarchy – based largely on his view that a temperate climate and societal success are closely correlated – led him to make some outlandish statements that were subsequently proved wrong by the global diffusion of economic power. When reading Kennan's diaries one agrees admiringly and enthusiastically with ninety percent of the content, while his usual prescience eludes him in the remainder.

*****

John Lukacs, Kennan's most sympathetic and intuitive biographer – and a scholar for whom Kennan had the utmost respect – makes a strong case that Kennan's greatest achievements lay in the realm of his scholarship and literary achievements, not in respect to his diplomatic career, distinguished as it was. Lukacs believes that scholars have focused too much on the period 1946 to 1949, when Kennan's foreign policy influence in Washington was its height. This emphasis is regrettable because 'that chapter of his life was brief and transitory. To concentrate on those few years is as insufficient as it is wrong.'[33] Kennan played an important role in establishing America's basic foreign policy posture towards the Soviet Union during those first few postwar years, and his contribution here should not be underestimated. Indeed, John Lewis Gaddis' *Strategies of Containment* remains the best available account of Kennan's important diplomatic role in the early Cold War.[34] Yet when US foreign policy ran away from Kennan, when Paul Nitze's NSC 68 displaced the 'long telegram' and the 'X Article' to assume blueprint status in Washington, Kennan's quality of insight did not follow the same trajectory as his diminished status as a foreign policy actor. Here, John Lukacs is worth quoting at length:

> [F]or the sake of an American posterity, Kennan the writer and thinker is, or should be, even more important and enduring than Kennan the political advocate; that Kennan about America is even more important and enduring than Kennan about Russia; that Kennan the actual historian and essayist has left us even more valuable

things than Kennan the potential statesman. Though he was often withdrawn and unsure of himself, his character was both more stable and more inspiring than that of Henry Adams. He was a better writer and a better thinker than Adams. The qualities of his achievements were, largely, the results of his mind, of his character, of his conscious employment of his talents.[35]

The elegance and eloquence of Kennan's diary largely justifies Lukacs' ostensibly startling claims (with the exception of his views on America, which will be discussed below.) There was a great deal of literary experimentation in some of the early entries, which produce an evocative and memorable effect. While based in Moscow in 1935, for example, Kennan recorded the following observations:

> Back in Moscow – and extremely unhappy. Boulevards on summer nights. In it and not of. The stark reality of Soviet life compared to the neurotic unreality of our own. The almost theatrical vividness and directness of all things human. More human flesh lives in our seething intimate mass – far more even than in New York. It streams slowly, guilelessly, in thick, full currents, along the boulevards, between the dark trees, under the gleam of the street lights; it is carried – as herded, tired animals are carried in box-cars – in the long trains of street-cars. And it is human life on the new, humanity brought down to its fundamentals – good and evil, drunk and sober, loving and quarrelling, laughing and weeping – all that human life is and does anywhere – but all much more simple and direct and therefore stronger.[36]

These are the observational skills of a first-rate novelist. Much of Kennan's intellectual identity was vested in the quality of his writing for it gave him his greatest sustenance. Through the diaries one gets the strongest sense yet of the importance that Kennan attached to the artistry of his prose and to bequeathing a major literary legacy. It is in Kennan's diaries that his brilliance as a writer and perceptiveness as an observer of people, nations, and ideologies is given truest expression. A year later in Moscow, for example, Kennan composed an updated Burkean view – finished with an Orwellian flourish – on the Russia the revolution had created:

> Has not the Russian experiment proven – if it has proven anything – that the proletariat, once given power, does not necessarily

exercise it with any particular altruism or intelligence by virtue of its own economic chastity, but readily hands it over to the most ruthless and determined political element, which in turn, as a consequence of its ruling position, only inherits the fears and interests of former regimes and exploits the people, under appeals to their patriotism, for the maintenance of its own foreign and domestic position.[37]

This is a marvelous description of Marxism-Leninism in practice. It is a fairly typical entry in that it's beautifully written and revealing. And Kennan, more than anyone, had the requisite skills to offer the most penetrating and elegant insights on the phenomena he observed. In Germany and Russia, his linguistic ability allowed him to assimilate and read these societies from a perspective that most foreign visitors were incapable of assuming. His close and vast reading of history allowed him to draw linkages across eras and empires that a novelist might miss. Yet his written English was also magnificent. This combination of attributes makes the Kennan diaries compulsive to read and truly enlightening. How might the generic American diplomat have reflected on the fall of Paris in 1940? Compare that reconstruction with Kennan's thoughts:

Could one not say to the Germans that the spirit of Paris had been too delicate and shy a thing to stand their determination and had melted away before them just as they thought to have in their grasp? Was there not some Greek myth about the man who tried to ravish the Goddess, only to have her turn to stone when he touched her? That is literally what had happened to Paris. When the Germans came, the soul simply went out of it; and what is left is only stone. As long as they stay – and it will probably be a long time – it will remain stone... In short, the Germans have in their embrace the pallid corpse of Paris.[38]

Kennan's poetic sensitivity took its toll on him through his lifetime. Having lived a peripatetic life up to 1946, when the influence exerted by his Long Telegram led to his recall to Washington, Kennan spent most of the remainder of his life either in Princeton, at the Institute for Advanced Study, or at his farm in Pennsylvania. For over fifty years he found it extremely difficult to gaze at his home nation without falling into despair. Kennan was a staunch opponent of the Vietnam War but he was equally scathing in his assessment of the nihilistic student protests and societal splintering that blighted American society through the 1960s and 1970s. On August 26, 1968, during the chaos of the Democratic Party's convention in Chicago, Kennan expressed his alienation from America in stronger terms than usual:

> I have often returned home in a state of depression, but never anything like this... One thing does seem clear to me. I ought in the interests of my disposition, to avoid as far as possible all confrontation with American life. This means: the absolute minimum of travel (and even that, as far as possible, with closed eyes) but also avoidance of the media: radio, TV, newspapers. Anything, in other words, to avoid the sight and awareness of my country. I must learn to live in it as though I did not live in it... The purpose is not to remain ignorant of American life; the purpose is to avoid seeing it, or encountering it, in the flesh... Scholarship and the farm are the two final refuges, both significantly devoid of every sort of involvement with other people.[39]

In this instance, Kennan's anti-Americanism is remarkable in its intensity. Kennan was hugely gifted in finessing the virtues and failings of other nations, but he fell short in offering a nuanced assessment of his own. His contempt for American values – his amplification of the problems that beset the United States – is surely overdrawn and overwrought. There is much to admire in his identification and critique of the environmental and societal degradation caused by the proliferation of the automobile, and the ugly urban sprawl that was erected to facilitate the demographic shift to the suburbs. But through Kennan's lifetime the United States had an intellectual, economic, and societal vibrancy that was worthy of greater respect. Kennan was sharp, and often correct, in identifying America's shortcomings, but there was too little by way of accompanying balance in his recognition of the nation's virtues.

'Scholarship and the farm' were indeed Kennan's preferred refuges, and historians should be thankful that the former, in particular, satisfied him so completely. The release of Kennan's diaries will likely change the way in which scholars assess his broad significance. Instead of focusing on the early Cold War, and the influence or otherwise of Kennan's containment doctrine, scholars will likely be drawn more into an assessment of the quality of his thought as a reluctant outsider – from the Korean War to the Second Iraq War. Eighty years is a long time to keep a diary. In a diary of this quality, the narrative effect is remarkable. Kennan's moment of recognition was indeed transitory, and the diaries remind us that his absence from the highest government circles was regrettable, for US foreign policy might have been spared many of its missteps had his counsel prevailed. But Kennan, as he recognized painfully, was never likely to enjoy a sustained level of respect and recognition in the United States. His hostility towards the aspects of Cold War America that supposedly defined its moral, social, and political superiority over the Soviet Union guaranteed his distance from the mainstream. This was a man, after all, whose alienation was such that he confided his intention to avoid encountering any aspect of America 'in the flesh.' The life revealed in the pages of these diaries is that of a scholar and writer of the deepest significance; a cosmopolitan who made the conscious decision to live most of as life as an 'edge person,' in Tony Judt's evocative phrase, 'where countries, communities, allegiances, affinities, and roots bump uncomfortably up against one another – where cosmopolitanism is not so much an identity as the normal condition of life.'[40] This is the Kennan that will emerge more clearly in the historiography in the coming decades.

Notes

1. See Arthur M. Schlesinger Jr., *Journals: 1952–2000* (New York: The Penguin Press, 2007) and Lyndon Baines Johnson, *The Vantage Point: Perspectives on the Presidency, 1963–1969* (New York: Henry Holt and Co., 1971).
2. See George F. Kennan, *Memoirs, 1925–1950* (Boston: Little Brown, 1967); George F. Kennan, *Memoirs, 1950–1963* (Boston: Little Brown, 1972); George F. Kennan, *Sketches from a Life* (New York: Pantheon, 1989).
3. Henry Kissinger's three volumes of memoirs are revealing mainly in the sense that he reveals little – in over three thousand pages – that is truly illuminating for scholars (as was intended.) It is a remarkable performance, in many respects. See Henry Kissinger, *The White House Years* (London: Weidenfeld and Nicholson, 1979); Henry Kissinger, *Years of Upheaval* (London: Weidenfeld and Nicholson, 1982), and Henry Kissinger, *Years of Renewal* (New York: Simon and Schuster, 1999).
4. Quoted in Robert L. Beisner, *Dean Acheson: A Life in the Cold War* (New York: Oxford University Press), 118, 355.
5. Eugene Rostow, 'Searching for Kennan's Grand Design,' *The Yale Law Journal*, Vol. 87, No. 7 (June 1978), 1528.
6. Walter L. Hixson, *George F. Kennan: Cold War Iconoclast* (New York: Columbia University Press, 1989), xii.
7. Barton Gellman, *Contending with Kennan: Toward a Philosophy of American Power* (New York: Praeger, 1984), 18.
8. David Mayers, *George Kennan and the Dilemmas of US Foreign Policy* (New York: Oxford University Press, 1988).

9. Anders Stephanson, *Kennan and the Art of Foreign Policy* (Cambridge, MA: Harvard University Press, 1989), 191.
10. George F. Kennan Diaries (GFKD), August 4, 1944, Box 231, Department of Rare Books and Special Collections, Princeton University Library (PUL).
11. See John J. Mearsheimer and Stephen M. Walt, *The Israel Lobby and US Foreign Policy* (New York: Farrar, Straus and Giroux, 2007).
12. GFKD, March 21, 1940, Box 231, PUL.
13. GFKD, April 15, 1951, Box 232, PUL.
14. GFKD, October 6, 1959, Box 233, PUL.
15. See Nicholas Thompson, *The Hawk and the Dove: Paul Nitze, George Kennan, and the History of the Cold War* (New York: Henry Holt and Company, 2009), 9.
16. GFKD, July 1, 1944, Box 231, PUL.
17. GFKD, July 13, 1999, Box 239, PUL.
18. Kennan was fascinated by his family history and wrote a book on the subject: George F. Kennan, *An American Family: The Kennans* (New York: W.W. Norton, 2000).
19. Quoted in Henry Kissinger, *Diplomacy* (New York: Simon and Schuster, 1994), 97.
20. See George F. Kennan, *American Diplomacy, 1900–1950* (Chicago: University of Chicago Press, 1951).
21. GFKD, September 18, 1944, Box 231, PUL.
22. W. Scott Lucas and Kaeten Mistry present a strong case that Kennan was not driven by a single unifying theory, and offer an insightful assessment of how this affected his views on 'political warfare.' See Scott Lucas and Kaeten Mistry, 'Illusions of Coherence: George F. Kennan, US Strategy and Political Warfare in the Early Cold War,' *Diplomatic History*, Vol. 33, Issue 1 (January 2009). Frank Costgliola offers a marvelously creative interpretation of Kennan's mindset in '"Unceasing Pressure for Penetration": Gender, Pathology, and Emotion in George Kennan's Formation of the Cold War,' *The Journal of American History*, Vol. 83, No. 4 (March 1997), 1309–39.
23. Quoted in William James (edited with an introduction by Bruce Kuklick), *Pragmatism* (Indianapolis, IN: Hackett Publishing, 1981), xii.
24. See Walter Isaacson, *Henry Kissinger: A Biography* (London: Faber and Faber, 1992), 60.
25. GFKD, January 28, 1948, Box 231, PUL.
26. GFKD, July 17, 1950, Box 232, PUL.
27. GFKD, March 13, 1953, Box 233, PUL.
28. GFKD, April 29, 1959, Box 233, PUL.
29. George F. Kennan, 'A Fateful Error,' *New York Times*, February 5, 1997, A19.
30. Stobe Talbott to George F. Kennan, February 13, 1997, Box 47, Papers of George F. Kennan, PUL.
31. GFKD, October 7, 1998, Box 239, PUL.
32. Letter from George F. Kennan to Walt Rostow, May 15, 1962, *Foreign Relations of the United States: National Security Policy*, 1962, 286–7.
33. John Lukacs, *George Kennan: A Study of Character* (New Haven: Yale University Press, 2007), 2.
34. John Lewis Gaddis, *Strategies of Containment: A Critical Appraisal of American National Security Policy During the Cold War* (New York: Oxford University Press, 1982).

35 John Lukacs, *George Kennan*, 6.
36 GFKD, September 3, 1934, Box 230, PUL.
37 GFKD, May 10, 1935, Box 230, PUL.
38 GFKD, July 3, 1940, Box 230, PUL.
39 GFKD, August 26, 1968, Box 237, PUL.
40 See Tony Judt, 'Edge People,' *New York Review of Books*, February 23, 2010.

4
Ideology, Race and Nonalignment in US Cold War Foreign Relations: or, How the Cold War Racialized Neutralism Without Neutralizing Race

Jason Parker

In an irony that would likely have both surprised and gratified its founders, the Non-Aligned Movement (NAM) has outlived the bipolar Cold War alignments that inspired its creation in the first place. It has come to be seen as synonymous with the so-called 'Third World,' another entity which the superpower conflict helped to create. As such, the persuasion that NAM champions – originally dubbed 'neutralism' but purposefully renamed 'nonalignment' by its founders – has historically been perceived as race- (and class-) inflected; as being the *de facto* collective stance of the non-European developing-nations of the global South.[1] This membership was not, or not entirely, a grouping imposed by the Western camp. Although it was a French demographer who coined the term 'Third World,' there was always – most critically in the rhetoric of many global-South actors themselves – a racial dimension to the concept and the neutralist-nonaligned ideology that accompanied it. As a consequence, for contemporaries and scholars, NAM seemed by extension to equal non-white as well. But it is important to remember that neutralism-nonalignment, as a response to the Cold War, didn't start out that way. 'Race,' broadly understood, shaped its conceptual and linguistic evolution in important ways. This historical relationship between Cold War neutralism-nonalignment – an ideological position that could be adopted by movements of various stripes – and race – a complex subject central to the postwar age of decolonization and civil rights – raises fascinating questions. How did neutralism-nonalignment, once incarnate as the NAM, see its Third World membership transform the persuasion into a 'racial' matter? Given the crippling paradox of the US superpower – the 'land of the free' being the home of Jim Crow

– was there an American role in driving the racialization of a putatively non-racial Cold War bloc? Is this turn of events thus best understood as an ideological construct of the East-West Cold War, or as a transnationally ethno-cultural construct of the North-South global race revolution?[2]

This chapter argues that the answer to the last question depends on the timing: it is first the former, and then the latter. In recent decades, a flowering of scholarship on race and diplomacy now allows us to examine topics such as this one, located at that intellectual intersection, in their proper depth.[3] While that literature is not without its flaws – it has, for example, on occasion succumbed to romantic temptation at the expense of empirical grounding – it nevertheless allows us to see the interplay of race and neutralism-nonalignment as a microcosm of two competing visions of modern international history. One sees through what Matthew Connelly calls the 'Cold War lenses' of the East-West strategic-ideological contest, in which the two sides presented 'universalist' templates for modernity and nation-statehood to a global South seeking independence and development. The other sees through the prism of the longer-running, incomplete, 'Wilsonian' transition from imperial rule via 'particularist' ethnic-nationalism, race relations, and the nation-state.[4] Odd Arne Westad's magisterial work shows that the two visions clashed repeatedly in the global South, pitting the internal politics of nation-making against external connections to the superpowers. The results were often violent and felt far afield, producing the truly 'global Cold War.' Yet before that time, the two visions had first converged in the formation of a racially-inflected, non-aligned geopolitical bloc, whose coalescence carved a North-South axis on the Cold War landscape.

In the later 1950s, the persuasion began to evolve in ways that left it not quite fully – but nonetheless predominantly and identifiably – racialized, both in the minds of US policymakers and many self-identifying Third World actors alike. It did so even as the initial Afro-Asian push for neutralism-nonalignment split and diffused among competing proponents. The early signs of this split were evident at the April 1955 Bandung meeting which purportedly affirmed both neutralism and the pan-racial solidarity of Afro-Asian peoples. The legacy of that meeting meant different things to the political leaders who organized and participated in it, to the contemporary enthusiasts of pan-racial identity and solidarity who praised it, and to subsequent generations of scholars who have assessed it. Recent contributions by Bob Vitalis, Itty Abraham, Christopher Lee, and others reveal that as these diverse legacies of Bandung and its companion developments filtered through subsequent East-West and North-South relations, they created a complex interplay of ideology and race on the Cold War landscape, in which the establishment of NAM ultimately represented the ascendancy of one strain of neutralism-nonalignment over another.[5] The terms 'neutralism' and 'nonalignment' denoted two slightly different strains of an ideological stance, in competition in the years after Bandung. The change in terminology held twofold significance. On the one hand, as Mark Lawrence notes, was the deliberate choice to highlight nonaligned agency: 'while [neutralism] implied a passive kind of withdrawal from the global stage, non-alignment entailed the possibility of activism.'[6] On the other, while that agency was intended to be non-racial in nature, its assertion – concurrent with the near-tandem rise of the 'Third World' – meant that in practice the movement was seen to have been largely repossessed by the avatars of pan- and trans-racial global-South solidarity.

This essay argues that the convergence of these two entities – neutralism-nonalignment and the Third World – produced the 'racialization' of the former, to the extent that in many First and Third World minds alike during the Cold War, nonaligned more or less equaled non-white. The hybrid term neutralism-nonalignment underlines the shared foundational principle – opposition to the Cold War's bipolarity – which predated the founding of NAM.[7] Although neutralism-nonalignment began as an ostentatiously non-racial persuasion, to which any global actor from Yugoslavia to India could in theory subscribe, it evolved in tension with the fact that virtually all the newly-independent peoples were non-white, and many of their leaders inferred a collective 'Third World' identity from this seemingly millennial phenomenon of decolonization. Their multiple and ongoing 'insider' conversations drove the process, leaving actor-observers in Washington to tease out its contending meanings for American Cold War strategy. By the time neutralism-nonalignment took the form of NAM, and despite the efforts of that body's organizers, the stance had become synonymous with the Third World, as seen by many actors at the time, and enduringly by many scholars since.

* * * * *

By way of background, it is worth emphasizing both the fluidity of the terms here in play – neutralism-nonalignment, anticolonialism, nationalism, and perhaps 'race' above all – and the fact that the relationship of each term to the others evolved over the decades of the

Cold War. 'Race,' for example, in European and American officials' experience with empire abroad or segregation at home, tended to denote and reinforce a hierarchy of the world's peoples.[8] On the other hand, for many on the receiving end of empire or segregation, an ethno-racial identity could undergird the solidarity necessary for the overthrow of the colonial regime, as pan-African, pan-Asian, or pan-Arab sentiment could erase the lines of imperial rule. In between these points, several of those who would become prominent colonial-nationalist leaders would have recoiled at being lumped into a catchall bloc defined vaguely by 'race.' But the power of the concept to create categories within and among societies in the still-imperial world was undeniable.

Early Cold War neutralism, for its part and before it had come to be used more or less interchangeably with 'nonalignment,' was neither necessarily race-inflected nor a colonial-nationalist matter.[9] In the United States, its close cousin neutrality had been a respectable stance in the world crisis of the 1930s, until it was discredited by Pearl Harbor and the subsequent course of World War II. Its decline continued more or less steadily through the transition years between world war and Cold War, and its fall from grace was finally complete by the onset of the latter. But the latter years of the 1940s seemed to show that neutralism-nonalignment abroad had two faces, and neither was specifically or essentially racial in nature or impression. Unlike, for example, the rhetorical currents of Muslim solidarity that had helped to cleave Pakistan from India, or of trans-island Caribbean nationalism that encouraged the creation of a West Indian Federation, little about late-1940s neutralism-nonalignment suggested any racial or other-communal dimension. At this early moment in the Cold War, the Truman administration thus ranked it much more as an ideological foreign policy concern – potentially endangering above all the political soul of Europe – than as a 'movement' of any discernible kind, racial or otherwise. This was in keeping with the greater weight Washington tended to assign to ideology over most other geopolitical factors.[10] That is, if neutralism-nonalignment was seen as possessing both ideological *and* regional, racial, or some other dimensions, the first concern was the Truman administration's chief one.

US analysts of the time even put literal faces on the proverbial 'two faces' of late-1940s neutralism-nonalignment: Marshal Josip Broz Tito in Yugoslavia, and Prime Minister Jawaharlal Nehru in India. Tito offers the clearest evidence that the persuasion was, in some basic sense, seen as non-racially-specific in nature. In some respects, though, this made it a potentially even greater challenge, as far as Washington was concerned. Although few American officials saw it this way at the time, if neutralism-nonalignment *à la* Tito was racially non-specific, then in theory any country might fall under its sway. It might, that is, make its way into western Europe. This conclusion would not gel in most minds until the middle Eisenhower years; until then, Tito's stance was on balance seen as a net gain for the Western side.[11] US policymakers wrestled with its uncertainties, but ultimately embraced it as a defection from the Eastern camp. They also, on the whole, understood it as confirmation that neutralism-nonalignment was primarily an ideological identification, leavened with a healthy dose of power-politics.

The other half of the late-1940s duo, Nehru, did little at first to undercut this conclusion. His eloquent and passionate advocacy of neutralism-nonalignment showed that sentiment to be afoot in decolonizing areas. Many of Nehru's pronouncements on the subject had at least as much to do with domestic politics as with world circumstances as South Asia approached independence, but his external listeners, in Washington and elsewhere, often failed to register that nuance. Before and well after the transfer of power to an independent India in August 1947, he had argued for such a 'neutral' course in the still-nascent Cold War.[12]

Such a position, seen from Washington that missed many of its subtleties, could not help but have racial-ethnic overtones. The end of 'white' rule over the 'brown' subcontinent would have an unavoidably racial tinge to it. At the often-overlooked Asian Relations Conference of April 1947, neutralism-nonalignment was more implicit than explicit – and indeed, 'racial' identity, in the form of the glories of a shared Asian civilization and in Gandhi's repeated use of the term 'coolie' in his remarks at the Conference, was for the moment more in the foreground. But the Conference was, somewhat by default, perhaps the first prominent platform of neutralism-nonalignment. In its aftermath, participants, as Abraham shows, began to transcend the inherited imperial legacy of thinking in 'racial logics' of 'Asian civilization.'[13]

After the Asian Relations Conference, race moved largely to the margins of Nehru's rhetorics of neutralism, both toward the wider world and toward India's peer countries in the 'first wave' of decolonization. The shift was not always a smooth one. Some colonial and diasporan voices from South Asia to the West Indies had been proposing race-consciousness as an engine of romantic anticolonialism for decades. As those areas approached both individual and collective independence, such 'racial logics' were bound to remain in tension with the avowedly non-racial doctrine of neutralism-nonalignment advanced by Nehru and his fellow proponents. The other new independent states of South and Southeast Asia – the Philippines, Burma, Pakistan, Ceylon, and Indonesia – embraced some parts of the neutralist philosophy to varying degrees, but for reasons other than some vague sense of racial solidarity. The same was largely true of Nehru's public pronouncements. Various US and British officials suspected him of harboring mistrust and even ill-will of whites, but his elucidations of neutralist philosophy did not offer much evidence of this. Rather, in addition to expressing a genuinely-held philosophical conviction, they also arguably fit into the same category as Tito's neutralism: a savvy, *realpolitik* stance befitting India's position in regional and world affairs, one with the ostensible additional virtue of its organic connection to Hinduism.[14] If race was a passenger in the neutralist vehicle, ideology seemed to be in the driver's seat, with power-politics riding shotgun.

The one-two punch of the communist triumph in China in autumn 1949 and the outbreak of the Korean War in June 1950 changed the equation. The former showed Washington that a country on the periphery, at least as much as those on the Cold War's European frontlines, could succumb to communism. It showed, moreover, that communism could triumph among the peoples of Asia – that the 'red menace,' that is, was not at the same time an exclusively white one. If the ideological appeal of communism could be fused with the 'racial' currents of nationalism elsewhere in Asia and Africa, it could potentially change the geostrategic picture, greatly endangering American prospects in the Cold War. The war in Korea, for its part, demonstrated the now-higher stakes of *any* transition from 'colonial' status; it should not be forgotten that postwar Korea was itself a decolonizing area, though one held by a defeated Asian power rather than a European empire, and one occupied by American and Soviet forces. The combination convinced all observers that the Cold War had been unleashed on the Asian mainland. For Nehru, this bolstered his case for neutralism, which became a kind of containment doctrine meant to keep the military and nuclear standoff from spreading inland south and west from the Pacific littoral. On these grounds he kept India, and neutralism, at the center of the Korean armistice diplomacy at the United Nations.[15]

This, however, also raised the concern in the minds of American observers – and, they thought, reading Nehru's mind, in the Indian premier's as well – that the heretofore subtle racial dimension of neutralism might become more pronounced. On the one hand, some US officials recognized other factors driving the persuasion. One American propagandist argued in the early months of the Korean War that 'the "neutrality" of the young Asian nations is only another name for the "isolation" that so long prevailed in the US and that we have only recently outgrown. It is natural and inevitable for the Asians who have been free of Western domination for such a short time to wish to stay out of the conflicts which have been thrust upon the West.'[16] At the same time, Washington wondered if Nehru believed that neutralism could transcend communism as a unifying agent of a pan-Asian identity. As one report assessed, Nehru 'thinks of himself as the potential leader of Asia... [he] sees himself as leader of colored masses in a world struggle for equality.'[17] Some feared, not wholly realistically, the possible emergence of an 'Asian bloc' under an entente of militant Chinese communism and a disingenuous and acquiescent Indian neutralism. The main American worries about the latter continued to stem less from race-related fears than from the suspicion that Nehru's neutralism made him a dupe, willing or unwilling, of communism. But race-tinged rhetoric of the 'yellow peril,' long present in American culture, suggested that even the Korean armistice would not settle all the strategic, ideological, and racial issues raised by China and Korea in the 1950s.[18] If the first two categories were ranked most important, the third could nonetheless not be dismissed. Moreover, it was the one arguably least controllable, not to say least comprehensible, by an American government itself at that moment wrestling with desegregation in the streets of its federal capital.[19]

Such intimations were not soothed by the creation of the Colombo Powers, and were apparently confirmed by the powers' first fruit. The powers were the above-named South- and Southeast Asian countries, minus the Philippines. They did not constitute a formal alliance, but the meeting of their foreign ministers in April 1954 had fleshed out the nucleus of an informal neutralist bloc, minus Pakistan. Their determination to avoid entanglement with either side in the Cold War – to keep it from further intrusion into Asia, and to avoid the militarization of the continent – received a rude reply in September when the Eisenhower administration led the two 'outside' Asian allies (Pakistan and the Philippines) plus Thailand, Australia, New Zealand, Great Britain, and France in the formation of the Southeast Asia Treaty Organization (SEATO). Given that the membership included two members of that first wave of Asian decolonization, it might be seen as a device for holding the proverbial line against neutralism as much as against communism. If the latter was more crucial for SEATO architect John Foster

Dulles, the former's chief representatives nevertheless saw SEATO's establishment as a gauntlet thrown their way. In the following months, Nehru and Sukarno rallied their Colombo compatriots to the idea of responding – not with a neutralist-nonaligned bloc *per se*, but with an event that might bring together peoples of the potentially-neutralist world in a roughly common cause. The fruit of these efforts was the Afro-Asian Peoples conference, announced in December 1954 and to be held the following April in Bandung, Indonesia. Soon to be known by the shorthand of the Bandung Conference, it marked a milestone in the 'racializing' of neutralism-nonalignment, both in the romantic imaginations of the champions of race-solidarity and in the strategic calculations of the Cold War players.[20]

Why was this so? It was because 'committed' or 'non-committed' had less to do with the final list of attendees than did 'white' or 'non-white.'[21] During the planning stages of the conference in early 1955, the agenda was fuzzy among insiders and harder still to discern from the outside. That which could be gleaned from Washington appeared neutralist in substance and tone, despite the prospect that 'neutrals' at the meeting might be outnumbered by a distinctly 'aligned' majority, as turned out to be the case.[22] The final communiqué issued at the close of the conference on April 24 remained somewhat vague, which as Abraham argues was crucial to maintaining the fragile consensus among the participants.[23] The document referred to the shared struggle with colonialism and imperialism, but even these were couched in the language of transracial cooperation – to the point that Dulles could report to the National Security Council (NSC) that the United States largely agreed, the communiqué being in line with what 'we [Americans] feel in our hearts.'[24] In addition, thanks to the presence of decidedly aligned attendees like the Philippines, which acted as Washington's proxy at the conference, the communiqué was so even-handed that it denounced equally both Soviet and Western imperialism. Even other aligned, or non-neutral at least, attendees like China registered little or no dissent in this progression.

However, if the communiqué's prose was racially neutral, its authors were not, especially as perceived corporately by Western observers. The roster of the two and half dozen attending countries held, according to CIA chief Allen Dulles, 'little in common save the shared experience of recent Western colonialism or imperialism.' The African American writer Richard Wright concurred though with considerably more enthusiasm and from a different point of view, avowing that the act of coming together of various non-white peoples engendered a potent, foundational solidarity. Wright gave the title *The Color Curtain* to his memoir of the meeting, and exulted that 'every religion under the sun, almost every race on earth, every shade of political opinion, and one and a half thousand million people... were represented here.' In this he echoed Sukarno's opening statement to the conference, cited by countless scholars since: 'We can mobilise all the spiritual, all the moral, all the political strength of Asia and Africa on the side of peace. Yes, we! We, the peoples of Asia and Africa, 1,400,000,000 strong, far more than half the human population of the world, we can mobilise.'[25]

Observers could be forgiven for assuming that such rhetoric would resonate given the attendees' list, which included countries newly-independent and soon-to-be-independent from around the Afro-Asian globe – but none from the 'white world,' not even Nehru's ostensible partner in neutralism, Yugoslavia. Nehru and Sukarno no doubt truly believed that neutralism-nonalignment as a Cold War position could exist independent of color. But the conceptualization, design, and execution of Bandung suggested the possibility, perhaps the likelihood, of a convergence of the two. Nehru was quite explicit that the creation of a new 'bloc' on the geopolitical map was not a purpose of the conclave.[26] However, the communiqué's references to working together, plus the rhetoric of anticolonial Afro-Asian-Arab solidarity, affirmed a kind of global-South common ground. That solidarity's serious internal fissures were not obvious from the outside. But it could nonetheless have potential going forward – perhaps even coming to overshadow its putative assertion of neutralism-nonalignment. As Christopher Lee observes, 'only India, Burma, and Indonesia supported the idea [nonalignment] explicitly. However, the more momentous result was the *feeling* of political possibility presented through this first occasion of "Third World" solidarity, what was soon referred to as the Bandung Spirit.'[27]

Richard Wright was not the only American observer to perceive this prospect. African American Congressman Adam Clayton Powell, who went to Bandung with a journalist's rather than a diplomatic emissary's credentials, thought so too.[28] Bandung's impact could be felt in the contemporary conversation and culture of what John Munro calls the anticolonial front of the Black International. Wright was thus not alone in testifying to the power of the moment; Alpaheus Hunton, Frank London Brown, and Malcolm X, among others, wrote it up as well.[29] Nor were those who heard a call to pan-racial destiny alone in perceiving an epochal moment in race relations, with the obvious follow-on questions about the impact of such possible 'unity' on world affairs. As Matt Jones writes, before the conference some members of the Eisenhower administration had worried that Bandung signified the possibility of a '"segregated" Asia.'[30]

In the event, the conference presented Washington with a plot twist: the Bandung brand of neutralism-nonalignment seemed to have simultaneously become *more* racial and *less* threatening. As noted above, Bandung attendees hailed exclusively from non-white nations and nations-to-be. This, on its face, would seem to confirm the 'segregated' thesis. But it did not – because the Afro-Asian aspect of neutralism-nonalignment espoused in the final document did not strike the Eisenhower administration as the main story in the aftermath. American officials starting with Dulles instead peered through the lens of power-politics. Whatever the prospects of a Bandung-born 'black-brown-yellow menace' of pan-racial unity, they paled in comparison to the overarching Red one. US analysts drew this conclusion from their judgment that Nehru had suffered a 'very severe reverse' at his own meeting, whereas Zhou Enlai came away with his and China's prestige enlarged.[31] The two leaders had affirmed, in their speeches at Bandung and in the final conference communiqué, the 'five principles' of *panscheel* that the two countries had jointly first declared the year before.[32] Yet given that China was both non-white and un-neutral, Enlai's embrace of Bandung forced all parties to make a choice. China could submit its blessing of neutralism-nonalignment as a way to jockey for position with Moscow as the leader of worldwide communism, especially in the competition in the emerging Third World. Nehru, seeing un-neutral China stake its claim, would be obliged to reclaim true neutralism-nonalignment by distinguishing it from the communist-inflected kind.[33]

In this he would have help from Nasser. The two leaders had bonded at Bandung, and Nasser added a stopover in New Delhi to his return trip home so that they might talk further. But the Egyptian premier was nonetheless also a potential competitor for the role of Third World spokesman, albeit one with his own reasons for keeping China and communism at arm's length. The conference's rhetoric of cooperation notwithstanding, the Eisenhower administration ultimately concluded that these interactions held at least as much promise for dissension on political grounds as for unity along 'racial' lines constructed around the Bandung cohort.[34] A 'segregated Asia' or a mobilized Afro-Asian bloc ranked as more background than foreground concern; the opposite was true of the nexus of ideology, strategy, and power-politics that emerged from Bandung in the middle 1950s.

Viewed from Washington, then, these developments added up to a phenomenon whose racial dimension might still in some vague and yet uncertain ways damage some American interests.[35] However, its ideological dimension might in the end actually serve other ones. Among these were the prospects that Bandung-style 'neutralism' might pull China and the Soviet Union apart, in fashion similar to Tito's distancing from Moscow; that if China did successfully co-opt Afro-Asian sentiment, it might nudge India westward, or at least towards a 'purer' neutralism-nonalignment untainted by the explicit bond with Beijing; and that China's enhanced stature gave it the legitimacy and confidence to negotiate crises, like those recurring over the offshore islands, with the US. None of these developments were guaranteed, of course, and all brought potential disadvantages as well – but any one of them would amount to a reasonably shiny silver lining around the cloud of Asian neutralism-nonalignment.

Beyond the Asian theater, the future possibility of a more racial and less ideological neutralism-nonalignment could even come to serve as a bedrock for US interest. Although a racially-identified strain of the persuasion reinforced other currents troublesome to Washington – most of all, the burgeoning African American civil rights movement and the consequent world attention on Jim Crow in the self-proclaimed 'land of the free' – it also had one constructive aspect for American diplomacy.[36] It is interesting to note that one of the main lessons the Eisenhower administration took from Bandung was on the threat of neutralism *in Europe*. After the conference, the administration conducted studies, on both an individual-country- and continental-basis, of the danger that neutralism-nonalignment bore for Western unity in the Cold War. The studies concluded that the chances of neutralism taking root in Europe were less than in Third World – but that the damage to US interests, should that occur, would be far greater. Hence a more-ideological-than-racial strain of neutralism would pose, in a way, the greater risk. If the persuasion, flying from Bandung under Nehru et al.'s wings, had the potential to become a basically non-white phenomenon, then the theoretical risk of it taking hold in Europe seemed to Eisenhower's team to be much reduced.

This is not to underplay the significance of neutralism-nonalignment's potential racial dimension, either for US policy or for postwar global history. Bandung and Jim Crow, noted above, formed part of a broader worldwide context, one which Tim Borstelmann calls the '*Brown*-Bandung-Montgomery' watershed in global race relations.[37] Lengthening the chronology into 1956–58 allows for the inclusion of four more 'supporting' events pointing in that same direction: the Suez Crisis, the independence of Ghana, the Little Rock Crisis, and the All African Peoples Congress. Each of these events has been well-covered elsewhere, and need not be described here in great detail. What is of interest is their rough concurrence, and cumulative effect. The watershed they represented was unmistakable. It helped to further the perception of an Afro-Asian-Arab neutralism-nonalignment begun at Bandung, even if, ironically, the authors of that original conference found themselves leaning in the other direction by the end of decade. The set of putatively unrelated events, across a four-year stretch and spanning the globe, taken together signaled the arrival of what we might call the global race revolution. The Richard Wright assessment of Bandung, though increasingly at odds in these years with the actual jockeying and competition among its authors, nonetheless harmonized with other claimants of its legacy such as Nkrumah. This kept Bandung in conversations about the changing international dynamics of race. As James Meriwether's excellent study demonstrates, the high if often largely symbolic global profile of these events drew mutual interest from activists on all continents, who as a consequence began to conceive of their own respective struggles differently.[38]

This international environment all but guaranteed that neutralism-nonalignment would evolve into being synonymous with race in many minds by the turn of the decade – ironically, even as some of the persuasion's most visible spokesmen consciously sought to *distance* themselves from race while wrestling with each other for leadership of the persuasion. As Vitalis has argued, the later 1950s witnessed a heated competition for possession of the 'Bandung legacy,' including the neutralism-nonalignment banner. Nehru, Nasser, Nkrumah, Sukarno, and a handful of others deployed various initiatives – hosting or attending conferences, conducting public relations campaigns, seeking allies abroad – meant to play up one or another aspect of neutralism-nonalignment, and thereby to claim a kind of ownership of the persuasion.[39] Each of these initiatives had weaknesses. Nkrumah's Pan-African strain, on vivid display at the All African Peoples Congress noted above, limited its possible membership. Sukarno's strain of the Bandung spirit was not as neutral as advertised, although perhaps less egregious on that front than the communist-sponsored Afro-Asian Peoples Solidarity Organization.[40] Nasser's obvious regional focus constrained the broader appeal of whatever 'neutral' agenda he attached to it. The mere fact of this competition ensured that neutralism-nonalignment had many faces – almost all non-white and non-

Western, and all seemingly at some odds with one another. If the persuasion was coming to be identified with the global South, it did not escape notice that its avatars were hardly a vision of unity in its name.

The groundwork for victory in this competition was laid down at an event coincident with, but in other ways an outlier to, the 'watershed' timeline noted above: the meeting of Nehru, Nasser, and Tito at Brioni in July 1956. The meeting was an accident in its inception, but an outlier by design in its execution.[41] The triumvirate sought to strengthen the connections between them, and to discuss and coordinate, to the degree possible, a 'third way' neutralist-nonaligned agenda to be led by them. The degree possible was less than it might have been given the timing, as Nasser's seizure of the Suez Canal complicated the prospects for unity. But Brioni did help to strengthen the coalition for a broad-based, multicontinental, and both ostensibly and ostentatiously nonracial neutralism-nonalignment, which the triumvirate would affirm five years later.

The triumvirate's unity itself was an important statement. Its mere existence as a multilateral, autonomous entity was more than competitors like Sukarno could claim, and it brought victory: the formalization of neutralism-nonalignment in the vehicle of the Non-Aligned Movement, founded by Nehru, Nasser, and Tito in Belgrade in September 1961. The triumvirate established an entity that would prove to have staying power. It endured throughout the rest of the Cold War, and gained a certain legitimacy as the 'official' voice of the global South in the UN General Assembly.[42] But Belgrade was also where, in a sense, avowedly non-racial neutralism-nonalignment had its swansong. The triumvirate had made great efforts to distance NAM from the rhetoric of race-unity, underlining time and again the ideological role they envisioned for the entity on the Cold War stage. NAM was, it would appear, a rebuke to the implicit idea that neutralism-nonalignment equaled non-white, if for no other reason than that Tito was one of the founders, and that the founding took place in Belgrade.[43]

However, Belgrade would be the only 'white' city ever to play host, as circumstances conspired to fuse neutralism-nonalignment with a kind of globalized race-consciousness. Chief among these was the contemporaneous coalescing of an intellectual and geopolitical entity long imagined: the 'Third World.' Though some scholars date the emergence of this entity earlier on the century's timeline – Vijay Prashad, for example, finds the moment of birth to have been the 1927 inauguration of the League against Imperialism in Brussels – most would agree that the identity-*cum*-bloc became full-fledged during the first half of the Cold War.⁴⁴ This, in turn, owed to the interplay of several factors. Among these were the basic metrics of decolonization. The year before Belgrade had been dubbed the 'Year of Africa,' during which seventeen new sub-Saharan countries gained independence, followed in the next few years by a half-dozen more. Thus as a matter of numbers, all of the new countries to enter the atlas were majority non-white, so that even if only a portion of these chose a neutralist-nonaligned path, the net effect would still be to push neutralism-nonalignment away from any identification with the global North.

Certainly this was the case in the minds of contemporaries. The USA, for example, consistently judged that this tendency was organic, if misguided: 'Underestimating Sino-Soviet interest in Africa or in world domination and viewing the East-West conflict as almost ephemeral, some Africans hold that the more important division of the world is a North-South one between the 'have' and 'have not' nations and that East and West ought to cooperate in redressing it.'⁴⁵ As Leslie Wolf-Phillips puts it in his history of the term 'Third World,' quoting Peter Worsley's contemporary definition: 'What the Third World originally was, then, is clear; it was the non-aligned world.'⁴⁶ Moreover, echoing some of the rhetoric if not the reality of Bandung, its proponents asserted before the United Nations that the nonaligned Afro-Asian group was, in the words of the Minister of Foreign Affairs of newly independent Guinea, a 'spiritual family.'⁴⁷

Perhaps as important was what one might call a matter of philosophy, or perhaps morality. This was not in the condemnatory Dullesian sense of neutralism as an essentially moral failing, nor of the 'supremacist' Gandhian reading of a higher Afro-Asian sensibility about world affairs, both of which senses could be found in the rhetoric of the previous decade. Nonetheless important is that to the extent non-alignment was perceived to have a 'moral' dimension, it was one in line with other philosophies of independence. Nkrumah's Pan-Africanism, for example, perhaps helped to crystallize the racial component of nonalignment.⁴⁸ Nkrumah contended that the version of the persuasion which he (and Nasser alike) called 'positive neutralism' was all but required by true Pan-Africanism.⁴⁹ For Nkrumah, this was not only a moral obligation but practically necessary for the full achievement of the continent's liberation and unification.⁵⁰ As Pan-Africanism suggests, the conviction that Third World independence was a moral necessity raised the question of what *true* independence was. Rather than a strictly political-juridical status, its more abstract dimensions engaged a set of deeper meanings. As Tanzanian premier Julius Nyerere put it, 'non-alignment comes back to the question of freedom for our nation. If we are to rely upon one of the contending power blocs and be hostile to the other, then... the freedom to determine our own policies would have to be surrendered.'[51] For Africa specifically, Nyerere argued, 'African nationalism is meaningless, is dangerous, is anachronistic if it is not at the same time pan-Africanism.'[52] If non-alignment at Belgrade signified a kind of declaration of independence from the ideological East-West strictures of the Cold War, non-alignment as understood and defined by Nkrumah, Nyerere, and their fellow Third World actors themselves went further, asserting solidarity along a global North-South axis as well.

* * * * *

Below such airy, romantic visions, both the East-West and North-South aspects of neutralism-nonalignment had a *realpolitik* rationale too; the position simply made good sense for powers of a certain size. It justified keeping their militaries at a modest, reasonable scale, it left the maximum number of regional and international doors open, and for its savviest practitioners, it allowed them to play one side off the other in the Cold War. But the more idealistic aspects of the persuasion should not be overlooked. Thus perhaps there is to be found a middle ground in the scholarship. That is, Lee, Vitalis, Abraham et al. are correct that the 'Bandung spirit' was far less than advertised at the time, or by most scholars since, and that the intricacies of nationalist leaders' intramural competitions and domestic politics best explain the crooked lines running through neutralism-nonalignment as it evolved from Bandung to Belgrade. Meanwhile a concurrent story unfolded as this fractured neutralism-nonalignment melded with race-consciousness to take on a life of its own, as the Third World evolved from intellectual concept to geopolitical voting bloc. The story is still imperfectly understood in its local-particular and broader-holistic dimensions alike, both of which are further distorted by scholars' inherited 'Cold War lenses.' There were, in effect, several simultaneous conversations underway during these years regarding neutralism-nonalignment, all in competition for its soul. Understanding the persuasion and movement as essentially a Cold War story does not do justice to its complications or implications. More empirical research is thus needed across the global-South sites to tease out the warp-and-woof of power-politics, strategic competition, and race-consciousness that wove the fraught, tangled threads of neutralism-nonalignment and the Third World.[53]

This course of events presents some intriguing implications for understanding US Cold War foreign relations. For one, though a counterintuitive point, the increasing identification over time of neutralism-nonalignment with the non-white world might actually have come as something of a relief to Washington. The real US fear of neutralism-nonalignment during the first decade-plus of the Cold War was twofold: that it was simply communism in drag, and that it posed the greatest danger in Europe, at the very front-line of the superpower conflict. To the extent neutralism-nonalignment became identified with the non-West – to the extent that it became the credo of the Third World – this minimized the risk of it taking root in the First. (Recall that the Eisenhower team's reaction after Bandung was to study the phenomenon of neutralism in greater detail in Europe than anywhere else.) This counts as 'counterintuitive' insofar as the literature on race and foreign relations holds that Third World resentment of American racism damaged US standing in the worldwide battle for 'hearts and minds.'

This was true – and increasingly so as the superpowers came to see the Third World become a key battleground in the Cold War's second decade – but not always and in every way. Viewed slightly differently, it is plausible to surmise that a racialized neutralism-nonalignment, for all the headaches it could cause at the U.N. General Assembly, could assist American strategy by pulling neutralism out of practical play in the most crucial Cold War battleground. At several points in the story, the United States worried that racial dynamics might help a nonaligned bloc to coalesce, because race could add credibility to neutralist appeals among global-South peoples overcoming imperialism and white-supremacy. However, Washington ultimately concluded that the power of a bloc thus constituted would be less worrisome than one driven by 'simple' neutralism-by-ideological-principle – and might help to inoculate Europe against the persuasion.

Beyond US foreign policy, the continuing permeation of domestic and international affairs by race-consciousness in the next decades makes the racialization of neutralism-nonalignment, in hindsight, seem practically predestined. The world's most visible non-white leader, whose nation led the first wave of Third World independence, had championed the persuasion. Even after he repudiated race-solidarity as an organizing principle, as a simple matter of nose-counting, the rest of the Third World which followed the Colombo Powers into independent nationhood was also majority non-white, so that the pool of potential new neutralist-nonaligned countries was weighted in that direction. Philosophically, as noted above, neutralism-nonalignment held a special appeal for newly-independent countries. It was the logical extension of independence broadly conceived. It meshed smoothly with the various racially-inscribed, pan-ethnic proto-nationalist and nationalist visions of earlier decades, which had animated the drive to decolonization.

In retrospect, NAM proved to have less power than its proponents had hoped. But it should not be forgotten that at the time, as Antoinette Burton puts it, even if it proved ultimately unfounded, there was a 'presumption of Afro-Asian solidarity – as the foundation of post-imperial political community and as a guarantor of Third World non-alignment – which was at once feared and maligned in the West and so perpetually invoked by people of color and others as the aspirational standard-bearer of radical postcolonial politics.'[54] Nor should the staying-power of this identification and bloc be underestimated, both in the eyes of US foreign-policymakers and the self-identification of the global South alike. After all, NAM still exists, and in its almost-wholly-Third World incarnation, despite the end of the Cold War to which it was ostensibly opposed. Yet despite this air of apparent predestination, the racialization of neutralism-nonalignment in fact had a complicated and long-continuing relationship with both the ideological roots of the persuasion and with the more romantic visions of solidarity that accompanied the postwar emergence of the global South.

Notes

1 A glance at the membership of the Non-Aligned Movement (NAM) today includes only one nation – Belarus – which might be categorized as phenotypically majority-white and non-Latin. Interestingly, Yugoslavia – a founding member of NAM – was 'suspended' from the organization in 1992, and as of 2004 none of its successor states in the Balkans had joined.
2 On the 'global race revolution,' see Jason Parker '"Made-in-America Revolutions"? The "Black University" and the Decolonization of the Black Atlantic,' *Journal of American History*, Vol. 96, No. 3 (December 2009), 727–8. The burgeoning literature on this and other 'north-south' dimensions of the east-west Cold War has already produced some landmark scholarship, including Matthew Connelly, 'Taking off the Cold War Lens: Visions of North-South Conflict During the Algerian War for Independence,' *American Historical Review*, 105 (June 2000), 739–69; Thomas Borstelmann, *The Cold War and the Color Line: American Race Relations in the Global Arena* (Cambridge, Mass.: Harvard University Press, 2001); and the Bancroft-Prizewinning Odd Arne Westad, *The Global Cold War: Third World Interventions and the Making of Our Times* (Cambridge UK: Cambridge University Press, 2005).
3 Michael Hunt, *Ideology and US Foreign Policy* (New Haven: Yale University Press, 1987); Paul Gordon Lauren, *Power and Prejudice: The Politics and Diplomacy of*

Racial Discrimination (Boulder: University of Colorado Press, 1988); Thomas Noer, *Cold War and Black Liberation: The United States and White Rule in Africa, 1948–1968* (Columbia: Columbia University Press, 1988); Brenda Gayle Plummer, *Rising Wind: Black Americans and US Foreign Affairs, 1935–1960* (Chapel Hill: University of North Carolina Press, 1996); Penny Von Eschen, *Race Against Empire: Black Americans and Anticolonialism, 1937–1957* (Ithaca: Cornell University Press, 1997); Borstelmann, *The Cold War and the Color Line* (Cambridge, Mass.: Harvard University Press, 2001); Mary Dudziak, *Cold War Civil Rights: Race and American Democracy* (Princeton: Princeton University Press, 2000); Carol Anderson, *Eyes off the Prize: The United Nations and the African American Struggle for Human Rights, 1944–1955* (New York: Cambridge University Press, 2003). See also Gerald Horne, *Black and Red: W.E.B. DuBois and the Afro-American Response to the Cold War* (Albany: State University of New York Press, 1986); Plummer, ed., *Window on Freedom: Race, Civil Rights, and Foreign Affairs, 1945–1988* (Chapel Hill: University of North Carolina Press, 2003); Jonathan Rosenberg, *How Far the Promised Land?: World Affairs and the American Civil Rights Movement from the First World War to Vietnam* (Princeton: Princeton University Press, 2005).

4 Connelly, 'Cold War Lens'; Erez Manela, *The Wilsonian Moment: Self-Determination and the International Origins of Anticolonial Nationalism* (New York: Oxford University Press, 2007); Frank Ninkovich, *The Wilsonian Century: US Foreign Policy Since 1900* (Chicago: Chicago University Press, 2001).

5 Robert Vitalis, 'The Midnight Ride of Kwame Nkrumah and Other Fables of Bandung,' unpublished paper (2009), in author's possession; Itty Abraham, 'From Bandung to NAM: Non-alignment and Indian Foreign Policy, 1947–1965,' *Commonwealth & Comparative Politics*, Vol. 46, No. 2 (April 2008), 195–219; Christopher J. Lee, *Making a World after Empire: The Bandung Moment and its Political Afterlives* (Athens OH: University of Georgia Press, 2010).

6 Mark Lawrence, 'The Rise and Fall of Nonalignment,' in Robert McMahon, ed., *The Cold War in the Third World* (forthcoming 2011, Oxford University Press), 7.

7 A brief note on style: although the term 'Third World' has come to be seen as passé, its use by contemporary actors argues for its use here. In addition, when the two parts of the hybrid term 'neutralism-nonalignment' are used individually, it is meant to reflect the historicity of its usage: neutralism was more common before the middle 1950s, nonalignment afterward. As for the term 'Third World,' see Arturo Escobar, *Encountering Development: The Making and Unmaking of the Third World* (Princeton: Princeton University Press, 1994), chapters 1 and 2; and Leslie Wolf-Phillips, 'Why "Third World": Origin, Definition and Usage,' *Third World Quarterly*, Vol. 9, No. 4 (October 1987), 1311–27.

8 In addition to the works in note 4, the insights of Ivan Hannaford and Kenan Malik have been especially useful in exploring the subject. Ivan Hannaford, *Race: The History of an Idea in the West* (Baltimore: John Hopkins University Press 1996); Kenan Malik, *The Meaning of Race: Race, History, and Culture in Western Society* (New York: Palgrave Macmillan, 1996).

9 On neutralism-nonalignment, see Lawrence, 'Rise and Fall'; Robert Rakove, 'A Genuine Departure: Kennedy, Johnson, and the Nonaligned World' (PhD

Diss.), University of Virginia, December 2008; H.W. Brands, *The Specter of Neutralism, 1947–1960* (New York: Columbia University Press, 1990); and contemporary accounts, above all G.H. Jansen, *Nonalignment and the Afro-Asian States* (New York, 1966); also Lawrence W. Martin, ed., *Neutralism and Nonalignment: The New States in World Affairs* (New York, 1962).
10 Melvyn Leffler, *For the Soul of Mankind: The United States, the Soviet Union, and the Cold War* (New York: Hill & Wang, 2008), chapter 1.
11 Brands, *Specter of Neutralism*.
12 Robert McMahon, *The Cold War on the Periphery: The United States, India, and Pakistan* (New York: Columbia University Press, 1996); Andrew Rotter, *Comrades at Odds: The United States and India, 1947–1964* (Ithaca: Cornell University Press, 2000); Kenton J. Clymer, *Quest for Freedom: The United States and India's Independence* (New York: Columbia University Press, 1995).
13 Abraham, 'From Bandung to NAM,' 202.
14 McMahon, *Cold War on the Periphery*, 38–9. See also U.S. Bajpai, ed., *Nonalignment, Perspectives and Prospects* (Delhi: Lancer Books, 1983); C.R. Mohan, *Crossing the Rubicon: The Shaping of India's New Foreign Policy* (Delhi: Palgrave Macmillan, 2003), and K.P. Mishra and K.R. Narayanan, eds., *Non-alignment in Contemporary International Relations* (New Delhi, 1981), cited in Abraham, 'From Bandung to NAM,' 195.
15 McMahon, *Cold War on the Periphery*, chapter 3; Rotter, *Comrades at Odds*, 169–70, 211–13; William Stueck, *The Korean War: An International History* (Princeton: Princeton University Press, 1997), 153–7.
16 Ogburn to Connors, 8 November 1950, folder: 'Political & Psychological Warfare,' Box 11a, Lot File 64D563: Records of Policy Planning Staff 1947–1953, Lot Files, Record Group 59: State Department Records (RG 59), US National Archives (NA), College Park, Maryland.
17 Report, 'Country Paper: India,' USIA, 1952, folder 'USIA Country Papers,' Box 5, Lot 62D385: Misc Lot Files: International Information Administration – Office of Administration Subject Files, 1952–53, RG 59, NA.
18 On this strain in American views of Asia, see William F. Wu, *The Yellow Peril: Chinese-Americans in American Fiction, 1850–1940* (Hamden, 1982); and John R. Eperjesi, *The Imperialist Imaginary: Visions of Asia and the Pacific in American Culture* (Hanover, 2005). However, in her article on the conference, journalist Peggy Durdin explicitly dismissed the notion that Bandung would call forth the 'Yellow Peril.' *New York Times Magazine*, 5 June 1955, cited in Jones, 'A "Segregated" Asia?,' 862.
19 After lamenting discrimination against non-white visitors to Washington on the campaign trail, Eisenhower in 1953 desegregated all federal facilities in the District of Columbia, and in subsequent years 'worked behind the scenes to secure desegregation of [Washington] theaters and hotels.' Philip Klinkner and Rogers Smith, *Unsteady March: The Rise and Decline of Racial Equality in America* (Chicago: Chicago University Press, 1999), 237. See also Dudziak, *Cold War Civil Rights*, 96, 99.
20 The Bandung conference was the subject of both contemporary and recent scholarly analysis, receiving relatively less attention in the middle period between. Accounts of the time include George McTurnan Kahin, *The Asian-African Conference* (Ithaca: Cornell University Press, 1956); Richard Wright, *The Color Curtain* (New York, 1956; reprinted Oxford University Press, 1995);

Carlos Romulo, *The Meaning of Bandung* (Chapel Hill: University of North Carolina Press, 1956); A. Appadorai, *The Bandung Conference* (New Delhi: Indian Council of World Affairs, 1955); David Kimche, *The Afro-Asian Movement: Ideology and Foreign Policy of the Third World* (New York: Halstead Press, 1973); and more recently, Nicholas Tarling, 'Ah-Ah: Britain and the Bandung Conference of 1955,' *Journal of Southeast Asian Studies*, Vol. 23, No. 1 (March 1992), 74–112; Samir Amin calls it the 'Bandung Era' in *Re-reading the Postwar Period: An Intellectual Itinerary* (New York: Monthly Review Press, 1994); Cary Fraser, 'An American Dilemma: Race and Realpolitik in the American Response to the Bandung Conference, 1955,' in Brenda Gayle Plummer, ed., *Window on Freedom* (Chapel Hill: University of North Carolina Press, 2003), 115–40; Jason Parker, 'Cold War II: The Eisenhower Administration, the Bandung Conference, and the Re-periodization of the Postwar Era,' *Diplomatic History* (November 2006), 867–92; Matthew Jones, 'A "Segregated" Asia? Race, the Bandung Conference, and Pan-Asianist Fears in American Thought and Policy, 1954–55,' *Diplomatic History*, Vol. 29, No. 5 (November 2005), 841–68; Heike Raphael-Hernandez and Shannon Steen, eds., *Afro-Asian Encounters: Culture, History, Politics* (New York: New York University Press, 2006); Fred Ho and Bill V. Mullen, eds., *Afro Asia: Revolutionary Political and Cultural Connections between African Americans and Asian Americans* (Durham: Duke University Press, 2008); Lee, *Making a World After Empire*. For treatments of Bandung in the race-diplomacy literature, see Von Eschen, *Race Against Empire*, 167–73; Plummer, *Rising Wind*, 247–56; Lauren, *Power and Prejudice*, 209; Borstelmann, *The Cold War and the Color Line*; Brands, *Specter*, 117–18; Horne, *Black and Red*, 190–1.

21 This was not, contrary to much of the literature, due to a policy of deliberate exclusion on the organizers' part. Wright, *The Color Curtain*, 88, cited in Vitalis, 'Midnight Ride,' 27. At the same time, the invitation extended to the multiracial but white-dominated Central African Federation was done 'in order to establish the principle that the conference would not be merely a gathering of coloured races.' Sarvepalli Gopal, *Jawaharlal Nehru: A Biography*, abridged ed. (New Delhi: Oxford University Press, 2004), 283.

22 Robert Vitalis, 'Lessons of 1970,' Conference Paper in author's possession, 48.

23 Abraham, 'From Bandung to NAM,' 208

24 Jason Parker, 'Cold War II,' 882.

25 Wright, *The Color Curtain*, 135; Sukarno, 'Opening Speech of Bandung Conference,' *Asia-Africa Speaks from Bandung* (Jakarta, 1955), 24.

26 Nehru was far from alone in this. For example, as Vitalis notes, Indonesian socialist Soetan Sjahrir opposed the race-tinted 'self-glorifying and egocentric tone of anti-colonial nationalism' that accompanied much of the rhetoric of neutralism-nonalignment at and after Bandung. Clive J. Christie, *Ideology and Revolution in Southeast Asia 1900–1980: Political Ideas of the Anticolonial Era* (Richmond, 2001), 70–2, cited in Vitalis, 'Midnight Ride,' 27.

27 Lee, *Making a World After Empire*, 15. Lee here cites Vijay Prashad, who writes, 'What [the conference] meant was simple: that the colonized world had now emerged to claim its space in world affairs... the Bandung Spirit was a refusal of both economic subordination and cultural suppression...

The audacity of Bandung produced its own image.' Vijay Prashad, *The Darker Nations: A People's History of the Third World* (New York: The New Press, 2007), 45–6.
28 Parker, 'Cold War II,' 884; Fraser, 'An American Dilemma,' 133–5.
29 John Munro demonstrates this in his dissertation, noting the raft of mentions of the conference by African American figures: W. Alphaeus Hunton, *Decision in Africa: Sources of Current Conflict* (New York: International Publishers, 1957); Frank London Brown, *Trumbull Park* (2005; Boston: Northeastern University Press, 1959), Malcolm X, 'Message to the Grassroots,' in George Breitman, ed., *Malcolm X Speaks* (New York: Pathfinder, 1965), 3–18; 'General Baker,' in Robert H., Mast, ed., *Detroit Lives* (Philadelphia: Temple University Press, 1994), 305–13; Robin D.G. Kelley, *Freedom Dreams: The Black Radical Imagination* (Boston: Beacon Press, 2002), 81–2. John Munro, 'The Anticolonial Front: Cold War Imperialism and the Struggle Against Global White Supremacy, 1945–1960,' PhD Diss., University of California-Santa Barbara (December 2010), 12. See also Nikhil Pal Singh, *Black is a Country: Race and the Unfinished Struggle for Democracy* (Cambridge, Mass.: Harvard University Press, 2004); Michael Denning, *Culture in the Age of Three Worlds* (New York: Verso Books, 2004); Manning Marable and Vanessa Agard-Jones, eds., *Transnational Blackness: Navigating the Global Color Line* (London: Palgrave Macmillan, 2008); Fanon Che Wilkins, 'Beyond Bandung: The Critical Nationalism of Lorraine Hansberry, 1950–65,' *Radical History Review*, 95 (Spring 2006), 191–210.
30 As Jones puts it, 'the specter that loomed largest for US policymakers was of the Chinese leading pan-Asian sentiment in a struggle to reject Western, and more specifically, white influence and tutelage.' Jones, 'A "Segregated" Asia?,' 854.
31 Minutes, Cabinet Meeting, 29 April 1955, Cabinet Series, Whitman File, Box 5, Dwight D. Eisenhower Library (DDEL), Abilene, Kansas.
32 Rahul Mukherji, 'Appraising the Legacy of Bandung: A View From India,' in See Seng Tan and Amitav Acharya, eds., *Bandung Revisited: The Legacy of the 1955 Asian-African Conference for International Order* (Singapore: Singapore University Press, 2008), 167–9. Pancheel's five principles, according to N. Jayapalan, can be summarized as: mutual respect for territorial integrity and sovereignty; non-aggression; non-intervention; mutual benefit and equality; and peaceful co-existence. N. Jayapalan, *The Foreign Policy of India* (New York, 2001), 55.
33 This tension would persist in the conference aftermath as various actors weighed the merits of a 'second Bandung' as opposed to the 'nonaligned conference' envisioned at Brioni. John Garver, *Protracted Contest: Sino-Indian Rivalry in the Twentieth Century* (Seattle: University of Washington Press, 2001), 123.
34 Minutes, Cabinet Meeting, 29 April 1955; Report CA-7532, 'Preliminary Evaluation of Results of Afro-Asian Conference,' 2 May 1955, attached to Memorandum, Staats to OCB, 12 May 1955, OCB Central File Series, WHO-NSC, folder 'OCB 092.3 (2),' DDEL.
35 Fraser, 'An American Dilemma,' 133–7.
36 The timing was important; as Dudziak notes regarding these months, 'Emmet Till's brutal murder in 1955 had outraged the world, the 1955–56 Montgomery bus boycott had focused international media attention on

civil rights protest, and Autherine Lucy's attempt to cross the color line at the University of Alabama in 1956 had become a civil rights crisis with international impact.' Dudziak, *Cold War Civil Rights*, 118.
37 Borstelmann, *The Cold War and the Color Line*, 93.
38 James Meriwether, *Proudly We Can Be Africans: Black Americans and African, 1935–1961* (Chapel Hill: University of North Carolina Press, 2002).
39 The conferences were of course the highest-profile activities of this kind, but the 'mutual infiltration' took place on a day-to-day basis as well. No less so than the superpowers, the competing neutralist-nonaligned powers such as India and the United Arab Republic (Egypt) opened public-diplomacy shops in Ghana soon after independence, in recognition of 'strategic importance... of Ghana's leadership in the drive for independence sweeping Africa.' USIA Inspectors to USIA, 28 March 1959, folder 'Ghana,' Box 4, USIA, Inspection Reports and Related Records 1954–62, Record Group 306: Records of the United States Information Agency (RG 306), NA. Certain of the themes of these campaigns would find support, US analysts surmised, in communist propaganda – but others might in the end work at cross purposes. Report, 'S-17-58: Estimate of the Situation in Africa in 1961,' 21 October 1958, USIA Office of Research and Intelligence, Box 15, Office of Research, Special Reports 1953–63, RG 306. See also James R. Brennan, 'Radio Cairo and the Decolonization of East Africa, 1953–64,' in Lee, *Making A World*, 173–95.
40 On the AAPSO, see Charles Neuhauser, *Third World Politics: China and the Afro-Asian People's Solidarity Organization, 1957–1967* (Cambridge, Mass.: Harvard University Press, 1968).
41 'The State of the Nation and the World' (Speech at meeting of Congress Parliamentary Party, New Delhi), 27 July 1956, H.Y. Sharada Prasad, A.K. Damodaran, Mushirul Hasan, eds., *Selected Works of Jawaharlal Nehru*, 2nd series, Vol. 34 (New Delhi: Oxford University Press, 2005), 19.
42 Though Mark Lawrence is correct in describing a 'rise and fall of nonalignment' given that NAM turned out to have less power than its architects hoped, the entity nonetheless had a large impact on international affairs and institutions (especially the UN) at a critical moment, 'bending' them in unexpected ways. Lawrence, 'Rise and Fall.'
43 As Prashad puts it, '[Brioni] and Belgrade augured the creation of an association that would seek more room for the darker nations – but not necessarily for the reconstruction of the world in their image.' Prashad, *The Darker Nations*, 96.
44 Prashad, *The Darker Nations*, 27. See also Escobar, *Encountering Development*; and Westad, *The Global Cold War*.
45 USIA-IRI, 'R-21-60: Communist Propaganda Activities in Near East, South Asia, and Africa 1959,' 15 April 1960, Box 1, Ofc Rsch, 'R' Repts 1960–63, RG 306. Moreover, it was expected at the time that the 'have-nots' would cooperate, to a greater degree than ultimately turned out to be the case, given 'the likelihood that many of these newly independent nations will follow a neutralist course, and... their natural inclination to support the interests of other less developed countries.' Halla to Gray, 11 May 1959, folder 'New Independent Countries – US Policy Toward, 1959,' Box 14, Briefing Notes Subseries, NSC Series, WHO-OSANSA: Records 1952–61, DDEL.

46 Wolf-Phillips, 'Why "Third World",' 1313.
47 Louis Lansana Beavogui, in 'Africa Speaks to the United Nations: A Symposium of Aspirations and Concerns Voiced by Representative Leaders at the UN,' *International Organization*, Vol. 16, No. 2 (Spring 1962), 319. This 'family' found purchase outside the realm of geopolitics. Martin Luther King alluded to it in his 'Letter from a Birmingham Jail': Consciously or unconsciously, he [the American Negro] has been caught up by the Zeitgeist, and with his black brothers of Africa and his brown and yellow brothers of Asia, South America and the Caribbean, the United States Negro is moving with a sense of great urgency toward the promised land of racial justice.' http://www.mlkonline.net/jail.html, accessed 20 March 2010.
48 It was taken seriously by US analysts at the time; as one report eighteen months after Ghana's independence put it, 'Pan-Africanism can be expected to become a magnetic force, supplementing but not necessarily conflicting with communist-supported Afro-Asian solidarity movements.' 'Estimate of the Situation in Africa in 1961,' 21 October 1958.
49 Nkrumah made 'positive neutralism,' 'non-alignment,' and 'Pan-Africanism' central to his public-relations efforts both at home and abroad – and used the terms more or less interchangeably. USIS-Accra to USIA, 2 February 1960, folder #3, Box 1, Foreign Service Despatches 1954–65: Africa & Australia, RG 306. See also Evan White, 'Kwame Nkrumah: Cold War Modernity, Pan-African Ideology and the Geopolitics of Development,' *Geopolitics*, Vol. 8, No. 2 (Summer 2003), 99–124. Nasser used the coinage 'positive neutralism' tirelessly; see for example 'Speech Delivered to Delegation of Arabs from the United States, 10 August 1959'; 'Speech at Inaugural Session of National Assembly, 9 July 1960'; and 'Speech on Return from General Assembly of United Nations, 5 October 1960,' all in Gamal Abdel Nasser, *Gamal Abdel Nasser on Nonalignment* (Cairo, no publication date).
50 See especially 'Introduction,' Kwame Nkrumah, *I Speak of Freedom: A Statement of African Ideology* (London, 1961); and Opoku Agyeman, *Nkrumah's Ghana and East Africa: Pan-Africanism and African Interstate Relations* (Rutherford New Jersey: Fairleigh Dickinson University Press, 1992), 28. Though as Agyeman shows important parts of East Africa – above all Kenya – disagreed. See *ibid.*, 184–6, and Agyeman, *The Failure of Grassroots Pan-Africanism: The Case of the All-African Trade Union Federation* (Lanham, Maryland: Rowman & Littlefield, 2003). See also Daryl Zizwe Poe, *Kwame Nkrumah's Contribution to Pan-Africanism* (New York: Routledge, 2003).
51 'Memorandum for the June 1966 Meeting of the National Executive of TANU,' in Julius Nyerere, *Uhuru Na Ujamaa: Freedom and Socialism* (Dar Es Salaam, 1968).
52 Nyerere, *World Assembly of Youth Forum*, 40 (September 1961), 14, cited in Rupert Emerson, 'Pan-Africanism,' *International Organization*, Vol. 16, No. 2 (Spring 1962), 290.
53 As Lawrence observes, 'The scope and complexity of this development surely accounts for the fact that remarkably few scholars have studied non-alignment during the Cold War in any sort of all-encompassing way. Rather, historians have mostly examined small slices of the larger arc, isolating either particular moments' or places. Lawrence, 'Rise and Fall,' 3. The exceptions are Prashad, *The Darker Nations*; Jansen, *Nonalignment and the*

Afro-Asian State; Westad, *The Global Cold War*; and D.K. Fieldhouse, *The West and the Third World* (Oxford: Wiley-Blackwell, 1999).

54 Antoinette Burton, 'The Sodalities of Bandung: Toward a Critical 21st-century History,' in Lee, *Making a World*, 354. Burton rightly laments the ways in which this same presumption underlay a 'romance of racialism' that befogged much popular and scholarly memory and visions of the Bandung conference and the Third World. *Ibid.*, 352.

5
America's Great Game: The CIA and the Middle East, 1947–67
Hugh Wilford

Considering the history of its involvement in the Middle East, it is easy to see why, for many Arabs and Muslims today, the Central Intelligence Agency (CIA) has an almost diabolical reputation. In recent years, the CIA has been responsible for the most infamous American measures in the 'War on Terror', including waterboarding, secret prisons, and extraordinary rendition. Earlier, when it functioned as the US's main weapon for waging Cold War in the region, the Agency was known for engineering the destruction of nationalist governments, shoring up pro-western autocracies in the oil-rich Gulf States, and anchoring the growing American-Israeli alliance. The events of the early Cold War era are widely interpreted as foundational to the current, fraught relationship between America and the Middle East; as Yale scholar Abbas Amanat has described the baleful consequences of covert meddling in the region by generations of western spies, 'the thread of memory led clearly from the Great Game to the Great Satan'.[1]

It therefore comes as a surprise to learn that, at least during the first years of its existence, the CIA contained a number of intelligence officers noted for their expert knowledge of and their sympathy with the Arab and Muslim worlds. This tendency, often referred to by contemporaries as 'Arabism', had a complex set of origins in previous western encounters with the Middle East, including first-hand, non-governmental American experience of the region. It found expression in a variety of forms, among them a secret effort to counter Zionist influence on American public opinion through a 'front' organization called the American Friends of the Middle East. Ultimately, though, it failed to prevent the rise of what later critics would call the 'Israel Lobby' in the US, just as in the Middle East it could not halt a calamitous deterioration in American-Arab relations, especially after the overwhelming Israeli victory in the Six Day War of 1967.

Previous writers have examined (usually, it has to be said, from a hostile perspective) the phenomenon of Arabism in the US foreign service, the overt arm of the American government in the Middle East.[2] However, CIA Arabism – arguably more consequential historically than State Department Arabism, at least in the early Cold War period – has gone largely unexplored. This essay is an initial attempt to remedy this gap in our knowledge by tracing the origins, values, and decline of a core group of CIA Arabists, focusing mainly on the years between 1947, when the Agency was founded, to the watershed Arab-Israeli war of 1967. The analysis reflects the influence of the recent 'cultural turn' taken by historians of American foreign relations in that it constantly relates the attitudes and actions of the CIA Arabists to their domestic political culture, including state-private networks that blur the distinction between government apparatus and civil society.[3] It also situates them squarely in the longer-term history of western imperial encounters with the 'Orient', considering the relationship between 'Arabism' and 'Orientalism', the predominantly European tradition of perceiving and representing the 'East' based on its colonial subjugation.[4] In doing so, it draws heavily on the Arabists' own (surprisingly plentiful) published writings, which will be read not so much as transparent historical records as constructed literary texts which nonetheless reveal much about their authors' values and beliefs. This approach relates to the interest recently shown by several historians of US foreign relations in the emotional lives of leading American foreign policy-makers and diplomats,[5] as well as a new scholarly awareness of intelligence memoirs as a distinct literary genre of their own.[6]

Overall, what this chapter reveals is a moment at the beginning of the modern era of official US engagement with the Middle East when there appeared to be the possibility of a very different kind of relationship between Americans on the one hand, and Arabs and Muslims on the other, from the one that eventually came to prevail.

* * * * *

In part, CIA Arabism was descended from British orientalism, in particular the archive of imperial texts about and images of the Middle East accumulated by Britain since its rise to imperial dominance of the area in the late nineteenth and early twentieth centuries. That the early Agency should have exhibited British influence was perhaps only to be expected given that, as several historians have noted, it recruited much of its personnel from US educational institutions modeled after English private schools (the 'public schools', as they were known). The most important of these was Groton, an elite New England academy whose long-serving headmaster Endicott Peabody strove to foster in his pupils the kind of manly, Victorian virtues he believed the American governing class would need if it was to shoulder the imperial responsibilities it was bound one day to inherit from Britain (tellingly, Groton's motto, roughly translated from the Latin, was 'For whom to serve is to rule').[7] Some Grotonians were especially fascinated by the British imperial experience for personal reasons. Kermit Roosevelt, for example, grandson of President Theodore Roosevelt and future head of the CIA's Near East division, had grown up reading the fiction of Rudyard Kipling, the great novelist and poet of the British empire, and a Roosevelt family friend. Indeed, the young Kermit's nickname 'Kim' was inspired by Kipling's picaresque novel of the same title, in which the eponymous hero, the orphaned son of an Irish soldier and nursemaid, travels through northern India playing the 'Great Game', the spy war between Britain and Russia for control of central Asia.[8] Not only that, Kermit's father had fought with the British Army during World War I in Mesopotamia (modern-day Iraq), befriending among other British Arabists T.E. Lawrence, the young archaeologist-turned-intelligence officer who appeared to have absorbed the fictional Kim's ability to pass as the 'native' other.[9] The two men maintained their relationship by corresponding after the war, at the same time Lawrence and his circle were helping build for Britain in the Middle East what historian Priya Satia has insightfully called a 'Covert Empire'.[10] Hence, the 15-year old Kim Roosevelt was evoking a specifically British orientalist tradition (significantly, one strongly associated with spying) when in 1931 he rhymed in the pages of an American boy's journal, 'I've read of the East for years unnumbered/I've dreamed about it since first I slumbered....'[11]

This is not to say, though, that CIA Arabism was *merely* a US imitation of British orientalism. Equally influential was a uniquely American history of interaction with the Middle East also dating back to the previous century, when, long before the US government began taking an interest in the region, private American citizens began traveling to the 'Holy Land' as missionaries. Although predictably unsuccessful in their bid to convert Muslims, these evangelists nonetheless left a lasting impression on the Middle East in the shape of the schools and universities they founded there, such as the Syrian Protestant College (later known as the American University of Beirut, or AUB). Moreover, they appear to have earned considerable good will among the Arabs with whom they came into contact, if only because their relatively selfless interest in the region contrasted favorably with the colonial designs of the European powers; indeed, institutions such as AUB became important sites for the incubation of new strains of Arab nationalism.[12] This US reputation for 'disinterested benevolence' (as one Protestant theologian described it) was slightly eroded later by the arrival of, first, American archaeologists intent on excavating (and carrying off) the Middle East's ancient artifacts, then oilmen wanting to exploit its natural resources.[13] However, even in the late 1940s, there still existed large reserves of American-Arab friendship, and a perception in the Middle East of the US as a non-colonial, even *anti*-colonial, western power. This pre-history of private engagement fed into the early CIA, most notably through the person of William Eddy, the Lebanon-born descendant of a prominent family of missionaries and educators who played a major part in the discussions leading to the Agency's creation in 1947 and continued to act as an important CIA link to the world of non-governmental Arabism while working as a senior executive of US oil company ARAMCO.[14]

Such, then, were the origins of CIA Arabism, a mixture of quasi-British, imperial and American, non-colonial impulses. Chronologically speaking, it would probably be true to say that, while always present, the British influence became more visible later in the period under examination here. Initially, however, during the late 1940s and early 1950s, as Britain's power in the region receded and the US government, fearful of Soviet expansion into this strategically vital region, rushed to fill the vacuum, it was the American strand that was most evident, as discussion of the forms of early CIA Arabism will now show.

* * * * *

To begin with, there was a definite desire among the first American intelligence officers in the Middle East to shake off the influence of European colonialism, to do something different in the region. As Kim Roosevelt pointed out in his 1949 book *Arabs, Oil and History*, which might be read as a manifesto for early CIA Arabism, the US was 'alone among the major powers' in having previously had a relationship with the Middle East based not on 'political domination and economic exploitation' but rather 'on common interests, … without unfair advantage to either side'. The 'different attitude toward us' that resulted was, Roosevelt believed, a 'great national asset in the crossroads of the world', one that the US could 'ill afford to lose'.[15] Anti-colonial statements directed toward other western powers tended to be quite mild in the case of Britain, presumably because of many American spies' Anglophile upbringing and the continuing utility in the region of British area knowledge and contacts: as Miles Copeland, a senior CIA Middle East hand and Kim Roosevelt's right-hand man for much of the period, later recalled of the early Cold War, the 'former missionaries and romantics' who staffed the US's new government apparatus in the Middle East liked to indulge in 'naïve criticism of the old masters, the British', while at the same time relying 'on British diplomatic and intelligence resources'.[16] However, the French received no such quarter, especially from Kermit's cousin and fellow Grotonian, Archibald Roosevelt. Posted as a military intelligence officer to French North Africa during World War II, Archie befriended a number of Arab nationalists (including the future first president of the republic of Tunisia, Habib Bourguiba) and criticized the colonial authorities so loudly that, at French insistence, he was eventually recalled to the US.[17] It was almost as if in the eyes of CIA Arabists France served as a kind of negative template for post-war US dealings with the Middle East. There are parallels here with events in other French colonies, Vietnam, for example, where legendary CIA officer Edward Lansdale had a number of similarly bad-tempered exchanges with colonial officials.

Archie Roosevelt's friendship with Habib Bourguiba points toward a second distinct form of CIA Arabism: support for Arab nationalism. Again, it was Kermit Roosevelt who most explicitly enunciated this principle in *Arabs, Oil and History*. The 'Young Effendis', as Roosevelt called them, following British Arabist Freya Stark, were 'sober crusaders in education, government and medicine'. Politically moderate, 'progressive as distinct from revolutionary', and pro-western 'by education and by example', they deserved the support of the US in trying to advance their countries 'along Western liberal lines' and even in forming 'a federation of existing Arab states....'[18] This enthusiasm for modernizing nationalists (perhaps surprising in the case of Kim Roosevelt, considering later developments in Iran, of which more below) led the new CIA's Middle East hands to consider ways of ensuring, as Miles Copeland recalled later, 'the rise of "the right kind of leader"', by for example, 'removing certain artificial props which were keeping in power leaders who, by rights, shouldn't be there in the first place'.[19]

This tactic – the removal of unpopular European client rulers and their replacement by progressive nationalists – reached its apotheosis in Egypt where, in July 1952, the so-called Free Officers, among them a young colonel by the name of Gamal Abdel Nasser, overthrew the corrupt regime of the British-backed King Farouk. The exact extent of the CIA's involvement in the 1952 revolution is still difficult to determine – in the continuing absence of declassified Agency records, Miles Copeland's not necessarily reliable memoirs remain the fullest source available to researchers – but clearly there was some contact between Kim Roosevelt, Copeland and the Free Officers in the months leading up to the coup. Copeland's memoirs also relate how his and Roosevelt's relationship with Nasser deepened during the years afterwards when the Egyptian emerged as the dominant figure in the Arab nationalist movement region-wide.[20] An under-cover CIA team based in Cairo provided the new government with security training, public relations advice, and possibly even a bullet-proof vest that protected Nasser's life during an assassination attempt in October 1954.[21] Of course, Roosevelt and Copeland were motivated by other considerations besides simple idealism, and it would not be long before an about-turn in US foreign policy meant that the CIA was plotting *against* Nasser. Nevertheless, there was clearly more to the relationship than pragmatic calculations of tactical advantage, at least on the American side. Several observers noted at the time how Kermit Roosevelt and his associates constantly defended Nasser against the growing suspicion in Washington that he was a Soviet stooge, earning the (implicitly racist) tag of 'Nasser lovers' from one disapproving CIA colleague.[22] Years later, recalling the early Cold War era in the late 1980s, Archie Roosevelt still regretted the anti-Nasser turn taken by the US in the mid-1950s, insisting 'that here was a man we could work with... in seeking... solutions for the area's problems'.[23] For Miles Copeland, who when back home from the Middle East was often called on to play the role of Nasser in the US government's Washington Games Center (the British Great Game having undergone a reincarnation of sorts during the Cold War era in the American, social science-influenced shape of 'Game Theory'), trying to understand the Egyptian leader became something of a personal obsession.[24] It might not be too fanciful to suggest that the CIA Arabists felt a personal attraction to this warrior-intellectual cast in the same mould as their own idealized, masculine self-image. There are similarities here to John F. Kennedy's initial attraction to, and eventual repulsion by, Fidel Castro.

Linked to this was a third, vaguer form of Arabism: cultural identification with the Arab world. As already noted, a number of important recent studies have remarked on the importance of personal, psychological and emotional factors in the shaping of US officials' attitudes and actions toward the wider world. In the case of those CIA Arabists who, like the Roosevelt cousins, had grown up reading such stories as the *Arabian Nights*, there was about the region not just a sense of exotic fascination but also a comforting feeling of the familiar, a place known since childhood. Archie Roosevelt framed his memoirs around the trope of a journey on the 'Golden Road to Samarkand', a quotation from James Elroy Flecker's orientalist classic *Hassan* (which Archie had first read at Groton) and a metaphor for his life-long quest for knowledge about the Middle East, figured as a spiritual pilgrimage to the ancient Islamic city.[25] The notion of going back in time might also have been linked to feelings of a recent loss of status within US society, not uncommon among East Coast patricians in post-war America, and perhaps especially acute in the Oyster Bay line of the Roosevelt family, whose fortunes had certainly not prospered since the days of Theodore's presidency (TR hovers over Archie's memoirs like a benign ghost). Arabia was a place where one could escape from, as British politician Richard Crossman put it, 'the vulgarity, the tempo and the commercialism' of modern life and find 'an inner tranquility'.[26] Traveling with the Arabist diplomat Hooker Dolittle through Tunisia during World War II, Archie Roosevelt rested among olive groves and white houses near the site of ancient Carthage, watching a group of Arabs wash a camel. The two Americans felt 'like Connecticut Yankees', Roosevelt remembered later, 'transferred to an earlier, more tranquil century'.[27]

As for those Arabists like William Eddy who had themselves grown up in the Middle East, returning to serve there literally felt like going home. The movement of this particular group of intelligence officers between the region and the US heightened their awareness of the cultural heritage that East and West shared in common, especially the inter-connectedness of the great monotheistic religions. Eddy in particular harped on the theme of the fundamental similarity of Christianity and Islam, envisioning a Cold War 'moral alliance' of these faiths against godless communism.[28] Later, of course, the US would adopt the tactic, originally conceived by the British, of covertly supporting fundamentalist Islamism as a defense against Russian penetration of the region, and a possible means of destabilizing the Soviet empire itself – with unforeseen and disastrous long-term consequences, or 'blowback'.[29] At this early stage of US involvement, however, what Eddy and others imagined was something more like an inter-faith dialogue which would help bind the East and West closer together, achieving not only a partial westernization of the Islamic world but also conveying some of the spiritual intensity of modern Islam back to America. Discomfort with the growing materialism of American culture was a nagging undercurrent in the pronouncements of these Arabists, not unlike the aristocratic distress evident in some of Archie Roosevelt's statements.

Even CIA Arabists like Kim Roosevelt who favored a modern, secular approach to the problems of the Middle East were alert to the need for cultural exchange in American-Arab relations, proposing the area as 'the most promising ground for Occident and Orient to meet and understand each other'. Yet, as Roosevelt pointed out, US officials often displayed regrettable insensitivity toward Arab feelings, as he himself witnessed in 1944 when accompanying a good-will military mission to Jidda that backfired badly due to the boorish behavior of several US Army officers, including a doctor who loudly advised his companions not to touch the food being served them at a banquet. 'Even when our intentions are good', Roosevelt lamented, 'our ignorance of the people often makes our efforts... totally worthless'.[30] There were limits to Kermit Roosevelt's own knowledge of the Arab world: he never learned to speak Arabic, for example, restricting his ability to pass like earlier British spies in Arabia or, for that matter, Kipling's Kim. (Archie Roosevelt's Arabism was more profound: he spoke Arabic as well as several other Middle Eastern languages, and sought out Arab-American companions; his second marriage was to the daughter of Lebanese immigrants, Selwa 'Lucky' Showker). Still, at the very least Kim Roosevelt appreciated the tactical need for intercultural understanding. As such, he was articulating a discourse that would become increasingly powerful in Cold War America, recently explored brilliantly by cultural historian Christina Klein, which emphasized sentimental identification between Americans and other peoples as a means of integrating, and thereby strengthening, the 'free world'.[31] Several writers have echoed British double-agent Kim Philby's description of Kim Roosevelt as the 'Quiet American', evoking Graham Greene's harshly critical fictional portrayal of misguided US actions in 1950s Vietnam.[32] While this sobriquet is partly deserved, the CIA Arabist is perhaps even more reminiscent of the 'Ugly American', the hero of William J. Lederer and Eugene Burdick's best-selling 1958 novel, who, despite his physical unattractiveness, displays the cultural sensitivity toward foreign cultures enjoined by Klein's integrationist ethic.

The final form of CIA Arabism to be explored here is the most controversial: anti-Zionism. There were several different impulses involved here. One was fear that excessive American support for the new state of Israel would damage the reputation of the US in the Arab world and thereby harm American interests there. Another was humanitarian concern for the plight of the Palestinian refugees, evidently a particularly strong consideration for those Arabists who had grown up in the 'Holy Land'. A third possibility, one raised repeatedly at the time by American Zionists, was that anti-Zionism in elite American government circles was really anti-Semitism in disguise. There is no conclusive documentary evidence to confirm this charge, but it certainly was true that most Arabists had been raised and educated in environments, whether Protestant communities in the Middle East or upper-class enclaves on the East Coast (or both), where there was only a minimal Jewish presence, if any, something that might have made them, if nothing else, insensitive to the feelings about Israel of post-Holocaust American Jews. The sense of status anxiety already mentioned above might also have played into Arabist anti-Zionism, with the growing influence of the emergent 'Israel Lobby' on the media and Congress antagonizing men used to the unchallenged exercise of political power in American society. Finally, it is possible that organizational politics within the CIA also played a part: a number of former intelligence officers have testified to tensions between Kim Roosevelt's Near East division and the Agency's Israeli desk, then run more or less as a separate operation by the counter-intelligence chief James Jesus Angleton, who enjoyed extremely close relations with the Israeli secret service, *Mossad*.[33]

In any case, Kim Roosevelt was particularly vocal on this score, alluding constantly throughout *Arabs, Oil and History* to the damage US support for Israel was doing not only to American interests in the Middle East but also to the positions of the Young Effendis, who were in danger of being outflanked by extremists willing to exploit the growing mood of Arab anger, and for that matter the Jews themselves, who faced an unhappy future as an embattled minority in the region if they did not settle their differences with the surrounding Arab states. Nor was Roosevelt's anti-Zionism limited to writing. During the late 1940s he helped establish a series of American citizen associations whose aim was to bring about a reduction in US support for Israel and relieve the Palestinian refugees. Joining him in these organizations – first the Committee for Justice and Peace in the Holy Land, then the Holy Land Emergency Liaison Program – were Arabist former missionaries and educators, oilmen (William Eddy arranged funding from ARAMCO) and, perhaps less to be expected, a group of Reform Jews led by Michigan Rabbi Elmer Berger who objected to Zionism's insistence on a distinct Jewish national identity. Together, these various groups and individuals composed a dynamic, intensely committed, elite state-private network. However, even at this early stage their best efforts to overcome the forces of American Zionism and public indifference were not enough, and both organizations soon fizzled out.

Far longer-lived was a third organization created in 1951 under the leadership of famous journalist Dorothy Thompson, the New York-based American Friends of the Middle East (AFME). The main reason for AFME's survival only became apparent much later, in 1967: it was receiving regular covert subsidies from the CIA, channeled through dummy foundations. This money was used to run a variety of intercultural programs in the Middle East itself, including student exchange, technical training, and a convocation of Christian and Muslim theologians. Less usually for a CIA 'front' group, AFME also maintained a high profile at home in the US, where it strove to educate American citizens about Islam and Arab civilization while keeping up a running fire on the Zionist movement, in the process becoming a number one target of denunciation by I. L. 'Si' Kenen, editor of the *Near East Report* and founder of the American Israel Public Affairs Committee (AIPAC). Thompson and other officers of the group also made a number of provocative statements against European colonialism in the Middle East and in support of Nasser. The Presbyterian minister Edward Elson even used his position as pastor to both President Dwight Eisenhower and Secretary of State John Foster Dulles to lobby top US officials for a more anti-Zionist, pro-Nasser foreign policy. As such, AFME might be regarded as the fullest and clearest organizational expression of early CIA Arabism.[34]

In the final analysis, CIA Arabism could not be viewed as transcending entirely its orientalist antecedents. As a body of ideas and representations, it shared orientalism's tendency to construct the Middle East as a place of faded ancient glory that now invited western domination, except in this case the dominance would be benevolent rather than exploitative. Still, the Arabists' emphasis on the spiritual values East and West held in common, as well as the importance of interpersonal contact, were directly opposed to the binary and self-referential nature of classic orientalist thought. Perhaps the best single descriptor of this intellectual tradition is '*post*-Orientalist', a term recently coined by cultural historian Melani McAlister to describe a moment in the early years of the Cold War when 'American power [in the Middle East] worked very hard to fracture the old European logic and to install new frameworks'. According to McAlister, this discourse was less about 'disinterested benevolence' than 'benevolent supremacy', positioning Middle Eastern countries as consensual partners in a new American hegemony in the region. Nevertheless, it did explicitly reject the legacy of European colonialism and orientalism, emphasizing the values of 'affiliation, appropriation and co-optation' as opposed to 'distance, othering, and containment'.[35] McAlister's post-orientalism sounds a lot like CIA Arabism.

*****

The heyday of CIA Arabism was the early 1950s. The reputation of the Agency was yet to be tarnished by such failures as the Bay of Pigs, and

Kim Roosevelt enjoyed extraordinary personal prestige, thanks in no small part to his crucial contribution to the 1953 coup that toppled Prime Minister Mohammed Mossadegh in Iran and restored the power of the Shah. Unlike his definitely pro-Israel predecessor, Harry Truman, President Eisenhower preferred a policy of 'friendly impartiality' in the Middle East; diplomatic advances toward Nasser, often handled personally by Roosevelt and his Cairo-based CIA team, culminated in Project Alpha, a comprehensive Middle Eastern peace plan launched in late 1954. Meanwhile, Israel and Zionist groups in the US struggled to regain the influence over official and popular opinion they had wielded in the Truman era.[36]

Within a few years, however, all this had changed. The Eisenhower peace plan unraveled, thanks to renewed Arab-Israeli conflict and growing US mistrust of Nasser, leading to the replacement of Project Alpha by Omega, a joint British-American plan to isolate the Egyptian leader in the Arab world. At the same time, a process of organizational consolidation within the American Zionist movement, which included the launch of AIPAC, and a stepping up of Israeli publicity efforts, or *hasbara*, in the US, accelerated the decline of the Arabist cause domestically. Despite an early effort by the Kennedy administration to mend fences with Nasser and other Arab leaders, these trends gained additional momentum during the 1960s, especially after the strongly pro-Israel Lyndon Johnson became President. The denouement came in 1967, first with the dramatic exposure of AFME as a front group – one in a series of revelations about CIA covert operations which greatly damaged the Agency's reputation in the US and delighted Zionist groups who had long suspected secret governmental backing of the Arabists – then, later in the year, the Israeli rout of Arab forces in the Six Day War. The original core group of CIA Arabists had already broken up by this point, with Kim Roosevelt and Miles Copeland having quit the Agency for private employment in the late 1950s, Eddy having died in 1962, and Archie Roosevelt having been assigned to posts outside the Middle East. Those left behind in the Agency after 1967 would witness the further rise of US Zionism (allied with fundamentalist forms of Christianity that perceived Israel as the fulfillment of apocalyptic biblical prophesies), the growing currency of anti-Arab and anti-Islamic sentiment in American society, and the hardening of the US's reputation in the Middle East as a neo-colonial power.

Clearly, it was a concatenation of external forces – changes in US foreign policy, Arab defeats in the Middle East, and the growing power of Zionist groups at home – that led to the demise of CIA Arabism. However, these were not the only reasons. Arguably, the Arabist impulse had been doomed from the outset by the contradictory nature of its own origins.

On the one hand, there was the pre-history of non-governmental American engagement with the Middle East, constantly invoked by Kim Roosevelt and his group as a guide for official US behavior in the region after World War II. This tradition manifested itself in anticolonialism, support for Arab nationalism, and intercultural understanding and exchange. On the other hand, there was the British imperial precedent, and its particular association with the romance of spying. Eventually, the CIA repeated almost all the colonial techniques used (and mistakes made) by Britain in the region, deploying repressive monarchs and Islamic fundamentalists against a nationalist movement suspected of Russian orchestration, even to the point that the CIA, having helped bring Nasser to power, and protected him once there, colluded with Britain's MI6 to eliminate him (it is striking how many of the coups and attempted coups in the Middle East with which the CIA was linked were first hatched by the British). The similarities between the 'cryptodiplomacy' (Miles Copeland's term) practiced by the US during the Cold War and Britain's earlier 'Covert Empire', as described by Priya Satia, are manifold and unnerving. Even the trope of the Game cropped up again in the American era, with Copeland constantly using it to describe his activities in Egypt and elsewhere, sometimes apparently meaning simply *Kim*-like scrapes and adventures (something for which he plainly had a huge, possibly pathological appetite), at other times a high-stakes, international chess-match played according to the abstract rules of Game Theory. In Kipling's novel, the narrative arc is provided by a journey the young hero Kim undertakes in the company of his beloved guru, an other-worldly Tibetan lama, partly as a cover so that he can play the Great Game for his British spy-masters, but also as a personal Quest for spiritual enlightenment. For CIA Arabists like Archie Roosevelt who had set out on the road to Samarkand in search of insight and understanding about the Middle East, it was if the Great Game had distracted them from their Quest.

Told in the context of the early twenty-first century, after decades of American-Arab discord and US-Israel alliance, the story of CIA Arabism is a surprising one. Of course, how one feels about the Arabists depends to a large extent on where one stands on the present-day Arab-Israeli conflict. If one identifies with Israel, then they probably tend to resemble an aristocratic cabal whose nefarious cause was eventually defeated by the forces of popular representation and free expression. If one sympathizes with the Arab cause, they might appear instead as admirable idealists who tried to counter the growing power of the Israel Lobby and serve both America's true interests in the Middle East and those of the region itself. Despite their obvious differences, both these readings of the Arabist story recognize that it contradicts dominant narratives of US-Middle East relations, ones premised either on the notion that American and Arab civilizations are 'naturally' prone to conflict or concepts of a historically inevitable 'special relationship' between America and Israel. As such, it speaks interestingly to the present moment of relative fluidity in US attitudes towards and relations with the region as shown by, for example, the resurgence of anti-Zionist Jewish organizations such as the American Council for Judaism.[37] Again, the conclusions one draws from this understanding depend on one's politics. Either the story of CIA Arabism is a cautionary tale of what might happen if the US-Israel special relationship is not carefully nurtured – or it is a tragedy of promising beginnings and wrong turnings which nonetheless teaches the useful lesson that things were different once, and therefore could be again.

Notes

1. Quoted in Karl E. Meyer and Shareen Blair Brysac, *Kingmakers: The Invention of the Modern Middle East* (New York: W.W. Norton, 2008), 347.
2. See, for example, Robert D. Kaplan, *The Arabists: The Romance of an American Elite* (New York: Free Press, 1993).
3. For examples of this approach, see Helen Laville and Hugh Wilford, eds., *The US Government, Citizen Groups and the Cold War: The State-Private Network* (London: Routledge, 2006).
4. See Andrew J. Rotter, 'Saidism Without Said: *Orientalism* and US Diplomatic History', *American Historical Review*, CV (2000), 1205–17.
5. For a recent example of this approach by a leading practitioner, see Frank Costigliola, 'After Roosevelt's Death: Dangerous Emotions, Divisive Discourses, and the Abandoned Alliance', *Diplomatic History*, XXXIV (2010), 1–23.
6. This is one of major strands of the collaborative research project funded by the British Arts and Humanities Research Council and based at the Universities of Nottingham and Warwick, 'Landscapes of Secrecy: The CIA and the Contested Record of US Foreign Policy, 1947–2001'.
7. See Robert D. Dean, *Imperial Brotherhood: Gender and the Making of Cold War Foreign Policy* (Amherst: University of Massachusetts Press, 2001), ch. 2.
8. The young Kermit Roosevelt identified with his fictional namesake so strongly that he once convinced a gullible family tutor that he actually *was* Kim. See Kermit Roosevelt, Jr., *A Sentimental Safari* (New York: Alfred A. Knopf, 1963), xiii.
9. Kermit Roosevelt, *War in the Garden of Eden* (New York: Charles Scribner's Sons, 1919), 201–4.
10. Priya Satia, *Spies in Arabia: The Great War and the Cultural Foundations of Britain's Covert Empire in the Middle East* (New York: Oxford University Press, 2008).
11. Kermit Roosevelt, Jr., 'The Lure of the East', *The American Boy – Youth's Companion*, LVIII. Box 14, folder Roosevelt, Kermit, Jr., Kermit and Belle Roosevelt Papers, Library of Congress, Washington, DC.
12. For a recent account of this tradition, see Ussama Makdisi, *Faith Misplaced: The Broken Promise of US-Arab Relations* (New York: Public Affairs, 2010).

13 Theologian Samuel Hopkins, quoted in Abbas Amanat and Magnus T. Bernhardsson, eds., *US-Middle East Historical Encounters: A Critical Survey* (Gainesville: University Press of Florida, 2007), 2.
14 See the informative biography of Eddy, Thomas W. Lippman, *Arabian Knight: Colonel Bill Eddy USMC and the Rise of American Power in the Middle East* (Vista, CA: Selwa Press, 2008).
15 Kermit Roosevelt, Jr., *Arabs, Oil and History: The Story of the Middle East*, 2nd edn (Port Washington, NY: Kennikat Press, 1967), 7.
16 Miles Copeland, *The Game of Nations: The Amorality of Power Politics* (London: Weidenfeld and Nicolson, 1969), 34–6.
17 See Archie Roosevelt, *For Lust of Knowing: Memoirs of an Intelligence Officer* (Boston: Little, Brown, 1988), esp. ch. 9.
18 Kermit Roosevelt, Jr., *Arabs, Oil, and History...*, 43, 44, 68.
19 Copeland, *The Game of Nations...*, 34–5.
20 See Copeland, *The Game of Nations...*, chs 3–6, and Miles Copeland, *The Game Player: Confessions of the CIA's Original Political Operative* (London: Aurum Press, 1989), ch. 16.
21 Douglas Little, 'Mission Impossible: The CIA and the Cult of Covert Action in the Middle East', *Diplomatic History*, XXVIII (2004), 678.
22 Quoted in Robert Dreyfuss, *Devil's Game: How the United States Helped Islamic Fundamentalism* (New York: Metropolitan Books/Henry Holt, 2005), 107.
23 Archie Roosevelt, *For Lust of Knowing...*, 443.
24 Much of Copeland's 1969 *Game of Nations* is devoted to solving the Nasser riddle.
25 Archie Roosevelt, *For Lust of Knowing...*, 27, 337–8.
26 Quoted in Kaplan, *The Arabists...*, 101
27 Archie Roosevelt, *For Lust of Knowing...*, 110.
28 Quoted in Lippmann, *Arabian Knight...*, 277.
29 See Dreyfuss, *Devil's Game...*
30 Kermit Roosevelt, Jr., *Arabs, Oil, and History...*, 8, 34.
31 Christina Klein, *Cold War Orientalism: Asia in the Middlebrow Imagination, 1945–61* (Berkeley: University of California Press, 2003).
32 See, for example, Meyer and Brysac, *Kingmakers...*, ch. 10.
33 See Michael Holzman, *James Jesus Angleton, the CIA, and the Craft of Counterintelligence* (Amherst: University of Massachusetts Press, 2008), 151–5.
34 For a fuller account of the history of AFME, see Hugh Wilford, 'The American Friends of the Middle East: American Citizens, the CIA, and American-Arab Relations, 1947–67', forthcoming.
35 Melani McAlister, *Epic Encounters: Culture, Media, and US Interests in the Middle East since 1945*, 2nd edn (Berkeley: University of California Press, 2005), 2, 11.
36 For more on the strains in US-Israeli relations in this period, see Peter L. Hahn, 'The United States and Israel in the Eisenhower Era: The "Special Relationship" Revisited', in Kathryn C. Statler and Andrew L. Johns, eds., *The Eisenhower Administration, the Third World, and the Globalization of the Cold War* (Lanham: Rowman and Littlefield, 2006), 225–43.
37 See Samuel G. Freedman, 'American Jews Who Reject Zionism Say Events Aid Cause', *New York Times*, 26 June 2010, A14.

6
The Perfect and Sustainable Road to Economic Development?: The Eisenhower Administration and Latin America

Bevan Sewell

'We who are all young nations, in whom the pioneering spirit is still vitally alive, need neither to fear the future nor be satisfied with the present,' President Dwight D. Eisenhower told the Organization of American States (OAS) in April, 1953.

> In our spiritual, cultural and material life, in all that concerns our daily bread and our daily learning, we do and should seek an ever better world... I do not think it unjust to claim for the government and the people of the United States a readiness, rarely matched in history, to help other nations improve their living standards and guard their security. Despite unprecedented burdens of national debt and world wide responsibility, our people have continued to demonstrate this readiness.[1]

Though pitched at improving the climate of inter-American relations, the speech also portrayed the US as being firmly behind the concept of progress in Latin America.[2] Not in any specific detail, to be sure, but the notion of development in the region was nevertheless clearly apparent. The US supported development in the region, Eisenhower went on to state, but this should be achieved gradually; progress in the region could best be achieved by holding true to America's guiding principles. 'Private investment has been the major stimulus for economic development throughout this hemisphere,' he argued. 'Beyond this, the United States government is today engaged with our sister republics in important efforts to increase agricultural productivity, improve health conditions, encourage new industries, extend transportation facilities, and develop new sources of power. The pursuit of each of these goals in any one nation of the Americas serves the good of all the Americas.'[3]

For the duration of his presidency, this indistinct but nonetheless rigid sense of Latin American development would remain at the heart of Eisenhower's economic approach. And despite some disputes among his advisors as to the exact shape that this policy should take, it would continue to hold true until the administration left office in January, 1961. Traditionally, scholars of Eisenhower's Latin American policies have viewed the administration's approach as having been motivated either by the overwhelming exigencies of the Cold War or the desire to quell Latin American economic nationalism.[4] Both arguments have numerous merits. A close analysis of the administration's economic approach toward the region, however, also reveals something else – that the approach that Eisenhower and his advisors took with respect to fostering economic development in the region was unfailingly consistent. Latin American nations should develop steadily and in accordance with the US model of private investment, limited state intervention and with increasingly free markets. So entrenched was this mantra, in fact, that it continued to hold true even when the administration's approach was coming under significant fire from international and domestic critics. Indeed, as a pre-presidential task force reported to president-elect John F. Kennedy in early 1961: 'In Latin America the [economic] philosophy of the Eisenhower Administration is everywhere disliked... [it] amounted to saying that whatever was good for General Motors would be good for the Latin American countries.'[5] By 1961, it was suggested that the US had done far too little, far too late in terms of altering its economic approach. A new administration, enthused by ideas constructed on notions of modernisation theory, would subsequently seek to redress this problem.[6]

Yet this does not tell the whole story. Kennedy and his advisors did usher in shifts in US policy toward the region, but their model was constructed on top of what already existed. Their stated endpoint, meanwhile, was not so very different from that of their predecessor. Both Eisenhower and Kennedy supported the notion of Latin American development; both wanted the region to be (eventually) democratic; and both believed that improved living standards and greater prosperity was the key to achieving this. Without doubt, their methods for achieving these goals differed, as did their timescales. Nevertheless, the similarities between their stated endpoints suggest a need to reappraise the difficulties that the Eisenhower administration faced in Latin America. Eisenhower's policy undoubtedly failed: development in the region was painfully slow, anti-American sentiment was increasing rapidly and the policy of supporting authoritarian leaders for Cold War expediency had backfired horribly. The impact of an ideology of development in US policy, though, suggests a different approach to explaining the administration's failure. The problem on the economic front was less one of disinterest in the region, and more one of a rigid ideological blueprint.[7]

This chapter will trace the presence of this ideological commitment to development in Eisenhower's Latin American policy. In doing so it will not suggest that this was the sole aim of US policy, as pressing strategic or political concerns could undoubtedly predominate; rather, it will argue that throughout its two terms the administration's approach toward the question of development remained unaltered and that this helps to explain why, when its approach was so unpopular, the administration did not change its approach more significantly. There was no major change because neither Eisenhower nor his advisors believed there to be anything substantially wrong with their original approach.

* * * * *

The idea of fostering US-style development in Latin America was, of course, boosted by the abundant financial links that existed before Eisenhower came to office. 'Our $7 billion of trade with our sister republics is greater than our commercial trade with Europe or any other part of the world,' one of Eisenhower's Latin American advisors stated in 1953. 'Our $6 billion of investments in Latin America surpass those in any other single area except Canada.'[8] These pre-existing financial ties helped US officials to believe that it was certainly possible to extend American capital into other areas of the Latin American economy. This was believed to be the precursor to US-style development: the influence of American finance and business practices, coupled with ongoing advice from Washington, would result in economic growth that was steady and based on sound fiscal principles.

The administration's first policy deliberations on the region emphasised the mode of development that should be encouraged, as well as promoting the idea of utilising US businesses as a conduit to a successful policy.[9] At a National Security Council (NSC) meeting on March 18, 1953, Harold Stassen, the former Governor of Massachusetts and head of the Foreign Operations Administration (FOA), suggested that the Latin American nations needed to be offered greater encouragement to implement sound business practices. While he was generally very happy with the report, Stassen said, 'it failed to take into account with sufficient force one point that he felt to be of very great importance. It did not reflect the need for Latin American capitalists and business men to provide better treatment for their workers and to take a more progressive and responsible role in the development of the economies of their countries.' Treasury Secretary George Humphrey – a strident fiscal conservative, opposed to extending foreign economic assistance – supported Stassen's broader point with his own recommendation. 'If we could find a few first-rate business men and send them as our ambassadors to the key Latin American nations,' Humphrey said, 'it would do far more good than any amount of money we could dole out.'[10]

More important than these forms of commercial links, however, was the concept of development. Though its short-term reliance on military assistance agreements and supporting dictators was believed to be a catch-all solution to emerging political problems that would keep the area 'safe' in terms of the Cold War, the administration was aware that, in the mid- to long term, a move toward modernisation in the region was necessary in order to stave off discontent.[11] The Latin Americans, one State Department report noted, 'have a driving urge toward economic development' with 'which we can cooperate to achieve our common ends.'[12] Hence, the administration's first policy reports set out how this should be achieved. 'Our objective is to facilitate the supporting role of US capital in developing Latin American economies... this role is principally played by US private capital, and we seek to maximize it by encouraging a better climate in Latin America for foreign enterprise,' an annex to the administration's first Latin American policy statement explained.[13] The reductive nature of this discussion was elucidated upon further by the President for his Cabinet. 'We put a coin in the tin cup,' he told them, 'and yet we know that the tin cup is still going to be there tomorrow.' US policy, he inferred, should focus on ensuring that the 'cup' did not reappear in the future.[14] NSC 144/1, the administration's finalised version of its Latin American policy, thus stated that:

> Most Latin American governments are under intense domestic political pressures to increase production and to diversify their economies. A realistic and constructive approach to this need which recognizes the importance of bettering conditions for the general population, is essential to arrest the drift in the area toward radical and nationalistic regimes... The United States should seek to assist in the economic development of Latin America by... Encouraging Latin American gov-

ernments to recognize that the bulk of the capital required for their economic development can best be supplied by private enterprise and that their own self-interests requires the creation of a climate which will attract private investment... Continuing the present level of International Bank loans and Export-Import Bank loans and, where appropriate, accelerating and increasing them, as a necessary supplement to foreign private investment... Undertaking a thorough study of the means by which we can assist Latin American capital to play a more vigorous and responsible role in economic development of the area.[15]

Beyond the rather generic goals outlined in NSC 144/1, though, the administration's policy was far from clear about how economic development was to be achieved in Latin America (and, more broadly, the Third World). And yet herein lays a crucial point: the administration's stance on development was ill-defined and vague, because US officials were suggesting that developing nations imitate the American model. There was very little scientific or economic analysis taking place; the approach was instead born out of an innate faith in the US economic system.[16]

This lack of clarity, coupled with the administration's sense that development should be a gradual process, buttressed the ideology of development when early reports noted that NSC 144/1 had hardly had a transformative economic impact in Latin America. To the contrary, the climate for attracting private investment in Latin America in 1953 had worsened. 'Nothing irretrievable has occurred,' the *New York Times* editorialised in May, 'but it is time to call attention to the fact that nothing positive, and little that is favourable in the sphere of inter-American relations has happened, either.'[17] But the Eisenhower administration – thanks to its very American sense of development – was able to ignore negative appraisals. Rather, the administration sought to incorporate minor tweaks to its approach in order to address specific problems in attracting private capital. Following a tour of the region in the summer of 1953, the president's brother Milton recommended a series of small adjustments to US developmental policy. 'Latin Americans,' he reported,

> hold a persistent feeling that the United States could, if it wished, have made substantial sums for development available to them when it was providing billions for the rest of the world. This feeling is enhanced by the fact that Latin America does not seek financial

grants, but rather, loans to satisfy its driving demands for broad and immediate economic development.

And while future development was certainly being imperilled by a 'lack of dollar exchange and investment capital', this could be addressed through judicious use of public loans in order to bridge the gap and further encourage private capital to flow to the region.[18] The subsequent implementation of NSC 5407 with little internal debate – a document which implemented many of the recommendations outlined in Dr. Eisenhower's report, including that of making 'sound development loans which are in our national interest, but which might not be made by an international agency' – suggested the report was in keeping with prevailing sentiments.[19]

Such adjustments, it was hoped, would encourage the Latin American governments to adopt the policies believed to be necessary to attract greater levels of private capital. Foreign investments needed to be protected; companies needed to be allowed to remit their profits; high inflation and balance of payments difficulties needed to be addressed; and, important natural resources like oil needed to be open to investors. Simple enough on the surface, but measures such as these were unconscionable for a significant number of Latin American governments. Some, such as Brazil, recognised that encouraging greater US corporate involvement in this way would provoke a backlash from powerful nationalist forces firmly opposed to their nation being in thrall to US finances. Others, such as those in El Salvador or Paraguay, lacked the nationwide control necessary to adopt such approaches. Still others, such as those in Bolivia or Guatemala, were simply not willing to tow the American line (leading, in both cases, to very different forms of intervention). Finally, some authoritarian governments, such as those in Venezuela or the Dominican Republic, were starting to tread a fine line between obsequiousness toward the US and the need to restrain the will of the people.[20] Across the region, then, the prospects for the Eisenhower administration actually being able to implement this ideological form of development were far from hopeful. So entrenched was it, though, that these abundant problems failed to affect the faith that US officials had in their stated economic model.

The relative stability in the political sphere – which only seemed to be strengthened by the successful ousting of Jacobo Arbenz in Guatemala and the simultaneous de-radicalising of the Bolivian Government in 1953–54 – reinforced this belief.[21] Evidence of the administration's steadfast stance on development came at an inter-American conference in

Caracas, Venezuela in the spring of 1954, which became dominated by the run-up to the US move against Arbenz. Even so, John Foster Dulles forcefully reasserted the administration's position on economic matters at Caracas in a speech whose implications, amid the mounting crisis over Guatemala, was not fully recognised.

> We would, however, like to see the economies of our American friends and neighbours more vigorous than in some cases they are... In the United States private capital and free enterprise constitute the great source of our own economic well-being. That is a source which we do not try to keep at home. It is free to go abroad, and we welcome its international activities... private capital cannot be driven. It has to be attracted. Therefore, the decision rests with you.[22]

This was a clear encapsulation of where precisely the Eisenhower administration stood on the question of development. Again, the evident unpopularity of such sentiments was overlooked. Sidney Gruson, writing in the *New York Times*, reported that there 'is no masking the fact that there was disappointment with the Secretary's economic statement'; an internal administration report, meanwhile, was equally forthright: 'Latin Americans are dissatisfied with the present state of their economic relations with the United States... the Communists are increasingly taking advantage of this dissatisfaction.'[23]

If the intractability of the US position in Caracas was hardly surprising, it was nevertheless hugely disappointing for the Latin Americans that the administration adopted an almost identical approach for another conference later that year in Rio de Janeiro. In preparation for the conference in Rio, in fact, the administration took the time to reaffirm its position on development as it prepared a new regional policy document. 'Economic development in Latin America must be speeded up by increasing Latin American trade, helping to finance sound projects and encouraging a climate conducive to private investment,' an early draft explained, 'but without providing grant aid except to fulfil special commitments and in emergency situations.'[24] Although some officials, notably those in the Foreign Operations Administration, voiced concerns over the political ramifications of this the US economic position for Rio remained unaltered.[25] Hence, the finalised version of the document – NSC 5432/1 – stated:

> While recognizing the sovereign right of Latin American countries to undertake such economic measures as they may conclude are best

adapted to their own conditions, encourage them by economic assistance and other means to base their economies on a system of private enterprise and, as essential thereto, to create a political and economic climate conducive to private investment, of both domestic and foreign capital.[26]

At the Rio Economic Conference, then, the US position on development remained wholly consistent. Like in Caracas, the US position was made clear from the start. In his opening address, Treasury Secretary George Humphrey stated that:

> Our agenda is admirably fashioned to help us appraise not only our place on the road which has already brought us so far toward our goal, but also the measures which we can take jointly and severally to hasten our progress on that road. It is our conviction that to accomplish this purpose two basic principles should underlie all our thinking. The first is our belief that the road which will lead most surely and most directly to the goals which we seek is that of the vigorous free enterprise system. This system in its modern form builds new industries, new enterprises, and opens new areas to development. And it does all these things without endangering those free institutions which are the very foundation of the social and human progress which we have achieved in this hemisphere. The other is our belief that we as governments should reduce to a minimum the scope and duration of our own intervention in the fields of commerce and industry... Our own belief in the principles I have stated derives from the fact that wherever they have been applied in the Americas and elsewhere in the world they have bought improvements in the lives of our peoples...[27]

And though part of this would involve slightly increasing loans available through existing financial institutions, it was – as the *New York Times* reported – made 'with the understanding that this was to be an encouragement to free enterprise rather than a displacement of it.'[28] Inevitably, this was met with little enthusiasm by the Latin Americans, while the simultaneous emergence of Raul Prebisch and the United Nations Economic Commission for Latin America demonstrated the development of an alternative economic model in the region. But the unyielding nature of the US position left little intellectual room for manoeuvre.[29]

In its first two years in office, the Eisenhower administration determinedly set out its developmental stance toward Latin America. There had been some slight modifications, in accordance with the recommendations made by the president's brother, but the wider intellectual conceptualisation of development remained unaltered. The abiding power of this ideology, however, can only be ascertained by examining the way it held firm during Eisenhower's second term in office. For during this period, a series of political and strategic crises compelled the administration to reconsider its Latin American strategy as US interests appeared to come under threat. In strategic terms, this led to a fluid situation in US policy. In developmental terms, however, significant changes to existing policies were rejected; if anything, the administration's innate belief in its vision was strengthened.

* * * * *

The first major challenge came with the emergence of a tangible Soviet presence in the region. In January 1956 the Soviet leadership extended an offer of economic and technical assistance to the countries of the region, which was part of their wider effort to promote links with the Third World. Viewed with great suspicion in Washington, US officials feared that Moscow was aiming to undermine inter-American unity by agreeing to provide funding in areas that the US would not (such as state-owned companies controlling oil resources) and without imposing economic pre-conditions.[30] But while this forced US officials to reconsider their position in Latin America, it did not challenge the prevailing constructs of their developmental vision. Emerging strategic threats did not undermine the ideology of development. Later challenges, such as the anti-American protests during a trip by Richard Nixon in 1958 and the Cuban Revolution, elicited similar responses.[31]

In the first instance, the global outbreak of the Soviet Economic Offensive (SEO) forced US officials to consider whether or not they should alter their economic policies in response. The obvious fear was that the Soviet model of rapid industrialisation – and willingness to lend in areas the US would not – would be highly attractive for developing nations. Quickly, though, US officials determined that they remained fully committed to their developmental model. Some form of response – likely to involve propaganda and wider use of binding military agreements – would, of course, be necessary; but, in economic terms, there seemed little or no point in getting drawn into a battle of financial one-upmanship with Moscow. 'The Soviets have every opportunity to play us for suckers,' Eisenhower warned his NSC. 'We must be careful not to be drawn into matching every Soviet offer of assistance to foreign nations.'[32]

The administration determined this despite noting its unpopularity in Latin America, and the fact that private investment was not exactly pouring into the region. An NSC progress report had outlined this several months before the Soviet offer. 'The United States,' the report noted, 'will continue to be concerned with maintaining economic stability and accelerating economic development,' but would also have 'to face the desire of Latin Americans to have the US assume a larger share of the financial burden involved in solving their economic problems than the US is willing to bear.' Similarly, briefing papers prepared for officials in advance of the Quantico meetings in the autumn of 1955 detailed a lack of dynamism in existing policy. 'Progress has not halted,' one report explained, 'but its rate has fallen sufficiently to change the picture of improvement in per capita living standards... to one that is far lower than that upon which we have counted in this country.' The problem, the report went on, was not in the theory of development; rather, it was because the flow of private capital to the region had decreased.[33]

With even the most critical of reports not finding fault with the concept of US-style development *per se* and instead blaming it on Latin American deficiencies in attracting investment, it only took one or two positive reports to restore balance. After touring the region in 1955, for example, Richard Nixon told the NSC he was 'glad indeed that our current Latin American policy put such heavy emphasis on private capital and private enterprise' and that Rafael Trujillo, the dictator in power in the Dominican Republic, had had unequivocally stated during his visit that 'grants and gifts simply made beggars and loafers.'[34] It was highly noteworthy how little impact any problems had on the way US policymakers conceived of development in the region. The US economic response to the SEO, neatly summarised for Foster Dulles by Henry Holland in February 1956, was thus one of continuity. 'We need something new that does not involve broad grant aid, soft loans, loans to the oil industry or loans to projects for which private capital is available,' he wrote. 'We must put the other country in a position where it is obvious to her that if she accepts Soviet credits we can quietly diminish or cut off continuing benefits which are more important to her than anything Russia can offer.'[35] At the same time, a renewed effort would begin to clearly portray the US as being supportive of Latin American desires.[36]

Because the SEO soon petered out, the US response was not subjected to detailed scrutiny.[37] Instead, US perceptions about the sanctity of their existing approach were buttressed; as far as US officials were concerned, their response had proven to be successful. This was apparent a year later, at the Buenos Aires Economic Conference, when US officials once again took the opportunity to firmly restate their basic developmental principles to increasingly frustrated Latin American delegates.

Before the meeting in the Argentine capital, US regional policy had been reconfigured slightly in NSC 5613/1. Given the heightened strategic climate in the region, efforts to strengthen inter-American relations were inevitably to the fore. On the economic side, though, it was very much business as usual. A summarised version of the new paper for Eisenhower explained: 'Existing policy relies primarily on private trade and investment in the economic development of Latin America. These activities, particularly trade, are to be pushed more vigorously to forestall Soviet economic penetration.'[38] The finalised version of the document outlined the litany of Latin American complaints to this approach; but once more, this had little impact on policy. Soviet attempts to infiltrate the region economically, the document explained, 'only serve to emphasize the urgency and necessity of carrying out US policies vigorously, especially loan and trade policies, in order to demonstrate the benefits to be derived from a free private enterprise system and from close relations with the United States.'[39]

Prior to the Buenos Aires Conference, some US officials raised concerns with existing policy. Development via this model was perfectly right, they suggested, yet wasn't it damaging Washington's political position in the region? Accordingly, they proposed some alterations – specifically, greater levels of public loan assistance in order to generate the impression of greater US assistance and to help to create a climate more conducive to private investment-led growth, as well as social reforms to address chronic disparity in many Latin American nations.[40] But though these suggestions marked a change, they did not challenge the dominant ideology of development. Debates over whether or not the US should alter its stance on public loans and social reform – discussions that foreshadowed those that would come under John F. Kennedy – were subsequently subsumed into the existing model. It is little surprise, then, that the US position for Buenos Aires was primarily the same as it had been for Rio de Janeiro three years earlier.[41]

The same pattern – strategic concerns leading to some alterations, but concluding, on the economic side, with a restatement of the existing developmental model – was apparent in the wake of both the Nixon trip in 1958 and the Cuban Revolution a year later. Both events led to substantial discussions among US officials about how the US could salvage its position in Latin America; at no stage, though, did they question the validity of their stance on development.[42]

After the Nixon trip, which saw fervent anti-American protests against the Vice President in Venezuela, one State Department official told a congressional committee that the protests had been caused by 'the intensive exploitation of communist and other anti-American elements of grievances against our policies'; this, however, merely served to give the recommendations of officials like Milton Eisenhower more traction in policy discussions, rather than leading to any consideration of wholesale changes.[43] At a key NSC meeting following the trip, furthermore, Nixon outlined his belief that 'US policy and what the United States is doing in Latin America is not subject to very much criticism'; 'our policies and actions were generally correct,' he continued, 'but the problem was essentially more subtle and hence more difficult to solve.' Eisenhower, agreeing with this assessment, mused whether there needed to be a re-branding of capitalism – one that stopped it being erroneously equated with 'imperialism'. 'We should try,' the president suggested, 'to coin a new phrase to represent our own modern brand of capitalism.'[44] To be sure, US officials accepted that there would need to be some alterations; continuing in the same vein, after all, was only going to provoke further outbursts of anti-American discontent. Ideas such as regional commodity agreements to stabilise prices were subsequently approved, while a sense that development in the region would take even longer to occur than previously forecast led to the creation of a new Inter-American Development Bank.[45]

Like the earlier period, though, this recalibration did not amount to a scientific study of developing economic trends in the region. Nor, indeed, did it point to an evolving sense of how development in the region should take place. Rather, it was a mildly different route to the same endpoint. All of this came together, effectively, in a new report by Milton Eisenhower following a second trip to the region in the summer of 1958. The resultant report was much more significant than that which had resulted from his previous trip. Even so, its core message was essentially unchanged: inter-American relations can be improved through judicious use of economic measures, but significant development must take place via the private investment model. Thus while public capital, in the shape of increased loans, could be utilised to break funding log-jams, this was supposed to support, rather than replace, the role of private capital. Attracting private capital to the region, therefore, remained crucial if problematic. 'This problem is largely out of our hands,' the Eisenhower report noted. 'Private capital cannot be driven. It must be attracted.'[46] Milton Eisenhower's sentiments, moreover, sat neatly alongside the policy that the administration was outlining publicly. At the same time that the Eisenhower report was being finalised, Under Secretary of State,

Douglas Dillon, told the OAS: 'In Latin America, as in the United States we have experienced a dynamic economic expansion. If we all set ourselves resolutely to our task, if each does his share, and if we work cooperatively for an integrated program of development... we can demonstrate that free peoples can outproduce enslaved peoples and can do so without sacrificing their way of life.'[47]

Strategically, US policy was moving in new directions. The level of anti-American sentiment demonstrated during the Nixon trip, coupled with rising fears about the stability of the region, meant a change in approach was required. In 1958 and 1959, the administration worked to achieve this by creating NSC 5902/1 – a document whose importance only increased following Fidel Castro's seizure of power in Cuba in early 1959.[48] However, the course of events in Latin America had done little to dispel the belief among Eisenhower and his leading advisors that their economic vision was correct.

A powerful example of this came with the administration's response to an attempt by the Brazilian government to alter the developmental discourse in the area, a shift that compelled John Foster Dulles to forcefully restate the US position on development to Brazilian president, Juscelino Kubitschek, in the summer of 1958. Kubitschek, pursuing his own goals of turning Brazil into a modern state, had sought to use the fall-out from the Nixon trip to push forward an idea named 'Operation Pan America' (OPA). Essentially, Kubitschek called for vastly increased governmental funding to Latin America in an effort to promote more rapid development. After initial enthusiasm for OPA's political aspects, the US turned against Kubitschek's plan as it posited a model of development too far removed from that of the US.[49] Later, Dulles told Kubitschek that the US did not support his contention that the root of all political problems lay in 'underdevelopment'. It was 'an oversimplification to say that the communist problem can be solved by solving the problem of underdevelopment'; 'development of resources,' Dulles went on, 'is primarily a job for private capital.'[50]

The broader implication of the events surrounding OPA was that it confirmed the US position on development, while also demonstrating Washington's determination to continue adhering to this even though analysts were beginning to question whether it was ever going to prove possible to closely associate the US with Latin American aspirations. After both the SEO and the Nixon trip, the administration's reappraisal of policy had focused heavily on being seen to be behind Latin American aspirations. Now, just a few months later, an internal report cast significant doubt over this approach. 'We have not found – and it may not be possible to find – an approach which will entirely meet the problem of identifying the United States satisfactorily as a wholly constructive force in the area,' the report stated.[51] Shortly afterwards, a National Intelligence Estimate informed the president that 'we believe there is little likelihood that Latin America attitudes toward the US will change substantially for the better during the next few years', especially against a backdrop of rapid population growth and ongoing Latin American efforts to 'attempt economic development beyond their own capabilities.'[52]

When framed against a backdrop of such gloomy appraisals, the unremitting faith that US officials continually demonstrated in their economic model continues to jar. It is here that the role of ideology stands out most clearly – serving as a conceptual framework by which US officials could situate the hugely complex issue of development into a much simpler understanding and leading to a situation whereby US officials crafted policy 'less to fit the facts than their own preconceptions'.[53] Measured against entrenched preconceptions and ideas on the US side, Eisenhower's policy of development in Latin America made sense as the local situation was rendered irrelevant in the minds of US policymakers. Some changes were, undoubtedly, necessary – a point demonstrated by the creation of the Inter-American Development Bank (IADB) and, in 1960, Eisenhower's announcement of a Social Progress Fund to tackle the unremitting poverty in much of the region – but these were modifications to achieve the same goal not a major shift in thinking. The rising importance of the Caribbean, with a developing row between Cuba, the Dominican Republic and Venezuela exercising US minds, did not alter this salient fact. NSC 5902/1, introduced after the Nixon trip but before US-Cuban relations deteriorated, made few alterations to the economic covenants set out in NSC 144/1 in 1953.[54]

For the majority of Eisenhower's advisors this seemed to be the only way to proceed: results thus far had been far from spectacular, they concurred, but the US model nevertheless remained the only viable method of development. This much was made clear to the NSC by Thomas Mann – a long-serving State Department official, who would later become Lyndon Johnson's leading Latin American advisor. In actual terms, Mann told the NSC, Latin American growth was not unimpressive; the problem was that it had been accompanied by exponential population growth that had limited its impact. 'In the light of these developments,' Mann stated, 'if we in the United States hoped somehow to help meet the aspirations of the people of Latin America, the task is going to be extremely difficult.' The only hope, he concluded, lay in convincing the Latin Americans 'to follow consistent and sound economic policies.'[55]

Similar sentiments were in evidence when Eisenhower himself toured the region in 1960. 'It is expected that the President's trip will involve no negotiations,' a State Department instructional memo explained before the trip. 'While the President will be glad to confer with the leaders of the countries visited on subjects of mutual concern, he does not intend to negotiate solutions to problems... the President must not be expected to make new commitments nor alter present United States policy regarding area problems while on this trip.'[56] Latin American responses to the trip were accordingly circumspect. While appreciating the effort taken to demonstrate his commitment to the region, Secretary of State Christian Herter (who had replaced the terminally ill Dulles in the spring of 1959) reported to Eisenhower, a few Latin American leaders 'qualified their remarks with the proviso that the high hopes raised should be followed by action to solve the many problems facing Latin America.'[57] Eisenhower recognised this and, in a portent of what would come under Kennedy, announced a $500 million Social Progress Fund to tackle the worst deprivations in the region, especially with respect to housing and schooling. With respect to development, though, little had altered. Just a few months after his trip, Eisenhower told a press conference in Rhode Island: 'The only real investment that is going to flow into countries that will be useful to them in the long term, is private investment. It is many times the amount that can be put in from the public coffers.'[58]

* * * * *

Remarkably, toward the end of Eisenhower's second term, a report was produced by a mid-level official in the Department of Defense that challenged the overarching principles that had guided the administration's policies since 1953. 'Our essential conclusion,' the report began, 'is that the United States has not succeeded, either politically through the machinery of the OAS, or economically through existing levels or techniques of assistance, to accord to the countries of Latin America the recognition, consideration or treatment commensurate with their partnership status in the Western Hemisphere or with the minimum economic development requirements which arise from an evolving socio-politico-economic revolution.' Worse, the report continued, this failure could be traced 'to the inadequacies or outright invalidation of certain concepts underlying United States policy vis-a-vis Latin America.' The report challenged the fundamental principles that had guided the Eisenhower administration's position on Latin American development, arguing that the approach of fostering development in the region via private investment and the US model was deeply flawed. Instead, the report advocated more direct public funding similar to that which had been utilised in India, Pakistan and Indonesia; such funding, the author argued, was critical if funding gaps were to be addressed. The biggest problem, the report concluded, was that Eisenhower's approach had failed to significantly accelerate regional growth and that the entire nature of intra-hemispheric relations was thus being undermined to the ultimate benefit of the Soviet Union.[59]

The report provided a sharp critique of Eisenhower's approach, none worse than the allegation that his policies had threatened America's national security. Furthermore, these were criticisms that were also being made to the president-elect, John Kennedy, by his own advisory group. Kennedy's specially convened Task Force on Latin America brusquely asserted that Eisenhower's policies had 'lent plausibility to the Communist charge that America's only interest was to enlarge her investment opportunities and markets, and to the Marxian charge that American capitalism equated to imperialism.'[60] These sentiments, coupled with the alarmist condemnations of Eisenhower's policies that had characterised the Kennedy campaign's statements on the region and the predominantly negative tone in the American press, meant that there was little argument over how successful Eisenhower had been in Latin America.

Strategically, Eisenhower would likely have accepted some of the charges against him. The support of dictators and reliance on military assistance agreements, coupled with an absence of support for democracy, had undoubtedly impacted heavily on the state of the inter-American relationship. Intervention in Guatemala, meanwhile, had been undertaken in spite of the fact that meeting what was deemed to be a necessary strategic threat would also be overwhelmingly unpopular among the other Latin American states.[61] Economically, however, Eisenhower would have disputed the allegation that his administration had pursued the wrong developmental policy in the area. It had unquestionably proven to be unpopular with the Latin Americans. But neither Eisenhower nor the bulk of his advisors believed this to be the same as it being the wrong policy.

More importantly, few in the incoming Kennedy administration would have disputed this central point: their recommendations, based predominantly on the theories of social scientists and modernisation theorists, recognised the necessity of long-term development being funded by private capital. Where they differed was in their belief that, in the short term, widespread use of loans and aid could be used to accelerate this process and achieve much-needed social reforms in order to improve inter-American relations.[62] Viewed outside of the maelstrom of 1960s international relations, it seems less certain that Eisenhower's economic approach was necessarily as wrong as his critics suggest. For his envisioned endpoint – of a region developed and supportive of the US – was not so far removed from Kennedy's. Though it was undoubtedly unpopular, he may have been right that Latin American development would be a gradual process and should be guided more by private capital than public (and indeed that it should – at least to some degree – be viewed outside of the confines of the Cold War).[63]

Ultimately, the Eisenhower model fell into the same trap as modernisation-era assumptions that one model could apply to all Latin American nations – heralding the universality of the American model while, at the same time, wholly neglecting to consider the situation on the ground in the individual Latin American countries in anything like enough detail.[64] Eisenhower may, therefore, have unconsciously recognised the inherent limits on US power to act as the fount of modernisation. Unfortunately for both him and the Latin Americans, squaring this particular circle proved to be highly difficult.

Notes

1 Address by President Eisenhower before the Council of the Organization of American States, April 12 1953, *Public Papers of the Presidents: 1953 Dwight D. Eisenhower* (hereafter *PPPUS* and year). These sources accessed via www.presidency.ucsb.edu/ws/index
2 Kenneth Osgood, *Total Cold War: Eisenhower's Secret Propaganda Battle at Home and Abroad* (Lawrence, Kansas: University Press of Kansas, 2006), 144.
3 Address by President Eisenhower before the Council of the Organization of American States, April 12 1953, *PPPUS 1953*.
4 For the Cold War argument, the main work remains: Stephen Rabe, *Eisenhower: The Foreign Policy of Anticommunism and Latin America* (Chapel Hill: University of North Carolina Press, 1988), 174–8; also in this vein: Mark Gilderhus, *The Second Century: US-Latin American Relations since 1889* (Wilmington, Delaware: Scholarly Resources Inc, 2000), 139–71; Joseph Smith, *The United States and Latin America: A History of American Diplomacy, 1776–2000* (London: Routledge, 2005); Thomas Zoumaras, 'Eisenhower's Foreign Economic Policy – The Case of Latin America', in Richard Melanson and David Mayers, eds., *Re-evaluating Eisenhower* (Urbana, Illinois: University of Illinois Press, 1987), 155–91. For the argument that the administration was more concerned with the fight against Latin American economic nationalism: James

Siekmeier, *Aid, Nationalism, and Inter-American Relations: Bolivia, Guatemala and the United States, 1953–1961* (New York: Edwin Mellen Press, 1999); Matthew Loayza, 'An Aladdin's Lamp for Free Enterprise: Eisenhower, Fiscal Conservatism, and Latin American Nationalism, 1953–1961', *Diplomacy and Statecraft*, Vol. 14, No. 3 (September 2003), 83–105.

5 'Report to the President-elect of the Task Force on Immediate Latin American Problems', January 4 1961, 'Task Force Reports', Box 1074, Papers of President Kennedy: Pre-Presidential Papers, John F. Kennedy Presidential Library, Boston, Massachusetts; On domestic criticisms of Eisenhower's approach, Stephen Rabe, *The Most Dangerous Area in the World: John F. Kennedy Confronts Communism in Latin America* (Chapel Hill: University of North Carolina Press, 1999); for details of anti-American sentiments in Latin America, Alan McPherson, *Yankee No!: Anti-Americanism in US-Latin American Relations* (Cambridge, Massachusetts: Harvard University Press, 2003), 1–38.

6 Michael Latham, *Modernization as Ideology: American Social Science and 'Nation Building' in the Kennedy Era* (Chapel Hill: University of North Carolina Press, 2000); Jeffrey Taffet, *Foreign Aid as Foreign Policy: The Alliance for Progress in Latin America* (New York: Routledge, 2007).

7 To an extent, this cuts against the scholarly consensus of Eisenhower's approach toward the Third World, which has argued that the administration's approach failed due to a lack of interest in these regions or because it stolidly applied broader Cold War maxims to these areas. See: Robert McMahon, 'Eisenhower and Third World Nationalism: A Critique of Revisionists', *Political Science Quarterly*, Vol. 101, No. 3 (1986), 453–73; Odd Arne Westad, *The Global Cold War: Third World Interventions and the Making of Our Times* (Cambridge, UK: Cambridge University Press, 2005), 26–7; Gabriel Kolko, *Confronting the Third World: United States Foreign Policy, 1945–1980* (New York: Pantheon Books, 1988); Kathryn Statler and Andrew Johns, eds., *The Eisenhower Administration, the Third World, and the Globalization of the Cold War* (Lanham, Maryland: Rowman & Littlefield, 2006).

8 Address made by Assistant Secretary of State for Inter-American Affairs John Moors Cabot before the Export-Import Club of the Columbus Chamber of Commerce, Ohio, December 16 1953, *Department of State Bulletin* (*DOSB*) 30, January 11 1954, 48; Gilderhus, *The Second Century*, 153.

9 On the links between Eisenhower and the US business community, Thomas DiBacco, 'American Business and Foreign Aid: The Eisenhower Years', *Business History Review*, Vol. XVI, No. 1 (Spring 1967); Jessica Martin, 'Corporate Cold Warriors: American Business Leaders and Foreign Relations in the Eisenhower Era' (PhD Diss.: University of Colorado, Bolder, 2006), Chapter 2.

10 Memorandum of Discussion at the 137th Meeting of the National Security Council, March 18 1953, *Foreign Relations of the United States* (hereafter *FRUS*) *1952–1954 Volume IV*, 2–6.

11 On the administration's support of undemocratic regimes, Stephen Rabe, *Eisenhower...* Chs 2–3.

12 Memorandum by Norman Pearson of the Bureau of Inter-American Affairs to the Assistant Secretary of State for Inter-American Affairs John Moors Cabot, March 13 1953, *FRUS 1952–1954 Volume IV*, 187–9.

13 NSC Staff Study – Annex to NSC 144, March 6 1953, NSC 144 – Latin America (2), Box No 4, Office of the Special Assistant for National Security

Affairs, Eisenhower Library, Abilene, Kansas (hereafter EL); James William Park, *Latin American Underdevelopment: A History of Perspectives in the United States, 1870–1965* (Baton Rouge: Louisiana State University Press, 1995), 167–77.
14 Minutes of Cabinet Meeting, July 3 1953. Quoted in: Loayza, 'An Aladdin's Lamp for Free Enterprise', 83.
15 NSC 144/1 Statement of Policy by the National Security Council, March 18 1953, *FRUS 1952–1954 Volume IV*, 6–10.
16 This would, of course, change in the coming years as the US social sciences began to consider in more detail the question of whether development theory could be integrated into US Cold War policy more fully, and whether a more scientific approach to the issue could solve some of its challenges. See Nils Gilman, *Mandarins of the Future: Modernization Theory in Cold War America* (Baltimore: John Hopkins University Press, 2003).
17 'Latin American Relations', *New York Times* (hereafter *NYT*), May 26 1953, 28; also see Memorandum from the Under Secretary of State Walter Bedell Smith to the Executive Secretary of the National Security Council James Lay, 'First Progress Report on NSC 144/1', July 23 1953, *FRUS 1952–1954 Volume IV*, 15–19; Memorandum from the Under Secretary of State Walter Bedell Smith to the Executive Secretary of the National Security Council James Lay, 'Second Progress Report on NSC 144/1', November 20 1953, *FRUS 1952–1954 Volume IV*, 31–2.
18 A Summary of Dr. Milton Eisenhower's Report to the President on United States – Latin American Relations, November 1953, Box No. 4, Milton Eisenhower Papers 1938–1973, EL; 'Dr. Eisenhower says South America Needs US Capital for Development', *NYT*, August 5 1953, 6; Loayza, 'An Aladdin's Lamp…', 96; these sentiments, it bears noting, were similar to those being put forward by economists – and, later, critics of the Eisenhower administration – Max Millikan and Walt Rostow. Mark Haefele, 'Walt Rostow's Stages of Economic Growth: Ideas and Action', in David Engerman, Nils Gilman, Mark Haefele and Michael Latham, eds., *Staging Growth: Modernization, Development and the Global Cold War* (Boston: University of Massachusetts Press, 2003); Kimber Charles Pearce, *Rostow, Kennedy, and the Rhetoric of Foreign Aid* (East Lansing, Michigan: Michigan State University Press, 2001), 49–75.
19 NSC 5407 Report Prepared for the National Security Council, February 17 1954, *FRUS 1952–1954 Volume IV*, 208–16.
20 For details on US efforts in the region at this time, and relations with these various governments, Rabe, *Eisenhower…*, Chs 2–4; Siekmeier, *Aid, Nationalism and Inter-American Relations…*, Chs 2–5; Adamson, *The Single Most Important Aspect…*
21 On Guatemala: Piero Gleijeses, *Shattered Hope: The Guatemalan Revolution and the United States, 1944–1954* (New Jersey: Princeton University Press, 1991); Richard Immerman, *The CIA in Guatemala* (Texas: University of Texas Press, 1983); On Bolivia: Kenneth Lehman, 'Revolutions and Attributions: Making Sense of Eisenhower Administration Policies in Latin America', in *Diplomatic History*, Vol. 21, No. 2 (Spring 1997), 195–6; James Siekmeier, 'Persistent Condor and Predatory Eagle: The Bolivian Revolution and the United States, 1952–1964', in Statler and Johns, eds., *The Eisenhower Administration, the Third World, and the Globalization of the Cold War*, 197–221.

22 'The Spirit of Inter-American Unity', Address by Secretary of State Dulles to the Tenth Inter-American Conference, Caracas, Venezuela, March 4 1954, *Department of State Bulletin*, Vol. 30, March 15 1954, 379–83.
23 Sidney Gruson, 'Pan-Americanism Gets New Lift at Caracas', *NYT*, March 14 1954, E6; Memorandum from Daniel Arzac of the Operations Coordinating Board to Dr. Horace Craig, Containing a Requested Survey on Latin America, February 4 1954, OCB 091.4 Latin America (FILE#1) (1) December 1953–March 1954, Box No. 71, OCB Central File Series, EL.
24 Draft Policy Document by the NSC Planning Board for the National Security Council, August 18 1954, Box No. 13, NSC 5432/1 Policy Toward Latin America, White House Office – Office of the Special Assistant for National Security Affairs, NSC Series – Policy Papers Sub-series, EL.
25 The FOA, in fact, was solely concerned about the political ramifications; it most assuredly did not believe that the development strategy itself was wrong, just that it needed to be modified to alleviate potential political problems. See: Minutes of a Meeting of the Foreign Operations Administration, June 21 1954, *FRUS 1952–1954 Volume IV*, 321–5; Suggested FOA Draft Letter for Transmittal from the OCB to the NSC, July 16 1954, OCB 091.4 Latin America (FILE#2) (2) July–December 1954, Box No. 72, OCB Central Files Series, EL; Memorandum of Discussion at the 224th Meeting of the National Security Council, November 15 1954, *FRUS 1952–1954 Volume IV*, 344–52.
26 NSC 5432/1 'United States Objectives and Courses of Action with Respect to Latin America', September 3 1954, *FRUS 1952–1954 Volume IV*, 81–6.
27 Statement by Treasury Secretary George Humphrey at the Meeting of Ministers of Finance or Economy at the Rio de Janeiro Economic Conference, November 23 1954, *Department of State Bulletin*, Vol. 31, December 6 1954, 863–9.
28 Forwarded Clip of *New York Times* Article, November 24 1954, Henry Cabot Lodge 1954 (3), Box No. 24, Administration Series, Whitman File, EL.
29 On the Rio Conference, see: Siekmeier, *Aid, Nationalism and Inter-American Relations*, 184–5; Rabe, *Eisenhower*, 70–6; Michael Weis, *Cold Warriors & Coup D'Etats: Brazilian-American Relations, 1945–1964* (Albuquerque: University of New Mexico Press, 1993), 82–5.
30 Arne Westad, *Global Cold War*; Osgood, *Total Cold War*, 67–71; William Taubman, *Khrushchev: The Man, His Era* (USA: Free Press, 2003), 325–60; Joseph Nogee & Robert Donaldson, *Soviet Foreign Policy since World War II* (New York: Pergamon Press, 1984) Second Edition 1985, 101–12, 146–60.
31 I have outlined these events more fully in Bevan Sewell, 'A Perfect (Free Market) World: Economics, the Eisenhower Administration, and the Soviet Economic Offensive in Latin America', *Diplomatic History*, Vol. 32, No. 5 (November 2008), 841–69. Here, a brief summary will suffice to illustrate the broader point.
32 David Engerman, 'The Romance of Economic Development and New Histories of the Cold War', *Diplomatic History*, Vol. 28, No. 1 (January 2004), 23–54; Michael Adamson, 'The Most Important Single Aspect'…, 55–66; Osgood, *Total Cold War*, 113–50; Memorandum of Discussion at the 277th Meeting of the National Security Council, February 2 1956, *FRUS 1955–1957 Basic National Security Policy Volume XIX*, 215–16.
33 National Security Council Progress Report on NSC 5432/1, February 3 1955, NSC 5432/1 – Policy Toward Latin America, Box No. 13, White House

Office of the Special Assistant for National Security Affairs, Whitman File, EL; Draft Paper Number 11: Latin America – As a Demonstration Area of US Foreign Policy in Action, by Stacy May, September 24 1955, attached to: Memorandum by Robert Crenshaw of the OCB for the Members of the OCB Working Group on Latin America, October 6 1955, OCB 091.4 – Latin America (FILE#4) (5) August–November 1955, Box No. 73, OCB Central File Series, EL.
34 Report by Vice President Richard Nixon on his trip to Latin America at the 240th Meeting of the National Security Council, March 10 1955, Box No. 6, NSC Series, Whitman File, EL.
35 Memorandum from Assistant Secretary of State for Inter-American Affairs Henry Holland to the Secretary of State John Foster Dulles, February 24 1956, CFEP 537/1 – US Position With Respect to an International Coffee Agreement Box No. 6, CFEP Series, EL.
36 National Security Council Progress Report, March 28 1956, *FRUS 1955–1957 Volume VI*, 46–58; 'Outline Plan of Operations Against Communism in Latin America', Prepared by the Operations Coordinating Board, April 18 1956, *FRUS 1955–1957 Volume VI*, 61–6. On a meeting in Panama where public relations were uppermost in US thoughts: Sewell, 'A Perfect (Free Market) World'…; Milton Eisenhower, *The Wine is Bitter*, 202–4.
37 Stephen Rabe, *Eisenhower*…, 90–4.
38 Briefing note for President Eisenhower on NSC 5613, September 4 1956, Latin America (2), Box No. 63, Disaster File, White House Office, EL.
39 5613/1 'Statement of Policy on US Policy Toward Latin America', National Security Council Report, September 25 1956, *FRUS 1955–1957 Volume VI*, 119–32.
40 For more on the group of advisors behind these arguments and their growing opinion that social reform was needed as well as economic development, Milton Eisenhower, *The Wine is Bitter*, 160–3; Rabe, *Eisenhower*…, 93–4.
41 Summary Notes of a Meeting of the Subcommittee on the Buenos Aires Economic Conference, Department of State, May 28 1957, *FRUS 1955–1957 Volume VI*, 503–7; Siekmeier, *Aid, Nationalism and Inter-American Relations*, 30.
42 On the Nixon Trip: Alan McPherson, *Yankee No!: Anti-Americanism in US-Latin American Relations* (Cambridge, Massachusetts: Harvard University Press, 2003), Ch. 1; Marvin Zahniser and Michael Weis, 'A Diplomatic Pearl Harbor?: Richard Nixon's Goodwill Visit to Latin America in 1958', *Diplomatic History* Vol. 13, No. 2 (Spring 1989), 163–90; Rabe, *Eisenhower*, Ch. 6; On the Cuban Revolution, Thomas Paterson, *Contesting Castro: The United States and the Triumph of the Cuban Revolution* (New York: Oxford University Press, 1994); Lars Schoultz, *That Infernal Little Cuban Republic: The United States and the Cuban Revolution* (Chapel Hill: University of North Carolina Press, 2009), 52–109.
43 State Department official quoted in Lars Schoultz, *Beneath the United States: A History of US Policy Toward Latin America* (Cambridge, Massachusetts: Harvard University Press, 1998), 353.
44 Memorandum of Discussion at the 366th Meeting of the National Security Council, May 22 1958, *FRUS 1958–1960 Volume V*, 239–46.
45 Milton Eisenhower, *The Wine is Bitter*, 209; E.W. Kenworthy, 'US Backs Move in Latin America for a Loan Bank', *NYT*, August 13 1958, 1; 'A New

Hemispheric Policy', *NYT*, August 15 1958, 20; Siekmeier, *Aid, Nationalism and Inter-American Relations*, 320–1; Loayza, 'An Aladdin's Lamp'..., 99–100.

46 Milton Eisenhower, 'Report to the President: US-Latin American Relations', December 27 1958, Box No. 7, Milton Eisenhower Papers, EL. Intriguingly, this model was one that was not viewed unfavourably by the Latin Americans; a gap remained, however, between what the US was prepared to contribute and what the Latin Americans requested (and what for).

47 'An Integrated Program of Development for Latin America', Speech by Under Secretary of State Douglas Dillon to the Special Committee of the Council of the Organization of American States, November 18 1958, *Department of State Bulletin*, Vol. 39, December 8 1958, 918–22.

48 On the rise in importance of the Caribbean: Jason Parker, *Brother's Keeper: The United States, Race, and Empire in the British Caribbean, 1937–1962* (New York: Oxford University Press, 2008), 119–40; Stephen Rabe, 'The Caribbean Triangle: Betancourt, Castro, and Trujillo and US Foreign Policy, 1958–1963', *Diplomatic History*, Vol. 20, No. 1, Winter 1996.

49 Bevan Sewell, 'Early Modernization Theory? The Eisenhower Administration and the Foreign Policy of Development in Brazil', *English Historical Review*, Vol. 125, No. 517 (December 2010), 1449–80; Weis, *Cold Warriors & Coup D'Etats*...

50 Memorandum of a Conversation between Secretary Dulles and President Kubitschek, 6 Aug. 1958, *FRUS 1958–1960 Volume V*, 696–9.

51 Special Report by the Operations Coordinating Board to the NSC, November 26 1958, *FRUS 1958–1968 Volume V*, 36–60.

52 NIE 80/90–58, National Intelligence Estimate, 'Latin American Attitudes Toward the US', December 2 1958, *FRUS 1958–1960 Volume V*, 60–78.

53 Seth Jacobs, *America's Miracle Man in Vietnam: Ngo Dinh Diem, Religion, Race, and US Intervention in South Vietnam* (Durham, NC: University of North Carolina Press, 2004), 8–9.

54 NSC 5902/1, 'Statement of US Policy toward Latin America', February 16 1959, *FRUS 1958–1960 Volume V*, 91–103; Rabe, *Eisenhower*, 100–36.

55 Memorandum of Discussion at the 407th Meeting of the National Security Council, May 21 1959, NSC Series, EL.

56 Memorandum of a Conversation, December 3 1959, *FRUS 1958–1960 Volume V*, 267–9; Memorandum of a Conference with the President, Augusta, Georgia, December 29 1959, *FRUS 1958–1960 Volume V*, 272–3; Instruction from the Department of State to All Diplomatic Posts in Latin America, February 4 1960, *FRUS 1958–1960 Volume V*, 274–8.

57 Memorandum from Secretary of State Christian Herter to President Eisenhower, March 12 1960, *FRUS 1958–1960 Volume V*, 279–80.

58 News Conference by President Eisenhower, Newport, Rhode Island, July 11 1960, *PPPUS 1960–61*.

59 Memorandum from the Deputy Coordinator for Mutual Security John Bell to Assistant Secretary of State for Policy Planning Gerard Smith, July 5 1960, *FRUS 1958–1960 Volume V*, 198–208.

60 Task Force Report on Immediate Latin American Problems, January 4 1961, 'Task Force Reports', Box 1074, Pre-Presidential Papers, Papers of President Kennedy, Kennedy Library, Boston, Mass.

61 Michael Grow, *US Presidents and Latin American Interventions: Pursuing Regime Change in the Cold War* (Lawrence, Kansas: University Press of Kansas, 2008), 17–20.
62 Michael Latham, 'Ideology, Social Science, and Destiny: Modernization and the Kennedy-era Alliance for Progress', *Diplomatic History*, Vol. 22, No. 2 (Spring 1998), 199–229; Gilman, *Mandarins of the Future*…
63 Francis Fukuyama, *Falling Behind: Explaining the Development Gap Between Latin America and the United States* (New York: Oxford University Press, 2008).
64 For more on this see the essays in David Engerman and Corinna Unger, eds., 'Special Forum: Modernization as a Global Project', *Diplomatic History*, Vol. 33, No. 3 (June 2009).

7
The Defeat of Ernest Lefever's Nomination: Keeping Human Rights on the United States Foreign Policy Agenda

*Sarah Snyder**

To those committed to human rights, Ronald Reagan's election on 4 November 1980 raised widespread apprehension. Their basic concern was that Reagan would abandon Jimmy Carter's human rights policies. Joshua Rubenstein of Amnesty International spoke for many human rights activists when he said, 'We are concerned that the Reagan administration will not have a positive emphasis on human rights and in some parts of the world his election has been taken as a green light, an encouragement for repressive forces.'[1] The role of human rights in US foreign policy had slowly emerged in the 1960s and gained considerable ground in the years that followed, culminating with Carter's declaration in his 1977 inaugural address that the US commitment to human rights must be 'absolute.'[2] To those focused on the issue, Reagan's electoral victory threatened that progress. The persistence of human rights as an element of US foreign policy under Reagan is thus a testament to the power of the issue against communist regimes, but also to the efforts of the human rights community to keep the issue on the American foreign policy agenda and to its resonance with the broader American public.

Reagan, and many within his administration, had criticized elements of Carter's human rights policy before entering the White House, charging that Carter's policy had not improved human rights meaningfully and had neglected the US national interests.[3] For example, Reagan's appointee to serve as US Ambassador to the United Nations, Jeane Kirkpatrick, had reproached Carter for not prioritizing East-West issues above human rights.[4] Condemnation of this type was interpreted by many to mean the Reagan administration would decrease the prominence of human rights in its foreign policy once in office, and furthermore, at the outset of his presidency, Reagan's aides suggested he wanted to emphasize spreading democracy and defeating terrorism rather than championing human rights. Furthermore, Reagan's nomination of Ernest W. Lefever, a vocal critic of Carter's human rights policy, to head the State Department's Bureau of Human Rights and Humanitarian Affairs raised serious questions about the administration's dedication to human rights and strengthened early concerns about Reagan's commitment. The nomination failed in the face of opposition to his record on human rights, leaving the administration without a senior official focused on the issue for some time.[5]

Four months passed without a new nominee, leading to consternation from human rights activists and their supporters. The administration, however, learned from the opposition to the Lefever nomination, appointed a new candidate who garnered bipartisan support, and leaked parts of a State Department memorandum entitled 'Reinvigoration of Human Rights Policy,' which stated, 'human rights is at the core of our foreign policy.'[6] The administration's efforts in the wake of the nomination's defeat reflected recognition of the salience of human rights, and the White House worked to convey its concern for the issue to Congress, the American public, and an international audience. This chapter argues the defeat of Lefever's nomination should be seen as a significant victory for those determined to maintain a commitment to human rights as an element of US foreign policy, representing a key test for America's human rights policy and ensuring that it would remain an essential component of US policy in the years to come.[7]

* * * * *

Lefever's nomination was seen as threatening to the human rights community not only because he was viewed as personally opposed to the cause but also because it fit into a broader pattern of administration actions. After criticizing Carter's policy on human rights during the 1980 campaign, Reagan and his aides indicated that they wanted to transform US policy when they took office.[8] The White House charged that Carter's policy had not improved human rights and had neglected United States national interests; the administration instead announced it would shift its focus to combating international terrorism. In his first press conference as Secretary of State, Alexander Haig said, 'International terrorism will take the place of human rights in our concern because it is the ultimate of abuse of human rights. And it's time that it be addressed with better clarity and greater effectiveness by Western nations and the United States as well.'[9] Furthermore, naming

Kirkpatrick, a harsh critic of Carter's human rights policy, to serve as ambassador to the United Nations indicated a divergence in policy.

The Reagan administration was cognizant of external concerns about its commitment to human rights. One National Security Council (NSC) staffer wrote soon after Reagan's inauguration, 'The impression of Administration policy created thus far has been that human rights are being jettisoned or severely downgraded in favor of countering terrorism or supporting authoritarian allies.' The author suggested the administration needed to articulate how a commitment to human rights complemented its other policy priorities and outlined the proposed role of human rights in Reagan's foreign policy: that fighting terrorism advanced human rights, that the administration would balance strategic relationships with authoritarian regimes with concerns about human rights, and that it was opposed to 'public lecturing' of other states.[10]

Whatever efforts the NSC and White House made to convince skeptical observers of their dedication to human rights, they were weakened by Reagan's nomination of Lefever to head the State Department's Bureau of Human Rights and Humanitarian Affairs.[11] The nomination, announced in early February 1981, provoked considerable controversy. Many observers questioned the appropriateness of his appointment, setting the stage for extensive, and ultimately contentious, congressional hearings that undermined Lefever's candidacy.

Opposition to Lefever was driven by policy differences, doubts about his qualifications for the role, and his personal disposition. The most significant obstacle was a concern that Lefever would not be an effective champion of human rights, as he had a record of questioning the issue's relevance to US policy. Shortly after Carter's inauguration, Lefever had written in the *New York Times* that 'a consistent and single-minded invocation of the "human rights" standard in making United States foreign policy decisions would serve neither our interests nor the cause of freedom.'[12] In other writings, Lefever argued Carter's approach neglected the fundamental differences between totalitarian and authoritarian governments and diminished the more far-reaching human rights abuses under totalitarian regimes.[13] As an editorial in *The Nation* pointed out, 'Even in the long procession of Reagan appointees professing their antagonism to the objectives of the agencies they have been chosen to lead, Lefever stands out. He is an outspoken apologist for the barbarous practices of right-wing dictatorships.'[14]

Before Lefever's confirmation hearings began, Haig gave a speech to the Trilateral Commission seemingly designed to assure domestic and international audiences that the US was not completely abandoning its commitment to human rights. In it, Haig asserted, 'Human rights are therefore not only compatible with our national interest, they are an integral element of the American approach – at home and abroad.' He went on to promise 'the United States opposes the violation of human rights by ally or adversary, friend or foe. We are not going to pursue a policy of "selective" indignation.' Haig declared, 'Concern for human rights is compatible, indeed even integral to our national interest: We have great principles to defend and a great example to give the world.'[15] Nevertheless, in the context of other administration initiatives, Haig's speech was viewed by many as empty rhetoric and did not assuage those opposed to Lefever.

A range of groups and individuals mobilized against Lefever's nomination. Many sought to influence his confirmation hearings, and a significant number testified or submitted written materials outlining their opposition. Representative Tom Harkin (D-IA), who was active on human rights issues in the House, testified against Lefever's nomination, expressing frustration at Lefever's stated intention to move away from linking US assistance with the human rights practices of aid recipients: '[B]ecause Mr. Lefever has no concept of the strategic or political importance of linkage in the human rights efforts of American foreign policy, I find his nomination to the position of Assistant Secretary of State for Human Rights and Humanitarian Affairs to be particularly inappropriate.'[16] Similarly, Donald Fraser, who had led Congressional efforts on human rights in the late 1960s and early 1970s, testified that 'instead of an advocate we are getting a denigrator of human rights.'[17]

Lefever's nomination rehashed debates over Carter's human rights policy, including claims that it represented a double standard, criticized only the human rights policies of Washington's Cold War allies, and remained silent on Soviet and other communist repression.[18] A second principal point of criticism by the Reagan administration and its allies was that the Carter administration had relied too heavily on public shaming of human rights abuses. Lefever disparaged the Carter administration for 'excessive scolding in public' and 'selective morality.' In his view, such actions by the Carter administration had actually worsened the human rights situation in some countries.[19] The Reagan administration promised a more discreet approach. Lefever argued the US should lead through its actions, rather than its criticisms of other regimes: 'We become a beacon of hope primarily by responsible and just behavior at home, our deeds are well known.'[20] His stance, however, led some to fear the administration would remain silent on human rights abuses; Senator Alan Cranston (D-CA) asked, 'If we do not indicate our disapproval of gross violations of human rights that go on in country after country after country in any way that can become public knowledge, how do we become a beacon of hope?'[21] Cranston pushed Lefever for evidence that quiet diplomacy was an effective means to protect human rights; Lefever refused, arguing that to do so could 'hamper future successes.'[22] A memorandum drafted in Cranston's office before the hearings began indicates the degree to which Lefever was viewed as disputing the central tenets of US human rights policy:

> [Lefever] – opposes any human rights legislation
> – opposes public US support for human rights
> – opposes Human Rights Bureau
> – views human rights in Communist countries as Red-baiting opportunities; opposes Jackson-Vanik.[23]

Other members of the Senate Foreign Relations Committee, including its chair, Senator Charles Percy (R-IL), at times seemed offended by Lefever's positions; Percy said, 'You seem in doubt about whether your job should exist, and then you want quiet diplomacy. It takes an advocate fighting, not just quiet diplomacy. These battles are not won by kid gloves.'[24]

A significant obstacle to Lefever's confirmation was testimony he gave before the House Foreign Affairs Subcommittee on International Organizations on 12 July 1979. Lefever's comments, which condemned US human rights policy, were repeatedly cited during his confirmation hearings as evidence that he was unfit for the Assistant Secretary position. At the outset of his 1979 testimony, Lefever had asserted, 'a consistent and single-minded invocation of the human rights standard, in making it U.S. foreign policy, would serve neither our interest nor the cause of freedom.' He went on to say, 'giving human rights a central place tends to subordinate, blur, or distort all other relevant policy consideration.' Lefever also criticized legislation mandating the consideration of human rights in formulating US policy, saying:

> In my view the United States should remove from the statute books all clauses that establish a human rights standard or condition that must be met by another sovereign government before our Government transacts normal business with it, unless specifically waived by the President... It shouldn't be necessary for any friendly state to pass a human rights test before we extend normal trade relations, before we sell arms or before we provide economic or security assistance... We have no moral mandate to remake the world in our

own image. It is arrogant of us to attempt to reform the domestic behaviors of our allies and even of our adversaries.

In Lefever's view, the US could best advance the global cause of human rights by its own example, or 'serving as an example of decency,' and preventing the fall of American allies to communism.[25]

When addressing his earlier opposition to human rights statutes in his confirmation hearings before the Senate Foreign Relations Committee, Lefever said he had 'goofed.' He repeatedly tried to disavow what he said had been 'too flat a statement.'[26] Neither this concession, nor others he made during the four days of hearings held by the Committee, won him sufficient supporters, as a number of senators questioned if he had changed his position only as a result of his nomination.

Moreover, although Lefever rescinded or qualified some of his earlier positions, he maintained that there should not be a human rights 'test.'[27] In his confirmation hearings, Lefever resisted requirements that recipients of US military and financial assistance adhere to certain human rights practices; in his view, preventing a country's slip into communism was a more important goal: 'In some cases, Mr. Chairman, we must provide economic or military aid to a besieged ally whose human rights record is not blameless.'[28] Critics argued he would adopt an imbalanced and selective approach and ignore human rights abuses in authoritarian regimes.[29] He similarly angered a number of senators with his refusal to name noncommunist countries he regarded as human rights abusers, saying, 'I don't normally name countries. That's not my style.'[30] Eschewing suggestions that the US should vocally criticize international human rights abuses, Lefever's view of the role of the US in the world echoed Reagan's formulation that the country should be a 'city on a hill' and shine as an example to the broader international community. Lefever also emphasized the limits to American influence in the world, noting, 'We must recognize there are moral and political limits to what the U.S. Government can and should do to modify the internal behavior of other sovereign states.'[31]

More specifically, Lefever's opponents criticized his foreign policy positions. Some witnesses questioned his commitment to ending apartheid in South Africa given his view that 'it would be impossible for sophisticated, industrialized South Africa to integrate culturally and politically 19 million largely illiterate Bantu without catastrophic consequences.'[32] Such comments provoked Senator Paul Tsongas (D-MA) to suggest Lefever expressed 'a basic contempt for Africa.'[33] In addition, critics charged that the Ethics and Public Policy Center, which Lefever headed, had received money from the South African government.

Furthermore, detractors alleged that Lefever exhibited cultural arrogance. They pointed specifically to his 1978 article, 'The Trivialization of Human Rights,' in which Lefever argued, 'Many of these Western democratic rights are unknown and unattainable in large parts of the world where both history and culture preclude the development of full-fledged democratic institutions.'[34] His opponents similarly questioned his attitude toward Latin America given that Lefever had attributed abuses by police officers there to 'the residual practices of the Iberian tradition.'[35] In addition, Lefever came under fire for his dismissal of human rights activists in South Korea as 'a mixture of naïve utopians and power-hungry ideologues.'[36] His critics suggested such beliefs would inhibit effective human rights advocacy. Lefever also faced repeated questions about his ethics and personal judgment. A significant obstacle was the relationship between a report on the infant formula boycott commissioned by the Center and subsequent financial contributions by the Nestlé Corporation.

Finally, Lefever's demeanor in meetings with Senators and during his confirmation hearings imperiled his nomination. Senator Rudy Boschwitz (R-MN) suggested Lefever's personal style made him unfit for the position, saying he 'lacks the diplomatic skills needed for the post.'[37] In addition, Percy repeatedly expressed irritation over Lefever's assertion that his opponents were part of a 'communist-inspired' conspiracy.[38] Lefever engaged in extensive debate with members of the Committee on a range of issues and frustrated some with his refusal to offer his opinions on existing human rights legislation, the political situation in certain African countries, human rights treaties including the Genocide Convention, whether or not the Pol Pot regime should be seated at the United Nations, and the degree of repression in China. Senator Claiborne Pell (D-RI) declared Lefever was the first nominee that he could remember in his sixteen years of service on the Foreign Relations Committee who had declined to give his or her personal views on issues. Pell went on to say, 'I will just note that the Genocide Convention was written in the late 1940s. You have had a lifetime to form an opinion on it, and I am not impressed with your reply.'[39] Lefever said he was unwilling to share his views in principle, as they were not yet 'mature and disciplined,' but would say that the 'signing of treaties does not necessarily change the behavior of the states that violate rights the most.'[40]

Given the leading role played by Congress in US human rights policy in the 1970s – with the statutes Lefever had in 1979 suggested be erased, including a key amendment to the 1974 Foreign Assistance Act, predating Carter's term in office – many members of Congress interpreted Lefever's criticisms of Carter's policy as opposition to their own efforts.⁴¹ Thus, there was a considerable degree of executive-legislative branch rivalry evident in Lefever's confirmation hearings.

Not surprisingly, many in the human rights community actively opposed Lefever. Human rights groups in Washington, DC and New York City reached out to one another and worked to defeat the nomination.⁴² Helsinki Watch, a prominent human rights organization, opposed Lefever's nomination because, as its chair Robert Bernstein testified, 'he himself opposes the purposes for which Congress created the post he seeks.'⁴³ Helsinki Watch officials such as Bernstein, Jeri Laber, Aryeh Neier, and Orville Schell had met with Lefever in advance of his confirmation hearings, but their meetings did not mitigate their position. They continued to oppose his nomination, making repeated trips to Washington to campaign against his confirmation, including attending and testifying at his confirmation hearings and hosting a dinner in Washington honoring former Argentine political prisoner Jacobo Timerman that coincided with the hearings. The group, and Neier in particular, was firmly committed to defeating Lefever's nomination: 'We thought it vital for the future of the human rights cause to defeat him.'⁴⁴

Jacobo Timerman's presence at Lefever's confirmation hearings heightened the drama of the proceedings. Timerman was acknowledged at the hearing, his memoir cited, and his presence greeted with applause. Although he did not testify, Timerman represented a stark counterpoint to Lefever's testimony on behalf of quiet diplomacy as he attributed his release in part to the efforts of Carter's Assistant Secretary of State for Human Rights and Humanitarian Affairs, Patt Derian, and he asserted that Carter's human rights policy saved 'thousands of lives all over the world.' Through interviews with journalists and members of Congress, Timerman made his position clear: 'Silent diplomacy is silence. Quiet diplomacy is surrender.'⁴⁵ In Helsinki Watch Executive Director Jeri Laber's view, Timerman's appearance at Lefever's hearings helped seal the nomination's fate:

> A factor in [Lefever's] defeat was a well-timed appearance by the Argentinean newspaper publisher Jacobo Timerman, who had described his experiences as a former political prisoner and torture victim to a select group of senators at a dinner we hosted in Washington the night before. Lefever was finished once Timerman stood before the Senate committee.⁴⁶

A number of expert witnesses also testified against Lefever's nomination. Prominent human rights scholar Louis Henkin testified that Lefever was 'wholly disqualified for this job.' Henkin disagreed with

Lefever's characterization of human rights criticism as unwarranted interference in the internal affairs of sovereign states, arguing that quiet diplomacy had become no diplomacy under earlier administrations. Similarly, Marvin Frankel, a prominent lawyer and human rights activist, testified that Lefever's concerns about interfering in the internal affairs of a sovereign state were in line with the views of Soviet leaders, who also disavowed public condemnation of human rights abuses. Henkin and other witnesses also questioned Lefever's contention that he had 'goofed' in earlier congressional testimony, noting, 'The "goof" may suggest a minor slip; in fact his opposition has been clearly part of a coherent position, firmly expressed over several years, and so far as I know, held at least until he was nominated.' Henkin said, 'I do not believe that this law can be faithfully executed by someone who thinks there should be no such law, who has been firmly opposed to it in its spirit and in every detail.'[47] Emphasizing the importance of governmental support for human rights, the Western representative of the Moscow Helsinki Watch Group, a human rights monitoring group in the Soviet Union, Ludmilla Alekseeva said, 'The United States has achieved respectability and credibility in speaking out publicly and forcefully against human rights violations around the world. A continuation of this universal policy is essential to the human rights movement in the Soviet Union.'[48]

In contrast to the opposition his nomination engendered from Helsinki Watch and other human rights groups, Lefever's nomination garnered support from a range of Eastern European ethnic interest groups, no doubt drawn to his sharp condemnations of the communist regimes there.[49] Fifty individuals representing predominantly Eastern European and Vietnamese interest groups endorsed Lefever's nomination under the umbrella group, Committee for a Balanced Human Rights Policy, citing their conviction that Lefever 'has dedicated his life towards those self-same principles of freedom, democracy and independence on which this country is based.'[50] The group argued that Lefever was 'fully qualified to restore balance in the nation's human rights policy, and [would] implement policies and programs designed to strengthen human rights around the world consistent with the freedom and independence of the United States and its allies.'[51] Quite often, Lefever's supporters explicitly cited what they viewed as Carter's weak stance against human rights abuses in communist countries; many repeatedly accused the Carter administration of having maintained a 'double standard' in assessing countries' human rights records.[52] A number of other academics and former government officials wrote to the Senate Foreign Relations Committee to defend Lefever's approach to human rights and personal record.[53] For example, philosopher Sidney Hook wrote to the committee, 'I have been appalled by the evidence of a veritable campaign of misrepresentation of his position by those who are more hostile to current American foreign policy than dedicated to the even handed defense of human rights.'[54]

Some administration supporters argued that criticism of Lefever reflected opposition to Reagan's human rights approach, which in columnist William Safire's words 'has just won an election.'[55] Testifying before the Senate Committee, Representative Charles Wilson (R-TX) said:

> I would point out to my friends with a differing viewpoint from mine, that Mr. Lefever is not the only man in the United States that believes that human rights can best be achieved by using less pyrotechnics and more diplomacy. The President can certainly find others to represent his policy, but I can assure you he is not going to appoint Pat [sic] Derian as Assistant Secretary for Human Rights, no matter what my friends say.[56]

Indeed, in questions to former Representative Donald Fraser, members of the Committee suggested no Reagan nominee would meet with his approval.[57] Briefing materials for Tsongas, however, pointed out many instances in which Haig and Lefever diverged in their stated approaches to human rights treaties and assistance to governments that abuse human rights. On the latter question, Haig had stated, 'I do not believe we should, other than in the most exceptional circumstances, provide aid to any country which consistently and in the harshest manner violate the human rights of its citizens.'[58] These differences raised questions about whose pronouncements on human rights most closely reflected Reagan's policy and if criticism of Lefever could be easily reduced to opposition to Reagan's approach.

Lefever's performance at the hearings did not mitigate congressional concerns about the appropriateness of his nomination. After the first two days of hearings, Cranston, Tsongas, and Senator Christopher Dodd (D-CT) called upon Lefever to withdraw his name from nomination: 'We believe Lefever's misleading and evasive testimony should disqualify him from further consideration for a post which requires a forthright advocate and champion of human rights.' In their view, his nomination 'imperils the credibility and reputation of the Bureau of Human Rights and Humanitarian Affairs itself.'[59] According to reports, Percy privately asked the White House to withdraw Lefever's nomination, although the State Department asserted, 'The President is determined to stand by his nominee.'[60]

Other members of Congress increasingly spoke out against Lefever's nomination, while Cranston raised the specter of a filibuster to prevent a vote on Lefever's confirmation: 'there are many others who feel that the Lefever nomination is so inconsistent with high American ideals that we would oppose sending his nomination to the floor and would feel it our duty to try to prevent the Senate from voting on this nomination by resorting to extended debate.'[61] Given congressional opposition, former Nixon aide Patrick Buchanan argued 'the White House will have to intervene to save him.'[62] By early June, however, Tsongas alleged administration support for Lefever was waning, saying on NBC's 'Meet the Press': 'The Secretary of State is not beating down the halls and the doors of members of the Senate to support Dr. Lefever.' He further asserted, 'I have spoken to no one in this Administration who is strongly supporting this nominee.'[63] The lack of administration lobbying on Lefever's behalf might be explained by reports in *Newsweek* suggesting that Lefever was selected to 'placate' conservatives such as Senator Jesse Helms (R-NC) rather than due to Haig or Reagan's initiative.[64] Furthermore, as Reagan indicated through his comments in his March 1981 interview with Cronkite, the President did not have a close personal relationship with the nominee, making Reagan's prestige less connected with Lefever's confirmation.

Lefever's nomination also stimulated wider concern. The American public had supported the United States' attention to human rights and resisted efforts to downgrade its importance.[65] For example, Senator Nancy Kassebaum (R-KS) received thirty-three letters regarding Lefever's nomination, and all but one opposed him.[66] One correspondent wrote to Kassebaum to express her concerns that Lefever 'is not capable of functioning as a protector of human rights.'[67] Percy received 554 letters supporting Lefever's nomination and 1,046 opposed to it.[68] Congressional and popular apprehension was echoed in the media; one critical columnist likened Lefever's nomination to putting 'the fox in charge of the chicken coop.'[69] On May 24, the *New York Times* came out strongly against Lefever's nomination, labeling him 'unworthy' and suggesting it sent 'the worst possible signal.'[70] The administration recognized the resistance to Lefever's nomination with one official describing him as 'the most controversial guy we've got.'[71]

In a recess in Lefever's hearings, Reagan administration officials attempted to address concerns about the nomination.[72] First, the State Department worked to counter claims about South African funding of the Ethics and Public Policy Center as well as to diminish the controversy surrounding the Center's work on infant formula.[73] Administration officials also compiled a package of information on 'false charges' against Lefever.[74] Briefing materials for Lefever urged him to avoid using 'overbroad generalizations that you may be forced to retract later' and warned him to 'never be defensive.'[75] Lefever also embarked upon a series of television and radio appearances to rebut his critics. In one interview, Lefever asserted a close correlation between his views and the President's: 'There is no difference between my view and that of the president's, so opposition to me is opposition to the president of the United States, and his mandate to carry out foreign policy in a different way.'[76] His interviews, however, were curtailed after two days when administration officials became concerned Lefever was worsening his position.[77]

The hearings resumed on 4 June, in an executive session to enable Lefever to respond to the objections that had been raised against him. Lefever tried to refute allegations that he was insensitive to human rights abuses in authoritarian regimes arguing, 'I care about human rights everywhere, in democracies, in our own country, and in friendly countries and in enemy countries. I make no distinction. There is one moral yardstick.'[78] For the executive session, Senator Samuel Hayakawa (R-CA), who was charged with shepherding Lefever's nomination, prepared a packet for the Committee outlining broad support for Lefever among academics, human rights leaders, theologians, former government officials, and other leaders. Furthermore, forty-two House members wrote to Percy to express their support for Lefever's nomination. Questions in the executive session dealt extensively with the timeline of Nestlé's contributions to the Ethics and Public Policy Center, and a number of Senators indicated their belief that Lefever had a conflict of interest by accepting funds from Nestlé at the same time as he was commissioning an investigative piece on the infant formula boycott. Furthermore, some Senators suggested Lefever had been misleading in his earlier testimony on the subject.

The following day, the Committee voted thirteen to four against him.[79] Senate historians at the time said that it was the first instance since 1959 that a president's nominee had been rejected by a Senate committee.[80] In explaining his vote, Percy expressed apprehension about Lefever's commitment to human rights and personal integrity: 'Concern for human rights is not just a policy of the United States. It is an underlying principle of our political system and a fundamental factor in the appeal of democracy to people throughout the world.'[81] Percy also questioned Lefever's knowledge of policy issues, saying Lefever had 'very little familiarity with the [human rights] provisions themselves' and characterized his testimony as 'a series of broad generalizations without a willingness to discuss specific issues.'[82]

Other members of Congress explained their votes against his nomination. Pell suggested Lefever could not be a credible voice supporting human rights internationally given his earlier writings on South Africa and South Korea as well as the absence of formulated positions on treaties such as the Genocide Convention. Tsongas criticized what he considered to be 'an intolerant view of his opponent and a tendency to divide the world in friends and enemies, left and right, Communist and non-Communist.' Cranston declared he was disturbed by what he saw as inconsistencies in Lefever's testimony: 'I believe he has demonstrated a highly disturbing disregard for adherence to the facts and a propensity for "loose" statements, to use his own word. This kind of cavalier approach would ill serve our national interests and should not be institutionalized by confirmation to a vital position of public trust.'[83] Dodd, in explaining his vote against Lefever, said he found him 'to be totally unreliable as an advocate of human rights, to be entirely inconsistent in his own testimony before this committee, and to lack the necessary balance to assume a sensitive position of high public trust.'[84] Lefever withdrew from consideration shortly thereafter, writing: 'I am blameless of all the charges and innuendos that have been made against my integrity and my compassion. I do not wish any longer to put up with the kind of suspicion and character-assassination that some of my opponents have used to besmirch my name.'[85]

In the wake of Lefever's withdrawal, the administration did not move quickly to propose a second nominee. Instead, the Reagan administration contemplated disbanding the Bureau and eliminating the Assistant Secretary for Human Rights and Humanitarian Affairs position, leading to consternation from human rights groups and members of Congress. Four months passed without a new nominee.[86] The White House, however, argued that such changes, if undertaken, would not signal a lessening of concern for human rights by the administration, reiterating that Reagan was committed to a strategy more focused on quiet diplomacy.[87] Vice President George Bush declared the 'administration is pledged to human rights' but will not 'shout from the rooftops and beat our breasts.'[88]

An ongoing element of this debate was the Congressional legislation that mandated the Assistant Secretary position.[89] To leave the position empty seemed an effort to avoid compliance with the law. Fifty-seven members of Congress wrote to Reagan in late June to express their concern at the unfilled seat, asking him to make a nomination 'as soon as possible.'[90] Representative Don Bonker (D-WA) noted on the floor of the House the 282nd day of the Reagan administration in which there was no Assistant Secretary of State for Human Rights and Humanitarian Affairs.[91]

The concern and complaints from human rights advocates were not lost on the administration. Under Secretary of State Richard Kennedy wrote, 'Congressional belief that we have no consistent human rights policy threatens to disrupt important foreign-policy initiatives…. Human rights has become one of the main avenues for domestic attack on the administration's foreign policy.'[92] Kennedy, working alongside State Department officials Charles Fairbanks, Jr. and Paul Wolfowitz, sought to shift the administration's approach.[93] Acting Assistant Secretary of State for Human Rights and Humanitarian Affairs Stephen Palmer sees Fairbanks as key to the transformation in attitudes toward human rights at the State Department: '[Fairbanks] became convinced that the new administration could usefully use human rights in a constructive way, could stay with the country reports, and emphasize more quiet diplomacy.'[94] To address persistent concerns and signal a new approach, Haig gave a speech saying that human rights was 'the major focus' of Reagan's foreign policy.

The administration also leaked parts of a State Department memorandum entitled 'Reinvigoration of Human Rights Policy' to the *New York Times*. It stated, 'Human rights is at the core of our foreign policy because it is central to what America is and stands for. "Human rights" is not something we tack on to our foreign policy, but is its very purpose.'[95] In the memorandum, State Department officials argued human rights 'gives us the best opportunity to convey what is ultimately at issue in our contest with the Soviet bloc' and 'must be central to our assault on them.' In addition to identifying support for human rights as useful in the Soviet-American struggle, the memorandum's authors also noted the issue was essential to garner public and Congressional support: '<u>We will never maintain wide public support for our foreign policy unless we can relate it to American ideals and the defense of freedom</u>.'[96] By not articulating its commitment to human rights, the administration was subjecting itself to considerable domestic criticism according to the authors. The memorandum also attempted to clarify the meaning of 'quiet diplomacy' suggesting a softer voice would 'not neglect the goal' of enhancing freedom, particularly in the Soviet Union.[97] In addition, it outlined a greater commitment to a balanced approach to human rights abuses than Lefever had advocated in his confirmation hearings. The memorandum's authors conceded, 'A human rights policy means trouble, for it means hard choices which may adversely affect certain bilateral relations. At the very least, we will have to speak honestly about our friends' human rights violations.'[98] The memorandum was greeted warmly when leaked to the *New York Times* and when a similar version was disseminated to human rights organizations such as Helsinki Watch.[99]

In advance of the planned announcement of a new nominee to head the Human Rights Bureau, the State Department asserted the Bureau was to be 'strengthened and reinvigorated' as opposed to the reduction in influence many had feared.[100] The State Department also communicated with human rights organizations such as Helsinki Watch to reassure them of the administration's commitment to the issue. Writing to Helsinki Watch Chair Robert Bernstein, Palmer asserted the administration was not contemplating any decreased emphasis on human rights. In addition, he maintained a nomination to head the Human Rights Bureau would 'not be unduly delayed.'[101]

Faced with rising concerns among members of Congress and interested non-governmental organizations, the administration sought to articulate its human rights policy. Testifying before a House Foreign Affairs Subcommittee, Under Secretary of State for Political Affairs Walter Stoessel suggested the Reagan administration would express concern about violations of human rights irrespective of the friendliness of the government to the US, a shift from earlier articulations. He said it would oppose human rights violations 'whether by ally or adversary, friend or foe.'[102] The Reagan administration further proclaimed what it argued was a consistent approach to human rights abusers, writing in the 1981 *Country Reports on Human Rights Practices*, 'U.S. human rights policy will not pursue a policy of selective indignation.'[103]

Most significantly, the White House announced its nomination of Elliott Abrams, who was serving as Assistant Secretary of State for International Organization Affairs, to head the State Department's Human Rights Bureau on 30 October 1981. After consulting with Wolfowitz and Fairbanks on the Department's new approach to human rights, Abrams had decided that he wanted to move over to be Assistant Secretary for Human Rights and Humanitarian Affairs.[104] According to Teresa Tull, who served in the human rights bureau at the time, Abrams' decision was due in part to his frustration with his relationship with Kirkpatrick who was said to resist direction from Washington.[105] Abrams' nomination had bipartisan support in Congress, having previously worked for Senators Daniel Patrick Moynihan (D-NY) and Henry Jackson (D-WA). Moynihan declared Abrams had a 'great commitment to the issue of human rights,' and Jackson proclaimed him 'an excellent choice.'[106] According to State Department official George Lister, although Don Bonker believed the Reagan administration had 'reversed most of the major human rights positions we had taken earlier,' he regarded Abrams' nomination as a positive step.[107] Similarly, Lister reported that Tom Harkin expressed a positive response to Abrams' nomination, regarding him as 'light years ahead' of Lefever in his 'understanding of human rights.'[108] Skeptics, however, expressed less than overwhelming enthusiasm for Abrams appointment, with one saying, 'Everyone's saying Elliott Abrams is so great just because he's not Darth Vader.'[109]

At Abrams' confirmation hearings, Percy asserted the nomination 'signals a real commitment by the administration to take the high road when it comes to human rights.'[110] Abrams faced few difficult questions in his confirmation hearings, and Republicans and Democrats alike expressed pleasure at his nomination. For example, Senator Pell told him,

> I think an example of the President's and the Secretary's belief in human rights is shown by the fact that they are going to appoint an activist secretary in the job...
>
> I am delighted both that the job is being filled and that you are the man who is filling it.[111]

The Senate Foreign Relations Committee unanimously approved Abrams' nomination on 17 November 1981. The Senate unanimously confirmed him several days later.

In the aftermath of Abrams' confirmation, the administration adopted a new approach publicly, working to convey a concern for human rights to the American public and an international audience. For example, the White House organized a meeting between Reagan and Soviet émigrés at which the president particularly stressed his commitment to religious freedom in Eastern Europe.[112] Similarly, National Security Adviser William P. Clark scheduled a meeting with Helsinki Watch members, and the NSC arranged a call between Reagan and a relative of internally exiled Soviet human rights activist Andrei Sakharov.[113] These largely superficial events illustrate the political importance human rights had developed for the American public.

The new approach, however, went beyond superficiality. After Abrams' confirmation, Haig distributed a memorandum directing all regional bureaus to work with the human rights bureau to ensure that 'the promotion of political freedom... not be considered only as an afterthought.'[114] Haig also urged State Department officials, in their contacts with foreign governments, to 'be sure to convey... the continuing interest of Congress, the American people, and the Administration in the expansion of personal and political freedom.'[115] Furthermore, Abrams articulated an intention to pursue a more active approach than had been predicted of Lefever: 'There has been and will be less public criticism of friendly country governments... [but] you cannot make a clear distinction between East and West on the basis of freedom if the United States is supporting dictators around the world.'[116] Such steps suggested the administration hoped to put the controversy raised by Lefever's nomination behind it.

At the outset of his presidency, Reagan and his aides made clear their intention to shift away from the emphasis that had been placed on human rights by the previous administration, in particular by lowering the volume and limiting the number of American pronouncements. Reagan may have been able to accomplish such a change through an evolutionary process, but his selection of Ernest Lefever to head the State Department's Bureau of Human Rights and Humanitarian Affairs was viewed as extremist. Lefever's nomination elicited a groundswell of opposition among members of Congress, human rights activists, and the broader public that prevented a complete abandonment of Carter's emphasis on human rights. Although human rights never regained the prominence they had enjoyed under Carter, the issue remained a rhetorical and substantive element of US foreign policy in the years that followed. The shift was due largely to the campaign to defeat Lefever's nomination. In his memoirs, Helsinki Watch Vice Chair Aryeh Neier emphasizes the lasting significance of Lefever's withdrawal to the US human rights movement: 'It was, I now believe, the turning point in establishing the human rights cause as a factor in U.S. foreign policy and not the passing fad or even folly of the Carter administration, as it was considered in 1981 by the man who nominated Lefever and by his foreign policy team.'[117]

The evolution of the Reagan administration's attitude toward human rights over the course of 1981 offers important evidence of the critical role played by members of Congress and concerned citizens in shaping US policy and keeping human rights on the foreign policy agenda. Lefever's disavowal of years of human rights legislation and struggle to articulate his support for international human rights undermined many Americans' sense of the positive role the US could play in the world. Similarly, it raised important questions about what values and ideals should shape American diplomacy. The outcome of Lefever's nomination suggested concern for human rights had gained greater salience than the administration had realized.

The administration's overall human rights record, however, remains controversial. After George Shultz became Secretary of State in July 1982, he devoted considerable attention to the question of protection of human rights in the Soviet Union and Eastern Europe, heightening the administration's commitment to the issue.[118] Yet, concern for human rights was highly compartmentalized as well as dependent on geopolitics and strategic interests. Despite its claims that it was pursuing an 'evenhanded' human rights policy, the Reagan administration was less willing than Carter to criticize states and leaders it considered America's friends. Such an approach led the administration to overlook human rights abuses in Argentina, Chile, the Philippines, South Korea, and Turkey as well as ignore congressional legislation related to human rights.[119] Furthermore, Abrams and others in the administration prioritized the prevention of communist takeovers as they believed democratic governments were more likely to respect human rights. This worldview, which stressed anti-communism over concerns about violations of human rights, shaped the administration's approach to widespread abuses in Nicaragua and El Salvador.[120] Abrams' nomination and the Reagan administration's rhetoric in subsequent years demonstrated recognition that it could not publicly eschew human rights as a priority in US foreign policy. Yet, the content of US human rights policy during the Reagan years and under the administrations that have followed has remained far from assured.

Notes

*The author wishes to express her appreciation to Anthony Sampas of the O'Leary Library at the University of Massachusetts Lowell; David Kessler of the Bancroft Library at the University of California, Berkeley; and Teresa Coble of the Kansas Historical Society. The Open Society Archives, Yale University, and Georgetown University all generously supported this research.

1 Associated Press (AP), 'Soviet Dissident Calls Reagan Human Rights Policy Dangerous,' 10 February 1981, Human Rights, 1982–1983, Box 691, Old Code Subject Files, 1953–1994, Soviet Red Archives, Records of Radio Free Europe/Radio Liberty Research Institute, Open Society Archives, Budapest, Hungary.

2 Jimmy Carter, Inaugural Address, 20 January 1977 in *Public Papers of the Presidents: Jimmy Carter 1977: I* (Washington: Government Printing Office, 1977), 2.

3 David Carleton and Michael Stohl, 'The Foreign Policy of Human Rights: Rhetoric and Reality from Jimmy Carter to Ronald Reagan,' *Human Rights Quarterly*, Vol. 7, No. 2 (May 1985), 208–9; and David P. Forsythe, 'Human Rights in U.S. Foreign Policy: Retrospect and Prospect,' *Political Science Quarterly*, Vol. 105, No. 3 (Autumn 1990), 444–5.
4 Tamar Jacoby, 'The Reagan Turnaround on Human Rights,' *Foreign Affairs*, Vol. 64, No. 5 (1986), 1068–9.
5 Forsythe, 'Human Rights in U.S. Foreign Policy,' 442; John Dumbrell, *American Foreign Policy: Carter to Clinton* (New York: St. Martin's Press, 1997), 57; Hauke Hartmann, 'US Human Rights Policy Under Carter and Reagan, 1977–1981,' *Human Rights Quarterly*, 23 (2001), 403, 424; Carleton and Stohl, 'The Foreign Policy of Human Rights,' 208–9; Charles Mohr, 'Haig Aide Insists U.S. Rights Policy is Evenhanded,' *New York Times*, 15 July 1981, A10; and Sandy Vogelgesang, 'Diplomacy of Human Rights,' *International Studies Quarterly*, Vol. 23, No. 2 (June 1979), 230–1.
6 Kennedy to Haig, 26 October 1981, released to the author under the Freedom of Information Act.
7 Lefever's failed nomination has not previously received significant scholarly attention.
8 Carleton and Stohl, 'The Foreign Policy of Human Rights,' 205.
9 'Excerpts from Haig's Remarks at First News Conference as Secretary of State,' *New York Times*, 29 January 1981, A10. Richard Schifter, who served as Assistant Secretary of State for Human Rights and Humanitarian Affairs in Reagan's second term, suggests the extent to which the Reagan administration intended to replace concern for human rights with attention to international terrorism was misinterpreted due to a verbal fumble by Haig. Richard Schifter, 'Building Firm Foundations: The Institutionalization of United States Human Rights Policy in the Reagan Years,' *Harvard Human Rights* Journal, 2 (1989), 4.
10 Lord to Allen, 17 February 1981, Folder 1, Box 1, HU, White House Office of Records Management (WHORM) Subject File, Ronald Reagan Library, Simi Valley, California. (Hereafter RRL.)
11 Lefever was the director of the Ethics and Public Policy Center, a research organization originally affiliated with Georgetown University. He had attended divinity school and then earned a PhD in Christian Ethics from Yale University and had written widely on the approach of theologians and church organizations toward the wider world and United States foreign policy in particular. In addition to Lefever's friendship with Kirkpatrick, some reports indicate that Lefever came to the attention of National Security Adviser Richard Allen through an article he had written on human rights. Summary of News Stories and Commentaries, 31 May 1981 [Lefever Material from Richard Hauser] (4), CFOA 113, Counsel to the President, Office of: Records, RRL. Other reports attributed Lefever's appointment to the increasing role of political adviser Lyn Nofziger in overseeing political appointments. 'Thunderers on the Rights,' *Time*, 16 March 1981, 32.
12 Vogelgesang, 'Diplomacy of Human Rights,' 230–1.
13 *Congressional Record*, 1 April 1981, 6084.
14 Editorial, 'The Worst Yet,' *The Nation*, 21 February 1981, 195.

15 The speech was on March 31. *Congressional Record*, 11 May 1981, 9217–9218; and Edwin S. Maynard, 'The Bureaucracy and Implementation of US Human Rights Policy,' *Human Rights Quarterly*, Vol. 11, No. 2 (May 1989), 182–3.
16 'Nomination of Ernest W. Lefever,' Hearings before the Committee on Foreign Relations, United States Senate, 97th Congress, 1st Session, 18, 19 May, and 4, 5 June 1981.
17 *Ibid.*
18 Such views neglected the intense frustration the Soviet Union, Czechoslovakia, and other Eastern European countries felt about Carter administration criticism.
19 'Nomination of Ernest W. Lefever.'
20 *Ibid.*
21 *Ibid.*
22 *Ibid.*
23 Memorandum, Warburg to File, 2 March 1981, Lefever Nomination, Carton 264, Alan MacGregor Cranston Papers, Bancroft Library, University of California, Berkeley, California. (Hereafter Cranston Papers.)
24 Anthony Lewis, 'Advice at Home; Advise and Consent,' *New York Times*, 21 May 1981, A27.
25 'Human Rights and U.S. Foreign Policy,' Hearings Before the Subcommittee on International Organizations of the Committee on Foreign Affairs, House of Representatives, 96th Congress, 1st Session, 12 July 1979. See also Dumbrell, *American Foreign Policy*, 57.
26 In a March 3, 1981 interview with Reagan, Walter Cronkite asked him about Lefever's previous 'statute books' statement, and Reagan responded, 'Well, I've never had a chance to discuss with him just how he views that or what he believes the course would take. I do, however, believe that contrary to some of the attacks against him, that he's as concerned about human rights as the rest of us. But I think what he means is that basic human rights and the violation of them are being ignored by us where they take place in the Communist bloc nations.' Excerpts from an Interview With Walter Cronkite of CBS News, 3 March 1981 in John T. Woolley and Gerhard Peters, *The American Presidency Project*, http:// www.presidency.ucsb.edu/ws/?pid=43497 (accessed 12 May 2010).
27 'Nomination of Ernest W. Lefever.'
28 *Ibid.* A *Saint Paul Pioneer Press* editorial termed Lefever's sharp distinction between authoritarian and totalitarian regimes as 'shaky political science at best.' Extension of Remarks, *Congressional Record*, 24 February 1981, 2974.
29 Representative Barney Frank (D-MA), *Congressional Record*, 13 May 1981, 9704; and Charles Mohr, 'Human Rights Choice Abhors Scolding as U.S. Tool,' *New York Times*, 13 February 1981, A2.
30 Judith Miller, 'Rights Choice Says He's a "Do-Gooder," not "Galahad,"' *New York Times*, 19 May 1981, A7; and 'Nomination of Ernest W. Lefever.'
31 'Nomination of Ernest W. Lefever.'
32 *Ibid.*
33 *Ibid.* Such views also prompted members of the Congressional Black Caucus to cable Reagan asking that he withdraw Lefever's nomination.

Fauntroy and Gray to Reagan, 4 June 1981, FG 011 027355, WHORM Subject File, RRL.
34   Ernest W. Lefever, 'The Trivialization of Human Rights,' *Policy* Review, 3 (Winter 1978), 11; and *Congressional Record*, 1 April 1981, 6084.
35   'Nomination of Ernest W. Lefever.' Such a characterization led the Mexican American Legal Defense and Educational Fund to oppose Lefever's nomination on the grounds of racial and cultural bias.
36   Ernest W. Lefever, 'Carter's Periling Seoul,' *New York Times*, 18 June 1980, A31; and 'Nomination of Ernest W. Lefever.'
37   Judith Miller, 'Reagan Firm on Rights Choice as Opposition Rises,' *New York Times*, 23 May 1981, 7.
38   Lewis, 'Advice at Home'; and 'Nomination of Ernest W. Lefever.' See also Cranston Statement, 4 June 1981, Lefever Nomination, Carton 264, Cranston Papers.
39   'Nomination of Ernest W. Lefever.'
40   *Ibid.*
41   Representative Don Bonker (D-WA) noted in *Christian Science Monitor* 'it was really Congress which laid the ground-work for our human rights policy.' Don Bonker, 'Human Rights: Will Reagan Learn From Congress?' *Christian Science Monitor*, 25 February 1981, 23. While awaiting confirmation, Lefever told Stephen Palmer, who was the Acting Assistant Secretary, that he wanted to end the Department's annual human rights reports. Palmer reports he said, 'Ernie, that's easier said that done. It's a law. I personally don't see that we're going to get Congress to withdraw that obligation from us.' Interview with Stephen E. Palmer, Jr., 31 June 1995, The Foreign Affairs Oral History Collection of the Association for Diplomatic Studies and Training, Library of Congress.
42   Charles Mohr, 'Coalition Assails Reagan's Choice for State Dept. Human Rights Job,' *New York Times*, 25 February 1981, A10; and New York Human Rights Organizations Coordinating Meeting Minutes, 28 October 1981, USSR: US: State Department: Human Rights Bureau: [General], 1979–1982, 1985–1987, Box 59, Country Files, Cathy Fitzpatrick Files, Human Rights Watch Records, Center for Human Rights Documentation and Research, Rare Book and Manuscript Library, Columbia University Library, New York, New York. (Hereafter HRWR.)
43   Testimony, Robert Bernstein, 19 May 1981, Folder 4, Box 151, Part I: Professional File, Conference on Security and Cooperation in Europe, Arthur J. Goldberg Papers, Manuscript Division, Library of Congress, Washington, District of Columbia; and 'Nomination of Ernest W. Lefever.' (Hereafter Goldberg Papers.)
44   Minutes of the Board of Directors Meeting US Helsinki Watch Committee, 4 June 1981, Folder 4, Box 151, Part I: Professional File, Conference on Security and Cooperation in Europe, Goldberg Papers; and Aryeh Neier, *Taking Liberties: Four Decades in the Struggle for Rights* (New York: Public Affairs, 2003), 177.
45   Judith Miller, 'Rights Victim is a Potent Presence as Senators Assess Reagan Choice,' *New York Times*, 20 May 1981, A14; Daniel Southerland, 'Ex-Argentine Torture Victim Decries Lefever Nomination,' *Christian Science Monitor*, 20 May 1981; Jeri Laber, *The Courage of Strangers: Coming of Age*

with the Human Rights Movement (New York: PublicAffairs, 2002), 129; and 'Nomination of Ernest W. Lefever.'
46 Laber, *The Courage of Strangers*, 129.
47 'Nomination of Ernest W. Lefever.' Lefever's supporters countered that he was not unsympathetic to human rights abuses, but rather that he approached the issue with a realist outlook on the role of the United States in the world.
48 Ludmilla Alekseeva Statement, 19 May 1981, Folder 4, Box 151, Part I: Professional File, Conference on Security and Cooperation in Europe, Goldberg Papers; and *Congressional Record*, 14 May 1981, 9877. See also Anthony Lewis, 'Lefever: Why It Matters,' 31 May 1981, *New York Times*, 4: 19.
49 Lefever also gained the support of some human rights activists, such as Amnesty International USA's general consul, Mark Benenson.
50 Extension of Remarks, *Congressional Record*, 2 April 1981, 6393; and Open Letter, 7 March 1981 [Lefever Nomination – Clippings] (2), CFOA 114, Counsel to the President, Office of: Records, RRL.
51 Furthermore, the Committee argued that 'One of the promises made by President Reagan in the course of his campaign was that the direction of U.S. foreign policy in the area of human rights would be changed. Polls had indicated widespread concern by the American people that human rights considerations had been allowed to influence and even determine policy towards Third World and allied countries—often in a manner inconsistent with U.S. and Free World security interests.' Statement of Purpose, 7 March 1981 [Lefever Nomination – Clippings] (2), CFOA 114, Counsel to the President, Office of: Records, RRL.
52 'Nomination of Ernest W. Lefever.'
53 *Congressional Record*, 10 April 1981, 7287–90; and 'Nomination of Ernest W. Lefever.'
54 'Nomination of Ernest W. Lefever.'
55 William Safire, 'The New Haynsworth,' 28 May 1981, *New York Times*, A19.
56 'Nomination of Ernest W. Lefever.'
57 Fraser responded that a nominee who agreed with Reagan's April 30 statement on the Holocaust would garner his approval. *Ibid.*
58 'An Attack on Lefever is an Attack on Reagan,' Folder 2, Box 69B, Paul E. Tsongas Papers, Center for Lowell History, University of Massachusetts Lowell Libraries, Lowell, Massachusetts. (Hereafter Tsongas Papers.)
59 Press Release, 22 May 1981, Lefever Nomination, Carton 264, Cranston Papers. See also Caroline Rand Herron, 'Lefever, the Man; They Love to Bait,' *New York Times*, 31 May 1981, 4:3; and Cranston Statement, 4 June 1981, Lefever Nomination, Carton 264, Cranston Papers.
60 'Percy Said to Urge New Rights Choice,' *New York Times*, 22 May 1981, A1. The subsequent day, the Reagan administration reiterated it support for Lefever; its spokesman said, 'The President wants his nominee. He is entitled to a philosophically compatible appointment in his administration.' Judith Miller, 'Reagan Firm on Rights Choice as Opposition Rises,' *New York Times*, 23 May 1981.

61 Cranston Statement, 4 June 1981, Lefever Nomination, Carton 264, Cranston Papers.
62 Patrick Buchanan, 'Reagan's Haynsworth,' *Chicago Tribune-N.Y. News Syndicate, Inc.* 28 May 1981.
63 AP, 'Tsongas Says Lefever Prospects for Rights Post Are Deteriorating,' *New York Times*, 1 June 1981, A6. Lefever's nomination was further imperiled by allegations from his brothers that he held racist views. Judith Miller, 'Reagan Aide Defends Lefever and Policy on Rights,' *New York Times*, 4 June 1981. Tsongas' congressional papers also contain reports on State Department gossip that Haig had never supported Lefever's nomination. 'Ernest Lefever: State Department Gossip,' Folder A-3, Box 69A, Tsongas Papers.
64 Summary of News Stories and Commentaries, 31 May 1981 [Lefever Material from Richard Hauser] (4), CFOA 113, Counsel to the President, Office of: Records, RRL.
65 Observers characterized Lefever as 'a rallying point' for liberals, perhaps the most galvanizing since the end of the Vietnam War. Daniel Southerland, 'Reagan "Signaled" on Human Rights,' *Christian Science Monitor*, 19 May 1981, 1.
66 Tracking congressional correspondence is obviously only one, limited way to measure public opinion. See 1981 CMS Letters 46–49, Box 50, Nancy Kassebaum Papers, Kansas Historical Society, Topeka, Kansas. (Hereafter Kassebaum Papers.)
67 Weeks to Kassebaum, 10 February 1983, 1981 CMS Letters 46–49, Box 50, Kassebaum Papers.
68 'Nomination of Ernest W. Lefever.' The proportion of letters opposing Lefever as well as his claims to have 'analyzed' them became contentious issues in his confirmation hearings. A Hill staffer alleged that the letters supporting Lefever have been 'generated' by a conservative mailing operation. The Ken Alvord Show, 'A Talk with Ernest Lefever,' 26 May 1981 [Lefever Nomination Material III] (1), CFOA 114, Counsel to the President, Office of: Records, RRL.
69 Tom Wicker, 'In the Nation: Mr. Lefever's Colors,' *New York Times*, 22 May 1981, A27.
70 Editorial, 'Semantic Antics Over Human Rights,' *New York Times*, 24 May 1981, 18.
71 He further said, 'We're spending a lot of time putting together his campaign. It will be a bloody battle, but we think we'll win in the end.' Roberta Hornig, 'Administration, Senators Brace for Lefever Battle,' *Washington Star*, 13 March 1981.
72 *New York Times* columnist Anthony Lewis had described Lefever's performance at the hearings 'self-destructive.' He wrote, 'Mr. Lefever was an extraordinarily evasive witness, unresponsive, disingenuous.' Lewis, 'Advice at Home.'
73 Fairbanks to Percy, 27 March 1981, HPG Lefever, Ernest W. General (1), CFOA 114, Counsel to the President, Office of: Records, RRL.
74 Press Release, 17 March 1981, Briefing Book – Nomination of Ernest W. Lefever (1), CFOA 114, Counsel to the President, Office of: Records, RRL.

75 Pointers for Dr. Lefever, [Lefever Material from Richard Hauser] (2), CFOA 113, Counsel to the President, Office of: Records, RRL.
76 The Ken Alvord Show, 'A Talk with Ernest Lefever.' Lefever reiterated this point in an interview with the 'Today' show on NBC. John M. Goshko, 'Lefever Says Reagan Is Critics' Target,' *Washington Post*, 27 May 1981.
77 State Department officials reported Lefever, not the administration, initiated the interviews. Scott Armstrong, 'Lefever Cancels TV Appearance,' *Washington Post*, 28 May 1981, A8; and Judith Miller, 'Senators Postpone Vote on Rights Nominee,' *New York Times*, 29 May 1981.
78 'Nomination of Ernest W. Lefever.'
79 The five Republicans who voted against Lefever were: Charles Mathias, Nancy Kassebaum, Rudolph Boschwitz, Larry Pressler, and Charles Percy. All of the Committees Democrats opposed his nomination: Claiborne Pell, Joseph Biden, John Glenn, Paul Sarbanes, Edward Zorinsky, Paul Tsongas, Alan Cranston, and Christopher Dodd. His sole supporters were: Howard Baker, Jesse Helms, Richard Lugar, and Samuel Hayakawa.
80 'Exit Lefever, With a Nudge,' *New York Times*, 7 June 1981, 4: 1.
81 'Nomination of Ernest W. Lefever'; and Extension of Remarks, *Congressional Record*, 9 June 1981, 11934–6.
82 'Nomination of Ernest W. Lefever.'
83 Cranston Statement, 5 June 1981, Lefever Nomination, Carton 264, Cranston Papers; and 'Nomination of Ernest W. Lefever.'
84 'Nomination of Ernest W. Lefever.'
85 Lefever to Reagan, 5 June 1981, FG 011 019543, WHORM Subject File, RRL. Reagan responded by thanking Lefever for his 'perseverance, in the face of hostile and often willfully uncomprehending criticism, in explaining for our public and for the world the foundations of our new human rights policy.' Reagan to Lefever, 15 June 1981 [Lefever Nomination – Notes and Clippings] (4), CFOA 113, Counsel to the President, Office of: Records, RRL.
86 AP, 'Dissidents Suffer from Chill in U.S.–Soviet Relations,' 1 November 1981, USA: Diplomatic Relations, 1981–1981, Box 971, Old Code Subject Files, 1953–1994, Soviet Red Archives, Records of Radio Free Europe/Radio Liberty Research Institute, Open Society Archives; and Molinari et al. to Reagan, 1 October 1981, Folder 4, Box 1, HU, WHORM Subject File, RRL. (Hereafter OSA.) The State Department considered changing the name of the Human Rights Bureau to the Bureau of Individual and Personal Rights as well as shifting the tasks of the office. Barbara Crosette, 'U.S. Postpones Filling Rights Position,' *New York Times*, 29 September 1981, A3; and Minutes of the Board of Directors Meeting US Helsinki Watch Committee, 1 October 1981, Folder 4, Box 151, Part I: Professional File, Conference on Security and Cooperation in Europe, Goldberg Papers. Helsinki Watch expressed its concern about proposals to change the name of the Bureau or abolish the post in a letter to Reagan. Bernstein et al. to Reagan, 5 October 1981, Folder 4, Box 1, HU, WHORM Subject File, RRL; and Press Release, 13 October 1981, Folder 4, Box 151, Part I: Professional File, Conference on Security and Cooperation in Europe, Goldberg Papers.

87 Palmer to Bernstein, 28 October 1981; Bernstein et al. to Reagan, 5 October 1981, Folder 4, Box 1, HU, WHORM Subject File, RRL; and Mohr, 'Haig Aide Insists U.S. Rights Policy is Evenhanded.'
88 The speech was delivered on May 24, 1981. *CSCE Digest*, 29 May 1981, Helsinki/Madrid, Box 112, Millicent Fenwick Papers, Rutgers University, New Brunswick, New Jersey; and 'Mondale Assails Reagan on Rights,' *New York Times*, 25 May 1981, A3.
89 Congress established the position with an amendment (Section 624 (f)) to the Foreign Assistance Act of 1961.
90 Extension of Remarks, *Congressional Record*, 9 July 1981, 1530–1.
91 Extension of Remarks, *Congressional Record*, 29 October 1981, 26125.
92 Kennedy to Haig, 26 October 1981, released to the author under the Freedom of Information Act. See also Jacoby, 'The Reagan Turnaround on Human Rights,' 1069–70.
93 Jefferson Morley, 'Rights and Reagan: Does the Appointment of Elliott Abrams Signal a Reversal in Human Rights Policy?,' *Foreign Service Journal* (March 1982): 20; and 'Elliott Abrams: A Neoconservative for Human Rights.'
94 Interview with Stephen E. Palmer, Jr., 31 June 1995, The Foreign Affairs Oral History Collection of the Association for Diplomatic Studies and Training, Library of Congress. See also Jerome Shestack, 'Human Rights, the National Interest, and U.S. Foreign Policy,' *Annals of the American Academy of Political and Social Science*, 506 (November 1989), 17.
95 Kennedy to Haig, 26 October 1981, released to the author under the Freedom of Information Act. See also Maynard, 182–3; and Hartmann, 'US Human Rights Policy Under Carter and Reagan, 1977–1981,' 425–6.
96 Underlining in original. Kennedy to Haig, 26 October 1981, released to the author under the Freedom of Information Act.
97 Kennedy to Haig, 27 October 1981, USSR: US: State Department: Human Rights Bureau [General], 1979–1982, 1985, 1987, Box 59, Country Files, Files of Cathy Fitzpatrick, HRWR.
98 Kennedy to Haig, 26 October 1981, released to the author under the Freedom of Information Act.
99 See, for example William Safire, 'Human Rights Victory,' *New York Times*, 5 November 1981, A27; and Pell to Haig, 12 November 1981, Alexander Haig, Box 54, Claiborne Pell Papers, University of Rhode Island, Kingston, Rhode Island.
100 Barbara Crossette, 'U.S. To Name Human Rights Aide,' *New York Times*, 30 October 1981, A3.
101 Palmer to Bernstein, 28 October 1981, Folder 4, Box 1, HU, WHORM Subject File, RRL.
102 Mohr, 'Haig Aide Insists U.S. Rights Policy is Evenhanded.'
103 A. Glenn Mower, *Human Rights and American Foreign Policy: The Carter and Reagan Experiences* (New York: Greenwood Press, 1987), 46–7.
104 'Elliott Abrams: A Neoconservative for Human Rights,' *National Journal*, 1 May 1982.
105 Interview with Theresa A. Tull, 9 November 2004, The Foreign Affairs Oral History Collection of the Association for Diplomatic Studies and Training, Library of Congress.

106 Judith Miller, 'Man in the News: A Neoconservative for Human Rights Post,' *New York Times*, 31 October 1981, 1: 7; and George Lardner, Jr., 'Human Rights Spokesman Reported Chosen,' *Washington Post*, 30 October 1981, A12.
107 Lister to Abrams, 14 December 1981, Folder 6, Box 2, George Lister Papers, Benson Latin American Collection, University of Texas Libraries, the University of Texas at Austin, Austin, Texas. (Hereafter Lister Papers.)
108 Lister to Abrams, 10 December 1981, Folder 6, Box 2, Lister Papers.
109 Morley, 'Rights and Reagan,' 25.
110 'Nomination of Elliott Abrams,' Hearing Before the Committee on Foreign Relations, United States Senate, 97th Congress, 1st Session, 17 November 1981. In contrast to the voluminous record of Lefever's hearings, Abrams' nomination was dispensed with quickly, and the record of his hearings only totals twenty-seven pages. The record of Lefever's hearings, on the other hand, runs 577 pages.
111 *Ibid.*
112 Pipes to Clark, 6 May 1982, Dissident Lunch – White House May 11, 1982 (2/2), Box 22, Jack Matlock Files, RRL; and 'Former Dissidents Reassured by Reagan on Human Rights,' 12 May 1982, Human Rights, 1980–1982, Box 691, Old Code Subject Files, 1953–1994, Soviet Red Archives, Records of Radio Free Europe/Radio Liberty Research Institute, OSA.
113 Lord to Clark, 22 June 1982, Folder 12, Box 1, WHORM Subject File, RRL. Clark was named National Security Adviser after Allen resigned in January 1982. Dobriansky and Blair to Clark, 23 December 1982, 'Vatican,' Box 91186, NSC: Records, European and Soviet Affairs Directorate, RRL.
114 Schifter, 'Building Firm Foundations,' 19.
115 *Ibid.*
116 'Abrams, State's Human Rights Chief, Tries to Tailor a Policy to Suit Reagan,' *National Journal*, 1 May 1982.
117 Neier, *Taking Liberties*, 189. See also Laber, *Courage of Strangers*, 128–9.
118 Shultz thought Haig's past experience working with Henry Kissinger may have led him to place insufficient emphasis on human rights. George Shultz Interview, Folder 2, Box 3, Don Oberdorfer Papers, Public Policy Papers, Department of Rare Books and Special Collections, Princeton University Library, Princeton, New Jersey.
119 Jacoby, 'The Reagan Turnaround on Human Rights,' 1068, 1078; and Jerome J. Shestack, 'An Unsteady Focus: The Vulnerabilities of the Reagan Administration's Human Rights Policy,' *Harvard Human Rights* Journal, 2 (1989), 33–4, 37–8.
120 Interview with Theresa A. Tull, 9 November 2004, The Foreign Affairs Oral History Collection of the Association for Diplomatic Studies and Training, Library of Congress.

8
Areas of Concern: Area Studies and the New American Studies
John Carlos Rowe

American Studies has thus far avoided the heated debates concerning the restructuring of area studies prompted by dramatic changes in the geopolitical and economic maps as a consequence of globalization. In view of the US role in the economic, political, and cultural changes produced by that globalization, we might expect that American Studies would be as fiercely contested in its disciplinary borders as East Asian, Middle Eastern, Southeast Asian, Soviet, and Latin American Studies, to mention only a few of the areas established by post-World War II scholarship and facing dramatic challenges since the 1970s and later the aftermath of Soviet decolonization.

Of course, the area studies model has defined primarily the social sciences – economics, political science, and sociology – and interdisciplinary conjunctures of history and the social sciences, including 'historical sociology' and 'social science history'.[1] Given the centrality of cultural production, especially literature and the visual arts, and traditional history in the field, it is not surprising that American Studies would be considered eccentric to the debates concerning the scholarly map of a new world order governed by new political, economic, and social forces. Whether treated as epiphenomenal or superstructural, the objects of study dominating post-World War II American Studies – 'myths and symbols' to use a convenient tag – hardly warranted the attention of serious scholars dealing with urgent issues of global political instability, economic crisis, war, genocide, famine and drought, and the spread of infectious diseases.

In the past twenty years, American Studies has posed a greater threat to the authority of the 'area studies' model and to the nation-specific knowledge it supports. Scholars of the 'new' American Studies have challenged traditional American Studies for its exclusive attention to the distinctive qualities of US citizenship and nationalism, condemning such 'exceptionalism' for its deliberate neglect of the demographic diversity of the US and the transnational networks on which the US state has traditionally relied.[2] The key post-World War II advocates of this American Exceptionalism were the scholars of the Myth-and-Symbol School, and the challenge posed by 'new Americanists' included broadening the field to consider the Americas and Canada. Such debates internal to the field of American Studies may appear to have little to do with US foreign policies, the power of the state, or its domestic authority; these are merely academic debates negotiated in specialist journals and conferences.

Yet the new Americanists' challenge to US national form, itself crucial to US state power, occurred in a historical period when national knowledges in general were called into question. Although dominated by liberal and left intellectuals, the field of American Studies had seldom played a significant role in the post-World War II restructuring of knowledge along lines best suited to US global power. By 2003, however, Alan Wolfe's review-essay 'Anti-American Studies' in the *New Republic* targeted work by the new Americanists as 'anti-American', in large part because such scholarship threatened familiar US national ideologies.[3] No longer merely academic, debates within American Studies threatened larger public efforts to bolster a tottering US state, whose exclusiveness relied on a stereotypical 'representative man' who was white, middle-class, and of European descent. As the justification for US neoimperialism increasingly relied on the exportation of 'American-style democracy' and its civic virtues, threats to its traditional archetypes challenged the moral tone in which US foreign policy so often disguised its ruthless political and economic interests.

American Studies was not one of the 'area studies' defined during World War II precisely to serve postwar US political and economic domination, because American Studies represented the 'area' of the US that was not subject to neoimperial domination. As long as American Studies focused on the US, however critically scholars may have treated this national form, the discipline posed no threat to state power. Within this ideological framework, we can understand why the US State Department readily agreed to send American Studies' scholars from the prevailing liberal-left spectrum overseas as 'representatives' of America, lecturing in a variety of State Department programs, including the Fulbright-Hays and International Exchange of Scholars.[4] The genuine political 'dissent' expressed by many of these traveling scholars was contained neatly within the form of American diversity, which today we identify as 'neoliberalism', whereby actual political dissent was neutralized by what Herbert Marcuse long ago termed 'repressive desublimation'.[5]

When American Studies challenged American Exceptionalism by calling for more work on the US in transnational contexts, especially on the US as a traditional and neoimperial power, then the new American Studies scholars threatened not only the US state but its 'cultural clients', those 'area studies' established during World War II to serve explicitly US postwar ambitions of global hegemony. Most scholars in the humanities and social sciences were familiar with US state involvement in funding the study of foreign languages and area studies during the Cold War, but few scholars knew much about the longer history in which postwar area studies developed. Underfunded and marginalized by the US federal government, except during foreign junkets when they did the cultural work of bolstering the US state, most postwar American Studies scholars had little reason to learn more about 'area studies' in which they had no specific stake.

Yet today when the postnationalist and transnational work of the new American Studies is rejected vigorously by area studies scholars and condemned generally by Alan Wolfe, a Boston College political scientist with little reason to be interested in the field, the relevance of this history of area studies has never been greater. And because the new American Studies threatens an explicit pact made between the postwar American state and scholarship in the social sciences, it has the opportunity to expose such intellectual and political complicity in productive ways. Of course, the new American Studies in its comparative, polylingual, hemispheric scope is itself decidedly ideological, despite the significant differences of its many practitioners. There is nothing 'objective' in the politically motivated work of scholars attempting to make American Studies more relevant to contemporary processes of globalization and offering their own internationalism as an alternative to US nationalism. No scholarly approach in any discipline is ever completely free of its social and political situation, no matter how vigorously that approach might claim scientific rigor.

In ancient Greece, geographers divided their field into three major continental areas: Europe, Asia, and Libya (Africa).[6] The sixteenth- to eighteenth-century voyages of European exploration and the consolidation of what Walter Mignolo terms the 'modern/colonial world system' expanded the ancient continental model while relying on many of its basic assumptions regarding both the hierarchy of civilizations and the uniqueness of the peoples in these different regions.[7] The 'seven-continent model of the modern elementary school classroom' led to refinements and subdivisions, most of them reflecting specific European colonial interests. As Martin Lewis and Kären Wigen have written, '[S]cholarly divisions of labor showed that the tripartite global model of the ancient Greeks was deeply entrenched. The West (North America and Europe) was conceptualized as the site for serious history and the social sciences; the East (stretching from Morocco to Japan), as the zone where Orientalists could ponder the cultural flowers of supposedly fossilized civilizations; and the rest of the world was the domain of anthropologists, who specialized in "primitive" cultural and social systems.'[8]

According to the 'Best is the West' thesis, the US and Canada shared the privileged status of Europe in the traditional area studies model that dominated the social sciences from their institutional inception in the nineteenth century through the formal reforms instituted by the Ethnogeographic Board commissioned by the US government in 1942.[9] Certainly the confusion of nationalist and racialist ideologies in the nineteenth and early twentieth century contributed to such myths as 'the March of the Anglo-Saxon', whose 'destiny' ranged from Northern Europe to England, Ireland, Scotland, and then across the Atlantic and the North American Continent in a manifest destiny' that would civilize triumphantly the rest of the world. According to this familiar notion that the United States in particular (although Canada first as colony and then as member of the British Commonwealth also qualifies) is merely an extension of European Civilization, creating the 'greater' Western Civilization that was thoroughly challenged from the 1970s onward, it would seem that the United States and Canada (North America) and their prototypes in Europe would constitute the most important 'area' for study and thus draw as much as possible on complementary fields such as American and Canadian Studies.

Yet this was obviously not the case when modern 'area studies' operated under the shadow of the modern/colonial world system. Neither American nor European Studies existed in the period of nineteenth-century nationalism, the consolidation of European imperialism, and the emergence of US imperial authority. The 'serious history and social sciences' that Lewis and Wigen contend were devoted to North America and Europe offered primarily a model to the rest of the world for 'civilization', both in its contemporarily achieved and its ideal or destined forms. Walt Whitman's *Democratic Vistas* (1871/1876) is neither sociology nor history, but its incorporation of the rest of the emerging world into the 'cosmic' destiny of US democracy and individualism exemplifies this paradox that the privileged 'areas' of Western Civilization – the US, Canada, Europe, and their Greco-Roman sources – are not 'areas' at all, but conceptualizations or idealisms capable of thriving anywhere and everywhere, like the mind of God.[10] Neither North American nor European Studies were necessary to 'study' such an historically and geographically specific suite of phenomena, because they were indeed the intellectual complements of the modern/colonial world system, hardly subject to the internal critique or metanarrative that might have resulted from taking 'America' or 'Europe' as 'objects of study'.

At the beginning of World War II, when the 'U.S. government called upon the Smithsonian Institution, the American Council of Learned Societies, the National Research Council, and the Social Science Research Council to form a body known as the Ethnogeographic Board', the charge to create 'a new system of global divisions' was hardly intended to do away with imperialist hierarchies of the older 'area studies' and their commitment to 'the West is the Best'.[11] The Ethnogeographic Board was formally established in June of 1942.[12] Carl E. Guthe, the anthropologist who chaired the new Board, characterized it as 'a non-governmental agency established in the name of the scientists and scholars of the country for the purpose of aiding the government'.[13] This curious alliance of putatively independent foundations, scholars, and governmental institutions – a 'state-scholarly complex' – continues to shape area studies to this day, even after Cold-War era and funding have passed. What motivated the US government then, and motivates it now, is the need for more effective 'language training' and 'cultural fluency' to enable the US and its allies to conduct 'the war effort across large spans of the globe'.[14]

The work of the Board is characterized by Guthe as 'interdisciplinary in scope, seeking to use the facilities and knowledge of the earth sciences, the biological sciences, the social sciences, and the humanities, in so far as these relate to regions outside of the continental United States'.[15] Lewis and Wigen note that geography played a much smaller role on the Board than was initially imagined; Robert B. Hall is the only geographer on the original eight-scholar Board.[16] The Board membership in 1943 listed by Guthe includes two archaeologists (if you count William Duncan Strong twice in this list), three anthropologists, a historian, a geographer, a biologist, a public health specialist, and an East Asian languages scholar.[17] Chaired by Guthe, the Board was directed by William Duncan Strong (1899–1962), the Columbia University archaeologist and anthropologist who specialized in the indigenous peoples of North and South America, especially the Incas of Peru.[18] Thus Guthe's specific exclusion of areas within the continental United States clearly did not include 'indigenous peoples and their cultures', reinforcing the notion that this 'area studies' model was fully committed to the modernization and development processes.[19] Archaeology and Anthropology (especially if you count Strong twice, as his expertise in both disciplines warrants) account for more than half of the disciplines represented on the Board. Only two of these scholars, the Sinologist Mortimer Graves and historian Carter Goodrich, can be considered vaguely connected with the 'humanities'.[20] Neither 'American Studies' nor 'American Literature', indeed *any* literary or cultural specializations, other than those covered by the anthropologists and archaeologists, are represented on the Board.

The unmanageable 'seven-continents' model and its 'European colonial' subtext of the prewar era was replaced by the more specific 'areas' proposed by the Ethnogeographic Commission: East Asia, Southeast Asia, South Asia, the Middle East, Africa, Latin America, North America, Russia and Eastern Europe, Western Europe, and Oceania.[21] The older colonial hierarchy was replaced by goals of 'modernization and development', whereby North America and Western Europe still retained their status as 'superior civilizations' by virtue of technological advances and claims to political innovations. The interdisciplinary alliance between the social sciences, the humanities, and geography was not realized. Lewis and Martin point out that although two 'prominent geographers, Isaiah Bowman and Robert Hall, were appointed' to the Ethnogeographic Board, 'few geographers became involved in the intellectual work of the board, and the task of delineating areas fell primarily to anthropologists and other social scientists'.[22] Indeed, 'the anthropological imprint is evident in the use of the term area (derived from ethnological studies of ("culture areas"), rather than *region*', a symptom to my mind of how such 'area studies' were already motivated by the 'modernization and development' models isomorphic with neoimperialism, especially later versions of free-trade imperialism, and third-stage, postindustrial capitalism in its global form.

Interestingly, the work of the Ethnogeographic Board occurs contemporaneously with the emergence of American Studies as an interdisciplinary field, however we might quibble over exact origins, in the influential work of F.O. Matthiessen, whose *American Renaissance* was published in 1941. And yet American Studies, especially in the Myth-and-Symbol School so often traced back to Matthiessen, is by no means an 'area studies' field as it was conceived by the anthropologists, geographers, biologists, and other scholars serving on the Ethnogeographic Board. If there is a connection, then it must be made through the cultural idealism of American Studies supporting, often unwittingly, the modernization and development ideology of the area studies developed by the

Ethnogeographic Board in the early 1940s and fully institutionalized during the Cold War, especially with the '1958 National Defense Education Act, Title VI,... which supplied the funds to establish university area-studies centers' that by 1990 totaled 'some 124 National Resource Centers,... each devoted to the interdisciplinary study of a particular world region'.[23]

Of course, since Donald Pease published his pioneering '*Moby-Dick* and the Cold War' in 1985, much valuable work has been done on how American Studies participated in Cold War ideology, especially its articulation of an American Exceptionalism subsequently challenged by a 'new' American Studies vigorously committed to transnational, postnational, postcolonial, indigenist, and multiethnic goals for understanding the 'United States' in global contexts.[24] This critique of Cold-War area studies, initiated largely by left intellectuals in the 1970s, once again coincides historically with the criticism of first-generation American Studies (primarily the ideology of the Myth-and-Symbol School) directed by feminists, ethnic studies, postmodernists, gay studies, and other minoritized intellectuals over how their interests and rights were at worst neglected or at best 'synthesized' in traditional American Studies. Lewis and Wigen attribute the 'crisis' in area studies that begins in the 1970s to 'the stalling out of the growth of U.S. universities in the 1970s,' the 'end of the Vietnam War' resulting in 'a major loss of funding for Southeast Asian Studies programs,' and extending to the more urgent crisis at the end of the 1980s 'when the end of the cold war undercut the geopolitical rational for area studies expertise just as the demise of the Soviet Union and its sphere of influence rendered the postwar area-studies map outdated.'[25] The Gulbenkian Commission, convened by Immanuel Wallerstein in the mid-1990s, proposed several alternatives to the area-studies model in its report, *Open the Social Sciences* (1996), which cited 'the challenge... from... "cultural studies"' according to three main themes: 'first the central importance of gender studies and all kinds of "non-Eurocentric" studies to the study of historical social systems; second, the importance of local, very situated historical analysis, associated by many with a new "hermeneutic turn"; third, the assessment of the values involved in technological achievements in relation to other values.'[26] The Report asserted that these developments promised new relationships among humanists (especially 'among scholars in literary studies of all kinds'), anthropology, and 'the new quasi-disciplines relating to the "forgotten" peoples of modernity (those neglected by virtue of gender, race, class, etc.), for whom it provided a theoretical ("postmodern") framework for their elaborations of difference'.[27]

But this promise to 'open the social sciences' beyond the Cold-War area studies model to include developments familiar to scholars of the 'new' American Studies does not sufficiently take into account the enormous institutional resistance of scholars trained in area studies, still committed to their specializations and in some areas, notably 'East Asian', 'South Asian', 'Middle Eastern', and 'Latin American', benefiting rather than suffering from the collapse of 'Southeast Asian Studies' and 'Soviet Studies'. Area studies are alive and well, defending their territories with the determination of scholars whose very existences depend on this fight and have at their command an impressive arsenal of 'common-sense' arguments opposing coalitions of 'new' American Studies, Postcolonial Studies, Cultural Studies, and virtually any version of 'postmodernism' and its assorted complements, 'cosmopolitanism' and 'post- or neo-Marxism'. In these intellectual fights, there are interesting figures at the vanguard: Walter Mignolo's 'border thinking' and Juan Poblete's *Critical Latin American and Latino Studies* force area-studies scholars to defend explicitly intellectual boundaries that still retain their imperial legacies, buried for a time beneath a certain pseudo-scientific reliance on empirical data and disguised in part by a post-World War II US provenance casting a vaguely 'democratic' aura in which the modernization and development ideology is clearly announced.

Why should American Studies scholars engage in these fights, which are often staged in terms of national languages, local and regional histories, and institutional politics in which we are unevenly trained? If we are committed, as I am, to the comparative study of Canada and the Americas, rather than merely US-centric American Studies, however diverse we may make it, then how do we respond to the familiar challenge from Latin American area specialists that our project is simply the next stage of US imperialism stretching from the Monroe doctrine through the Spanish-American War to the Pan-Americanism of the Cold War era? Finally, is not this commitment to 'hemispheric study' of Canada and the Americas merely a revival of the much older continental model for area studies, replacing contemporary problems with even more insidious difficulties haunting us from the European imperial past?

There are practical answers to each of these questions. American Studies must develop curricula that require foreign languages relevant to the different communities in Canada and the Americas, just as we should broaden our curricula to deal with local and regional histories beyond the United States. Of course, we must be attentive to the problems of linguistic, cultural, and epistemological imperialism, especially in a global era shaped by neoimperialist practices that work as much through cultural and intellectual means as through military, political, and economic tactics. But not all study of other societies is inevitably imperialist, especially when the method of scholarship is intended to investigate precisely the imperialist inclinations of knowledge to follow power. Comparative study of the different communities in the Western Hemisphere is intended to pay particularly close attention to the historical power dynamics that created hierarchies along the North-South axis as troubling as the imperial assumptions implicit in an earlier East-West divide (monumentalized in Hegel's ineluctable evolution of World-Historical Spirit from east to Western Civilization).

Finally, the 'Western Hemisphere' reproduces the older continental model of prewar area studies if we focus upon its 'exceptional' status, either in its pre-Columbian, premodern indigeneity or in its extraordinary uniqueness as the 'New World' that would realize the ideals of European imperialists. Understood as a particularly instructive instance of what Mignolo terms the 'modern/colonial world system', the Western Hemisphere cannot be disengaged finally from the global processes in which it has been historically involved, including those that traversed it long before the arrival of European invaders. In this context, we must begin to think less in terms of the pertinent 'rims' – Pacific, North Atlantic, mid-Atlantic, Caribbean – and more in terms of certain 'flows' describing the terrestrial, maritime, modern avian, and postmodern transits of outer (military and communications' satellites) and inner (bodily prostheses and virtual realities) spaces.[28]

These answers are not really what many area studies specialists want to hear, because the threat posed to their disciplines also involves an internal critique already well underway in US-centric American Studies and increasingly evident in Latin American Studies. Despite the very different European imperialisms and their historical modalities informing traditional studies of the 'Americas', they have in common the Creole nationalisms that developed in rebellion against their imperial masters. Following Enrique Dussel's *The Invention of America*, Mignolo points out:

> 'America', interestingly enough, is a name that became the territorial identification not for the Spanish crown, or for the Spanish in the Indias Occidentales, but for the Creole population and intellectuals, born in 'America' from Spanish descent and leaders of the independence during the nineteenth century. It was also the Creole population and its intellectuals who initiated a process of self-definition as 'Americans,' with all its possible variations ('Spanish,' 'Indo,'

'Latin'),.... The importance of the discourse of geocultural identity lies in the fact that it filled a space that was broken in the process of conquest and colonization.²⁹

The 'creoles' to whom Mignolo refers are the descendants of Spaniards or Portuguese born in the colonies, from whom 'liberators' like Simón Bolívar and José de San Martín would emerge to lead the national revolutions of the early nineteenth century in what they themselves would come to term 'Latin America'.

Although we do not refer to the US 'founding fathers' or cultural nationalists, such as Emerson and Hawthorne and Whitman, as 'Creoles', they fit Mignolo's conception of the anti-imperialist aura of national ideology in the Western Hemisphere.³⁰ Despite the enormous differences between Bolívar's struggle against Spanish imperial power in decline and Franklin and Adams's struggle against British imperialism, increasingly triumphant around the globe, South American and North American 'Creole nationalisms' commonly 'filled a space that was broken in the process of conquest and colonization'.³¹ Mignolo is referring to the massive destruction of indigenous societies by European conquest and colonization, and it is indeed remarkable how often US and Latin American revolutionaries would invoke the imperial destruction of indigenous peoples as a justification for Creole revolution, despite the open hostility most Creoles displayed to their own indigenous populations. From American rebels disguised as the native peoples that their forefathers had slaughtered in the Pequot War and King Philip's War to the melodramatic outrage expressed by Bolívar regarding Spanish atrocities against Amerindians or José Martí's paternalism with regard to North American Indians with whom he claims a tenuous bond, the political writings of the Creole nationalists in North and South America are full of passionate commitments to the liberation of indigenous peoples from the slavery and exploitation of their common imperial masters.³²

Despite very different national policies toward indigenous peoples throughout the Hemisphere, the 'national' stage of the modern/colonial world system displays the perpetuation of colonial oppression under the guise of 'national development' and 'necessary modernization'. And although these bourgeois, Creole nationalisms appear to have continued the policies of their imperial masters in ways that perpetuated the linguistic, ethnic, and cultural differences distinguishing Spanish, Portuguese, and British imperialisms (to deal with only the three most powerful between 1500 and 1800), they developed a certain strategic commonality that persists to this day and may well be one reason why scholars in Latin American area studies fight so vigorously against the hemispheric comparatism of the 'new' American Studies. Mignolo is particularly clear on the development of an intriguing 'commonality' of these diverse American 'nations':

> [I]t is clear that between 1820 and 1830 the future historical paths of the two Americas, Anglo and Latin, were being decided. Before then, roughly from 1500 to 1800, the differences between the two Americas were the differences dictated between the Spanish and British empires in the modern/colonial world system. Language and race... were two crucial components in the articulation of the modern/colonial world system imaginary.
>
> The commonality of the difference, however, lies in the way that, at the beginning of the nineteenth century, 'America' was appropriated by intellectuals of the emerging states as different from Europe but still within the West.... [P]olitical independence was accompanied by a symbolic independence in the geopolitical imagination.[33]

Mignolo identifies in this passage a nineteenth-century 'American Exceptionalism' of hemispheric and transnational scope. We recognize immediately a host of possible examples ranging from the fierce struggle for literary nationalism in the antebellum US, haunted by European allusions and models, to comparable struggles of Latin American intellectuals to break free of European sources by adapting them to South American, Caribbean, or Meso-American human and natural environments. The latter project is brilliantly represented and satirized in the Cuban novelist Alejo Carpentier's *Los pasos perdidos* (1953), often cited as one of the first works of the so-called 'Latin American Boom'.[34]

In the print-dominated era of nineteenth-century nationalism, literature played a crucial role in constructing and interpellating this national imaginary. The anti-imperialist rhetoric dominates not only the overtly democratic literature of the traditional American Renaissance, but also includes many key Latin American literary texts of the period. *Jicoténcal*, the anti-imperial Mexican novel published anonymously in Philadelphia in 1826 and attributed by some scholars to the revolutionary Cuban priest, Félix Varela, occupies a celebrated position in the Latin American literary canon, in part because its stinging indictment of Cortès, his consort, Doña Marina (La Malinche), and the Catholic priests accompanying his military invasion appears written in support of the Mexican revolution against Spain and of other revolutionary movements in Latin

America, and in part because the novel's vigorous defense of indigenous rights as equivalent to those of the Creole revolutionaries realizes, three centuries later, the failed democratic aspirations of the Tlaxcalan eponymous hero, Jicoténcal, and his long-suffering lover and wife, Teutila.[35]

The 'commonality of the difference' that Mignolo finds in Creole nationalisms in the Western Hemisphere links these emancipatory movements with the imperialist agendas they transcoded from their imperialist masters: Spain, Portugal, Netherlands, England, and France. Although the North-South divide in the Western Hemisphere has long been defined by the radical differences in public policies regarding ethnic and racial identities, there is also a 'commonality of the difference' across this border when we consider how these same Creole nationalisms treated indigenous peoples and Creoles of color. At the height of nineteenth-century nationalist ferment in the hemisphere, Creole revolutionaries rarely invoked the Haitian slave rebellion, arguably the first successful slave revolt in history, and consistently incorporated indigenous issues into their own nationalist platforms while perpetuating, and in many cases worsening, the social and human conditions under which indigenous peoples struggled to survive.[36] Immediately upon establishing national boundaries, most emerging nations also initiated vigorous campaigns of territorial expansion, entering into struggles with neighbors that in some cases last to the present day.

I repeat Mignolo's phrase 'the commonality of the difference' to stress that a comparative study of the communities of the Western Hemisphere is not a question of identifying their deep-structural unity or their distinct national exceptionalisms, as an older Comparative Literature did with its largely European models in the misnamed World Literatures project. The imperialist subtext I have interpreted as common to Creole nationalisms hardly leads to positive answers to such questions as posed by Gustavo Pérez Firmat's influential collection of 1990, *Do the Americas Have a Common Literature?*, or Marshall Eakin's more recent query, 'Does Latin America Have a Common History?'[37] There are nevertheless points of contact and commonality that allow us to conduct such comparative work at crucial intersections or contact zones, rather than producing yet another testament to a monumental 'exceptionalism' that is at root neo-imperialist.

National expansionist projects in contestation with other nationalist projects in the Hemisphere are particularly worthy of our attention. Mignolo focuses on 1848 and 1898 as crucial historical moments in 'the early division between Anglo and Latin America'.[38] The Treaty of

Guadalupe-Hidalgo concluding the Mexican War (1846–1848) 'was a conflict between new emerging nations', Mexico and the United States, and the open imperialism of the US has often been cited as one reason the War has until recently played such a small role in US cultural and social history.[39] However, its significance in shifting the 'border' between North and South, as well as incorporating in a very short span a significant 'Latinidad' into the United States, cannot be ignored by the new American Studies. In most accounts, the focus is on victimized Mexico only 25 years free from Spanish imperial control and continuing to struggle with internal political and economic problems at the time of the War's outbreak. Lost in the course of most accounts, including literary and cultural histories, are the indigenous peoples, already systematically displaced, enslaved, and murdered during the Spanish and subsequent Mexican colonization of Baja and Alta California, then subject to a host of new laws and rules imposed by postwar American officials and less formal, but accepted, practices of genocide practiced by US citizens well into the twentieth century.

For Mignolo, 1898 also redraws the hemispheric map, ostensibly by overtly asserting the imperialist agenda of the United States in its invocation of the Monroe Doctrine and the collapse of Spanish imperial claims in the Hemisphere.[40] I would add that US negotiations with Great Britain for a Canal Treaty and during Secretary of State John Hay's Open Door Policy in Asia have to be considered, since the result of these negotiations was that Great Britain agreed to US hegemony in the Western Hemisphere in exchange for British dominance in Asia.[41] Too often forgotten in the invocation of 1898, however, is the US cooptation of the republican struggles in Cuba and Puerto Rico, as well as in the Philippines. To study 1898, we must travel one of those strategic 'rims' or follow one of those historical 'flows' across the Pacific, recognizing that the US suppression of Philippine nationalism in the Philippine-American War (1899–1902) followed out the foreign policy the US applied in the Caribbean, especially to its current protectorate, Puerto Rico, and troublesome Cuba. The relationship between the US and Spain in the Spanish-American War cannot be understood adequately without also examining the US relationship to Cuban and Puerto Rican nationalisms. As scholars from Sundquist to Brickhouse have explained, the revolutionary ferment of Cuban nationalists in the nineteenth century is complexly entangled with different US political and economic interests, including pro-slavery interests in controlling Cuba as a source of slaves after the banning of the transatlantic slave trade in 1808.[42]

The 'border thinking' required to understand the historical development of these Creole nationalisms in contestation with each other must involve recognition of the forgotten populations on these islands. In Cuba and Puerto Rico, we cannot speak any longer in the ninth century of 'indigenous' peoples – although Puerto Rican activists still refer to themselves as 'Borricuans' in reference to the first inhabitants – because those indigenous populations were murdered by European imperialists. But in Cuba, Afro-Cubans and descendants of maroon communities must also be identified as the 'forgotten' populations who historically demonstrate a repertoire of means to resist and evade imperial extinction and national incorporation. Once we think of the intersection among the different peoples and communities marginalized by European and then nationalist imperialisms, we begin to recognize how 'border thinking' leads to the several versions of 'mondialization' Mignolo invokes in his recent work. Non-European populations in the Western Hemisphere brought with them and elaborated differently over time and in specific sites their African, Asian, Oceanic, and Amerindian heritages, including non-European languages and religions and cultural practices. Sometimes these non-European influences were hybridized with Euroamerican cultures, but there are many instances of 'maroon' styles, forms, and practices surviving as resistant discursive practices that powerfully mark the horizon of the Euroamerican imaginary.

The troublesome linguistic divisions of the Hemisphere seem to confirm the strict divisions of the Anglo North, the Spanish Southwest, and the Portuguese Southeast, with epiphenomenal traces of linguistic imperialism scattered here and there, especially in the polyglot Caribbean from Dutch Aruba through French Martinique. Yet when we take these linguistic divisions in the historical, cultural, and geographic contexts of the entire Hemisphere, we must recognize that we are following the tracks of European and Creole nationalist imperialisms, ignoring the massive destruction of Amerindian languages and their related cultures as well as the suppression of non-European languages occasioned by slavery's systematic detribalization and its customary ban on literary and other formal education for slaves.

Werner Sollors' and Marc Shell's wonderful *Multilingual Anthology of American Literature* (2000) gives us barely a hint of what a genuinely multilingual account of Canada and the Americas would be like, if we were to overcome what Mignolo terms the systematic imperial 'denial of coevalness' between European and Amerindian semiotics.[43] Colonial semiosis depended crucially upon the destruction of the Amerindian archive of knowledge and the repression of that history, just as slavery depends on the systematic denial of African retentions, including languages, religions, and cultural practices. A similar colonial semiosis is structurally integral to Creole nationalisms, as even the casual tourist cannot help but notice in the plethora of signs that testify to various nations' presumed 'rootedness' in their Amerindian histories, even as their policies toward indigenous peoples have been consistently genocidal. What would happen if we were to attempt 'border thinking' that, instead of adding Amerindian and diasporic semiotics to the variety of European-based languages, would challenge the 'commonality of the difference' in those imported languages and their epistemological protocols? In short, the traditional problem of different languages dividing the 'areas' of the Western Hemisphere turns out to be even more complicated when we factor in the numerous languages (and semiotic systems) occluded by this apparent diversity of the imperial legacy.

The neglect both by area studies and by American Studies, new or old, suggests how we might approach 'Hemispheric Studies' from beyond the shadow cast by European power/knowledge. Mignolo's emphasis on colonial semiosis at times ignores the biological transit of imperialism and the literal destruction not merely of the texts of pre-Columbian peoples but of their *bodies* and biochemistries. Charles Mann's *1491: New Revelations of the Americas before Columbus* (2005) summarizes the new scientific evidence of the impact of European diseases on indigenous peoples throughout the Hemisphere.[44] Infectious diseases like smallpox, influenza, and measles had dramatic impacts on Amerindian populations between 1500 and 1900, and for many Europeans appeared to support claims to the superiority of European civilization, even when crudely calculated according to a Social Darwinist standard of survival of the fittest. Area studies following the ideology of modernization and development would in many ways reinforce just such an ideology, often manifested in the 'conflictive encounters between Old World Europeans and pre-Columbian peoples of the Andes, Mesoamerican, and the Caribbean' in terms of a 'dialectic of the filthy and the clean, the fetid and the fresh', even the healthy and the sick.[45] Indeed, the prevalence of public health programs and policies in the rhetoric of modernization and development is just one example of how this binary continues to do imperialist work, even with the most benevolent and humanitarian purposes.

We now know that the immunities European acquired over the centuries against the infectious diseases they spread with such devastating consequences in the Western Hemisphere had much to do with the domestication of livestock they had learned from Middle Eastern agricultural practices they had followed and were thus hardly inherent to Europeans.⁴⁶ And the inoculation practices Europeans would adopt experimentally and unevenly in the eighteenth century were adapted from practices employed in China as early as 1100 to prevent the spread of smallpox. Add to all of this that the genetic differences between Amerindians and Europeans do not signal the superiority of one biology over the other, but are simply human differences whose contact produced extraordinarily negative results for one group. Western modernization and development take on rather different ethical meanings when we are forced to conclude that in the case of the Western Hemisphere, such progress required the deaths of anywhere from 40 to 60 million Amerinidian people between 1500 and 1900.

Border thinking should deconstruct the differences between European imperial powers and Creole national powers, amongst them European languages, and other manifest differences, such as those between the supposedly Catholic South and Protestant North. This should be done not only to expose the shared history of the modern/colonial world system, worked out systematically for the first time in the Western Hemisphere, but also to represent the histories and contemporary retentions of societies and communities that were overshadowed by the more imposing authority of their imperial masters. Adapting W.E.B. Du Bois's model of 'double consciousness' to the study of the Western Hemisphere and drawing thus explicitly from minority discourses, Mignolo suggests that such a comparative approach to the Western Hemisphere might open us to a broader worldly thinking he projects doubly as 'the future planetary epistemological and critical localism.'⁴⁷

I am not certain what Mignolo means by a 'border gnosis' that would allow us to think differentially across the divides of those geopolitical, imperial, and semiotic borders that have been imposed upon us as scholars, as citizens, and as humans. What I do know is that Mignolo's challenging methodology enables us to achieve the sort of double-consciousness the new and postnationalist American Studies should welcome. With one consciousness, it enables us to understand the 'conflicting homogeneous entities (Latin America, France, the United States, etc.) as… part of the imaginary of the modern/colonial world system'.⁴⁸ With another consciousness, we can understand that to 'think [of] "Latin America" otherwise, in its heterogeneity rather than in its homogeneity, in the local histories of changing global designs is not to question a particular form of identification (e.g., that of "Latin America") but all national/colonial forms of identification in the modern/colonial world system.'⁴⁹ Mignolo's project, ostensibly the deconstruction of Latin American area studies, applies as well to North American Studies and American Studies as we know it in its modern and postmodern versions.[50]

The conflict between area studies and the new American Studies impedes the development of a comparative study of the many different communities in the Western Hemisphere, but Mignolo's 'modern/colonial world system' is not restricted to this region. In the aftermath of 9/11, the ongoing US occupation of Iraq, its central role in the war in Afghanistan, foreign policies that contribute significantly to the imperial subjugation of the Palestinian people, and growing Arabic immigrant communities in the US, 'the Middle East' is a crucial field in the new American Studies. Yet the field itself is already defined by the area studies model I have traced back to the politically motivated work of the Ethnogeographic Board of the 1940s. Edward Said's criticism of nineteenth-century Western Orientalism needs to be updated to take into account more recent developments, and in that work the US role in restructuring what George W. Bush termed 'the Greater Middle East' needs to be challenged in relationship to US academic models for studying the Middle East, global Islamic communities, Arabic cultures, and specific immigrant groups from these regions and communities, now living outside their ancestral homelands as a consequence of diaspora or choice.

Paul Gilroy's *Black Atlantic: Modernity and Double Consciousness* fundamentally challenged the definitions of Caribbean, African American, and black British communities in area studies, directing us both literally and figuratively to the 'Atlantic world' in which transnational flows of people, goods, and cultures moved incessantly and diversely.[51] Green (Irish), Red (Communist), and still other 'Atlantics' have followed and broadened what we today understand as this oceanic complexity beyond the presumed stabilities of geopolitical states.[52] We need similarly flexible, transnational conceptions in the new American Studies that will work cooperatively with critical area studies of Latin America and the Middle East to respect the diverse communities we find in these regions and to provide the critical terms for challenging their marginalization, even exclusion, by more powerful nation states.

In reconceptualizing the global scope that American Studies must undertake to respond to US neoimperialism, we must remain vigilant regarding the specific ways knowledge and power have been coordinated historically. We would be naïve to think that the production and circulation of knowledge in the late-modern research university can remain separate from the economic, political, and social interests of the states and industries that fund such work. Whether public or private, the research university still functions as a representation of the nation in which it is permitted to exist, but such universities are also today pulled in a number of competitive directions by different state and corporate interests. We are already witnessing the globalization of the student, faculty, and research components of these educational institutions, and we must find the intellectual means to assure that such globalization works dialectically, offering those peoples who are rendered stateless and culture-less and who are otherwise economically and politically disempowered the means of the 'decolonizing mind'.[53]

Notes

1. Wallerstein, Immanuel; Juma, Calestous; Keller, Evelyn Fox; Kocka, Jürgen; Lecourt, Dominique; Mudimbe, V.Y.; Mushakoji; Prigogine, Ilya; Taylor, Peter J.; Trouillot, Michel-Rolph, *Open the Social Sciences*. Report of the Gulbenkian Commission on Restructuring of the Social Sciences (Stanford, Ca.: Stanford University Press, 1996), 44–5.
2. John Carlos Rowe, *The New American Studies* (Minneapolis: University of Minnesota Press, 2002), xiii–xviii.
3. Alan Wolfe, 'Anti-American Studies: The Difference between Criticism and Hate,' *New Republic* (10 February 2003), 25–32.
4. Richard P. Horwitz, *Exporting America: Essays on American Studies Abroad* (Greenwood, Conn.: Garland Press, 1993), 1–15.
5. Herbert Marcuse, *One-Dimensional Man: Studies in the Ideology of Advanced Industrial Society* (Boston: Beacon Press, 1964), 13–17.
6. Martin W. Lewis and Kären Wigen, 'A Maritime Response to the Crisis in Area Studies,' *The Geographical Review*, Vol. 89, No. 2 (April 1999), 162.
7. Walter D. Mignolo, *Local Histories/Global Designs: Coloniality, Subaltern Knowledges, and Border Thinking* (Princeton: Princeton University Press, 2000), 278–80.
8. Lewis and Wigen, *op. cit.*, 163.
9. *Ibid.*
10. Walt Whitman, *Democratic Vista*, in *Leaves of Grass*, eds., Sculley Bradley, Harold W. Blodgett and Michael Moon, Norton Critical Edition (New York: W.W. Norton and Col, 2004), represents most of the nineteenth-century US national myths regarding gender divisions (especially maternity and the 'separate spheres' ideology), Anglo-Saxon superiority, the 'western' (and tacitly 'southern') march of European civilization. Whitman's prose, a complement to his poetic corpus, suggests how nineteenth-century US literary culture (and the subsequent twentieth-century scholarly establishment that canonized it) helped shape the 'exceptional areas' of 'American' and 'European' Studies as disciplinary tools of imperialism's 'civilizing mission.'
11. Lewis and Wigen, *op. cit.*, 163.
12. Carl E. Guthe, 'The Ethnogeographic Board,' *The Scientific Monthly*, Vol. 57, No. 2 (August 1943), 188.
13. *Ibid.*, 189.

14 Lewis and Wigen, *op. cit.*, 163.
15 Guthe, *op. cit.*, 189.
16 Lewis and Wigen, *op. cit.*, 163.
17 *Ibid.* Board membership also included scholars who held positions on two relevant private foundations, Mortimer Graves, the Sinologist who was also Secretary of the American Council of Learned Societies (ACLS), and Wilbur A. Sawyer, a specialist on the treatment of malaria, who was Director (1935–1944) of the Rockefeller Foundation's International Health Division (IHD), and one governmental agency, the National School of Modern Oriental Languages and Civilizations, also chaired by Mortimer Graves. The Board in 1943 consisted of: William Duncan Strong (Director), an anthropologist; Carl E. Guthe (chair), an anthropologist from the University of Michigan; Wendell C. Bennett, an archaeologist; Carter Goodrich, a historian; John E. Graf, an anthropologist (perhaps with the National Anthropological Archive and/or Smithsonian?); Mortimer Graves, a Sinologist, who was also Secretary of the ACLS and Chair of the National School of Modern Oriental Languages and Civilizations; Robert B. Hall, a geographer; Wilbur A. Sawyer, a specialist on Yellow Fever, especially its treatment in Latin America, who directed (1935–1944) the Rockefeller Foundation's International Health Division; Douglas M. Whitaker, a biologist.
18 'William Duncan Strong,' *Wikipedia*.
19 Guthe, *op. cit.*, 189.
20 Carter Goodrich was a member of the faculty at the Wharton School of the University of Pennsylvania. Trained as an economic historian, he specialized in modernization and development, and was on the faculty of the 'Industrial School' at Wharton.
21 Lewis and Wigen, *op. cit.*, 163–4.
22 *Ibid.*, 163. The original Board (1942) seems to have no representation from sociology or political science, and only Goodrich suggests an explicit connection with economics. Isaiah Bowman, the geographer to whom Lewis and Wigen refer, was not a member of the original Board and must have been a later addition.
23 *Ibid.*, 164.
24 Donald Pease, 'Moby-Dick and the Cold War,' *The American Renaissance Reconsidered*, eds., Walter Benn Michaels and Donald E. Pease (Baltimore: The Johns Hopkins University, 1985), 113–55. Pease specifically traces the Cold-War interpretation of *Moby-Dick* back to Matthiessen, as in Pease's conclusion: 'Ever since Matthiessen's reading of [*Moby-Dick*] as a sign of the power of the freedom of figures in the American Renaissance to oppose totalitarianism, *Moby-Dick* has been a Cold War text, one that secures in Ishmael's survival a sign of the free world's triumph over a totalitarian power' (153).
25 Lewis and Wigen, *op. cit.*, 164.
26 Wallerstein et al., *op. cit.*, 64–5.
27 *Ibid.*, 65.
28 Martin Lewis and Kären Wigen, the cultural geographers on whom I have relied earlier in this essay, direct the 'Oceans Connect' initiative at Duke, which redefines area studies in terms of maritime connections. As they themselves acknowledge, one of the weaknesses of this new area studies

model is that it privileges older sites of transport, immigration, and commerce without taking sufficiently into account such new sites, such as 'Internet sites and airports' (Lewis and Wigen, *op. cit.*, 168). Even in the historical contexts in which oceans were the defining contact-zones or 'flows', the maritime model ends up proliferating ever-more complicated 'areas' – the Black Atlantic is now complemented by the Green Atlantic, the Red Atlantic, the North Atlantic (which also includes Black, Green, and Red variants) – that suggest the inherent problem with 'area' as a structural, geographical, or conceptual unit.
29 Mignolo, *Local Histories, op. cit.*, 130.
30 Technically, of course, Emerson, Hawthorne, and Whitman are not 'Creoles', because they are born after US independence from England, whereas Benjamin Franklin, John Adams, Thomas Jefferson et al. do qualify as 'Creoles'.
31 *Ibid.*
32 Bolívar's famous 'The Jamaica Letter: Response from a Southern American to a Gentleman from This Island' (September 6, 1815), in *El Libertador: Writings of Simón Bolívar*, trans. Frederick H. Fornoff, ed., David Bushnell (New York: Oxford University Press, 2003), p. 13, renews the revolutionary project against Spain in part by indicting the Spanish as a 'wicked stepmother', in part by transferring the 'atrocities' and 'perversities' of Spain against Amerindians to the 'slaves' he claims Spain wishes to make the Creole rebels. José Martí's 'The Indians in the United States' (1885), in *Selected Writings*, ed. and trans., Esther Allen (New York: Penguin Books, 2002), 157–64, reports on the Mohonk Conferences begun in 1883 and out of which came the passage of the hated Dawes General Allotment Act of 1887. Martí's conclusion, albeit written two years before the passage of the Dawes Act, is perfectly in keeping with the Dawes Act's goals of 'allotment and assimilation' of Native American lands and peoples to the US nation.
33 Mignolo, *Local Histories, op. cit.*, 134–5.
34 Alejo Carpentier, *The Lost Steps*, trans. Harriet de Onís (New York: Farrar, Straus and Giroux, 1956).
35 Félix Varela, *Jicoténcal*, eds., Luis Leal y Rodolfo and J. Cortina (Houston: Arte Publico Press, 1995). Leal and Cortina make the case for Varela's authorship of the novel in the 'Introducción', pp. vii–xlvii. Authorship of the novel remains disputed, as Guillermo I. Castillo-Feliú points out in his 'Introduction' to the English language translation of the novel, *Xicoténcatl: An Anonymous Historical Novel about the Events Leading up to the Conquest of the Aztec Empire*, trans. Guillermo I. Castillo-Feliú (Austin: University of Texas Press, 1999), 1–6. In her fascinating account of the transnational significance of this neglected 'American' novel, Anna Brickhouse, *Transamerican Literary Relations and the Nineteenth-Century Public Sphere* (New York: Cambridge University Press, 2004), 37–83, stresses the 'Pan-American' and 'anti-imperialist' features of the novel, but she does not read the allegory of nineteenth-century nationalism as an ideologically loaded way of 'using' Amerindians for nationalist purposes.
36 Mignolo, *Local Histories, op. cit.*, 139.
37 Gustavo Pérez Firmat, ed., *Do the Americas Have a Common Literature?* (Durham, N.C.: Duke University Press, 1990); Marshall C. Eakin, 'Does Latin America Have a Common History?'.

38 Mignolo, *Local Histories, op. cit.*, 136.
39 Shelley Streeby, *American Sensations: Class, Empire, and the Production of Popular Culture* (Berkeley: University of California Press, 2002).
40 Mignolo, *Local Histories, op. cit.*, 136.
41 John Carlos Rowe, *Literary Culture and U.S. Imperialism: From the Revolution to World War II* (New York: Oxford University Press, 2000), 174–5.
42 Spain did not sign the international agreement until 1817, and even after that date Cuba continued to be a source of illegal shipments of slaves from Africa. Cirilo Villaverde's Cuban nationalist novel, *Cecilia Valdés or El Angel Hill: A Novel of Nineteenth-Century Cuba* (1882), trans., Helen Lane, ed., Sibylle Fischer (New York: Oxford University Press, 2005), builds its plot around illegal slave shipments to Cuba, US planters living in Cuba, and the generally entangled political and economic fortunes of nineteenth-century US and Cuba.
43 Marc Shell and Werner Sollors, *The Multilingual Anthology of American Literature: A Reader of Original Texts with English Translations* (New York: New York University Press, 2000), which includes only four Native American selections out of the twenty-nine in the anthology; Walter Mignolo, *The Darker Side of the Renaissance: Literacy, Territoriality, and Colonization*, 2nd ed. (Ann Arbor: The University of Michigan Press, 2003), 136–60.
44 Charles C. Mann, *1491: New Revelations of the Americas before Columbus* (New York: Vintage Books, 2006).
45. Mignolo, *Local Histories, op. cit.*, 153.
46 Jared Diamond, *Guns, Germs, and Steel: The Fates of Human Societies* (New York: W.W. Norton, 1997).
47 Mignolo, *Local Histories, op. cit.*, 157.
48 *Ibid.*, 170.
49 *Ibid.*, 170–1.
50 'North American Studies' developed in post-World War II European universities, especially in Germany, as part of the 'area studies' model, as has 'European Studies' been formulated more recently in Europe and the US 'North American Studies' clearly displays in most instances the Cold-War 'area studies' model, whereas 'European Studies' seems to have emerged specifically in reaction to the limitations of such an area studies model while still preserving its basic terms. A thorough consideration of these two 'area studies' categories would require a more developed and independent argument.
51 Paul Gilroy, *The Black Atlantic: Modernity and Double Consciousness* (Cambridge: Harvard University Press, 1993), 4.
52 David Lloyd and Peter D. O'Neill, eds., *The Black and Green Atlantic: Crosscurrents of the African and Irish Diasporas* (Basingstoke: Palgrave Macmillan, 2009).
53 Ngũgi wa Thiong'o, *Decolonising the Mind: The Politics of Language in African Literature* (New York: New York University Press, 1986).

9
Libertas or *Fri*? On US Liberty, Decline, Freedom and Pluralism

David Ryan

> *Most revolutionaries believe, covertly or overtly, that in order to create the ideal world eggs must be broken, otherwise one cannot obtain the omelette. Eggs are certainly broken – never more violently or ubiquitously than in our times – but the omelette is far to seek, it recedes into an infinite distance. That is one of the corollaries of unbridled monism, as I call it – some call it fanaticism, but monism is at the root of every extremism.*
>
> Isaiah Berlin[1]

> *The end of empire is always present.*
>
> Charles S. Maier[2]

I

A few years into the latest US war in Iraq, Jürgen Habermas concluded that 'the normative authority of the United States of America lies in ruins'.[3] This war had taken the United States to the region in which so many other empires had contended; however, it was not that it was this particular region *per se* but the fact that the war in Iraq and especially the insurgencies faced there represented and became the symbol of imperial overstretch that simultaneously demonstrated how Washington could not easily contest the 'unpredictable outcomes' and the 'unwelcome results' that came from an attempt to control the waves through unilaterally defined objectives.

Michael Hunt suggests, 'Perhaps most challenging of all, thinking about decline involves accepting the importance of that insubstantial thing called legitimacy.'[4] In its war in Iraq and the preparatory documents that heralded its style of intervention, the Bush administration seriously eroded the goodwill often accorded the United States and undermined its position amongst the so-called 'community of nations'. Its unilateral actions and its inclinations to act alone or at least to lead alone alienated widespread opinion throughout the world, not least amongst its traditional allies. This particular inclination to avoid more multilateral, cooperative arrangements in the responses to 9/11 accelerated US decline.

Following periods of US difficulty in recent decades its leaders, seeking to avert isolation, opprobrium and further decline have looked to slow the pace through multilateral cooperation, burden sharing, and a distribution of the costs of foreign policy in terms of lives, resources and expenditure. It is also evident that the recurrent narratives of decline invite reactions within the United States by strategists who refuse to recognize the limits of US power and who stress the need for further US leadership and assertive policies on intervention; yet such unilateral engagement not only increases the costs of intervention to the United States, it also exacerbates the domestic fallout on how to meet the costs. The quest to maintain international legitimacy becomes even more fraught with tension.[5]

That the United States entered the period of *relative* decline in the late 1950s became even more obvious during the 1970s; the innovative technological bubble of the 1990s was dragged through the dollar-sapping war in Iraq and burst on the early recession of the twenty-first century.[6] US political decline accelerated as it resisted the centrifugal forces of the 1960s and the energy of decolonization and postcolonial forces and discourses. Its ideological force, still an incredibly attractive *concept*, nevertheless underwent severe testing across the Bush years. Anti-Americanism and anti-Americanization were frequently discussed and obvious. Early in those years, Emmanuel Wallerstein argued 'The eagle has crash landed.' Pax Americana was over: ultimately the United States found itself in a situation as 'a lone superpower that lacks true power, a world leader nobody follows and few respect, and a nation drifting dangerously amidst a global chaos it cannot control'.[7] Nevertheless, the Bush administration attempted to assert control in Iraq and Afghanistan; the projects failed, with extensive loss of life, extravagant expense, and strategic dislocation.

When Barack Obama entered the White House in 2009, he spoke of the 'tempering qualities of humility and restraint'[8] – he might also have spoken of the tempering quality of *necessity*. Observing his Inaugural, Timothy Garton Ash noted the 'melancholy defiance' of Obama's cry that 'we remain the most prosperous, powerful nation on earth'. The elegiac atmosphere of empire, captured so effectively in the work of Charles Maier's *Among Empires* attended the US celebrations of its new president. While Obama, a symbol of the 'American dream', its contemporary apotheosis, enacted fulfilment within the domestic sphere, the global political and economic trends were moving in other directions, and US influence needed to be calibrated to the new structures of power[9] evident by 2009. Even if Obama was ready to lead and ready to temper US power to ensure its attraction and endurance, others from allies to opponents had concluded, after eight years of Bush and of Iraq and of Afghanistan, that they were not prepared to follow. Garton Ash noted the restrained welcome Obama received from European leaders intent on amplifying their voices,[10] intent on tempering US power through multilateral engagement.

II

Isaiah Berlin, 'the explorer' in the history of ideas, wrote two essays on liberty in the late 1950s which were widely interpreted as a reading of Cold War ideologies.[11] Though initially repudiated by the Bush Sr. administration in 1992, the Defense Planning Guidance (DPG) document might have shocked Berlin in its scope and ambition. The document contained an ambition to achieve 'strategic depth'; it sought to 'discourage' advanced industrial nations 'from challenging our leadership or seeking to overturn the established political and economic order'. Competitors should be deterred 'from even aspiring to a larger regional or global role'.[12]

This vision of a unilateral American power, unimpeded even by its allies, had its roots in some of the writings of members of Ronald Reagan's National Security Council, as they pondered the dislocated power and position of the United States after the Vietnam War.[13] They both worried about renewed Soviet adventurism in the Third World and aspired to restore US pride and leadership. Much of that aspiration found its way into George W. Bush's National Security Strategy of 2002. The ambitions were articulated though the implementation was thwarted first in the 'field' and then 'at home'. The effects were devastating as disparate opponents pursuing a variety of ends,[14] checked US power and the more cautious and *realist* strategists within the United States reasserted their authority to stem the squandering of US power and prestige. Despite the long association of US thought with pragmatism, an ideological bent to lead and shape the world had frequently vitiated US policy, power and strategic position.

III

Berlin argued that subjection to a 'single ideology, no matter how reasonable and imaginative, robs men of freedom and vitality'. For the philosopher 'the richest development of human potentialities can occur only in societies in which there is a wide spectrum of opinions – the freedom for what J.S. Mill called "experiments in living" – in which there is liberty of thought and of expression, views and opinions clash with each other, societies in which friction and even conflict are permitted'.[15] Such pluralism and multilateralism have not consistently characterized US foreign policy. When it does, most famously in the form of the Marshall Plan, it produced a form of 'consensual hegemony'; outcomes and conditions into which most could buy. Yet the inclination toward the unilateral form not only exacerbated the US problem with decline but also undermined the pluralism associated with a more multipolar and multilateral world order.

The tensions between liberty and freedom have perpetually vitiated US foreign policy, yet they are commonly used interchangeably.[16] *Liberty*, according to David Hackett Fischer, derives from the Latin *libertas* meaning unbound, unrestricted or released from restraint. These words were related to other Greek words *eleutheria* and *eleutheros* 'which also meant the condition of being independent, separate, and distinct'. They described independent cities, those not 'ruled by another's will'. Liberty implied a form of 'separation and independence'. *Freedom* derived from the Norse, *fri* or the German *frei*. In the English the roots went back to the word *friend* – they held connotations of belonging and 'ties of kinship'. Fischer suggests, 'In that respect, the original meanings of freedom and liberty were not merely different but opposed. Liberty meant separation. Freedom implied connection.'[17]

Anders Stephanson makes the useful distinction between the 'empire *of* liberty' and the 'empire *for* liberty'.[18] Though he uses the same word, liberty, his intention was to draw a distinction between a more pluralistic world order and one dominated by US power. The latter formulation resonates through the 1992 Defense Planning Guidance and the 2002 National Security Strategy, it suggests an empire designed around US precepts, patterns and power, rather than the empire *of* liberty that might be associated with the creation and extension of conditions of pluralism (and an equality of freedom and the respect of the opinion of others, especially on matters of leadership).

While the United States has harkened after its nostalgic vision of liberty, independence, and leadership, since the inception of its relative decline from the late 1950s – accelerated through the 1960s and self-evident in the 1970s – it became important in the international arena to concentrate on and build on notions of *freedom*, friendship, alliances, and cooperative arrangements. The strategies of managing and, to the extent possible, averting decline or at least bringing about the conditions that make it most palatable have suggested engagement and integration: politically, economically, and culturally. Yet such constraints chafed against the yearning for *liberty* amongst strategists who longed to reach their nostalgic mirage of the United States on the horizon. The apotheosis of this vision occurred in the Bush years after 9/11.

Wolfgang Schivelbusch in his study of the *Culture of Defeat* wonders if the post-9/11 fever was really a response to the earlier, unresolved defeat in Vietnam. More disturbing is another one of his conclusions: 'The Bush doctrine of preventative military strikes eerily resembles the anti-Communist domino theory, that earlier expression of the horror of falling. Could it be that the decades of relative American peacefulness and readiness to cooperate that followed the defeat in Vietnam were merely an interim period, akin to the Weimar Republic, with its pleasant illusion of a pacified Germany?'[19] But it is important to note that the Bush doctrine did not emerge out of 9/11 alone; it had roots in the strategic dreams of the DPG and in the early Reagan years.[20]

The etymological tensions between these words rarely or explicitly rear their heads in the US culture in which they have appeared and constantly been reconstructed as a homogenous set of conditions, positing the United States as both the guarantor of certain negative liberties and simultaneously a power that is 'bound to lead' as, in Madeline Albright's words the 'indispensable nation'.[21] In its foreign policies these inclinations and temptations have to be juxtaposed with other narratives on US identity that characterize the country as one that has promoted by way of example or through more strenuous interventions: human rights – the Declaration's 'inalienable rights' – self-determination, decolonization, national independence, a force of political fragmentation, and the champion of pluralism. Yet in turn those identities need to be juggled with simultaneous processes of political and economic integration. The Rio and NATO alliances created in 1947 and 1949 which constrained US *liberty* to varying degrees, and the processes of transnational economic integration to the phenomenon of globalization have provided opportunities for *liberty* and *freedom*.[22] US identity and the exercise of its foreign policy have been confused by these competing tensions.

IV

The strategy for 'preponderance' advanced by the Truman administration[23] was prefaced by a cultural turn that implored Americans to increasingly look outward and abroad. That turn, that 'second chance',[24] was a tentative cultural rejection of John Quincy Adams' 1821 injunction to wish well to others and to venture not to go abroad to engage and slay the Other. Monsters, of course, were central to the efficacy of the internationalist cultural turn.[25] Hitler loomed large in the injunction of the owner of *Time* and *Life* magazines, Henry R. Luce of 'The American Century'. Franklin Roosevelt had failed to make democracy work within the national framework; the frontiers had been closed for some time so, for Luce, 'Our only chance now to make it work is in terms of a vital international economy and in terms of an international moral order.' The pressing question centred upon what terms the US should engage others. Luce asserted that Americans should 'accept wholeheartedly our duty and our opportunity as the most powerful and vital nation in the world and in consequence to exert upon the world the full impact of our influence, for such purposes as we see fit and by such means as we see fit.' He emphatically rejected the idea that the United States had to impose democratic institutions on all, including the 'Dalai Lama and the good shepherds of Tibet'; it did not have to be responsible for good behaviour throughout the world, but it did need to 'grasp the relationship between America and America's environment'. The US had missed the opportunity in 1919, to 'assume the leadership of the world': 'Wilson mishandled it. We rejected it. The opportunity persisted. We bungled it in the 1920's and in the confusions of the 1930's we killed it.'

Thus far then the American century was one filled with suffering and misery. Luce advanced four propositions: first, the two billion odd peoples of the world existed in an era of world history that was 'fundamentally indivisible'. Second, most people hated war and recognized its potential destructiveness. Third, the world was capable, in material terms, of producing the 'needs of the entire human family'. Fourth, if the twentieth century 'is to come to life in any nobility of health and vigor, it must be to a significant degree an American Century', a belief that Luce considered was shared 'by most men living'.

Luce's was to maintain and advance the fidelity to American ideals. He did not examine the cultural constructions of these ideals – the love of freedom, equality of opportunity, self-reliance, independence and cooperation – for they were an ideological given. The United States had a new destiny, a 'manifest duty' to assume the role of the 'Good Samaritan', 'to undertake to feed all the people of the world', 'really believing again that it is more blessed to give than to receive'.[26] Hunt notes that when Luce wrote to his countrymen, 'he did so as a therapist disturbed by national malaise'. Redemption was necessary to emerge from the emotional slough. National assertion and 'struggle would bring peace to the troubled heart'.[27]

Despite such fantasies of goodwill, US strategy relied, especially in Western Europe, Japan and other vital centres, on the creation of the politics of prosperity to dampen the appeals of more radical agendas that sought redistribution of material goods through other political formulae. In Europe the intention was to dampen the appeal of the left. In Asia, George Kennan advocated maintenance of the positions of the disparity of wealth.[28] Still, the cultural narrative associated with liberal internationalism, albeit tempered by Eisenhower's New Look, post-Korean War adjustments, and recognition of the wider parameters of security which involved the health of the US economy and the condition and standards of its health and education systems, largely advanced through the 1960s.

The divergent meanings of freedom and liberty, a tendency to recognize and practice a recognition of pluralism in foreign policy or to engage in the pursuit of empire and imposition of US ideals and/or power played themselves out in part in the swing and sway between the popular characterizations of realism, idealism, and neoconservatism in US policy over the subsequent decades. There is perhaps no irony that the narratives of decline return in cyclical form after periods of outreach and extension by presidents who fail to recognize the limits of US power. Kissinger articulated the changed circumstances and altered US position in the world at the end of the 1960s; he largely saw his own diplomatic craft as an attempt to reverse that decline.[29]

Of course this era was intimately related to the major cultural turn, the advent of postmodernity (the ideological disposition born out of defeat),[30] and the post-heroic age. The rightward turn across the 1980s sought to reverse such cultural relativism and associated sentiments.[31] Then President George H.W. Bush's realism posited an antidote to Reagan's early exceptionalism and the declinist narrative advanced by Paul Kennedy's *Rise and Fall of Great Powers* that captured attention in the waning days of the Reagan years. Obama's 'realism', prefaced by Robert Gates' tenure as Secretary of Defense in the later years of the George W. Bush presidency, injected the antidote to the neoconservative mirage of US power and supremacy. There was always a tempering adjustment.

For Walden Bello the moments of triumph 'also exhibit its vulnerabilities. The shadow of defeat accompanies every victory.' A few days after George W. Bush landed on the deck of the USS *Abraham Lincoln* in May 2003, Bello wrote, 'This point may sound surreal after the massive firepower we witnessed... [but] there is good reason to think that [the United States] is overextended. In fact, the main strategic result of the occupation of Iraq is to worsen this condition of overextension. Washington's goal is to achieve overwhelming military dominance over any rival or coalition of rivals. This quest for even greater global dominance, however, inevitably generates opposition, and it is in this resistance that we see the roots of overextension.'[32] The question is whether the dilemmas of domination are adjusted by recourse to more limited visions of US foreign policy implemented by the presidencies associated with the exercise of realism. The second question is whether the periods of *liberty* in US foreign policy are tempered by periods of *freedom* and a greater regard for pluralism and a deeper engagement in multilateral discussion and strategies *with* US allies.

V

After the US mounted its 'catastrophic victory' in Iraq, it entered a phase of prolonged counterinsurgency that Fareed Zakaria compared to the British war with the Boers, the 'long, arduous struggle, filled with political and military blunders and met with intense international opposition' provided opportunities and openings for US opponents from Iran to Venezuela, from China to Russia. Despite the still unknown outcome, the costs in Iraq '... have been massive. The United States has been overextended and distracted, its army stressed, its image sullied.'[33]

When Barack Obama came to power there were great expectations. Yet *Foreign Policy* caught an emerging frustration in its cover story as it juxtaposed the slogan of Obama's campaign: 'Yes, He Did But What If He Can't?'[34] The author of that article, a former speech writer for Condoleezza Rice, tried to attribute the realist adjustments to the late Bush years, suggesting Obama was likely to follow the trend.[35] Yet Obama was also constrained by far more direct circumstances. One year into his presidency he moved to wind down US engagement in Iraq providing tentative dates and conditions for withdrawal; though he simultaneously escalated the war in Afghanistan after agonizing reappraisal. Obama's announcement of an additional 30,000 troops for Afghanistan was coupled by a new limitation on the exercise of US power and the deployment of its troops that in part echoed experiences and strategies of both the Nixon and Reagan years. This time the limited deployment did not relate so directly to the impact of the Vietnam syndrome so much as to the US inability to stay the course for financial reasons. Obama clearly indicated that the surge would have to be short and that US troops would be brought home by 2011. The President reiterated an old message to the cadets at West Point: 'Our prosperity provides a foundation for our power. It pays for our military. It underwrites our diplomacy....' Even in the so-called 'war of necessity', although counterinsurgency experts repeatedly stressed the *long-term* nature of winning hearts and minds, Obama was in a hurry because 'our troop commitment in Afghanistan cannot be open-ended, because the nation that I'm most interested in building is our own'.[36] The United States was now a nation that needed rebuilding; gone were the assumptions of its exceptional condition. Gone was the ability to pay for and sustain the legitimacy of a war that increasingly looked like it could not be won.

The limitation resulted from a direct application of the numbers coming out of the budget predictions. The projected deficit for 2010 was nearly 11 percent of the country's entire economic output. Such deficits were features of the Civil War and the two World Wars. After those wars there was a return to some form of normalcy. Yet Obama's projections suggest that the United States will not return to 'sustainable levels over the next 10 years'. In fact they predict further rises after that period. There is little room for domestic initiatives let alone foreign policy adventures. Obama's desire to revive the liberalism of the 1940s to 1960s can only be paid for, if at all, by implementation of a old-style conservatism in foreign policy.[37]

Whereas Lyndon B. Johnson surmised that unless he prevailed in Vietnam his credibility at home would crumble, Obama must be seen and is inclined to do what he can in Afghanistan, but simultaneously he has to retract from Iraq and engage others on a more limited, realistic plane in pursuit of the US national interest. The nativist message of the post-Vietnam neoconservatives on the necessity of US primacy and the creation of a world dominated by their vision and leadership, that appeal to "America first" [did not] always leave America in first place'. The costs of unilateralism, of the US adventure in Iraq and the structure of world order premised on the 2002 National Security Strategy are counterbalanced by the more tempered return to a multilateralism that will ultimately bring about greater strength and prosperity.[38]

VI

In 2007 Michael Cox asked the question: Is the United States in decline – again? In doing so he traced the historiography of the declinist literature and the cyclical return of the questions asked of US power.[39] Indeed in 2010 James Fallows suggested that the recurrent fixation with decline in the United States was in part a call to rejuvenation.[40] For Cox, the United States was a country that represented a 'very special kind of polity preoccupied by status and consumed by inner doubt'.[41] That inner doubt was exacerbated by the Vietnam War, and was clearly identified by Kissinger as a world transformed by the centrifugal forces resulting from the readjustments of power after the 1960s coupled with the transformation of the international system resulting from decolonization. (More generally the entirety of the western-centric narratives of recent world history came under sceptical indictment through the postcolonial and postmodernist discourses.) Kissinger averred, 'Many of the salient characteristics of the present period of international politics spring from the diffusion of independent political activity among and within states following the decline of the cold war, the loosening of cold-war alliances, and the assertion of national and subnational loyalties in the wake of colonial dissolution.'[42]

Yet simultaneously, even as these declinist landscapes are cast across the social canvas, it became imperative to halt and reverse that particular 'sovereignty of collective consciousness' to prevent it from really emerging as the 'principle of unity and explanation'.[43] This particular 'order of things' in human consciousness had to be addressed. Indeed in each epoch of US decline the discursive reaction has also been swift, with renewed calls for reinvigorated US leadership, resolve and determination. But these reactions at the cultural level have also been accompanied by a period of a 'realist' application (or at least explanation) of US policy. The realist applications in turn might well be constructions in themselves, reflecting and legitimating or explaining what the United States is actually capable of doing (and casting it within the narrative of discerning choice).

For instance, President Carter was urged by his National Security Advisor, Zbigniew Brzezinski, to articulate his willingness to use force on occasion to protect US interests or those of its allies. He was advised to emphasize the need to forcefully oppose Soviet aggression and ambition and to 'emphasize less often the notion that we no longer have the capacity to interfere in the affairs of other countries (factually correct but inferentially an admission of weakness)…'.[44] Earlier, Kissinger's 'crisis discourse' centred on the expression of realism, was a convenient vehicle to advance a temporary consensus, yet it was, according to Del Pero, 'wrapped in typical European realpolitik rhetoric. Kissinger's argumentation was filled with slogans, explanations, and operative prescriptions of a peculiar American globalism that other realists – particularly George Kennan – explicitly contested.'[45] Such discourses are also designed to cast an image of the Commander in Chief as one in control, cautious, less ambitious, less adventurous, steady, concerned with the nation and the national interest – a realist; hence, in part, the extended use and reference to Eisenhower deployed by Obama in late 2009, even as he increased US troop numbers in Afghanistan.

The failure to readjust to the centrifugal forces accelerated US decline even as it stretched further in an attempt to control the waves in areas as far-flung as Angola to Central America. Though its commitments there were limited in terms of both troop numbers and financial expenditure, it was in these areas that its credibility was heavily strained (unlike 1980s Afghanistan). That strain deepened the scepticism of the United States amongst its allies. So when the curt, clipped rhetorical injunctions of the Bush administration to 'join us' in the fight against al Qaeda, the Taliban and Saddam Hussein were advanced, few followed.

Moreover, the profligate spending of the early Reagan years and the construction of the 'culture of contentment' accelerated further US decline because such attempts to rejuvenate the spirit of the United States after Vietnam were taken with the placebo of lowered taxes for the wealthy.[46] Reagan's defence expenditure was premised on spending more than security; the defence budget grew from $206 billion in 1980 to $314 billion in 1990. There was little initial resistance, but soon doubts were cast on the 'underlying strategic premises, economic sustainability and military necessity' of the expenditure.[47] Reagan's foreign policy was deeply driven by the internal perception of the administration of their 'loss of... strategic superiority'.[48]

So, just a year before the events of 1989, Paul Kennedy's thesis had such an impact because in the election year in which George H.W. Bush defeated Michael Dukakis, the Democrats desperately needed further intellectual credibility in their campaign, and Kennedy had linked the spending of the Reagan years to the longer cycle of decline that the US was experiencing. Furthermore, the analysis in which Kennedy studied the decline of various powers from the Romans to the British made the US experience seem all the more inevitable.[49]

Samuel Huntington accused Kennedy of not only misrepresentation, but also misinterpretation. Kennedy had singularly failed to understand 'the importance of primacy and the unique role played by the United States in the international system. America... was not merely different from all other great powers.... Far more importantly, it was situated at the apex of a global order, making the rules, punishing transgressors and showing through example what the free world was really about.' Cox suggests that the issue was not just academic; there was no policy option for a United States pullback, given the centrality of its power and leadership after the Second World War.[50]

Yet the form of engagement remained contentious. Amidst the Bush administration's bewildering response to the collapse of the Berlin Wall and ultimately to the collapse of the Soviet Union, Secretary of State James Baker's identification of a world without signposts, the Bush/Scowcroft identification of the world transformed, and the new agenda of the emerging neoconservatives to craft a temporary phenomenon into a permanent condition, buoyed by the sentiment of victory, the unipolar moment would not and could not endure.[51] Despite the collapse of the only extant global force capable of checking US power, it could not endure because ultimately it would confront the opposition to the pursuit of *liberty* by its opponents and its friends.[52]

VII

The US adventure in Iraq in 2003, in part, grew out of the narratives of decline and defeat. They related not just to the frustrations of the 'realist' decisions in 1991, to that sense of unfinished business and the unfulfilled promises of the unipolar illusion; they also related to the longer-term reaction to the psychological outcomes of the Vietnam Wars. The United States had always encountered resistance to its specific interventions throughout the twentieth century, but despite these forms of resistance in locations like Iran and Guatemala, generally the United States enjoyed a form of hegemony (though those two interventions did irreparable damage to its reputation with the development of a form of distant scepticism casting the US within the mould of an imperial power. Louis Halle of the State Department reported that the 'widespread impression' abroad was that the US had become 'hysterical' about communism and was 'losing its head in dealing with it' and that ultimately it was perceived as violating international law. (That perception and loss of legitimacy were echoed during the early years of the war in Iraq.)[53]

The multitude of phenomenal change across the 1960s shattered the hegemonic point of advantage. The postcolonial discourses threw back the meta-narratives at the various metropolitan powers. In many ways the United States escaped the full wrath of these forces despite its association with the European colonial powers; however, various Latin American experiences had evidenced similar double standards, further loosening the tenacity of the US narrative.[54] The Civil Rights and Feminist movements undermined the traditional discourses within the United States. The fragmentation of the Cold War, now characterized by the increasing participation of multiple independent actors and rival centres of power deconstructed the myth of the bipolar world and depictions of monolithic communism (just as there is still the need at the cultural level to deconstruct the various motivations and agency of the various groups, states, actors that Bush liked to simply term 'the enemy'). The Vietnam Wars undermined US hegemony, its traditional identity, its cultural appeal, its relative power, and its ability to convincingly request others to 'join us'. Pointless intervention and wars of choice frequently invoked such responses. Reagan's hyperbolic rhetoric on Nicaragua in the early 1980s and George W. Bush's constructions from 'the terrorists and the tyrants' to the 'axis of evil' enhanced scepticism of US intentions.

The rationale for these interventions lacked credibility in terms of the framework advanced by the president in question. But these rhetorical articulations also represented an attempt to restore a myopic sense of US leadership and its ability to ontologically define the framework that had been irreparably damaged. They were in ways an attempt to hark back to nostalgic visions of a world order in which the United States and Washington within the 'federal' system and for that matter the White House within the Constitutional balance of powers more or less determined the path along which they chose to walk; however, the mind-maps had been rendered problematical and the cartographers found that they were less in control of the signs and symbols they could place on their geopolitical maps. The silent spaces on these maps were being filled by a new set of cultural cartographers. These attempts at the US assertions of *liberty* were being met by other pursuits and narratives of *freedom*.

The dilemmas of domination and the age-old laws of international relations would play themselves out in US foreign policy too; in Cox's words: '*hubris* brought on by the temptation of empire will invariably produce its natural opposite in the form of *nemesis*'.[55] It is unsurprising that Walter LaFeber should choose to title his book on US-Central American relations *Inevitable Revolutions*[56] or that James Dunkerley's post-Cold War analysis of the region identified a temporary pacification.[57]

The broader dimensions of these themes are eloquently treated in the works of Victor Kiernan and Edward Said. For Said the process of building legitimacy centred on the power of narrative: 'The power to narrate, or to block other narratives from forming and emerging, is very important to culture and imperialism, and constitutes one of the main connections between them.' The grand narratives of 'emancipation and enlightenment' mobilized many across the modern era to throw off the imperial powers.[58] Bello's analysis of the recent past ascribes this reaction to the US-centred crisis, focusing on overproduction, overextension and the crisis of legitimacy. For him, 'there is one certainty: US democracy, celebrated by liberal writers like Joseph Nye, as the main source of Washington's "soft power", has long ceased to be a model for the rest of the world'. The ideological constructs and its spheres of discourse, created by the United States to justify its spheres of influence,[59] are increasingly questioned or ignored.

VIII

In part the explosion of the literature on the US empire represents attempts to understand the limits of its power and its overextension and to seek explanations of why the United States encounters the opposition that it does.[60] After 9/11 when Bush asked 'Why do they hate us?', his explanation further mystified the spheres of discourse. His conflation of the attacks with *their* hatred of US ideologies including *freedom* and *democracy* advanced the trope acceptable to US audiences, but that language and construction as explanation encountered a scepticism elsewhere and the limits of the US sphere of influence were evident.[61]

In that sense, while the US response to 9/11, by taking the 'war' to Afghanistan held a certain international legitimacy (though not one shared by this author),[62] the ties that bind were broken on Iraq. Apart from the difficulties after May 2003 experienced 'in the field', there was widespread international resistance taking various forms from the diplomatic to the symbolic to the actual. These were clearly further signs of the erosion of US influence and resistance to its 'leadership'. Cox explains that some played the United States at its own game and played it better, while others simply ignored the rules of the game and did their own thing. In that sense, the Iraq War not only demonstrated the weakness of Washington but did irreparable damage to the western liberal system '... with the result that we appear to be (once again) at another of those great transitional points in international relations where on one side stand a set of agreed international rules to which we all once paid homage, and on the other, deep uncertainty about what these rules should be following the US decision to ignore most of them after 2001'.[63]

So the real question for the Obama administration rests on how well it can adjust and recalibrate US power and position within the downward trend. Kissinger and Carter's response recognized the necessity to reposition: Kissinger through the articulation of *realpolitik* and hope and Carter through multilateralism, restraint, and diplomacy.

Obama clearly brought with him the potential to reverse the trend against the United States by capitalizing on the 'soft power',[64] that ability to win friends and persuade others in shared objectives that he generated in his campaign and through the early months of the presidency, though it was evident that his capital was eroding quickly. He recognized the need to shore up the alliances and to rebuild the US image in the world, but he also clearly articulated a deeper understanding of US security, one linked to the health of its economy. Invoking Eisenhower, Obama indicated that he was mindful of the necessity to balance foreign and domestic programmes: 'Over the past several years, we have lost that balance. We've failed to appreciate the connection between our national security and our economy.' And further, '... as we end the war in Iraq and transition to Afghanistan responsibly, we must rebuild our strength here at home. Our prosperity provides a foundation for our power. It pays for our military. It underwrites our diplomacy. It taps the potential of our people, and allows investment in new industry.'[65] It was incumbent on Obama to respond effectively to the pursuit of *liberty*, overstretch, and the costs of unilateral policies. The American military is stretched to the limit, its reputation, so carefully reconstructed after Vietnam,[66] lies shattered, 'diplomatically, it is out of moral capital. Economically, it is out of plain old capital'.[67] Paul Kennedy cogently argued that the Bush administration represented 'a spectacular example' of how to destroy the attraction to the United States 'once it appeared bent on unilateralist, heavy-handed, neoconservative actions, and didn't seem to care about world opinion'. Yet, whether the neoconservatives like it or not, the world reverted to a more multilateral order out of necessity because soft power cannot deal with the 'secular shifts in the world's economic balances' and Obama commands an economy and country less dominant than the 1940s, 1950s, or early 1960s.[68]

Global Trends 2025: A Transformed World released by the US National Intelligence Council (NIC) in November 2008 identified an international system that had evolved after the Second World War. It recognized that emerging powers, globalized market forces, non-state actors, and the rise of China and India by 2025 would witness 'an historic transfer of relative wealth and economic power from West to East...' and that 'although the United States is likely to remain the single most powerful actor, the United States' relative strength – even in the military realm – will decline and US leverage will become more constrained'.[69] Moreover, the NIC estimated, 'The most salient characteristics of the "new order" will be the shift from a unipolar world dominated by the United States to a relatively unstructured hierarchy of old powers and rising nations, and the diffusion of power from state to nonstate actors.'[70] Consequently the US ability to 'lead' or to 'call the shots' would diminish, unless it formed strong partnerships.[71] In other words, it needed to embrace *freedom* over *liberty*.

IX

Obama was conscious of the sense of crisis that he identified in the inauguration:

> We are in the midst of crisis is now well understood. Our nation is at war, against a far reaching network of violence and hatred. Our economy is badly weakened, a consequence of greed and irresponsibility on the part of some, but also our collective failure to make hard choices and prepare the nation for a new age. Homes have been lost; jobs shed; businesses shuttered. Our health care is too costly; our schools fail too many; and each day brings further evidence that the ways we use energy strengthen our adversaries and threaten our planet. ... Less measurable but no less profound is a sapping of confidence across our land – a nagging fear that America's decline is inevitable, and that the next generation must lower its sights.

Moreover, '[Our Founding Fathers] understood that our power alone cannot protect us, nor does it entitle us to do as we please. Instead, they knew that our power grows through its prudent use; our security emanates from the justness of our cause, the force of our example, the tempering qualities of humility and restraint.'[72]

Obama's speech on Afghanistan in late 2009 was characterized by the redeployment of elements of the Powell Doctrine: a narrow focus, identified objectives including eliminating al Qaeda safe havens, containing and reversing the Taliban's progress with concerted campaigns such as the February 2010 offensive in Marja, and building the government in Kabul, the fourth and crucial process of the recent adaptations of counterinsurgency: to capture, clear, hold *and* transfer. His speech was near-silent on the more liberal agendas. For Zakaria:

> He has been cool and calculating, whether dealing with Russia, Iran, Iraq, or Afghanistan. A great orator, he has, in this arena, kept his eloquence in check. Obama is a realist, by temperament, learning, and instinct. More than any president since Richard Nixon, he has focussed on defining American interests carefully, providing the resources to achieve them, and keeping his eyes on the prize.

Obama would ensure that there was a balance between commitment and capability and that extravagant foreign policy did not undermine long-term strategic depth. In that regard this speech echoed Eisenhower's 'Chance for Peace' speech in which he juxtaposed the costs of aircraft carriers against schools and hospitals.[73] 'It is now clear that Obama is attempting something quite ambitious – to reorientate American foreign policy toward something less extravagant and adversarial'; after all, Zakaria contends that although there were reversals for the US after Vietnam, from Angola to Nicaragua and Iran, ultimately the US recovered its position through domestic economic revival.[74] This time, however, it would be far more difficult: the economic prognosis was far worse and the perceptions and expectations of the US were in trouble.[75]

Moreover, periods of a more realist restraint in US foreign policy have often been followed by extravagant periods of engagement, exceptionalism, and unilateralism because that restraint for some represents the unacceptable face of decline that in their views call for a more muscular foreign policy. The transitions have occurred frequently, from Kennan to Nitze and Acheson, from Eisenhower to Kennedy, from the Nixon/Kissinger years to Reagan.[76] The yearnings for *liberty* in part threaten to accelerate US decline and undermine its power.

Notes

1. Isaiah Berlin cited by Nicholas Kristof, 'Explorer', *The New York Review of Books*, Vol. 57, No. 3 (February 25, 2010), 27.
2. Charles S. Maier, *Among Empires: American Ascendancy and Its Predecessors* (Cambridge: Harvard University Press, 2006), 286.
3. Jürgen Habermas, *The Divided West* (Cambridge: Polity, 2006).

4 Michael H. Hunt, *The American Ascendancy: How the United States Gained and Wielded Global Dominance* (Chapel Hill: University of North Carolina Press, 2007), 315–16.
5 Hunt, *The American Ascendancy*, 316.
6 Roger C. Altman, 'The Great Crash, 2008', *Foreign Affairs*, Vol. 88, No. 1 (January/February 2009), 2–14.
7 Immanuel Wallerstein, 'The Eagle Has Crash Landed', *Foreign Policy* (July/August 2002), 60–2. See also, Ahmed Rashid's, *Descent into Chaos* (New York: Viking, 2008); Niall Ferguson, 'The Axis of Upheaval', *Foreign Policy* (March/April 2009), 56–8.
8 Barack Obama, Inaugural Address, January 20, 2009, Washington D.C.
9 Politically, Washington was increasingly challenged and isolated on key global issues from climate change, its stance on the International Criminal Court, the fallout from Iraq, its choices and revisions on Guantanamo. Militarily, its forces were stretched in Iraq. Economically, Europe and the BRICs [Brazil-Russia-India-China] attracted increasing attention; across Latin America others forms of development were advanced. Ideologically, the 'end of History' seemed a distant mirage.
10 Timothy Garton Ash, 'Obama's Grand Narrative May Unite His Country but Divide the World', *The Guardian* (London), January 22, 2009.
11 David Hackett Fischer, *Liberty and Freedom* (Oxford: Oxford University Press, 2005), 3; see also: Isaiah Berlin, *Four Essays on Liberty* (Oxford: Oxford University Press, 1969); Berlin's conception was a considerable influence on my *US Foreign Policy in World History* (London: Routledge, 2000), though our readings of the United States might be quite different.
12 Patrick Tyler, 'US Strategy Plan Calls for Insuring No Rivals Develop', *The New York Times*, March 8, 1992; David Ryan, *US Foreign Policy in World History*, (London: Routledge, 2000), 190.
13 US National Security Strategy, and accompanying papers, April 1982, document 8290283 (NSDD 32) System II, NSC Records, The Reagan Presidential Library [hereafter RPL]; David Ryan, '"Vietnam", Victory Culture and Iraq: Struggling with Lessons, Constraints and Credibility from Saigon to Falluja', in John Dumbrell and David Ryan, eds., *Vietnam in Iraq: Tactics, Lessons, Legacies and Ghosts* (London: Routledge, 2007), 117.
14 Toby Dodge, *Iraq's Future: The Aftermath of Regime Change*, Adelphi Paper 372 (London: Routledge, 2005), 9–23.
15 Isaiah Berlin, *The Crooked Timber of Humanity* (London: Fontana, 1991), 46; Ryan, *World History*, 141.
16 See for instance George Bush's Inaugural 2005: 'America, in this young century, proclaims liberty throughout all the world, and to all the inhabitants thereof. Renewed in our strength – tested, but not weary – we are ready for the greatest achievements in the history of freedom.' George W. Bush, cited by Jonathan Raban, 'The Golden Trumpet', *The Guardian* (London), January 24, 2009.
17 David Hackett Fischer, *Liberty and Freedom* (Oxford: Oxford University Press, 2005), 4–5.
18 Anders Stephanson, 'A Most Interesting Empire', paper delivered to the symposium: Reviewing the Cold War: Interpretation, Approaches, Theory, Norwegian Nobel Institute, 1998.

19 Schivelbusch, *Culture of Defeat*, 294.
20 US National Security strategy and accompanying papers, April 1982, document 8290283 (NSDD 32), System II, NSC Records, RPL.
21 Eric Foner's study sets freedom within its historical contexts rather than studying it in the abstract. In that sense it investigates the competing forces of freedom in the United States and examines the colloquial use of the terms in that culture. It is important to note that the terms are also constantly redefined to suit the contemporary needs of the culture at any given time. See, Eric Foner, *The Story of American Freedom* (New York: W.W. Norton, 1998), xiii–xv; M. Patrick Cullinane, 'Fighting for "Freedom": The Language of "Liberty" and the US Anti-Imperialist Movement, 1898–1909', PhD thesis, University College Cork, Ireland 2010.
22 Ian Clark, *Globalization and Fragmentation: International Relations in the Twentieth Century* (Oxford: Oxford University Press, 1997).
23 Melvyn P. Leffler, *A Preponderance of Power: National Security, the Truman Administration, and the Cold War* (Stanford: Stanford University Press, 1992).
24 Robert A. Divine, *Second Chance: The Triumph of Internationalism in America during World War II* (New York: Atheneum, 1967).
25 George Kennan thought that the challenge of communism ought to be welcomed because it would make the United States more cohesive see X [George Kennan], 'The Sources of Soviet Conduct', *Foreign Affairs* 25 (July 1947), 582; Ryan, *US Foreign Policy in World History*; Ryan, *Frustrated Empire* (London: Pluto, 2007).
26 Henry R. Luce, 'The American Century', *Life* (February 17, 1941), 61–5.
27 Michael H. Hunt, 'East Asia in Henry Luce's "American Century"', *Diplomatic History*, Vol. 23, No. 2 (Spring 1999), 321.
28 Report by the Policy Planning Staff, PPS/23, Review of Current Trends in US Foreign Policy, February 24, 1948, *FRUS*, 1 (1948), 510–29.
29 See in particular, Jussi Hanhimäki, *The Flawed Architect: Henry Kissinger and American Foreign Policy* (Oxford: Oxford University Press, 2004); Mario Del Pero, *The Eccentric Realist: Henry Kissinger and the Shaping of American Foreign Policy* (Ithaca: Cornell University Press, 2010).
30 Fredric Jameson, *Postmodernism, or, The Cultural Logic of Late Capitalism* (London: Verso, 1991), xx; Perry Anderson, *The Origins of Postmodernity* (London: Verso, 1998), 91.
31 Michael Schaller, *Right Turn: American Life in the Reagan-Bush Era, 1980–1992* (New York: Oxford University Press, 2007); Sean Wilentz, *The Age of Reagan: A History 1974–2008* (New York: HarperCollins, 2008).
32 Walden Bello, *Dilemmas of Domination: The Unmaking of the American Empire* (New York: Metropolitan Books, 2005), 3.
33 Fareed Zakaria, 'The Future of American Power: How America Can Survive the Rise of the Rest', *Foreign Affairs*, Vol. 87, No. 3 (May/June 2008), 21–2. See also Fareed Zakaria, 'The Rise of the Rest', *Newsweek*, May 12, 2008, 20–8.
34 Christian Brose, 'The Making of George Obama', *Foreign Policy* (January/February 2009), 53–5.
35 Indeed Rice argued a similar line trying to regain ground that she had conceded and presided over the concession just a few years earlier. Condoleezza Rice, 'Rethinking the National Interest: American Realism for a New World', *Foreign Affairs*, Vol. 87, No. 4 (July/August 2008), 2–26.

36 David E. Sanger, 'Huge Deficits May Alter US Politics and Global Power', *New York Times*, February 2, 2010.
37 Sanger, 'Huge Deficits...'; Michael Tomasky, 'The Age of Obama Promises the Rebirth of US Liberalism', *The Guardian* (London), January 26, 2009.
38 *Ibid*.
39 Michael Cox, 'Is the United States in Decline – Again?' *International Affairs*, Vol. 83, No. 4 (2007), 643–53. See also, Robert D. Kaplan, 'America's Elegant Decline', *The Atlantic* (November 2007); Gina Hahn, 'As the Romans Did', *The Atlantic* (June 22, 2007).
40 James Fallows, 'How America Can Rise Again', *The Atlantic Online* (January/February 2010), 1–15.
41 Cox, 'Is the United States in Decline – Again?' 644.
42 Henry Kissinger, National Security Advisor [NSA], memorandum to Richard Nixon, Analysis of changes in international politics since World War II and their implications for our basic assumptions about US foreign policy, October 20, 1969, doc. 41, *FRUS: Foundation of Foreign Policy, 1969–1972*, Vol. 1, 131.
43 Michael Foucault, *The Archaeology of Knowledge* (London: Routledge, 1972), 22.
44 Zbigniew Brzezinski to the President, memorandum, NSC Weekly Report #94, 12 April 1979, Weekly Reports 91–101, 3/79–6/79 (11), JCL.
45 Mario Del Pero, *The Eccentric Realist: Henry Kissinger and the Shaping of American Foreign Policy* (Ithaca: Cornell University Press, 2010), 59, 66.
46 Schivelbusch observes, 'It is all the more surprising, then, how briefly the losing nation's depression tends to last before turning into a unique type of euphoria.' Wolfgang Schivelbusch, *The Culture of Defeat: On National Trauma, Mourning, and Recovery* (New York: Metropolitan Books, 2003), 10.
47 John Kenneth Galbraith, *The Culture of Contentment* (London: Sinclair-Stevenson, 1992), 126; Raymond L. Garthoff, *The Great Transition: American-Soviet Relations and the End of the Cold War* (Washington, D.C.: Brookings, 1994), 34–42; Ryan, *World History*, 169.
48 US National Security Strategy, and accompanying papers, April 1982, document 8290283 (NSDD 32) System II, NSC Records, the Reagan Presidential Library.
49 Cox, 'Is the United States in Decline – Again?', 646.
50 Cox, 'Is the United States in Decline – Again?', 647.
51 Cox, 'Is the United States in Decline – Again?', 648; George H.W. Bush and Brent Scowcroft, *A World Transformed* (New York: Alfred A. Knopf, 1998); Charles Krauthammer, 'The Unipolar Moment', *Foreign Affairs*, Vol. 70, No. 1 (1991), 23–33.
52 Despite all external signs there are the counter-narratives that insist on attention. 'The country is developing the prototypical knowledge economy of the 21st century, an economy in which the division between manufacturing and services becomes less clear cut, in a world where the deployment of knowledge, brain power and problem-solving are the sources of wealth generation.' Will Hutton, 'Forget the Naysayers – America Remains an Inspiration to Us All', *The Observer* (London), May 11, 2008.
53 Louise J. Halle to Robert Bowie, Policy Planning Staff, Department of State, June 23, 1954, Records of the Policy Planning Staff, RG 59, Lot 65 D101,

box 79, NARA; David Ryan, *Frustrated Empire: US Foreign Policy, 9/11 to Iraq* (London: Pluto, 2007), 17.
54 Amy Kaplan, '"Left Alone with America": The Absence of Empire in the Study of American Culture', in Amy Kaplan and Donald E. Pease, eds., *Culture of United States Imperialism* (Durham: Duke University Press, 1993), 11–14.
55 Cox, 'Is the United States in Decline – Again?' 649.
56 Walter LaFeber, *Inevitable Revolutions: The United States and Central America* (New York: W.W. Norton, 1993).
57 James Dunkerley, *The Pacification of Central America: Political Change in the Isthmus, 1987–1993* (London: Verso, 1994).
58 Edward Said, *Culture and Imperialism* (London: Chatto and Windus, 1993), xiii; V.G. Kiernan, *Imperialism and Its Contradictions* (New York: Routledge, 1995).
59 Bello, *Dilemmas of Domination*, 4–7, 209.
60 Cox, 'Is the United States in Decline – Again?' 650; The literature on US empire has grown exponentially of late, see Andrew Bacevich, *American Empire: The Realities and Consequences of US Diplomacy* (Cambridge: Harvard University Press, 2002); Niall Ferguson, *Colossus: The Price of America's Empire* (London: Allen Lane, 2004); Lloyd Gardner and Marilyn Young, eds., *The New American Empire* (New York: The New Press, 2005); Eric Hobsbawm, *On Empire: America, War and Global Supremacy* (New York: Pantheon, 2008); G. John Ikenberry, *Liberal Order and Imperial Ambition: Essays on American Power and World Politics* (Cambridge: Polity, 2006); Christopher Layne and Bradley A. Thayer, *American Empire: A Debate* (London: Routledge, 2007); Charles S. Maier, *Among Empires: American Ascendancy and its Predecessors* (Cambridge: Harvard University Press, 2006); Michael Mann, *Incoherent Empire* (London: Verso, 2003); Herfried Münkler, *Empires: The Logic of World Domination from Ancient Rome to the United States* (Cambridge: Polity, 2007); Bernard Porter, *Empire and Superempire: Britain, America and the World* (New Haven: Yale University Press, 2006); David Ryan and Victor Pungong, eds., *The United States and Decolonization: Power and Freedom*, (London: Palgrave Macmillan, 2000); Michael H. Hunt, *America Ascendant: How the United States Gain and Wielded Global Dominance* (Chapel Hill: University of North Carolina Press, 2007); Geir Lundestad, *'Empire' by Integration: The United States and European Integration, 1945–1997* (London: Oxford University Press, 1997); Richard N. Haass, *The Opportunity: America's Moment to Alter History's Course* (New York: Public Affairs, 2005); Anne Norton, *Leo Strauss and the Politics of American Empire* (New Haven: Yale, 2004); David Ryan, *Frustrated Empire: US Foreign Policy 9/11 to Iraq* (London: Pluto, 2007); Emmanuel Todd, *After the Empire: The Breakdown of the American Order* (London: Constable, 2003).
61 On the 'powers to convince', the 'play of homology' and especially the 'production of belief' see Pierre Bourdieu, *The Field of Cultural Production* (Cambridge: Polity, 1993). A recent analysis of US Public Diplomacy, almost a rearguard action against the recent anti-American sentiments, see Scott Lucas and Ali Fisher, *The Trials of Engagement: The Future of US Public Diplomacy* (Leiden, The Netherlands: Brill Publishers, forthcoming 2010).
62 See chapter 4: 'War and Just War: Terrorism and Afghanistan', in Ryan, *Frustrated Empire*, 53–76.

63 Cox, 'Is the United States in Decline – Again?', 651; NIC, 'For their part, China, India and Russia are not following the western liberal model for self-development but instead are using a different model, "state capitalism."' NIC, *Global Trends 2025*, vii. See also essays in G. John Ikenberry, *Liberal Order and Imperial Ambition: Essays on American Power and World Politics* (Cambridge: Polity, 2006); Jeffrey Anderson, G. John Ikenberry, Thomas Risse, eds., *The End of the West? Crisis and Change in the Atlantic Order* (Ithaca: Cornell University Press, 2008); Christopher S. Browning and Marko Lehti, eds., *The Struggle for the West: A Divided and Contested Legacy* (London: Routledge, 2010).
64 Joseph S. Nye, *Soft Power: The Means to Success in World Politics* (New York: Public Affairs, 2004).
65 President Barack Obama, Address to the Nation on the Way Forward in Afghanistan and Pakistan, Eisenhower Hall Theatre, West Point, New York, December 1, 2009.
66 David Fitzgerald, Learning to Forget?: The US Army and Counterinsurgency Doctrine and Practice from Vietnam to Iraq. PhD thesis, UCC, 2010.
67 Gary Young, 'Americans Have Never Felt So Excited, and Yet So Depressed', *The Guardian* (London), November 24, 2008.
68 Paul Kennedy, 'Soft Power is On the Up. But It Can Always Be Outmuscled', *The Guardian* (London), November 18, 2008; see also Niall Ferguson, 'Complexity and Collapse: Empires on the Edge of Chaos', *Foreign Affairs*, Vol. 89, No. 2 (March/April 2010), 18–32.
69 National Intelligence Council, *Global Trends 2025: A Transformed World* NIC 2008-003 (Washington D.C.: US Government Printing Office), vi.
70 NIC, *Global Trends 2025*, 1.
71 NIC cited by Julian Borger, 'Sun Sets on US Power: Report Predicts End of Dominance', *The Guardian* (London), November 21, 2008.
72 Barack Obama, Inaugural Address, January 20, 2009, Washington D.C.
73 Walter Russell Mead, 'The Carter Syndrome', *Foreign Policy* (January/February 2010), 61.
74 Fareed Zakaria, 'The Post-Imperial Presidency', *Newsweek*, December 14, 2009.
75 Ferguson, 'Complexity and Collapse', 31.
76 Russell Mead, 'The Carter Syndrome', 64.

10
The United States and the United Nations: Hegemony, Unilateralism and the Limits of Internationalism

Andrew Johnstone

The 2008 publication of Robert Kagan's *The Return of History and the End of Dreams* was the latest chapter in the ongoing debate over the nature of American internationalism. In it, Kagan argued that a new 'league of democracies' is required in foreign affairs. The idea is more than academic: Republican Presidential candidate John McCain promoted such an idea in his 2008 campaign.[1] Sympathetic reviewers have argued the promotion of such a league represents a move away from neoconservative idealism towards international legitimacy and offers a potential brake on US foreign policy. Critics, meanwhile, claim any such league merely represents an alternative forum or international community to the United Nations from which the US could legitimise its foreign policy actions.

What both perspectives have in common is a keen awareness of what Kagan refers to as America's 'tendency toward unilateralism'.[2] Whether the league of democracies idea is seen as a response to the perceived unilateral excesses of recent US foreign policy, or whether it is seen as a method for reinforcing America's dominant global position through an organisation of like-minded allies, the unilateralist tendency for the US to control its own destiny and retain freedom of action is at the core of the debate.

This tendency is nothing new. Unilateralism has been one of the defining characteristics of American foreign relations since George Washington's farewell address, and the most essential component of that unilateralism has been freedom of action. Throughout its history the US has sought to retain that freedom in international affairs and been wary of entangling alliances. As a result, despite providing the impetus for international organisations such as the League of Nations, the United Nations and the North Atlantic Treaty Organisation (NATO), the American relationship with those organisations has been complex and occasionally fraught with tension. This chapter seeks to examine the nature of what is often simplistically referred to as American internationalism by assessing the relationship between the US and the United Nations since 1945. In particular, it aims to examine the tension between internationalism and unilateralism, to highlight the reasons behind the unilateral approach to foreign affairs, and to consider if Kagan's approach offers a genuine way forward.

Ultimately, both the history of US-UN relations and the promotion of the league of democracies idea reveal the American desire for internationalism on its own terms. The American desire to use its power to pursue its national interest through international organisations explains why Tony Smith has argued that '"Multilateralism" was, and remains, a code word for American hegemony', and why 'multilateralism can be a disguised formula for what in practice may amount to unilateralism'.[3]

US internationalism

To his credit, Kagan defines American internationalism in a way that gives it genuine meaning. For too long, the phrase 'American internationalism' has been utilised in a way that deprives it of any real analytical value, and there is no consistent definition of what internationalism is with respect to US foreign policy. Warren Kuehl and Gary Ostrower have highlighted that internationalism 'has had different meanings for nearly every generation of citizens and diplomats', and that it has now reached the point where the term has so many definitions that it has effectively lost its meaning altogether.[4] Since 1945, when the United Nations was created with US involvement, American internationalism has largely been equated with the fact that the United States plays an active role in world affairs.[5] As Alan Dawley has pointed out, 'Cold War liberals counterposed internationalism to isolationism, which, in their view, had led to the blunder of Senate rejection of the League of Nations in 1919 and to the still worse American complicity in the appeasement of Hitler at Munich'.[6] In this respect, internationalism is merely the opposite of isolationism, an equally empty term used to describe America's world role prior to 1941 (and the interwar years in particular).[7] Given America's continued history of involvement in foreign affairs since the establishment of the nation in 1776, this most basic definition of internationalism has little value.[8]

In addition, this simple description does nothing to describe the nature of American internationalism. It can be, and often is, used to describe unilateral US involvement overseas. However, for many, American internationalism has a very distinct nature: multilateralism. In this sense, internationalism means far more than simply overseas involvement. It goes beyond a narrow unilateralism, and looks for an engaged and multilateral approach to foreign affairs. A full definition of internationalism reflects the efforts of those Americans who have sought a more just and peaceful world through international political, economic and cultural cooperation. There is a strong tradition of support for multilateral internationalism in the US. From the League to Enforce Peace during World War I, through the League of Nations Association in the interwar years, to the American Association for the United Nations and today's UNA-USA, there is an almost unbroken thread of public support for a distinctly multilateral internationalism.[9]

More significantly, for the last century, the US government has been the prime mover behind the creation of international organisations. International organisations are by no means an American idea.[10] Yet despite the unilateralist rhetoric of the younger Bush administration, there is a certain irony in the fact that the US has done more than any other nation to make international organisations a reality. President Woodrow Wilson almost single-handedly created the League of Nations during World War I, and while debate continues over the defining characteristics of his foreign policy, there is little doubt that multilateralism was a core element of Wilsonian thought. However, the unilateralist tendency quickly reappeared at the end of World War I, and the US Senate chose freedom of action over Wilson's League.[11]

Yet the idea of international organisation refused to go away, and the events of World War II provided a second chance for internationalism, convincing most Americans that the rejection of the League had been a mistake. As a result, the US again led the way in creating a new international organisation, and the final months of the war saw the creation of the United Nations Organisation. For a brief moment, it appeared to represent a triumph of internationalism.[12] However, tension between the multilateralism of the new UN system and the tradition of American unilateralism soon developed, affecting the US-UN relationship from the very beginning. As a result, for a variety of reasons, the general trend of the US-UN relationship has been a long, slow deterioration to the point where critics like Kagan seek alternatives vehicles for international legitimacy. It should be stated that the United States is not the sole party responsible for the limited nature of the US-UN relationship, and that the relationship has often broken down for historically specific reasons. It should also be noted that in many cases the

US has worked successfully with the UN. Yet as we shall see there is also no doubt that the broader history of US-UN relations is marked by tension created by an American tendency toward unilateralism, tension that has become more and more pronounced as the US has increasingly lost its hegemonic status at the UN.

The quest for hegemony: US-UN relations

The creation of the United Nations Organisation was extremely popular among Americans in 1945. A July 1945 poll reported that 85 percent of Americans wanted to join the new international organisation, and the Senate vote to ratify the UN Charter passed by a vote of 89 to two.[13] The popularity was built on the fact that the UN Charter was largely drafted and developed during World War II, by the US – in effect, a made-in-America United Nations. Consequently, it has been argued that from its inception there was an expectation of a hegemonic relationship between the US and the UN, and that that 'the UN would be a relatively pliant instrument of US policy'.[14]

Of course, this was not the case. US-UN relations were immediately affected by the almost simultaneous onset of the Cold War, which would prove to be the primary source of US-UN tension for the next decade, and a challenge to the functioning of the UN for over forty years. Despite some areas of agreement in 1945 and 1946 over issues including the choice of Secretary General and the location of the permanent headquarters, the cordial nature of the wartime grand alliance soon disappeared with dire consequences for the UN. The creation of veto power for permanent Security Council members meant that the US would always be able to veto Soviet proposals – and vice versa. Attempts to give the UN international control of atomic energy failed due to an American insistence on a plan that would ensure the Soviets were unable to develop their own bomb. Similarly, attempts to set up a Military Staff Committee to coordinate a UN military force fell through over basic disagreements as to how any such force might be arranged, let alone where it might be utilised.[15]

As the Cold War set in, the US had to reconcile the continued belief that international legitimacy was required in foreign affairs with the inability of the UN to deal effectively with security issues. This led to the first American efforts to seek an alternative multilateralism to the UN and to find collective security elsewhere, particularly with its allies in alternative organisations and regional groupings where the US would have greater power and control. The most notable example of this was the creation of NATO in 1949.[16] NATO obviously represented an alternative forum for the US to pursue its security, and as a purely military alliance it only sought to replace the element of the UN that was gridlocked by the veto. However, it had the effect of intensifying Cold War divisions, and led to the eventual Soviet creation of the Warsaw Pact. Nevertheless, despite the search for alternatives, in these first years it appeared that the US was more willing to utilise the UN than the Soviet Union, and their frustration with the organisation was less about the UN itself and more about Soviet obstructionism within it. This was understandable in an era when the UN was dominated by allies of the US. Yet it was still hoped that the US could successfully achieve its national security aims through the UN.

This faith was bolstered when the Korean War provided an opportunity for the US to get around Soviet obstructionism. This possibility was due to the ongoing Soviet boycott of the Security Council following its unwillingness to seat Mao Zedong's new revolutionary Chinese government in place of the defeated Nationalist forces (an unwillingness led by the US, with concerns about a second communist member with veto power). The Soviet boycott enabled the US to press the Security Council to authorise a military response to North Korean aggression. The fact that the US chose to utilise the UN when it had the opportunity displayed an understanding that international legitimacy mattered, and that the UN was still one of many diplomatic organs of potential use to the US. The force that subsequently went into Korea was UN authorised, but controlled by the US.

Once the Soviets ended their boycott, the US quickly found another way to circumvent the Soviet veto through the Uniting for Peace Resolution – an agreement that allowed the General Assembly to vote on security issues deadlocked by Security Council veto. This clearly represented an attempt to maintain US hegemony over the UN, but was nevertheless contingent upon the diplomatic influence of the US and its allies, and their ongoing ability to hold sway in any major votes. However, this sense of control was about to be challenged, and much more quickly than most Americans expected.[17]

Due to the rapid process of global decolonisation in the late 1950s, the nature of the UN shifted in a way that challenged the dominant status of the US. The UN, which consisted of 51 members upon creation in 1945, had 101 by 1961, and 145 by 1975 with most of the new nations from the developing regions of Africa and Asia. These new, non-aligned nations were given collective force and representation by the creation of the Group of 77 in 1968. With east-west relations increasingly deadlocked by the Security Council veto, the focus of these new nations shifted much of the UN's activity to the General Assembly, making that body increasingly significant. As a result of this shift, the US found that it was, for the first time, in the minority on many UN issues, and that the international body was less susceptible to US control.[18] This marked the beginning of growing US frustration with the UN as Americans increasingly felt that the UN was moving away from the American values upon which it was created. The different interpretations of terms such as freedom and democracy emanating from the new non-aligned countries did not necessarily fit with US strategic interests, while for many nations the Vietnam War represented the US moving away from both US and UN ideals.

In the face of southern domination, the US used its first Security Council veto in 1970 to stop a resolution issuing sanctions against Southern Rhodesia.[19] Since then, the US has wielded the veto more than any other nation – far more than the USSR/Russia. It is clear that once the US lost its dominant position in the UN, it became far more willing to use the veto and fight its own corner. This defensive posture was exacerbated by the appointment of Daniel Patrick Moynihan as permanent representative to the UN in 1975. The most bullish ambassador to that point, Moynihan fought to expose what he saw as the hypocrisy of fellow UN members, such as the General Assembly's denunciation of South African intervention in Angola while ignoring the intervention of Cuba (though Soviet support was equally troubling, and the main reason for US interest here). However, he was similarly guilty of such hypocrisy himself when ensuring that the UN was 'utterly ineffective' in acting over its ally Indonesia's invasion of East Timor. Despite his denunciations, most US action saw ideological and geopolitical concerns to the fore, rather than ideals.[20]

As the position of the US within the UN began to weaken, American attitudes towards the international body were also affected. American dissatisfaction with the UN had been developing for a number of years, but if there was a decisive shift in US-UN relations, it came with General Assembly Resolution 3379 which equated Zionism with racism. With Israel increasingly equated in the Arab world, and more broadly by the Group of 77, as an imperial entity, the Resolution described Zionism as a form of 'racism and racial discrimination'.[21] Moynihan's response in the UN was one of outrage, and was reflected in the country as a whole. US-UN relations hit a new low. More than any other incident, it sparked open discussion in the US regarding the future of US involvement (and indeed membership) in the UN. From then on, it became increasingly acceptable to denounce the UN, and calls for withdrawal from the organisation became much more vocal.

Despite some rhetorical improvements, the Carter administration did little to repair US-UN relations and in some respects the relationship deteriorated further. In 1977, the US withdrew from what it saw as the increasingly politicised, radical and G-77-led International Labour Organisation (ILO) for three years. In 1979, the US voted to seat the Khmer Rouge as the Cambodian delegation, rather than the recently installed Vietnamese/Soviet backed government. As Gary Ostrower has rightly pointed out, the US could have abstained, but instead chose to vote for the regime of Pol Pot.[22] This, combined with the earlier American veto of Vietnam's admission to the UN, again highlighted the willingness of the US to put its ideals to one side for political purposes, and did nothing to enhance the UN's standing in the eyes of both UN critics and US internationalists.

It would be left to the Reagan administration to fully spell out disillusionment with a UN that the US could no longer dominate and that – with its apparent disregard for free market principles, support for terrorists and disregard for human rights violations – had seemingly betrayed the Charter. In its most dramatic move, the US withdrew from the United Nations Educational, Scientific and Cultural Organisation (UNESCO) in 1984. In similar circumstances to the earlier withdrawal from the ILO, US leaders saw UNESCO as increasingly politicised over Middle Eastern issues.[23] More significantly, the US unilaterally reduced its financial contributions to the UN. But in many ways this mattered little to an administration that pursued (in its first term at least) an exceptionally unilateral foreign policy. Such attitudes were echoed outside of government by conservative think-tanks such as the Heritage Foundation, which, in the words of one UN practitioner, favoured US withdrawal from 'a UN system it can no longer dominate'.[24]

This unilateral attitude was seen again when the International Court of Justice (ICJ) ruled that US had acted illegally in aiding the Contra rebels in Nicaragua. The US responded by withdrawing its acceptance of the Court's jurisdiction, an action which even drew domestic condemnation for its disregard of international law (including criticism from Daniel Patrick Moynihan). The cumulative effect of these policies led one prominent internationalist to decry 'the twilight of internationalism'. In a 1985 *Foreign Policy* article, Carnegie Endowment head Thomas L Hughes argued that a rise in nationalist sentiment, coupled with factors including a fear of American decline and a desire for simple answers to complex questions, had led to a lack of support for international organisations, international law, economic interdependence, and leadership through education.[25]

Yet the worst fears of internationalists proved unfounded. Not only did the Reagan administration soften its diplomatic stance in its second term, but that softening was partly responsible for bringing first a thaw, and eventually an end, to the Cold War. Rather than twilight, the end of the Cold War offered an opportunity for American internationalism to renew its promise. As former permanent representative to the UN George H.W. Bush became president in 1989, it appeared that a window of opportunity was opening, and that perhaps the UN would see the kind of great power cooperation envisaged in 1945. This was seen in renewed peacekeeping operations, but most notably in the first Gulf War.

First, the great powers came together to introduce sanctions on Iraq; then they agreed on Security Council Resolution 678, approving 'all necessary means' to liberate Kuwait from Iraqi forces. As Bush argued, the UN provided 'a cloak of acceptability to our efforts'.[26] True, had the UN been unwilling, the US would have gone in anyway, and the forces of liberation were not UN forces, but US-led forces. Nevertheless, the coalition that supported the action was broad, had been created in the UN, and had the Resolutions to prove it. The success of US internationalism during the Gulf War offered fresh hope not just to American internationalists, but to internationalists worldwide and the UN itself. However, as Stanley Meisler has pointed out, the war convinced Americans 'that the UN was their UN'. In doing so it reinforced the idea that UN was only working properly when it worked in a way that supported the aims of the US.[27]

When it became clear that not every post-Cold War era crisis would be as easily or successfully resolved, belief in the UN and multilateralism quickly waned. The Clinton administration quickly found itself working with the UN to deal with famine and warfare in Somalia, but with little success. A lack of coordination between the US and other UN forces, followed by domestic dismay at the sight of American body bags led to the withdrawal of US troops from a region where many Americans saw no national interest. The situation was little better in Bosnia where the UN had limited success in keeping the peace in the wake of Yugoslavia's dissolution. But in the aftermath of public disillusionment with events in Somalia, the UN failed to act in any significant way over the genocide in Rwanda. It proved that the US was unwilling to commit forces to an area where it saw no clear national interest, even in the face of a humanitarian disaster.[28]

However, while the Clinton administration never fully engaged with the UN in a way that fulfilled the hopes of post-Cold War internationalists, it never turned its back on internationalism either. The latter approach was taken up by the George W. Bush administration, whose foreign policy was defined by a new aggressive unilateralism that cared little for existing institutions, commitments and laws. It was reflected in the first year of the Administration with the withdrawal from the 1972 anti-ballistic missile treaty, and the failure to ratify both the Kyoto treaty on the environment and the International Criminal Court. As Warren Cohen has put it, 'Bush and most of his advisers demonstrated to the world that the United States was law unto itself'.[29]

The administration's disregard for the UN became most apparent after 9/11. Even though the UN quickly authorised US action in Afghanistan, the US was not interested in putting together a broad coalition of forces.[30] Where Bush's father saw a coalition as a positive attribute, George W. and his advisers saw it as a possible source of constraint. The US was clearly going to go its own way, and the subsequent decision to invade Iraq represented American unilateralism at its most forceful. Security Council Resolution 1441 gave Iraq a last chance to disarm, though it did not spell out what the consequences would be. The vague phrasing left all sides to interpret it however they chose; the Americans believed it (and the many Resolutions before it) authorised war, the French and Russians did not. Only at the insistence of British Prime Minister Tony Blair did Bush allow the US to attempt to secure a binding resolution for intervention at the UN. Despite Secretary of State Colin Powell's attempt to convince the UN of Iraqi weaponry, the French made it clear they would veto any Resolution for war. The US went ahead regardless with a rather limited 'coalition of the willing', a slogan that attempted to secure the legitimacy only genuine multilateralism could provide.

The Bush administration's negative attitude towards the UN appeared to be encapsulated by the appointment of arch-unilateralist and vehemently anti-UN diplomat John Bolton as its permanent representative to the UN in 2005.[31] More outspoken than Moynihan had been, and far more ideologically opposed to the UN, Bolton was on record as stating in 1994 that 'there is no such thing as the United Nations. There is only the international community, which can only be led by the only remaining superpower, which is the United States'. He also famously stated that 'the Secretariat building in New York has 38 stories. If you lost ten stories today, it wouldn't make a bit of difference'.[32] Few would argue that the UN is not in need of reform, but sending Bolton to a UN already suspicious of US unilateralism sent a highly confrontational message, reflecting the fact that tensions between the US and the UN remained as fraught as ever.

Despite Bolton's brief sixteen-month appointment, there were hints late in its second term that the Bush administration was moving away from the unilateral end of the foreign policy spectrum. Yet the administration softened its tone not because of any ideological shift regarding the principles of multilateralism. Instead, as it became bogged down in Iraq and with operations continuing in Afghanistan, the administration finally appeared to recognise the limits of its own power. To the disappointment of some neoconservatives, a more pragmatic 'realist' approach came to the fore, as hawkish polices towards Iran were shelved, the US placed greater emphasis on finding an international solution to the Israeli-Palestinian conflict, and Bush increasingly sought to include the UN in plans for post-war Iraq. While it can be argued that multilateralism should have been the administration's first – rather than last – choice for diplomacy, the shift reflected a belated acknowledgement that a more international approach was required. In a broader sense, it suggested a recognition not only that the unilateralist tendency in US foreign policy had become overly dominant, but also that American power had limits.

The unilateralist tendency

Sixty years after the US had been the main driving force behind the creation of the UN, its attitude toward it had altered considerably. At best, the US appeared to be narrowly interested in the UN only when the US could direct it or it could do something for US interests. At worst, it seemed to be undermining the UN with both its words and actions. Yet as the history makes clear, this unilateral tendency to retain its freedom of action and desire for hegemonic control has always been present to varying degrees. Indeed, as has been noted, a unilateral thread in US foreign policy can be traced back to the earliest days of the Republic. In his farewell address, President George Washington warned against 'permanent alliances' with other nations.[33] Only with the creation of the United Nations did the US truly begin to break with this tradition. Though others prefer to describe US foreign policy through terms such as 'Independent Internationalism' or 'Instrumental Multilateralist', both are variants on unilateralism, as is Robert Kagan's own description of 'multilateralism, American style'.[34]

This unilateralism can be explained in a number of ways. It can be partially explained by practical issues at the UN. These include a genuine desire for reform, from reconfiguration of the Security Council to rationalisation in numerous areas of administration. In a nation with a tradition of small government, it is no great surprise that the US should look

– especially as the single biggest contributor to the UN budget – to ensure those contributions are spent as effectively as possible. It can also be explained by the minority status the US has held at the UN since the 1960s. Frequently outnumbered by nations that do not share Washington's perspective, interests, or ideals, the US has usually been powerful enough to be able to ignore any prevailing opinion that has attempted to limit US action (though the US has not always been able to stop dissenting views in the General Assembly, most notably the Zionism racism controversy).

Yet there is more to American unilateralism than practicalities on the East River. Equally significant is the vague and nebulous concept of American exceptionalism. While it is difficult to define, the sense that the United States is not merely different, but *superior* to other nations, plays a key role in its unilateralism. The idea that the American political and economic system (and its conceptions of democracy, freedom and liberty) should be the aspiration of all nations shines through in the rhetoric of those Americans who believe America should and indeed must lead the world. While there is much to admire about the American system, what the US sometimes fails to acknowledge is that it has often failed to live up to its ideals. As a result, the rest of the world has been justified in asking if the US is qualified to lead. In the lifetime of the United Nations, the Vietnam War is perhaps the most dramatic foreign policy example of such failure, with the Iraq War a more recent example. The worst excesses of American exceptionalism came with the unilateralism of the Bush administration, which appeared to see itself as above all existing forms of international law and institutions. Nevertheless, degrees of this sense of exceptionalism remain. It was evident in Barack Obama's inaugural address in which he claimed that America was 'ready to lead once more', albeit couched in the broader context of a multilateral approach to foreign affairs.[35]

One particular element of exceptionalism that has hindered cooperation with the UN has been the refusal of the US to cede national sovereignty. As Edward Luck has written, there is a sense that US sovereignty 'is a precious and fragile commodity that must be jealously guarded at all times within and from international organizations'.[36] With considerable opposition to any international laws that affect or supersede the US Constitution, the US is more reluctant than most nations to be led or governed by unelected international bodies. This is certainly true compared to European nations who saw the destructive power of the nation state in twentieth-century wars and have subsequently sought collective security.

Since the end of the Cold War, America's unipolar status and unmatched military strength has also provided a key component of American unilateralism. Whatever desire for internationalism remains, the strength of US military power has meant that the US has often been able to go it alone where necessary to achieve its aims. This has led some – especially in the Bush administration – to question the need for international organisations or cooperation at all. As G. John Ikenberry has highlighted, 'the United States alone has the capacity to act or stand in the way of action on behalf of the international community', which has led to US power being seen as 'controversial and even illegitimate'.[37]

There is also an element of frustration that other nations do not aspire to the exceptional American values that (somewhat paradoxically) seem so universal to American policymakers. It is perhaps unsurprising that because the US was responsible for creating the UN, this led to a belief that it had been made in America's image. In light of this belief, as Edward Luck has highlighted, 'some US representatives are still confounded at times to find themselves repeatedly in a minority status in "their" world body'.[38] This in turn has led to a frustration that the UN has proven to be a forum for conflict as much as consensus, and one in which a nation like Sudan could be on the Human Rights Commission while atrocities took place in Darfur. It is not simply the fact that the US is outnumbered at the UN; equally important is the political nature of the nations that outnumber it. This frustration has led to calls, like that from Robert Kagan, for a subgroup of democracies. A like-minded group of nations would share values and 'bestow legitimacy' upon their actions, which may go beyond traditional UN activity to include democracy promotion and political liberalisation.[39]

A league of democracies?

It should be noted that Kagan's plan and McCain's endorsement of it does not mean that this is merely a Republican or neoconservative approach. The idea has also been promoted, equally strongly, by some liberal scholars. The most notable examples are G. John Ikenberry and Anne-Marie Slaughter in their Princeton Project on National Security. Its final report argued that 'the United States should work with its friends and allies to develop a global "Concert of Democracies"' to 'institutionalize and ratify the "democratic peace"'.[40] In addition, the Clinton administration was instrumental in the creation of the Community of Democracies in 2000, an organisation which aims 'to work toward a global community increasingly based on democratic governance', and which has met at the UN since 2004.⁴¹ The primary difference between liberals and conservatives appears to be that liberals see any such league working alongside the UN, where conservative silence on the issue suggests they would prefer to see a league of democracies replace the UN. Nevertheless, the idea clearly has a degree of support from across the political spectrum. But does it have any merit?

Perhaps the most positive attribute of the league of democracies concept is that it promotes international engagement and an acceptance that the US cannot, and should not, go it alone. It may be a qualified form, but it represents an American internationalism that appeared to have vanished during the G.W. Bush administrations. As Thomas Carothers has highlighted, calls for a league of democracies 'are rooted in a useful recognition that the United States in recent years has operated too much on its own in the world'.⁴² This recognition appears to accept Joseph Nye's paradox: that despite being the most powerful nation on the planet, there are many things the US cannot deal with alone.⁴³ In this sense, then, the league of democracies idea merely represents the latest in a long line of international organisations created and developed by the US to further its foreign policy interests through multilateral channels.

The league of democracies concept also recognises an issue that is problematic for many Americans, namely the concept of one-nation one-vote at the UN. This is partly due to the fact that the US is clearly the dominant nation in the world, and that it should not be equivalent to other small sovereign nations such as (for example) Andorra, the Maldives, or the Federated States of Micronesia. More significant is that fact that many nations are represented by autocratic governments that have never been elected by their populations. A league of democracies could genuinely claim to speak for all of the people of all of its member nations. In John Bolton's words, the one-nation one-vote system is 'as fraudulent an analogy to real democracy as has ever been made'.⁴⁴

Yet while there are some positive elements to the concept, they are outweighed by the limitations. One of the principal criticisms of the league of democracies concept is that it will undermine the UN. Regardless of what its proponents might say about it merely offering another channel for US diplomacy, there is no question that it will erode the UN's credibility. Some might say that the UN's credibility has already been irreparably damaged, yet US policymakers and academics seem unwilling to make the kind of imaginative leaps with regard to the UN that have led to the creation of the new league concept. As Carothers has argued, 'attempting to push for meaningful UN reform... is apparently too time-consuming and... tailoring US policy to fit existing international norms rather than tailoring international institutions to fit US needs apparently just does not appeal'.[45] Yet this is exactly the combination that is necessary.[46]

Another significant problem is that the league concept splits the world into competing spheres. As in the Cold War, US policy will view the world as a zero-sum game – you would be with it or against it. As commentators have pointed out, it 'pits the good guys (market democracies) against the bad guys (autocracies)'.[47] Supporters may respond that this is not the aim, but even if that is true, there is no doubt that it could be perceived that way across the globe. This in turn could lead to the type of resentment seen by Russia's reaction to NATO's continued movement toward its borders. As a result, it has the potential to close off the opportunity for dialogue and engagement, ultimately limiting diplomacy.

An additional flaw with any league of democracies is that it creates a neat line between democracies and autocracies where one does not really exist – or not one that has any real meaning. There is no autocratic group of nations, although there might become one in response to any such league, just as the non-aligned movement joined together during the Cold War. More significantly, there is no coherent consensus even among democracies. After all, it was France that ensured there would be no second resolution in the UN on Iraq. Few western nations supported US involvement in Vietnam. Traditional US allies are more than capable of holding dissenting views. Democracy alone is an insufficient reason for nations to work together in a coherent and consistent manner, as seen in the efforts to create a common European Union foreign policy.

If coherence is not guaranteed among America's oldest allies, then the fact that democracy is messy is even more damaging to the cause, as it does not always lead to governments sympathetic to the US. Numerous recent examples – including Nicaragua, Venezuela, and Palestine – suggest that either the league would have to limit its membership quite rigidly (and risk criticism as a result), or be little better off than the current UN when it comes to matters of international security. If that is indeed the case, the question arises as to what the point of a league of democracies is? What would it be able to achieve that the US cannot already through ad hoc coalitions? It would, in fact, merely create another bureaucracy to support, which would merely add to the criticism of those on the right complaining about excessive waste of taxpayer dollars.

Indeed, the actual purpose of any such league is the biggest problem of all. As Tony Smith has highlighted, 'Such a concert is likely to be a convenient cloak for American hegemony'.[48] It certainly appears that promoters of the league concept are attempting to revert to a position of US hegemony resembling the early years of the Cold War, when the US was the dominant power in an organisation of sympathetic allies (with the added absence of a Soviet veto). Any desire to sidestep the UN to create a new international organisation more susceptible to US influence will be viewed with international scepticism. Even if the US chooses not to limit membership beyond creating certain conditions for entry (like Ikenberry and Slaughter's 'Charter for a Concert of Democracies'[49]), the international response may well see any such league as a tool for furthering US interests. Indeed, as Carothers has highlighted, the international response has been cool, and in the aftermath of Iraq 'people all over the world now see democracy promotion as a dishonest, dangerous cover for the projection of US power and influence'.[50]

Conclusion

Ultimately what is required is a more substantive change in the American mindset. Unilateralism is not the primary way forward, nor is a multilateralism that is simply unilateralism in disguise. Although the US is the sole remaining superpower, it is not always powerful enough to go it alone; there are new global issues that cannot be met unaided, and the challenges America faces will therefore best be met through engagement. As it becomes increasingly clear that the US cannot always impose its will unilaterally, even realist thinkers have acknowledged that there are limits to American power and that it is in US interests to work with other nations to achieve its goals.[51] The interconnected nature of a global society and the threats and challenges it provides requires a new stress on diplomacy. A renewed emphasis on dialogue and engagement is needed if the US is to seize a 'third chance' for internationalism; one that promotes the use of soft power where possible, and collective military action if necessary. Such an approach does not rule out the possibility of the use of force through ad hoc groupings or even unilaterally, but force must be the means to a legitimate and just end, within the boundaries of international law.

Yet despite initial optimism, history suggests that the Obama administration will not usher in a dramatic shift in policy, even if the rhetoric is moving ever more firmly in the direction of engagement. In his September 2009 address to the United Nations General Assembly, Obama conceded that the US was viewed negatively in parts of the world due to 'a belief that on certain critical issues, America had acted unilaterally, without regard for the interests of others'.[52] The case for engagement was put even more strongly in the 2010 National Security Strategy, which argued for enhanced cooperation with a stronger UN:

> ... we must focus American engagement on strengthening international institutions and galvanizing the collective action that can serve common interests such as combating violent extremism; stopping the spread of nuclear weapons and securing nuclear materials; achieving balanced and sustainable economic growth; and forging cooperative solutions to the threat of climate change, armed conflict, and pandemic disease.[53]

Yet while Obama's rhetoric has been characterised by constructive engagement, and the case for American hegemony has not been put as bluntly under Obama as it was under his predecessor, the broader structural issues remain: the unilateralist tendency remains strong, the US remains in the unipolar mindset, and the desire for internationalist alternatives is not restricted to one political party. In addition, as Craig Murphy has argued, any 'strong power will be tempted to use its power for short-term gain rather than to work collectively to institutionalize a longer-term vision'.[54]

Despite both the structural limitations and the negative trend in US-UN relations, the American belief in a multilateral internationalism has never completely disappeared.[55] As a result, an American commitment to multilateralism will continue, but it will be one in which the US continues to seek a hegemonic position. The ongoing desire for international legitimacy and a pragmatic acceptance of the benefits that can come with such an approach in an interconnected world has seen the US take an increasingly selective approach to multilateralism. This has seen the creation of numerous new multilateral organisations since 1945, whether long standing and institutionalised, like NATO, or post-Cold War creations such as the Middle East Quartet. Indeed, given that Obama's National Security Strategy left the door open to 'spur and harness a new diversity of instruments, alliances, and institutions in which a division of labor emerges on the basis of effectiveness, competency, and long-term reliability', the league of democracies idea may not disappear just yet.[56]

Yet it is the nature of American engagement with the rest of the world that remains in question. If the US really is ready to lead once more, it 'must learn to listen, as well as to preach'.[57] The ongoing US commitment to a selective multilateralism reflects American strength, with the US typically taking a hegemonic role, yet the very existence of such organisations also reflects an acknowledgement of the limits of American power. Even then, while the US may be the dominant power, it does not always have the monopoly on wisdom, whether on issues such as the wars in Iraq or Vietnam, or on policy towards Nicaragua and the World Court in the 1980s. There will be times when the UN binds the US and restricts its freedom of action. It should be clear in the aftermath of the war in Iraq that this will not always be a bad thing.[58] The US must work again, as it did during World War II, to define its interests 'in terms congenial to a world order based on a consensus of the community of nations'.[59]

Notes

1. See McCain's foreign policy speech to the Los Angeles World Affairs Council in March 2008: http://www.nytimes.com/2008/03/26/us/politics/26text-mccain.html?pagewanted=1&_r=3 (Accessed 20/04/10).
2. Robert Kagan, *The Return of History and the End of Dreams* (Atlantic Books: London, 2008), 85–6, 97–105. Despite Kagan's explicit dig at Francis Fukuyama in the book's title, Fukuyama had made a similar argument for a Community of Democracies in his *After the Neocons* (London: Profile Books, 2007), 176–7. A similar argument is also made by Ivo Daalder and James Lindsay in 'Democracies of the World, Unite', *The American Interest*, Vol. 2, No. 3 (January/February 2007).
3. G. John Ikenberry, Thomas Knock, Anne-Marie Slaughter and Tony Smith, *The Crisis of American Foreign Policy: Wilsonianism in the Twenty-first Century* (Princeton: Princeton University Press, 2009), 62, 63.
4. Warren Kuehl and Gary Ostrower, 'Internationalism', in Alexander DeConde, Richard Dean Burns and Frederik Logevall, eds., *Encyclopedia of American Foreign Policy*, Second Edition, Vol. 2 (New York, Scribner, 2002), 241, 254.
5. For an example of use of the term internationalism referring primarily to US involvement overseas, see David Schmitz, *The Triumph of Internationalism: Franklin D. Roosevelt and a World in Crisis, 1933–1941* (Washington: Potomac Books, 2007).
6. Alan Dawley, *Changing the World: American Progressives in War and Revolution* (Princeton: Princeton University Press, 2003), 347.
7. For an attempt to move beyond the term isolationist and adopt the more accurate 'anti-interventionist' for the interwar years, see Justus Doenecke, *Storm on the Horizon* (Lanham: Rowman and Littlefield, 2000).
8. See Robert Kagan, *Dangerous Nation: America and the World 1600–1898* (London: Atlantic Books, 2006).
9. See Ruhl Bartlett, *The League to Enforce Peace* (Chapel Hill: University of North Carolina Press, 1944); Warren Kuehl and Lynne Dunn, *Keeping the Covenant: American Internationalists and the League of Nations 1920–1939* (Kent, Ohio: Kent State University Press, 1997); Robert Divine, *Second Chance:*

The Triumph of Internationalism in America during World War II (New York: Atheneum, 1967); Andrew Johnstone, *Dilemmas of Internationalism: the American Association for the United Nations and US Foreign Policy 1941–1948* (Farnham: Ashgate, 2009); Robert Accinelli, 'Pro-UN Internationalists and the Early Cold War: The American Association for the United Nations and U.S. Foreign Policy', *Diplomatic History*, 9 (1985), 347–62.

10 For a survey of the development of international organisations, from William Penn, Jean-Jacques Rousseau and Immanuel Kant onwards, see F.H. Hinsley, *Power and the Pursuit of Peace* (Cambridge: Cambridge University Press, 1963).

11 For the ongoing debate over Wilson's legacy and the meaning of Wilsonianism, see G. John Ikenberry, Thomas J. Knock, Anne-Marie Slaughter and Tony Smith, *The Crisis of American Foreign Policy*; on Wilson's diplomacy, see Thomas Knock, *To End All Wars* (Princeton: Princeton University Press, 1992).

12 See Divine, *Second Chance*, and Townsend Hoopes and Douglas Brinkley, *FDR and the Creation of the UN* (New Haven: Yale University Press, 1997).

13 H. Schuyler Foster, *Activism Replaces Isolationism* (Washington: Foxhall Press, 1983), 31.

14 Robert W. Gregg, *About Face? The United States and the United Nations* (Boulder: Lynne Rienner, 1993), 6–7.

15 Evan Luard, *A History of the United Nations, Volume 1: The Years of Western Domination, 1945–1955* (London: Macmillan, 1982), 93–105.

16 The other major regional grouping was the Southeast Asian Treaty Organisation (SEATO). Created in 1954, SEATO was far less effective than NATO, and much more of a fig leaf for American power in the region.

17 Luard, *A History of the United Nations, Volume 1: The Years of Western Domination, 1945–1955*, 239–40, 253.

18 Gary Ostrower, *The United Nations and the United States* (New York: Twayne, 1998), 93, 125. The most striking decade of growth was between 1955 and 1965, where the membership increased from 60 to 119. See Evan Luard, *A History of the United Nations, Volume 2: The Age of Decolonization, 1955–1965* (Basingstoke: Palgrave, 1989), 517.

19 In contrast, the USSR had issued over 100 vetoes up to that point. Between 1946 and 1965, the USSR issued 101 vetoes compared to zero from the US. Between 1966 and 1992, the USSR issued just 13 vetoes compared to 69 from the US. See Adam Roberts and Benedict Kingsbury, eds., *United Nations, Divided World* (Oxford: Clarendon Press, 1993), 10.

20 Daniel Patrick Moynihan, *A Dangerous Place* (London: Secker and Warburg, 1979), 245–7; Ostrower, *The United Nations and the United States*, 135.

21 Roberts and Kingsbury (eds) *United Nations, Divided World*, 28.

22 Ostrower, *The United Nations and the United States*, 170.

23 See Roger Coate, *Unilateralism, Ideology, & US Foreign Policy: The United States In and Out of UNESCO* (Boulder: Lynne Rienner, 1988).

24 Yves Beigbeder, *Management Problems in United Nations Organizations: Reform or Decline?* (London: Frances Pinter, 1987), 12.

25 Thomas Hughes, 'The Twilight of Internationalism', *Foreign Policy*, 61 (Winter 1985–86), 25–48.

26 Quoted in James Traub, *The Best Intentions* (London: Bloomsbury, 2006), 24.

27 Warren Cohen, *America's Failing Empire* (Malden, MA: Blackwell, 2005), 24; Meisler quoted in Ostrower, *The United Nations and the United States*, 201.

28 Ostrower, *The United Nations and the United States*, 209–15, 218–19.
29 Cohen, *America's Failing Empire*, 129.
30 It even rejected most NATO support, offered for the first time ever under Article 5 which states that an attack on one NATO member is an attack on all.
31 Symptomatic of the Administration, Bolton's was a recess appointment unilaterally pushed through by Bush against the concerns of Congress.
32 http://www.democracynow.org/2005/3/31/john_bolton_in_his_own_words (Accessed 20/04/10).
33 Robert Kagan, *Dangerous Nation* (London: Atlantic, 2006), 115.
34 Joan Hoff recently revised her term 'independent internationalism' to 'unilateral internationalism'. See Joan Hoff, *A Faustian Foreign Policy* (Cambridge: Cambridge University Press, 2008), 7–9. For the concept of 'instrumental multilateralism', see Rosemary Foot, S. Neil MacFarlane and Michael Mastanduno, *US Hegemony and International Organizations* (Oxford: Oxford University Press, 2003), 265–72. Robert Kagan, *Washington Post*, 13 September 2002 (seen at https://carnegieendowment.org/publications/index.cfm?fa=view&id=1065&prog=zgp&proj=zusr (Accessed 20/04/10).
35 See Edward Luck, *Mixed Messages: American Politics and International Organization 1919–1999* (Washington: Brookings, 1999), 15–40; Obama's Inaugural Address: http://www.presidency.ucsb.edu/ws/index.php?pid=44 (Accessed 20/04/10).
36 Luck, *Mixed Messages*, 41.
37 Ikenberry et al., *The Crisis of American Foreign Policy*, 22.
38 Luck, *Mixed Messages*, 129; also see Craig N. Murphy, 'The US and the UN: Return of the Prodigal Son?' in Inderjeet Parmar, Linda B. Miller and Mark Ledwedge, eds., *New Directions in US Foreign Policy* (London: Routledge, 2009), 210–11.
39 Kagan, *The Return of History and the End of Dreams*, 97–105.
40 G. John Ikenberry and Anne-Marie Slaughter, *Forging a World of Liberty Under Law* (Princeton Project Papers, 2006), 7.
41 Council for a Community of Democracies: http://www.ccd21.org/about/index.html (Accessed 20/04/10).
42 Thomas Carothers, 'A League of Their Own', *Foreign Policy*, 167 (July–August 2008), 46.
43 Joseph Nye, *The Paradox of American Power* (Oxford: Oxford University Press, 2002).
44 John Bolton, *Surrender is Not an Option* (New York: Threshold Editions, 2008), 442.
45 Carothers, 'A League of their Own', 48.
46 For a recent assessment of the state of the UN, see Paul Kennedy, *The Parliament of Man: The Past, Present, and Future of the United Nations* (New York: Random House, 2006).
47 Ted Piccone and Morton Halperin, 'A League of Democracies: Doomed to Fail?', *International Herald Tribune*, 5 June 2008.
48 Ikenberry et al., *The Crisis of American Foreign Policy*, 61.
49 Ikenberry and Slaughter, *Forging a World of Liberty Under Law*, 61.
50 Carothers, 'A League of their Own', 47.
51 Andrew Bacevich, *The Limits of Power: The End of American Exceptionalism* (New York: Metropolitan Books, 2008).

52 Obama's Address to the United Nations General Assembly in New York City, 23 September 2009: http://www.presidency.ucsb.edu/ws/index.php?pid=86659&st=&st1 (Accessed 20/04/10).
53 US National Security Strategy, May 2010, 3: http://www.whitehouse.gov/sites/default/files/rss_viewer/national_security_strategy.pdf (Accessed 28/05/10).
54 Murphy, 'The US and the UN: Return of the Prodigal Son?', 219.
55 Indeed, such a position would be impossible: as Bruce Jentleson has highlighted, the distinction between unilateralism and multilateralism 'is one of degree and not a strict dichotomy'. Bruce Jentleson, *American Foreign Policy* (New York: W.W. Norton, 2010), 281.
56 US National Security Strategy, May 2010, 46: http://www.whitehouse.gov/sites/default/files/rss_viewer/national_security_strategy.pdf (Accessed 28/05/10).
57 Luck, *Mixed Messages*, 129.
58 Stephen Walt, *Taming American Power* (New York: W.W. Norton, 2005), 144–52.
59 Clyde Prestowitz, *Rogue Nation: American Unilateralism and the Failure of Good Intentions* (New York: Basic Books, 2003), 174.

11
The US War in Iraq: Confronting the Vietnam Analogy

Andrew Priest

In their pioneering study of the application of history to political decision-making, Richard E. Neustadt and Ernest R. May attempted to devise a model in which a protagonist can think about appropriate historical examples and analogies and utilise them in order to improve the decisions they make. By examining a number of different case studies, Neustadt and May argued history is useful and even essential in the way policymakers operate but that drawing the correct analogies and lessons is crucial in order to make good policy and avoid political disaster. If policymakers spent time thinking about history in a more systematic and structured way, they argued, the quality of the decisions they made would almost certainly improve.[1]

While Neustadt and May's suggestion that learning lessons and drawing analogies from the past is both natural and has much to commend it, identifying the 'correct' lessons of an episode is a highly subjective process. When a particular experience remains contested and its consequences disputed, this becomes more problematic. And when debates about a historical period are linked to broader questions of national identity and purpose, the process is made even more complex. So divisions over the meanings of historical episodes with deep cultural resonance in public life almost inevitably become appropriated for partisan causes.

In the United States this has especially been the case with the Vietnam War. Since 1975, 'Vietnam' has often been cited as the ultimate example of what not to do in war – how not to get drawn into a foreign conflict, how not to fight once there and how not to withdraw. It has become the dominant analogy of the age when discussing the US going to war, shorthand for all manner of disasters that might befall it if it enters into a conflict with another power on a flimsy pretext and without the full support of its political establishment and people. Yet the continuing controversy over the deeper significance of the Vietnam episode means that any use of the Vietnam analogy and the lessons that should be drawn from it remains highly contested.

The eventual US defeat in Vietnam was a profoundly shocking experience for most Americans and it led to a divisive and enduring debate about how this had occurred. Some suggested Vietnam was a misguided cause and that it should warn the US against any similar kind of venture in the future. Others disagreed, arguing that the people who decided to take the US into Vietnam did so for moral reasons and with the best intentions but they found it impossible to achieve their desired objectives. According to these people the US should not shy away from military confrontations because it feared 'another Vietnam', rather it should learn the lesson that it could not afford to undertake half-hearted military missions. Some have gone even further, suggesting the US was actually successful in Vietnam but that it ultimately failed because it was not allowed to win. Such people often blame various groups within American society for undermining the effort there and ultimately causing this failure. Thus, Vietnam still raises great passions and exposes deep ideological divisions that go to the heart of American understandings of how the United States should conduct itself around the world.

Since the events of 11 September 2001, debates about the Vietnam War have achieved even greater significance.[2] Many have resurrected the Vietnam analogy when discussing President George W. Bush's 'war on terror' and his decision to invade Afghanistan and Iraq. Perhaps naturally newspaper editors turned to those with in-depth knowledge of the Vietnam War – former politicians and military leaders, historians and political scientists – to provide explanations of the utility of the analogy. Most analysts have agreed that neither Afghanistan nor Iraq is like Vietnam, or at least that comparisons between the two wars are of limited value. Yet many of them have admitted that Vietnam can be useful to a certain extent to explain aspects of the ongoing conflicts and they have utilised the analogy in order to do so. This has once again brought the controversies surrounding Vietnam to the fore, often highlighting totally opposing viewpoints about the meanings of the war and what should be drawn from them.

This chapter traces some of these Vietnam debates and how they were applied especially to the Iraq War in the mainstream American press during the administration of George W. Bush. In particular it examines the influence of Vietnam-era policymakers and leading academics to illustrate the cultural conflict over meanings of the war. On the liberal left these figures included former official Daniel Ellsberg and writers such as Robert Dallek, George C. Herring, Stanley Karnow, Marilyn B. Young and Howard Zinn. They also include Andrew J. Bacevich, a conservative who draws inspiration from the left to inform his critique of US foreign policy and who was prominent in attacking the administration of George W. Bush. On the conservative right, former Secretary of Defense Melvin Laird, as well as authors such as Eliot A. Cohen, Robert Kagan, Norman Podhoretz, Max Boot, Andrew F. Krepinevich and Mark Moyar have all been prominent. The chapter argues that the utility of the debates comparing Vietnam and Iraq has been limited by their extremely partisan nature. In effect, an 'orthodox' versus 'revisionist' dichotomy in the literature on the Vietnam War has essentially been replayed in debates about Iraq and so the lessons a particular author draws from the Vietnam debacle depend largely on the school of thought to which they subscribe.[3] Following from this, the Vietnam analogy is deployed to support whichever line of argument the author favours regarding the Iraq war. So while two writers may examine the same issues on Iraq and relate them back to what they see as parallel issues in Vietnam, the conclusions they draw about the broader significance of the comparison are often totally different from another writer. In this way, historians re-configure their deeply held views on the consequences of Vietnam to support their positions on contemporary conflicts.

Debating Vietnam

The debates in the US about Vietnam reflect deep divisions in American society. Discussions have tended to focus on how and why the US became involved in Southeast Asia, why it did not achieve its objectives and what lessons can be drawn from the experience. In the aftermath of the war the debates grew in intensity as more histories of the war were written and different schools of thought emerged.[4]

The first school of thought on the war decried it as a misguided US attempt to relocate the containment doctrine that was so successfully applied in Western Europe to Southeast Asia. Authors such as historian Arthur M. Schlesinger and journalist David Halberstam led the way – with Schlesinger's maxim that the Vietnam War was a 'tragedy without villains' proving typical of their views.[5] Other writers, as diverse as Leslie H. Gelb, Richard K. Betts, Gabriel Kolko, Daniel Ellsberg and George Herring, developed and extended these critiques.[6] Many of these writers were from the political left and they tended to see the American misadventure in Vietnam as a warning to present US policymakers about making ill-advised commitments in the Third World. And the further to the left these writers were, the more they saw Vietnam as part of a broader malaise in US foreign policy.

The rebuttal came in the late 1970s, when the revisionist school offered a counter-argument that was much more sympathetic towards the war. These authors argued that the US had been correct to fight communism in Vietnam, but that it had chosen at least some wrong methods to do so. Works by such luminaries as former president Richard Nixon, commander of US forces in Vietnam, William C. Westmoreland, and commentator Norman Podhoretz all offered views of Vietnam as a war that was morally just and that the US could have won but for the timidity of those in the military, politics and the media.[7] Prominent studies by Harry G. Summers Jr, Bruce Palmer Jr and Andrew Krepinevich[8] all suggested that alternative approaches could have succeeded in Vietnam. Summers' hugely influential work – which won widespread praise and was widely distributed in political and military circles – argued that political and military authorities had fought the wrong type of war in Vietnam.[9] The book compelled a conservative turn in understanding Vietnam in the 1980s, which subsequently led to Ronald Reagan's re-appropriation of Vietnam as a 'noble cause' in which the US could take pride.[10]

In the following years any instances of US intervention saw these schools of thought competing to present the 'true' lesson of Vietnam and its relevance for contemporary policymakers. This applied especially to the first post-Cold War conflict the United States engaged in, the mission to expel Iraqi forces from Kuwait in early 1991 – a trend encouraged in large part by President George H.W. Bush, who was careful to stress that the war would not become 'another Vietnam' and mindful not to repeat what many had seen as major errors of judgement in Lyndon B. Johnson's escalation of the Vietnam War in the mid-1960s.[11] The crushing US victory over Iraq in 1991 subsequently led Bush to declare: 'by God, we've kicked the Vietnam syndrome once and for all.'[12] Summers agreed, claiming the president had run 'a masterful campaign... This time we had done it right', particularly in winning over the American people.[13]

The pattern of disagreement among historians and journalists about the lessons of Vietnam for current foreign policy continued under Bush's successor, Bill Clinton. The failed attempt to enforce peace in Somalia confirmed to many policymakers that interventionism should be treated extremely carefully and it cautioned against further expeditions to places such as Rwanda during the genocide of spring 1994 and, initially at least, in Bosnia-Herzegovina and later in Kosovo.[14] Moreover, it raised fears that the US could be drawn into potentially quagmire-like situations as a result of the unstable political order that now prevailed after the end of the Cold War. This, in turn, resurrected debates between the left and right about what lessons should be drawn from Vietnam in the post-Cold War world and their implications for America's global role.[15]

9/11 and Vietnam

By the time the new millennium dawned conservatives were becoming anxious to throw off the limits they believed still constrained the US in foreign affairs. The rise of neoconservatism in the United States that heralded the election of George W. Bush coincided with a renewed interest in revisionist readings of Vietnam and its consequences. In May 2001, reacting to accusations in the *New York Times* magazine about former Senator Bob Kerrey's service in Vietnam, conservative columnist William Safire complained: 'This story is another manifestation of the self-flagellation that led to the Vietnam Syndrome – that revulsion at the use of military power that afflicted our national psyche for decades after our defeat.'[16] This prompted reactions from those on the left, exposing the continued disagreements over the legacies of Vietnam and their use for partisan purposes. In an article appearing two months later in the *Nation* magazine, Richard Falk, a prominent professor of law at Princeton University, attacked Safire for overlooking the fact that the limits the Vietnam War had placed on the US had effectively saved countries from US adventurism in the years since the fall of Saigon. Falk also rounded on Republican senator and future presidential candidate John McCain for supporting Kerrey and claiming he was 'a war hero' when Kerrey had in effect admitted committing war crimes.[17]

With this baiting of the left by the right and vice versa, it was therefore hardly surprising that the events of 11 September 2001 and especially the Afghanistan and Iraq Wars set off another wave of introspection about US involvement in Vietnam.[18] While initially at least both sides were united in their disgust at the nature of the terrorist attacks on New York and Washington, DC, divisions over exactly how the lessons of Vietnam should be promoted quickly took hold. As in other areas, learning the lessons of Vietnam and applying them was a contentious matter because it was dependent on which lessons one chose to learn and promote. So while those on either side of the political spectrum might agree that there had been chronically poor planning and execution of the war in Vietnam and that carpet bombing Afghanistan and engaging in a large-scale conventional fight there would be counterproductive, here the agreement ended. Left-wing historian Howard Zinn writing in the *Los Angeles Times* implored politicians and military strategists to reconsider the consequences of what they were about to do in Afghanistan in light of the mistakes made in Vietnam: 'We need to think about the resentment all over the world felt by people who have been the victims of American military action. In Vietnam, [for example] where we carried out terrorizing bombing attacks, using napalm and cluster bombs, on peasant villages.' Use of the word 'terrorizing' here drove home Zinn's message that engaging in such a conflict made the US no better than the terrorists who had attacked the US, actions he made clear he absolutely abhorred.[19] In contrast, conservative historian and senior fellow of the Council on Foreign Relations Max Boot suggested 'Vietnam's lessons' were that the United States needed to think about military operations in Afghanistan in an unconventional way. The main US successes in Vietnam, Boot suggested, were seen in areas of counterinsurgency, most notably the highly controversial Phoenix programme involving the targeted capture and killing of enemy personnel and the Marines' Combined Action Program to secure villages against Viet Cong infiltration, and he argued that similar measures should now be attempted in Afghanistan.[20] Here he was building upon his new book *The Savage Wars of Peace* published earlier that year arguing for the importance of what he called 'small wars', including Vietnam, in the development of American power and in coming to an understanding of present US conduct in the war on terror.[21]

The routing of the Taliban and al Qaeda from the Afghan capital Kabul reduced the intensity of the Vietnam debates by early 2002. Moreover, by then it was clear that the next target on the Bush administration's list was Iraq and this time Saddam Hussein's failure to comply with US and United Nations (UN) demands to open sites to weapons inspectors was likely to lead to him being toppled. 'Regime change' was the phrase of the moment and the Vietnam pundits quickly re-entered the fray as the sense that the US had overcome the constraints of post-1975 foreign interventionism was rapidly dissipating. Towards the end of 2002, as the Bush administration sought to pass a congressional resolution in Washington and a UN resolution in New York to support military action against Iraq, commentators were already harking back to America's greatest foreign policy disaster and finding some troubling parallels. These seemed especially pertinent as some of the political elites on Capitol Hill and in the administration had been so heavily involved in the latter stages of the

American defeat in Southeast Asia.[22] Historian Robert Dallek suggested that declaring war was a *sine qua non* for success and yet he complained that 'a declaration of war – or even inviting debate and consultation – seems to be viewed by recent occupants of the White House as a quaint anachronism'. Dallek drew parallels between the present crisis and foreign policy follies in Korea and Vietnam, neither of which had been subject to searching congressional investigation in their early stages or to a declaration of war.[23] To some the massive publication demonstrations against the forthcoming Iraq war in major cities around the world in February 2003 also reminded them of protests during the Vietnam War era. Marilyn Young, author of a book about the Vietnam Wars, highlighted it as *the* striking parallel with the upcoming war as it was the most obvious way in which people in the West could connect with war in a foreign land.[24]

The main difference between liberals like Dallek and Young and conservative-revisionists was that they disagreed fundamentally about the threat presented by Iraq at this time. Thus liberals used the Vietnam parallel to argue against action being taken in the Middle East. Dallek implicitly challenged the Bush administration's pretext for invasion and seemed to suggest that the obstacle of gaining a congressional declaration of war would significantly raise the threshold and perhaps even prevent conflict. For her part, Young saw the importance of civilian participation, apparently so effective in opposing Vietnam, as the most resonant parallel for most people. Others (generally further to the left) were more vocal in their opposition. Zinn, for example, continued his attack on US war-making,[25] while Stanley I. Kutler, a historian at the University of Wisconsin Law School, berated the Bush administration and its supporters for refusing to acknowledge that any lessons could be learned from the Vietnam experience at all:

> History is not a selective litany for political agendas and purposes. The lessons of the past are problematic, and easily distorted for partisan gain. Yet the past can provide sober enlightenment; it will not go away, however the president might wish it so.... Our uses of history often border on the simplistic... But our history lessons from Vietnam, and the broader understanding we can learn from both our successes and failures in foreign policy, certainly are relevant to the moment. Where is the debate? History is worth remembering; after all, it is our ideas and memories that we are supposed to be defending.[26]

Iraq and Vietnam

The early success of the conventional battle in Iraq and the capitulation of Iraqi forces once again dampened down discussion of Vietnam in March and April 2003. Yet the subsequent American occupation and ensuing breakdown in law and order, particularly in the Iraqi capital Baghdad, then gave American commentators more opportunities to promote their versions of Vietnam's lessons in the months that followed. Again the fissures opened between the various pundits and what they expected the public to take from the Vietnam experience to help understand and even fight the present conflict.

In general, conservatives were far less likely to draw direct parallels between Iraq and Vietnam because they knew they were disturbing for many people. For example, Robert Kagan, a senior fellow at the Carnegie Endowment for Peace and co-founder of the conservative Project for the New American Century, chided the media for portraying divisions over the Iraq War as being like those over Vietnam: 'In fact, Americans have been remarkably supportive of the Iraq war'.[27] The following year, Kagan attacked the foreign polices of Democratic presidential nominee Senator John Kerry, noting that Kerry's claim that as president he would only fight 'wars of necessity' would lead to disaster and was flatly contradicted by Kerry's congressional vote in favour of war in Iraq. If his initial approval of the Iraq War was a blip, Kagan suggested, then Kerry's Vietnam experience had taught him precisely the wrong lessons about American foreign policy, namely that the US should retreat from the global stage.[28] Similarly Max Boot drew parallels with other successful 'small wars' that the US had fought rather than Vietnam.[29] Moreover, in typical revisionist style, when Boot did discuss Vietnam he emphasised US successes there while decrying the failure of the media to report these back to the home front. This was one of the favourite charges for those who believed that Vietnam was winnable and that perfidious press and TV reports undermined the American effort there. Boot, who had recently returned from Iraq, complained that the US media was repeating many of the same mistakes it had made in Vietnam, focusing on the negative aspects of the military campaign and refusing to relay the real story back to the American people. In fact, he argued (picking up a theme from his writing on Afghanistan) the troops were fighting a successful counter-insurgency campaign but the focus was unfairly being placed on the failure of the civilian aspects of rebuilding Iraq. This endangered the entire effort in the same way that irresponsible media reporting of the 1968 North Vietnamese Tet offensive had done in Vietnam.[30] In making such arguments Boot was in line with the Bush administration itself, which quickly refuted any comparison between the wars in Iraq and Vietnam.³¹

While those on the left were more likely to draw comparisons between the two wars, the majority of those who did accepted the limits of the analogy. During the first weeks of the war, Stanley Karnow, a veteran journalist who had covered Vietnam for many years and written what remains a standard history of the war, could not have been clearer: 'Do Not Compare Iraq with Vietnam' he warned readers of the *Boston Globe*. Citing differences in political situation and terrain, as well as arguing that Iraq 2003 was a conventional conflict unlike the guerrilla war the US fought for most of the 1960s, Karnow cautioned against reading too much into the situation. Indeed, he argued that the Iraq conflict was more challenging to the US because the diplomatic effort to rebuild relations with the Muslim world was so pressing.³² From the summer of 2003, however, Karnow and others who had rejected Vietnam parallels were forced to reassess as the Iraqi insurgency took hold and it seemed his doubts about US success began to grow. Retreating from his staunch opposition to the analogy, Karnow wrote in September that while the 'experiences in Southeast Asia and the Iraq conflict have many differences' they were in fact 'analogous in some respects'.³³ He was largely supported in this later assessment by Robert Dallek who explored other wars the US had fought (most notably in the Philippines after 1898) but who concluded that there was a case to consider similarities between the present conflict and the one in Vietnam, particularly in terms of the use of presidential rhetoric.³⁴ Over the course of the months and years that followed as the situation in Iraq deteriorated, their scepticism concerning the situation in Iraq and use of the Vietnam analogy grew as they attacked the military policies of the Bush administration.³⁵

Others such as prominent former government official Daniel Ellsberg were more concerned with inciting people to take action. Ellsberg's career had almost been a microcosm of the American struggle with the legacies of Vietnam. First visiting Vietnam in the early 1960s for the State Department, Ellsberg had become disillusioned with the war and in the early 1970s began leaking government documents to the press in order to demonstrate the extent of government duplicity regarding its involvement during the previous decade. These were the infamous 'Pentagon Papers' that so riled the Nixon administration and indirectly led to the Watergate scandal. More recently, with almost audacious timing, Ellsberg had published his memoirs *Secrets* in October 2002 just as the debates about the possible war in Iraq were reaching their peak.³⁶ The interviews he gave in the run up to the war made clear his opposition to current administration policies and he drew parallels with his experiences in Vietnam, giving succour to those on the left who opposed the war with Iraq.[37] In 2004, Ellsberg began to wonder aloud who would follow his example in leaking government papers on the war to the media.[38]

Commentators who had served in Vietnam also became involved in discussing Iraq. Andrew Bacevich, a Vietnam veteran and professor of international relations and history at Boston University, was a harsh critique of Bush's decision to invade Iraq and prolific in penning opinion pieces about it. Bacevich's inherent conservatism led him to question why the US should spend billions of dollars in the Middle East when it was failing to solve problems at home and even undermining many of the values it sought to promote. This brought him to remarkably similar conclusions as many classical leftist thinkers such as William Appleman Williams and Charles Beard and often meant that he seemed to straddle both sides of the argument. For example, while Bacevich continued to disagree with Bush's reasons for going to war, he pointed out in July 2003 that the US certainly had the potential to succeed in fighting guerrillas in Iraq but that history suggested the process would be long and unpopular with the American people.[39] Yet he also questioned the morality of the war and attacked the American military for its failure to acknowledge the deaths of Iraqi civilians in its attempts to escape from the 'body count' mentality it had employed in fighting guerrillas in Vietnam.[40]

Ironically, in response to the deepening crisis in Iraq and liberal critiques of US policies there that made reference to Vietnam, revisionists began to mount a defence of US actions in Iraq that now utilised rather than eschewed the lessons of Vietnam. Beginning in mid-2005, Boot, for example, argued that the difficulties the US encountered only reinforced the need to stay the course,[41] and neoconservative Norman Podhoretz published articles attacking those who undermined what he called 'World War IV' against 'Islamofacism' in places such as Iraq and Afghanistan.[42] On a broadly similar theme, Robert Kagan warned those who hoped that Iraq would dampen the spirit for American military adventurism abroad were likely to be disappointed. He claimed the long-held beliefs of Americans and what he called the 'messianic impulse' to help people around the world led them to places such as Vietnam and Iraq.[43] Kagan also asked what would have happened if the US had not gone to war with Iraq in 2003, just as others asked what would have occurred if it had not taken a stand during World War II and later in Vietnam. His answer was that the US would have been worse-off if it had not fought and he quoted a revisionist Vietnam historian, Michael Lind, to support his argument.[44]

In an echo of the 1980s when Summers' book was read by many in Washington, the symbiotic relationship between these revisionist historical accounts of Vietnam and policymaking on Iraq now became more pronounced as political and military leaders appropriated revisionist arguments to advance their own cause, claiming that the US army could have won in Vietnam if it had adopted different tactics and strategies there. While there were a number of books published in the previous twenty years that dealt with this subject, a new generation of Vietnam revisionist historians offered alternative perspectives that appeared relevant to the present foreign policy crisis. So books by Summers and Krepinevich were bolstered by newer accounts by H.R. McMaster, John Nagl and Lewis Sorley that became required reading for strategists who sought to revise the military's approach to Iraq and its overall doctrine.[45] In the last months of 2005, Krepinevich and former Secretary of Defense Melvin Laird both wrote major articles in *Foreign Affairs* magazine detailing the need for new thinking on the situation in Iraq based on revisionist readings of Vietnam. Placing the blame squarely on the US Congress, Laird in particular argued that to reduce funding for Iraq or contemplate withdrawal risked replicating the biggest mistake the US had made in Vietnam during his tenure, while Krepinevich suggested that a new strategy was necessary for the Bush administration.[46] In December, Matt Steinglass, an American journalist living in Hanoi, noted that the arguments made by Sorley, Laird and others were not new, '[b]ut in recent weeks as the issue of withdrawal from Iraq has become more pressing, the claim that congressional cowardice lost the Vietnam War has begun to be heard again'.[47] A new, detailed and controversial revisionist history of the war by Mark Moyar published in 2006 also stirred up the debate,[48] especially as Moyar himself wrote a number of articles comparing the two wars and arguing that mistakes could be learned. In an article in the *Christian Science Monitor*, Moyar heaped blame on Vietnam journalist-historians including David Halberstam and Stanley Karnow for turning against the war effort at a crucial time, thus undermining the American effort in Vietnam.[49]

Towards the end of his administration even President Bush began to sound the revisionist call, claiming the Vietnam analogy for himself to advance his cause in Iraq. As Bush's popularity plummeted and the Republicans endured a crushing defeat in the mid-term elections of November 2006, the president attempted to go on the offensive. Firing his Secretary of Defense Donald Rumsfeld, Bush began to draw up plans for a troop surge in Iraq. During a low-key trip to Vietnam, Bush said, 'One lesson [from the Vietnam War] is, is that we tend to want there to be instant success in the world, and the task in Iraq is going to take a while. We'll succeed unless we quit'.[50] Then in August 2007 Bush devoted a speech to the lessons the history of the Vietnam War offered for Iraq. Now instead of rejecting the analogy he was holding up Vietnam as an example of how America should and should not behave in the troubled Middle East. Speaking to the Veterans of Foreign Wars convention in Kansas City, Missouri, Bush acknowledged that there was 'a legitimate debate' about how the United States became involved in and how it withdrew from Vietnam during the Cold War. 'Whatever your position is on that debate', he continued, 'one unmistakable legacy of Vietnam is that the price of America's withdrawal was paid by millions of innocent civilians'. This was classic revisionism and he went on to detail the horrors that were perpetrated in Indochina by the Vietnamese communist government following its victory in South Vietnam in April 1975 and by the murderous Khmer Rouge regime in Cambodia, under which an estimated quarter of the Cambodian population perished.[51]

Bush's speech, made in the waning months of his administration when he was effectively already a lame duck president, elicited a flurry of responses from the US media who saw the move as being both significant and potentially risky.[52] Unsurprisingly, conservatives came out in support of his observations. Boot, for example, argued that while the analogies made should be treated with caution, Bush had been bold and brave in trying to wrestle it from the doves and, indeed, should have gone further in emphasising the negative consequences of US defeat in Vietnam.[53] Podhoretz was even stronger in his support: 'Never in American history had our honor been so besmirched as it was by the manner of our withdrawal [from Vietnam]'. The US should not, he argued, repeat these mistakes in Iraq.[54] Others were vocal in their opposition.[55] Andrew Bacevich excoriated Bush for his dubious use of history, calling his remarks 'self-serving and selective'. Laying out what he considered to be problems with Bush's analysis and highlighting what he believed were more telling comparisons between the Vietnam and Iraq Wars, he also noted that the Bush administration had rejected all parallels with Vietnam up to this point and now wanted to cherry-pick Vietnam's lessons to justify its own policies.[56] By this time, Bacevich's own relationship with the Iraq War was the subject of much scrutiny. Until 2007 Bacevich had kept private the fact that his son (also called Andrew) was actually fighting in Iraq while Bacevich senior continued to argue against the war. Then in May of 2007, his son was killed by a bomb in Balad, Iraq.[57] In a sign of how deep the divisions in the United States over Iraq were Bacevich reported that among the letters of condolence he and his wife had received, there had also been messages attacking his anti-war stance and blaming him directly for his son's death.[58]

Conclusion

The length of the ground wars in Iraq and Afghanistan has almost inevitably led to comparisons with America's greatest foreign policy failure, Vietnam. Yet the factors that continue to give Vietnam its power in American society – its close proximity and apparent relevance for contemporary conflicts – have also been severely limiting because the emotional response it evokes is still so raw. This is especially the case because so many who were involved in the Vietnam War, in whatever way, are intimately connected to policymaking and political commentary today.

While the Vietnam analogy remains enormously powerful in American public life, it does so not because of some shared cultural understanding of the event but rather the opposite; because it resonates with different communities in very different ways. So while writers who subscribe to the orthodox school on Vietnam have continued to see the war as a fundamentally misguided use of American power and its consequences as a reason for extreme caution around the world, revisionists in contrast tend to view US actions in Vietnam as laudable and its failure as a reason to strive for a reassertion of American power. This has generally been the case since the Vietnam War itself and the pattern has continued during the Afghanistan and Iraq campaigns. Thus writers choose to highlight or reject specific lessons of the war for present-day conflicts according to a pre-existing political agenda. This can be seen most clearly in the way that the revisionists originally dismissed comparisons with Vietnam as being irrelevant in the early stages of the Iraq War, while simultaneously many orthodox historians and social scientists were pointing out uncomfortable parallels that few of the revisionists wanted to address. Yet when the situation in Iraq became so dire, with ensuing fears that the US would be forced to withdraw ignominiously, revisionists began to deploy the lessons of Vietnam as a means for urging Americans to stay the course and not quit as they believed the US had done in Vietnam 30 years before. As this group saw the consequences of Vietnam in largely negative terms because it had apparently signalled a crisis of confidence in American global power, its members reasoned that Iraq could force a similar kind of reappraisal and sought to prevent it. In this respect, the continuing debates about the Vietnam War expose fundamentally different understandings among different groups regarding the use of American power in the world.

While there has been a great deal of intelligent debate by leading public intellectuals about the merits of the American decision to invade Afghanistan and Iraq as part of its war on terror, this chapter has argued that the utility of deploying the lessons of Vietnam in order to do so remains highly problematic. In part this is connected to broad issues about drawing the 'correct' lessons of a particular historical episode and applying them to a contemporary event in the way that Neustadt and May advocated in their study. But the continuing controversies over Vietnam mean that there are myriad lessons to be derived from the war, each politically charged. This suggests that it is difficult to drawing implications from an episode that remains as highly contested and, indeed, culturally divisive as Vietnam. Paradoxically then, the striking resonance of the Vietnam War in American public life also suggests the limited utility of applying its lessons to contemporary conflicts. Not only is this unlikely to be resolved soon, but it will almost certainly be further complicated as the lessons of Iraq and Afghanistan augment those of Vietnam.

Notes

1 R.E. Neustadt and E.R. May, *Thinking in Time: The Uses of History for Decision-Makers* (New York: Free Press, 1986).
2 Many academic studies have been published comparing the Vietnam and Iraq Wars. See, for example, R.K. Brigham, *Is Iraq Another Vietnam?* (New York: Public Affairs, 2006); K.J. Campbell, *A Tale of Two Quagmires: Iraq, Vietnam and the Hard Lessons of War* (Boulder, CO.: Paradigm, 2007); J. Dumbrell and D. Ryan, *Vietnam in Iraq: Tactics, Lessons, Legacies and Ghosts* (London and New York: Routledge, 2007); T.C. Jesperson, 'Analogies at War: Vietnam, the Bush Administration's War in Iraq, and the Search for a Usable Past', *Pacific Historical Review*, 74 (2005), 411–26; L.C. Gardner and M.B. Young, *Iraq and the Lessons of Vietnam* (New York and London: New Press, 2007); A. Priest, 'From Saigon to Baghdad: The Vietnam Syndrome, the Iraq War and American Foreign Policy', *Intelligence and National Security*, 24 (2009), 139–71; J. Record and W.A. Terrill, *Iraq and Vietnam: Differences, Similarities, and Insights* (Carlisle, PA: Strategic Studies Institute of the US Army War College, 2004). In contrast, very little has been published comparing the Afghan War with the war in Vietnam.
3 Lloyd Gardner and Marilyn Young have noted the prominence of Vietnam revisionism in the Iraq debates, although they suggest that liberals have incorporated revisionist critiques in contrast to the emphasis in this chapter

on the clash between these two groups. See Gardner and Young, 'Introduction', in Gardner and Young, *Iraq*, 2.
4 For good overviews of Vietnam scholarship, see R.A. Divine, 'Historiography: Vietnam Reconsidered', *Diplomatic History*, 12 (1988) 79–93; G.R. Hess, 'The Unending Debate: Historians and the Vietnam War', *Diplomatic History*, 18 (1994) 239–64; David Anderson, Christian Appy, Mark Philip Bradley and Robert P. Brigham, 'Interchange: Legacies of the Vietnam War', *Journal of American History*, 93 (2006) 452–90.
5 D. Halberstam, *The Making of a Quagmire* (London: Bodley Head, 1965); D. Halberstam, *The Best and the Brightest* (London: Barrie & Jenkins, 1972); A.M. Schlesinger, *The Bitter Heritage: Vietnam and American Democracy, 1941–1966* (Boston: Houghton Mifflin, 1966). The Schlesinger quote is on p. 32.
6 L.H. Gelb with R.K. Betts, *The Irony of Vietnam: The System Worked* (Washington: Brookings Institute, 1979); D. Ellsberg, *Papers on the War* (New York: Simon & Schuster, 1972); G. Kolko, *The Roots of American Foreign Policy: An Analysis of Power and Purpose* (Boston: Beacon Press, 1969); G. Kolko, *Vietnam: Anatomy of War, 1940–1975* (London and Sydney: Allen & Unwin, 1987); G.C. Herring, *America's Longest War: The United States and Vietnam, 1950–1975* (Fourth ed. Boston: McGraw-Hill, 2002).
7 R. Nixon, *No More Vietnams* (London: W.H. Allen, 1986); Norman Podhoretz, *Why We Were in Vietnam* (New York: Simon & Schuster, 1982); W.C. Westmoreland, *A Soldier Reports* (New York: Doubleday, 1976).
8 A.F. Krepinevich Jr, *The Army and Vietnam* (Baltimore and London: The Johns Hopkins University Press, 1986); B. Palmer Jr, *The 25-Year War: America's Military Role in Vietnam* (Lexington: University Press of Kentucky, 1984); H.G. Summers Jr, *On Strategy: The Vietnam War in Context* (Carlisle Barracks: Strategic Studies Institute, US Army War College, 1983).
9 For an early rebuttal of Summers' thesis, see J.M. Gates, 'Vietnam: The Debate Goes On', *Parameters: Journal of the US Army War College*, 14 (1984) 15–25. See also G. Hess, 'The Military Perspective on Strategy in Vietnam: Harry G. Summers's, *On Strategy* and Bruce Palmer's, *The 25-Year War*', *Diplomatic History*, 10 (1986) 91–106.
10 Remarks at the Conservative Political Action Conference Dinner, 18 February 1983, *Public Papers of the Presidents of the United States* (hereafter Public Papers), Ronald Reagan, 1983, Book I (Washington, DC: United States Government Printing Office, 1984), 249–56; Remarks at Memorial Day Ceremonies Honouring Unknown Servicemen of the Vietnam Conflict, 28 May 1984, Public Papers, Ronald Reagan, 1984, Book I (1986), 748–50. For discussion of Reagan's foreign policy and the legacies of Vietnam, see T.B. McCrisken, *American Exceptionalism and the Legacy of Vietnam: US Foreign Policy Since 1974* (Basingstoke and New York: Palgrave Macmillan, 2003), esp. 112–19; M.T. Klare, *Beyond the 'Vietnam Syndrome': US Interventionism in the 1980s* (Washington D.C.: Institute for Policy Studies, 1981); T.G. Paterson, 'Historical Memories and Illusive Victories: Vietnam and Central America', *Diplomatic History*, 12 (1988) 1–18; K.E. Sharpe, 'The Post-Vietnam Formula under Siege: The Imperial Presidency and Central America', *Political Science Quarterly*, 102 (1987–8) 549–69.
11 The President's New Conference on the Persian Gulf Crisis, 9 January 1991, Public Papers, George Bush, 1991, Book I (1992), 17–23.

12 Remarks to the American Legislative Exchange Council, 1 March 1991, Public Papers, George Bush, 1991, Book I, 195–7.
13 H.G. Summers Jr, 'The Vietnam Syndrome and the American People', *Journal of American Culture*, 17 (1994), 53–8. The quote is on p. 57. See also, *inter alia*, Summers, 'Putting Vietnam Syndrome to Rest', *Los Angeles Times*, 2 March 1991, 6. Others, such as Leslie H. Gelb, David Halberstam and Eric Alterman, were less convinced, however. See L.H. Gelb, 'Mr. Bush's War Strategy', *New York Times*, 16 January 1991, A23; E. Alterman, 'Is the Vietnam Syndrome Dead?', *New York Times*, 4 March 1991, A17; D. Halberstam, 'Out of the Quagmire', *Los Angeles Times*, 24 March 1991, 1.
14 For discussions of these issues in relation to Vietnam, see McCrisken, *American Exceptionalism*, 169–75; R.A. Melanson, *American Foreign Policy Since the Vietnam War: The Search for Consensus from Richard Nixon to George W. Bush* (New York: M.E. Sharpe, 2005), 248–56; Robert D. Schulzinger, *A Time for Peace: The Legacy of the Vietnam War* (New York: Oxford University Press, 2006), 194–6; R. Sobel, *The Impact of Public Opinion on US Foreign Policy Since Vietnam* (New York and Oxford: Oxford University Press, 2001), 175–230.
15 On this point concerning US intervention in Somalia, see especially G. Will, '60's Sensibility Shapes Interventionist Foreign Policy', *Seattle Post – Intelligencer*, 2 September 1993, A10. For other views on this episode, see, for example, K.B. Richburg, 'Aideed's Urban War: Propaganda Victories Echo Vietnam', *Washington Post*, 6 October 1993, A12; A. Quindlen, 'Admit Our Naivite and Bring Soldiers Home from Somalia', *Chicago Tribune*, 8 October 1993, 27; N.M. Horrock, 'Distant Echoes: In Somalia, Similarities to Vietnam', *Chicago Tribune*, 10 October 1993, 1.
16 W. Safire, 'Syndrome Returns', *New York Times*, 30 April 2001, A19.
17 R. Falk, 'The Vietnam Syndrome', *Nation*, 9 July 2001, 2, 18–23, 273.
18 See, for example, S. Mufson, 'For Bush's Veteran Team: What Lessons to Apply?', *Washington Post*, 15 September 2001, A05; J. Vennochi, 'Will this Jolt Put Vietnam Behind Us?', *Boston Globe*, 20 September 2001, A19; R.W. Apple, Jr, 'A Military Quagmire Remembered: Afghanistan as Vietnam', *New York Times*, 31 October 2001, B1; G.C. Herring, '9/11/01: The End of the Vietnam Syndrome?', www.mhhe.com/herring [2002], date accessed 1 February 2010.
19 H. Zinn, 'America's Course… and Peace', *Los Angeles Times*, 23 September 2001, M2.
20 M. Boot, 'Vietnam's Lessons on How to Fight Globo-Guerrillas', *Wall Street Journal*, 2 October 2001, A18.
21 M. Boot, *The Savage Wars of Peace: Small Wars and the Rise of American Power* (New York: Basic Books, 2002).
22 For example, S. Murray, 'Hagel Reins in Bush War Plans', *Wall Street Journal*, 12 September 2002, A4, S.R. Weisman, 'History Lessons for Wartime Presidents and Their Generals', *New York Times*, 15 September 2002, 4.14; M. Allen and C. Lane, 'Resolution Likened to '64 Vietnam Measure', *Washington Post*, 20 September 2002, A20; R.L. Bartley, 'Thinking Things Over: The Democrats Refight Vietnam', *Wall Street Journal*, 30 September 2002, A17; D.S. Broder, 'Still Reeling From Vietnam', *Washington Post*, 9 October 2002, A31; K. Phillips, 'Iraq; Of Politics and Vengeance', *Los*

Angeles Times, 13 October 2002, M1; R. Perlstein, 'Goodbye to the Vietnam Syndrome', *New York Times*, 15 October 2002, A27.
23 R. Dallek, 'Declaring War Is More Than a Formality', *Washington Post*, 5 May 2002, B01. Ironically, Dallek's call echoed a key argument made by the revisionist Harry Summers in the 1980s.
24 M. Young, 'Will Iraq Be Vietnam or WWII?', *Los Angeles Times*, 9 February 2003, M3; M.B. Young, *The Vietnam Wars* (New York: HarperCollins, 1991).
25 H. Zinn, 'The Case Against the War on Iraq', *Boston Globe*, 19 August 2002, A11.
26 S.I. Kutler, 'On Forgetting the Past', *Chicago Tribune*, 3 September 2002, 19; Kutler, 'The Vietnam Folly Calls Out to us as War Fever Burns', *Los Angeles Times*, 27 August 2002, B13.
27 R. Kagan, 'Divided on the War? Not Really', *Washington Post*, 19 December 2003, A37.
28 R. Kagan, 'The Kerry Doctrine', *Washington Post*, 1 August 2004, B7.
29 M. Boot, 'Forget Vietnam – History Deflates Guerrilla Mystique', *Los Angeles Times*, 6 April 2003, M3; Boot, 'A Century of Small Wars Shows They Can Be Won', *New York Times*, 6 July 2003, 4.10; Boot, 'The Lessons of a Quagmire', *New York Times*, 16 November 2003, 4.13.
30 M. Boot, 'Winning the Peace, Quietly', *Los Angeles Times*, 7 September 2003, M1
31 V. Loeb, 'No Iraq "Quagmire", Rumsfeld Asserts; Secretary Disputes Vietnam Comparison', *Washington Post*, 1 July 2003, A09.
32 S. Karnow, 'Do Not Compare Iraq with Vietnam', *Boston Globe*, 20 April 2003, D11. His study of Vietnam remains essential reading for scholars. See S. Karnow (1997) *Vietnam: A History* (Second ed. New York: Penguin).
33 S. Karnow, 'Vietnam's Shadow Lies Across Iraq', *Los Angeles Times*, 26 September 2003, B15.
34 R. Dallek, 'Patience May Not Be An Option: Will Public Pique Limit Bush's Time in Iraq?', *Washington Post*, 28 September 2003, B01. For a response to Dallek's book dealing with its contemporary relevance, see T. Van Dyk, 'JFK Biography Offers Lessons to Bush', *Seattle Post – Intelligencer*, 24 July 2003, B4.
35 T.S. Purdum, 'Flashback to the 60's: A Sinking Sensation of Parallels Between Iraq and Vietnam', *New York Times*, 29 January 2005, A12; S. Karnow, 'Worse Than McNamara?', *Washington Post*, 8 October 2006, B1; R. Dallek, 'Two Wars, Two Presidents, Two Eerily Similar Predicaments', *Boston Globe*, 14 January 2007, D1; Dallek, 'Iraq Isn't Like Vietnam – Except When It Is', *Washington Post*, 20 May 2007, B3.
36 D. Ellsberg *Secrets: A Memoir of Vietnam and the Pentagon Papers* (New York: Viking, 2002). In his review of the book, George Herring noted that its publication was coincidental but also timely. G.C. Herring, 'A Man For All Seasons', *Los Angeles Times*, 13 October 2002, R3.
37 For example, F. Branfman, 'The Salon Interview: Daniel Ellsberg', *Slate*, 19 November 2002, http://www.salon.com/news/feature/2002/11/19/ellsberg/index.html, date accessed 4 February 2010.
38 D. Ellsberg, 'Truths Worth Telling', *New York Times*, 28 September 2004, A25; Ellsberg, 'Where are Iraq's Pentagon Papers?', *Los Angeles Times*, 11 June 2006, M1.

39 A.J. Bacevich, 'The Long Battle Ahead', *Los Angeles Times*, 21 July 2003, B11.
40 A.J. Bacevich, 'What's an Iraqi Life Worth?', *Washington Post*, 9 July 2006, B1.
41 M. Boot, 'Why the Rebels Will Lose', *Los Angeles Times*, 23 June 2005, B13; Boot, 'Iraq isn't Vietnam, Henry', 22 July 2007, M5.
42 N. Podhoretz, *World War IV: The Long Struggle Against Islamofascism* (New York: Doubleday, 2007); J. Rago, 'Unrepentant Neocon', *Wall Street Journal*, 12 August 2006, A8. This built upon ideas developed by Eliot Cohen after the 9/11 attacks. See E.A. Cohen, 'World War IV: Let's Call This Conflict What It Is', *Wall Street Journal*, 20 November 2001. For a response, see A.J. Bacevich, 'This is not World War Three – or Four', *Spectator*, 22 July 2006.
43 R. Kagan, 'Our "Messianic Impulse"', *Washington Post*, 10 December 2006, B7; Kagan, 'Staying the Course, Win or Lose', *Washington Post*, 2 November 2006, A17.
44 R. Kagan, 'Whether This War Was Worth It: In Analyzing Iraq, Consider the Effects of Having Done Nothing', *Washington Post*, 19 June 2005, B07.
45 D. Ignatius, 'A Better Strategy For Iraq', *Washington Post*, 4 November 2005, A23; M. Steinglass, 'Vietnam and Victory', *Boston Globe*, 18 December 2005, K1; G. Jaffe, 'Next Chapter: As Iraq War Rages, Army Re-Examines Lessons of Vietnam', *Wall Street Journal*, 20 March 2006, A1.
46 A. Krepinevich Jr, 'How to Win in Iraq', *Foreign Affairs*, Vol. 84, No. 5 (2005), 87–104; M.R. Laird, 'Iraq: Learning the Lessons of Vietnam', *Foreign Affairs*, Vol. 84, No. 6 (2005), 22–43. Laird repeated these ideas in a number of subsequent articles. See, for example, Laird, 'A Model for Responsible Withdrawal: The Vietnam Plan Worked Until Aid Was Cut Off', *Washington Post*, 29 June 2007, A21.
47 Steinglass, 'Vietnam and Victory'.
48 M. Moyar, *Triumph Forsaken: The Vietnam War, 1954–1965* (Cambridge and New York: Cambridge University Press, 2006).
49 M. Moyar, 'The Vietnam History You Haven't Heard', *Christian Science Monitor*, 22 January 2007, 9. See also Moyar, 'An Iraqi Solution: Vietnam Style', *New York Times*, 21 November 2006, A29; Moyar, 'Knowing When to Let Go', *Washington Post*, 6 December 2006, A25; Moyar '"Worst in History"?', *Wall Street Journal*, 22 May 2007, A14.
50 D.E. Sanger, 'Vietnam War's Lesson: Don't Quit, Bush Says', *International Herald Tribune*, 18–19 November 2006, 1. Less than one week before this Bush had continued to reject the analogy. See D. Jackson, 'As Vietnam Trip Nears, Bush Rejects Iraq Link', *USA Today*, 13 November 2006, A4.
51 Transcript of President Bush's Speech at the Veterans of Foreign Wars Convention, Kansas City, 22 August 2007, http://www.nytimes.com/2007/08/22/washington/w23policytext.html, date accessed 17 February 2010.
52 For example, M.A. Fletcher, 'Bush Compares Iraq to Vietnam', *Washington Post*, 23 August 2007, A01; J. Rutenberg, S.G. Stolberg and M. Mazzetti, 'Bush Declares that "Free Iraq" is Within Reach', *New York Times*, 23 August 2007, A1.
53 M. Boot, 'Another Vietnam', *Wall Street Journal*, 24 August 2007, A15.
54 N. Podhoretz, 'America the Ugly', *Wall Street Journal*, 11 September 2007, A19.

55 See, for example, T. Shanker, 'Historians Question Bush's Reading of Lessons of Vietnam War for Iraq', *New York Times*, 23 August 2007, A8.
56 A.J. Bacevich, 'What Bush Didn't See in Vietnam', *Los Angeles Times*, 25 August 2007, A19.
57 B. MacQuarrie, 'Son of Professor Opposed to War is Killed in Iraq', *Boston Globe*, 15 May 2007, A1.
58 A.J. Bacevich, 'I Lost My Son to a War I Oppose', *Washington Post*, 27 May 2007, B1.

12
Domesticating Katrina: Eliding the International Coordinates of a 'Natural' Disaster

Anna Hartnell

In the years that have passed since Hurricane Katrina, the authorities in New Orleans have been quietly doing away with the city's remaining stock of affordable housing through measures characterized by the United Nations as violations of human rights. The demolition of public housing in New Orleans has prevented large numbers of very poor and mostly black residents from returning home, and it seems likely that for many, this displacement will be permanent.

In the years immediately following Katrina homelessness soared, house prices doubled, and public transportation and public health facilities remained closed. The city's housing market has now belatedly responded to the economic slow-down, and the scenes of widespread homelessness have in large part moved from the streets to the floors of family and friends. Some public facilities have now resumed operations, but it is hard to avoid the conclusion that the infrastructure which has supported the existence of low-income residents in the city for decades is being replaced by a set-up designed to attract wealthier, and some say whiter, residents.[1]

Perhaps unsurprisingly, the UN's intervention in February 2008 – which called for a halt to the demolition of public housing in the city, and which drew attention to the particular vulnerability of African Americans – went largely unnoticed by the national and international media.[2] Local news outlets effectively dressed up the incident as the pronouncement of a clunky international body remote from and ignorant about the situation on the ground in New Orleans. This treatment fits the trend of viewing Katrina and its aftermath as a predominantly local affair – at the most a domestic issue of national concern, with few global implications.

While the statement issued by UN human rights officials tells a different story from that told by the media, it is the grassroots organizing that most powerfully captures the international coordinates of the unfolding post-Katrina disaster. Increasingly, a burgeoning network of community-based organizations in New Orleans are calling for the 'right of return', a key element of the Guiding Principles on Internal Displacement which were adopted by the UN in 1998 and which are consistent with international humanitarian and human rights law. Such rhetoric shows how far many New Orleanians have come – from initially protesting against the use of the term 'refugee' to refer to Katrina evacuees, on the basis that it was an insulting and arguably racist denial of citizen status, to deploying a principle usually cited by those for whom citizenship has meant anything but protection.

I suggest that this path can be tracked by considering the ways in which Katrina's significance has been consistently played down in terms of its international implications. For some reason Katrina has been largely unavailable for interpretation and understanding – on the part of large segments of the media, government and public opinion – in the context of the US's wider role on the world stage. This is particularly clear when it is compared to other major events that have highlighted America's place in the world in the first decade of the twenty first century. In spite of the anger directed at the Bush administration's incompetent handling of the disaster, Katrina ultimately did not attract the same levels of public sympathy as did 9/11. And while it is now recognized as a major factor behind Bush's declining popularity in the latter years of his administration, Katrina did not become a rallying point for the American left to the extent that the disastrous Iraq war did. I suggest that this is in part because commentators have been unwilling or unable to translate the Katrina crisis into a clearly recognizable narrative. The conceptual confusion that has framed the Katrina narrative is part of a marked tendency to 'contain' the storm's significance, not just inside the borders of the United States but within the confines of a very specific region.

This paper is divided into three parts. The first section shows the way in which Hurricane Katrina has been framed as a largely regional event, and suggests that this framing, as compared to an event like 9/11 which had clear global dimensions, has played a significant role in marginalizing storm survivors. The second section suggests a link between this framing and the debate about how to rebuild New Orleans – and indeed the debate as to whether the city should be built back at all. What emerges in this section is that the storm's local impact – particularly in terms of the shortage in affordable housing – has potentially global resonance. This connection between the local and the global is evident on examination of the evolving human rights narrative that has been increasingly sounded by Gulf Coast activists since September 2005, the subject of the third section. This section explores the significance of this narrative within the wider contexts of human rights discourse within the US, and specifically the crucial role it has played in the African American struggle against racism. Current organizing in New Orleans and the Gulf Coast region can be seen, I suggest, as heir to a holistic vision of social justice that dates back to the abolition movement and which came to the fore in black American politics in the late 1930s and 1940s and again towards the latter stages of the Civil Rights movement.

Katrina, 9/11, Iraq

In the midst of the federal incompetence that characterized the initial response to the hurricane in September 2005, 9/11 served as an obvious example against which to measure the relief effort. This comparison belies huge differences: Ground Zero covered just 16 acres of New York City, whereas 80 percent of New Orleans was under water following the levee breaches. 9/11 raised the spectre of global terrorism whereas Katrina could be put down to a particularly gruelling episode in the yearly hurricane season.

These differences notwithstanding, the 9/11 comparison became a frequent rhetorical touchstone in the protestations against both the media coverage and the federal response to Hurricane Katrina. Where media responses to Katrina revealed stark divides in attitudes towards race and class, the overwhelming message promoted by the US media in the aftermath of 9/11 was one of national unity. What critics repeatedly pointed out was the fact that those who suffered as a consequence of 9/11 were presented to the world – by both media and elected officials – as innocent victims while those affected by Katrina emerged in the media as strangely culpable.

As Erica M. Czaja suggests in her discussion of Katrina's aftermath, while the relationship between government policy, media, and public opinion is complex and widely contested, there is evidence to suggest that public opinion often does drive government policy, and that 'the American public often bases its opinions on information it receives from the media'.[3] It's therefore reasonable to assume that while government policy and media representation are by no means synonymous, there is a relationship. This was all too evident in Katrina's aftermath, when the media colluded in portraying Katrina survivors as violent thugs, a portrait that served as part justification for the disastrously slow and inept government response. Fox commentator Bill O'Reilly's claim that survivors were only attempting to leave New Orleans because they could no longer get their 'fix' is just one example.[4]

The actions and behaviour of President Bush himself were hardly heroic in response to either event, and evidence accumulates to show that the long-term treatment of 9/11 victims has been far from exemplary. But studies show that the media played a crucial role in fanning the flames of national trauma and resentment in 2001 in a way that undoubtedly smoothed the course of the Bush administration's so-called 'war on terror'.[5] That both media and government embraced the victims of 9/11 – in rhetoric, in the case of government, if not in reality – and largely rejected Katrina survivors, in both rhetoric and reality, is what makes the comparison so striking, even if this difference is in itself unsurprising. Where 9/11 promoted the image of American innocence abroad, an exceptionalist myth that has long been a staple of US foreign policy, Katrina threatened to indict the US government, and in particular its stance on tackling racism, before the eyes of the world.

That this comparison has played a constitutive role in the way people have interpreted the deeply problematic responses to Katrina is evident throughout the growing body of scholarship on the hurricane, as well as in the many documentary films that have been made about the storm. Spike Lee's *When the Levees Broke: A Requiem in Four Acts* (2006) is a prime example. Including interview footage that focuses overwhelmingly on citizens that made New Orleans their home before the storm, the spectres of both 9/11 and Iraq are repeatedly raised as modes of comparison through which to critique the administration. Charles McHale captures much of the sentiment behind these comparisons when he points out in the film's epilogue that if 'the people of this country will see it [Katrina] more or less like 9/11 in New York' then they 'will do something to force the leaders in congress to do something about helping this city'.[6]

That attitudes towards Katrina survivors were so marked by division and ambivalence – where responses to September 11 victims were marked by consensus – is reflected in the conceptual confusion that, in Katrina's immediate aftermath, appeared to grip the government and media when speaking about the storm and its victims. Soon after the storm it was acknowledged that what started out as a natural disaster was fast evolving into a social one. It was a social disaster that was from the beginning coded in distinctly regional and national terms: as part of America's – and particularly the South's – unfolding story of poverty and racism, largely thought outside the contexts of the global legacies of slavery, colonialism, and the current realities of free market capitalism and climate change. Katrina memorably exposed a source of national shame, but one thought in the terms of a specifically 'American dilemma'. Yet while Katrina and its aftermath led to the recycling of clichés on US race relations, beneath the rhetoric there ran a recurring sense that the tragedy made only an uncertain impact on the national, let alone international, radar.

Where 9/11 was clearly an incident of global proportions with America at its centre, Katrina's location was much less clear; it was not perceived as an 'American event' in the way that 9/11 was. Early pronouncements on the storm portrayed it as a regional event peculiarly divorced from the nation, and its 'international' resonance seemed to go no deeper than vague parallels to a nebulous conception of the 'Third World'. The actor Sean Penn sums up his reaction to the devastation in his contribution to *When the Levees Broke* by saying: 'This was America, this was today, and this was a third world scene.' Katrina had produced what David Dante Troutt describes as 'an array of destruction unimaginable in a developed country',[7] and it is precisely the 'unimaginable' nature of the disaster that characterizes so much of the discourse.

This ambiguity marked President Bush's comments made on 2 September 2005 following his aerial tour of New Orleans – which, as many noted, did not involve him setting foot on Louisiana soil or confronting a single human being affected by the storm. He remarked, 'I've just completed a tour of some devastated country'; he also claimed to 'know the people of this part of the world are suffering'. People 'from this part of the world', Bush insisted, would not be forgotten. The president's sense of disconnect from the region was clear.[8]

Precisely who lay at the centre of this tragedy was similarly the source of some perplexity. This manifested itself in the widespread media labelling of Katrina evacuees as 'refugees'. Understandably, it was the African American community that reacted most strongly against this label – interpreted as yet another attempt to deny the citizen status of US blacks. By persisting with this description, the media enabled a racist discourse that has long served the US government in its denial of responsibility towards the nation's black population. Casting both the hurricane disaster zone and its victims into an uncertain location, this rhetoric worked curiously to deprive understandings of Katrina of wider terms of reference – whether national or international. Comparable only to a largely mythical notion of 'Third World' disaster, the storm's significance is markedly localized. By characterizing Katrina and its victims as somehow 'foreign' or 'placeless', sectors of the media, the president, and all who engaged in this rhetoric colluded in staging the hurricane as an isolated spectacle largely beyond the realms of identification.

As Stephanie Houston Grey points out, these rhetorical moves are consistent not only with the strategies deployed by the federal responders to the storm, but also with a narrative that has long marginalized the region and particularly the city of New Orleans. She writes, 'The federal response to Katrina demonstrated that the catastrophe was not to be addressed via outreach and rescue but through strategies of containment.' This strategy involved federal responders establishing 'a periphery around the city that blocked access to its main staging areas for at least five days'. Rather than seeing such a policy – which effectively abandoned people amidst unbearable heat and without food and medical supplies – as an aberration, Grey describes it as 'a logical extension of existing urban rationality' that specifically targets ethnic minorities. In Grey's analysis, New Orleans plays a special role in this narrative of racialized urban control: 'Residing as it does at the mouth of the Mississippi River, the city of New Orleans has been historically characterized as a site of expulsion, waste, and excess.' Whether or not Grey's 'geographical allegory of waste, pollution, and ethnic permeation' really did play a decisive role in the treatment of the storm survivors, it is hard not to agree with her conclusion that on some level, this strategy of regional containment, working both on a literal and metaphorical level, smoothed the process whereby human beings were cast as largely 'disposable'.[9]

On 3 September 2005, African American civil rights activist Al Sharpton called on the media to stop referring to evacuees as 'refugees'. He claimed that refugees are 'some others from somewhere lost, needing charity'. Seeking instead to define the place of Katrina evacuees in American national life, Sharpton insisted on their citizenship and their subsequent rights to protection; sarcastically he exclaimed: 'Activate the National Guard, activate the military. Oh I forgot, they were in Iraq making democracy free for those abroad, while those at home had nothing.'[10]

Certainly the fact that federal forces took five days to reach storm-struck Louisiana pointed to clear evidence of federal incompetence. But it also raised questions about the stationing of large numbers of troops in Iraq. By refuting the de-nationalizing implications of the 'refugee' status, and by emphasizing national over international imperatives, Sharpton's comments attempted to reinsert Katrina evacuees back into the identifiable and privileged terrains of American citizenship and identity. In so doing, he typified a trend of African American resistance to the racist discourses unleashed by the storm. Tonya Williams, former coordinator of the US Human Rights Network's campaign to have Katrina survivors recognized by the US government as Internally Displaced Persons, suggests that this attitude towards the 'refugee' label relates to a desire on the part of some African Americans to hold at a distance the 'visual pictures of Africans who had been displaced because of conflict'. The rejection of this implied analogy, Williams claims, derives from a larger discourse whereby 'African descendent peoples' in the US have 'conceptualized themselves against continental Africans'.[11]

Sharpton's articulation of this discourse illustrates the limitations of this kind of resistance. By emphasizing American benevolence abroad as compared with the neglect of a vulnerable home front, Sharpton revealed the conservative thrust of his own critique – which condemned the war but upheld the government line on it. His message amounted to not much more than 'charity should begin at home', and so laid claim to a higher form of patriotism. He thus side-stepped a more thorough-going critique of US power in favour of assuming an exceptionalist rhetoric – and in so doing missed the opportunity of interpreting the fallout from Katrina in wider global terms.

An important consequence of the widespread condemnation of the federal mishandling of Katrina by Sharpton and others was that it decisively turned the tide of popular opinion in the US against the Iraq war. Yet while the debate about the occupation of Iraq that resulted was fierce and ongoing, the aftermath of Katrina largely dropped out of national conversations. Katrina thus gained its significance as a catalyst for talking about something else.

More recent media attempts to brand the White House's handling of the Deepwater Horizon oil spill in the Gulf of Mexico 'Obama's Katrina' show that the 2005 hurricane has not been forgotten. Nonetheless, as the ambivalent nature of that designation reveals, it has been accorded a deeply uncertain place in the national imaginary. The inability to think the impact of Katrina very far beyond the immediate geography of the region has greatly benefited the forces that have driven New Orleans' controversial reconstruction programme. The fact that much grassroots activism that has sought to challenge developments in the city is now sounding the rhetoric of human rights and international law testifies to this, and offers an alternative line of resistance to the one represented by Al Sharpton. While Sharpton and others have appealed to an authorizing discourse in many ways far more powerful in the US than that of international human rights – American citizenship – its historical failure to deliver on its promises, particularly for US blacks, has made the opposite tactic of national shaming in the global arena appealing to an increasingly wide array of community activists.

Reclaiming New Orleans: Between the local and the global

The sound of human rights rhetoric as protest against the response to Hurricane Katrina became audible within weeks of the storm. In the following months and years, this rhetoric has been increasingly embraced by activists in New Orleans and the surrounding region, as the vulnerability of the rights of survivors within US law became ever more apparent. Where Al Sharpton and others were in part objecting to the casting of evacuees as somehow 'foreign' to the United States, organizations were soon embracing this 'foreign' terminology to describe their experiences.

Strategies of containment – the racist stereotyping of black New Orleanians in the storm's immediate aftermath, the labelling of the survivors 'refugees', and the narrow regional lens through which the storm was often viewed – laid the groundwork for a debate about whether New Orleans should be rebuilt at all. The uncertain conceptual mapping of Katrina led to a situation in which many claimed that New Orleans itself should be consigned to the scrap heap of history. This idea remained the vicious fantasy of those who believed that, unlike other precariously located cities like San Francisco, New Orleans, as a city built below sea level, did not deserve to be reconstructed: some conservative religious ministers, pointing out that 'Katrina' means 'to purify', claimed that the storm represented God's judgement on a city of 'sin'.[12] These ideas provided the climate in which the housing rights of New Orleans residents were seriously eroded. A response came from the emergence of a dynamic network of grassroots activism fast learning the language of community advocacy and self-determination.

Many residents were radicalized by an entity set up by Mayor Ray Nagin in the months following the storm. The euphemistically named 'Bring New Orleans Back Commission' recommended that flood-prone areas like the largely black Lower Ninth Ward and Village de L'Est – which houses the densest population of Vietnamese people outside of Vietnam – should be converted into 'green spaces'. Apart from bringing New Orleans 'back', such plans would have insured against the return of large numbers of the city's former residents – residents who happen to also fall within economic, racial, and national groupings consistently marginalized in the United States. Nagin's business-driven agenda created a situation that fits Naomi Klein's designation of 'disaster capitalism', whereby big business moved into post-Katrina Louisiana to cash in on the 'opportunities' provided by the relief industry – in moves that might be comparable to the colonization of a supposedly 'blank' space.[13] This excluded black businesses from the possibility of benefiting from reconstruction, foreshadowing the land grabs that would prevent the return of many poor black people to their homes.[14] Much of the city's public housing units, which before Katrina were inhabited mainly by African Americans, have been demolished. Some have claimed that the city's post-storm gentrification amounts to 'ethnic cleansing',[15] a claim fuelled by then US Secretary of Housing and Urban Development Alphonso Jackson (himself a black man), who in a press conference soon after the storm said, 'New Orleans is not going to be as black as it was for a long time, if ever again'.[16] What the commission did not anticipate was the mobilization of the city's scattered residents – evacuated after the storm to far-flung places all over the US. Large numbers of residents pitched tents on the sites of their former homes and presented human barriers to the bulldozers poised to tear down their neighbourhoods. As Rachel Luft explains, this was the beginning of developments that would see the convergence of 'three disparate human rights traditions – the Black Liberation Movement (BLM), the United Nations (UN) and nongovernmental organizations (NGOs)'.[17]

Evidence suggest that the city has returned to its pre-Katrina status as a majority-black city. Nonetheless, large numbers of poor people have not been able to regain their homes, and currently in New Orleans not just African Americans, but people of all ethnicities, are engaging in the rhetoric of self-determination and calling for the 'right of return'. In so doing, they lay human rights abuses on the part of the US government alongside those committed by national governments all over the world. Unable to gain proper recognition as US citizens, these people are mining the resources of an alternative vocabulary in a way that projects their plight onto a world stage. As the prominent civil rights lawyer and social justice activist William Quigley states, 'No principle has proven more helpful to Gulf Coast advocates than the international "right of return." The right to return has no parallel in U.S. law, which makes it even more important in advocacy and analysis.'[18]

Quigley's sense of the importance of Katrina's global dimensions emerged as a result of a trip made to the Gulf Coast in October 2005 by Dr. Arjun Sengupta, a United Nations Special Rapporteur on Human Rights and Extreme Poverty. After touring New Orleans, Baton Rouge, and the neighbouring state of Mississippi, Sengupta told a reporter that he found the current conditions 'shocking' and 'a gross violation of human rights'. This assessment was based in part on the devastation wrought by the storm, but even more on the fact that two months after the storm, so little had been done to reconstruct vast areas of New Orleans. Sengupta pointed out that 'the U.S. is the richest nation in the history of the world. Why cannot it restore electricity and water and help people rebuild their homes and neighbourhoods? If the U.S. can rebuild Afghanistan and Iraq, why not New Orleans?'[19]

The 'right of return': Human rights discourse in New Orleans

Sengupta's insight is borne out by the parallels with post-disaster situations in the developing world, most notably the displacement that resulted from the 2004 tsunami in South Asia. Comparable to the renters in New Orleans who inhabited the city's public housing projects, poor tsunami survivors had no legal rights to the land they had formerly inhabited, and in the disaster's aftermath many beach-front areas in which fishing communities had made their homes were snapped up by the tourist industry. The difference between the two situations is that tsunami survivors were not so widely displaced, and within days of the disaster they began building networks that appealed to human rights principles and campaigned for participation in the planning and rebuilding process. Following Katrina the Asian Coalition for Housing Rights formed an exchange with a number of human rights networks in the US and visited the Gulf Coast. They were shocked at the slow pace of recovery and promptly invited and funded a delegation from the Gulf Coast to travel to Thailand and Indonesia to observe the rebuilding process.

By the time the UN called for a halt to the demolition of public housing in February 2008, human rights advocacy on the ground in New Orleans was already well underway. Not only were grassroots activists calling for international observers very shortly after the disaster, but community groups from the Gulf Coast made representations before the UN Human Rights Committee in Geneva. Perhaps most notably, a number of human rights networks have been conducting extensive human rights training for local activists along the Gulf Coast. As human rights activist Sharda Sekaran writes, 'Human rights are certainly not a magic bullet for the many problems being faced in the post-hurricane U.S. Gulf Coast':

> There are no international bodies in a position powerful enough to effectively pressure the United States into ensuring human rights protections. However, as a grassroots approach, human rights could

provide a compelling framework for developing an analysis to describe what was so inherently reprehensible about the management of the disaster and the treatment of communities in the aftermath. Human rights offered a vision, along with concrete principles, for how state and local agencies should have responded to the crisis.[20]

This approach is self-consciously challenging a culture that has adopted what appears to be an almost principled resistance to human rights talk and action. The US Human Rights Network explains on their website that 'underlying all human rights work in the United States is a commitment to challenge the belief that the United States is inherently superior to other countries of the world and that neither the US government nor the US rights movements have anything to gain from the domestic application of human rights'.[21]

The notion that human rights are in some senses un-American once they are applied to US domestic law is borne out vividly by the experiences of judges who have come up against pointed and sometimes violent resistance to their invocations of international law. Supreme Court Justice Ruth Ginsberg, for example, revealed in February 2007 that she and fellow Justice Sandra Day O'Connor had received death threats due to their use of 'foreign' and international law in US jurisprudence. Dorothy Thomas notes that 'potential citation to the Geneva Conventions in the context of the so-called war on terror led one attorney general to denounce them as "quaint" and "outmoded"'.[22] The idea is of course that the US has an exemplary human rights record and therefore has no need of outside censors.

The notion that human rights activism is a direct challenge to American exceptionalism is a common theme amongst US human rights groups that have become increasingly vocal in the last two decades. The call for the right of return in and around New Orleans can be seen as part of this upsurge in the demands for human rights, and in some ways typifies the contemporary human rights movement in the United States. Key features of this include the commitment to view the US in a global, comparative framework, a desire to reconnect the often bifurcated domains of civil and political rights with economic, social and cultural rights, and in particular the desire to renew the incomplete struggle against racism.

Thomas claims:

> Before discussing the origins, nature, and future of the contemporary U.S. human rights movement in detail, it is important to understand what precipitates it. At its core is the question of racism

or, more broadly, supremacy. Its nearest roots lie in the sharp conflict of the mid-1940s and 1950s between the principles of human rights and the practice of discrimination based on race. At the time, the U.S. government chose explicitly and aggressively to protect domestic racial segregation at the cost of its own adherence to human rights, despite the origin of those rights in much of its own leadership and tradition.[23]

The contemporary call to 'bring human rights home' highlights what has been a consistently contradictory attitude towards human rights in the US, i.e. the notion that the US is the home of human rights coexisting with a sense that the application of those rights in domestic law somehow constitutes a foreign import. One of the defining experiences of the black struggle against US racism has been to fall precisely between the poles of American exceptionalism on the one hand and wider transnational understandings of justice on the other. Human rights talk therefore has played a very particular role in the articulation of racial equality.

Very shortly after Franklin Delano Roosevelt's famous articulation of 'the four freedoms' in 1941 – freedom of speech and worship, and freedom from want and fear – Southern Democrats along with allies in the Republican Party began to charge that the US Constitution and America were under attack from human rights. The UN was cast, in the words of Carol Anderson, as 'that foreigner-dominated organization set out to subvert American values with socialistic, even communistic, ideas about freedom and democracy'. Their primary concern was the protection of Jim Crow in Southern states, and Southern Democrats feared that the Genocide Convention, if ratified, could 'transform lynching into an international crime, and obligate the federal government to prosecute those who had, heretofore, killed black Americans with impunity'.[24]

It is no surprise then that W.E.B. Du Bois and the National Association for the Advancement of Colored People (NAACP) were among the early proponents of the post-World War II understanding of human rights in the US. Testimony to the resistance they faced is the incident that saw Eleanor Roosevelt, in her capacity as chair of the Commission on Human Rights, threaten to resign her position on the board of the NAACP in the late 1940s if it did not refrain from airing African American grievances before the UN. Their petition, she claimed, was an embarrassment to the US and exposed them to attack from the Soviet Union. It was within this climate that the NAACP under Walter White moved to an exclusive focus on fighting civil rights within the parameters of US law, much to Du Bois' dismay, who, during his various associations with the NAACP, always remained on its radical fringe. It was this repressive atmosphere of anti-communism and the conservative backlash against human rights that led to the birth of the Civil Rights movement. Undeniably one of the most successful liberation movement of modern times, Civil Rights began its life as a domestically-oriented and largely anti-communist affair that eschewed many of the transnational identifications that had marked previous upsurges in the African American fight against racism.

One of the switch-points in Martin Luther King's Civil Rights journey was his increasing invocation of human rights, as the successes of Civil Rights began to reveal limitations in the domain of economic and social rights. This was also the moment when King became an object of surveillance by the FBI. Branded gradualist by Black Power activists, King in his later, post-1965 phase was looking to form broad-based coalitions that both addressed racism and transcended race in an attempt to tackle the underlying causes of poverty. While his focus was still on the US, his outspoken criticism of the US role in the war in Vietnam and his identification with decolonizing countries across the world demonstrated that his perspective was increasingly a global one as well.

The contemporary human rights movement, now laying roots in the Gulf Coast and particularly in New Orleans, might be seen as heir to King's radical vision, a vision often lost to popular memory that has tended to brand him the prophet of the 'American Dream'. Early responses to Katrina on the part of African American spokespersons were keen to stress the American identity of US blacks, thus claiming a rightful share of this national dream. Yet alongside such sentiments now run tendencies committed to highlighting social justice within an international framework, not just because this is seen to be effective – indeed, as many human rights agencies readily admit, international treaties are routinely ignored – but because they articulate a holistic vision of social justice that refuses to separate political rights from what should be their material consequences. Clearly the human rights claims of Katrina survivors, like King's Poor People's Campaign, transcend issues of race but are by necessity deeply implicated in the struggle against racism.

Conclusion: Bringing human rights 'home'

As Penny Von Eschen argues, the formation of the UN in 1945 seemingly offered new opportunities to US blacks to expose American racism, and particularly Jim Crow, before the eyes of the world. Du Bois in particular used this opportunity to challenge the idea that individuals only have rights as citizens of nation-states. Thus Von Eschen identifies the late 1930s up until the early Cold War years as a unique moment in which the concerns of African American politics converged with the struggle against colonialism abroad.[25]

This snapshot of the collaboration of anti-colonial and anti-racist movements with the first cogent attempts to implement human rights ideals in practice provides an alternative picture of human rights discourse to the one that paints it as part and parcel of the triumph of western modernity.[26] Indeed, the very fact that successive US governments have been so resistant to the domestic application of human rights reveals a fissure at the heart of western triumphalism. While human rights discourse routinely colludes in narratives of superiority – wherein one nation claims the right to stand in judgement over another – its potential to pierce the myth of exceptionalism is manifold. The mentions of Hurricane Katrina on the UN website, alongside references to disasters that have taken place in South Asia and other parts of the developing world, is a vivid illustration of this. The resistance of Al Sharpton and others in the African American community to such comparisons reveals the contested role US exceptionalism has played in black American politics, which has long been caught between the competing poles of exceptionalism and transnational affiliation.[27]

In Katrina's immediate aftermath New Orleans, once a slave port, was flooded with largely undocumented Hispanic workers who provided cheap, exploitable sources of labour in the rebuilding process. Years after Katrina, highly vulnerable and traumatized families remained marooned outside the city in FEMA (Federal Emergency Management Administration) trailer parks, waiting to be evicted by the federal government. The Vietnamese-American community in New Orleans East drew historical parallels between their displacement after the storm and their earlier experience of refugee camps. A veritable 'Katrina diaspora' of internally displaced persons was scattered across the United States. It is easily forgotten that the wealthiest nation on the planet is home to levels of poverty, suffering and oppression familiar to some of the poorest regions in the world. The storm's aftermath gave rise to the astonishing anomaly that the US became the recipient of large amounts of foreign aid.

The search for 'Obama's Katrina' – discussion of which has not been confined to the oil spill in the Gulf of Mexico but has ranged from his administration's handling of swine flu in addition to aid to the victims of the Haiti earthquake – indicates that Katrina has become an ambivalent but pervasive symbol of American weakness, one that presented the world with a reflection of a nation whose star is on the wane. The Obama administration's feeble attempts to hide the fact of its own subordination to the oil industry cannot be compared to the gross negligence that was the Bush administration's response in 2005. Yet Katrina similarly highlighted the limits of state capabilities and thus US power – limits that are all the more vivid when highlighted by a human rights campaign committed to the deconstruction of the myth of American exceptionalism. If part of the failure of Katrina was incomprehension on the part of a national government unable to recognize a monster of its own making, its lessons seems to lie not in continued investment in national mythology but rather in the exposure of those national limits to the rest of the world. In this vein – and against the tendency to 'naturalize' the destruction wrought by Katrina and its ongoing legacy, and in so doing 'contain' the Katrina narrative – the current calls for the 'right of return' point emphatically to the international coordinates of a profoundly human storm.

Notes

1 These issues have been perhaps most urgently raised in relation to the apparently unnecessary post-Katrina closure of Charity Hospital, and the ongoing campaign for it to be re-opened. See *Save Charity Hospital*, http://savecharityhospital.com/ (accessed 14 June 2010).
2 See 'UN Experts Call for Protection of Housing Rights of Hurricane Katrina Victims', *UN News Centre*, 28 February 2008, http://www.un.org/apps/news/story.asp?NewsID=25782&Cr=housing&Cr1 (accessed 14 June 2010).
3 Erica M. Czaja, 'Katrina's Southern "Exposure": The Kanye Race Debate and the Repercussions of Discussion', in Manning Marable and Kristen Clarke, eds., *Seeking Higher Ground: The Hurricane Katrina Crisis, Race, and Public Policy Reader* (New York: Palgrave Macmillan, 2008), 203–23 (205).
4 Stephanie Houston Grey, '(Re)Imagining Ethnicity in the City of New Orleans: Katrina's Geographical Allegory', in *Seeking Higher Ground*, 129–40 (132).
5 See Fritz Breithaupt, 'Rituals of Trauma: How the Media Fabricated September 11', in Steven Chermak, Frankie Y. Bailey and Michelle Brown, eds., *Media Representations of September 11* (Westport, Connecticut and London: Praeger, 2003), 67–81.
6 Spike Lee, *When the Levees Broke: A Requiem in Four Acts*, DVD (HBO, 2006).
7 David Dante Troutt, 'Many Thousands Gone, Again', in David Dante Troutt, ed., *After the Storm: Black Intellectuals Explore the Meaning of Hurricane Katrina* (New York and London: The New Press, 2006), 3–27 (5).
8 Mukoma Wa Ngugi, 'The "Third World" and New Orleans', *Pambazuka News*, 221, 14 September 2005, http://www.pambazuka.org/en/category/comment/29483 (accessed 14 June 2010).
9 Grey, 130–3.

10 *When the Levees Broke.*
11 Tonya Williams, interview with Anna Hartnell, 1 April 2009.
12 Michael Eric Dyson, *Come Hell or High Water: Hurricane Katrina and the Color of Disaster* (New York: Basic Civitas, 2006), 179–82.
13 Naomi Klein, *The Shock Doctrine: The Rise of Disaster Capitalism* (London: Penguin, 2008), 406–22.
14 Dyson, 128–38.
15 See, for example, Naomi Klein, 'This is Turning into the Ethnic Cleansing of New Orleans', *The Guardian*, 24 September 2005, http://www.guardian.co.uk/environment/2005/sep/24/usnews.hurricanes2005 (accessed 25 October 2009) and Ghali Hassan, '"Ethnic Cleansing" in New Orleans', *Global Research*, 25 June 2006, http://www.globalresearch.ca/index.php?context=viewArticle&code= HAS20060625&articleId=2688 (accessed 25 October 2009).
16 Alphonso Jackson quoted by Anya Kamenetz, 'Black Out', *Village Voice*, 29 November 2005, http://www.villagevoice.com/2005-11-29/news/black-out/ (accessed 24 October 2009).
17 Rachel E. Luft, 'Beyond Disaster Exceptionalism: Social Movement Developments in New Orleans after Hurricane Katrina', *American Quarterly*, 61.3 (2009), 499–527 (500).
18 William P. Quigley, 'Thirteen Ways of Looking at Katrina: Human and Civil Rights Left Behind Again', *Tulane Law Review*, 81.4 (2007), 955–1017 (1007).
19 William Quigley and Sharda Sekaran, 'A Call for the Right to Return in the Gulf Coast', in Cynthia Soohoo, Catherine Albisa and Martha F. Davis, eds., *Bringing Human Rights Home: Portraits of the Movement* (Westport, Connecticut; London: Praeger, 2008), 291–305 (293).
20 Quigley and Sekaran, 295–6.
21 *US Human Rights Network*, http://www.ushrnetwork.org/about_us (accessed 14 June 2010).
22 Dorothy Q. Thomas, 'Against American Supremacy: Rebuilding Human Rights Culture in the United States', in Cynthia Soohoo, Catherine Albisa and Martha F. Davis, eds., *Bringing Human Rights Home: From Civil Rights to Human Rights* (Westport, Connecticut and London: Praeger, 2008), 1–23 (16).
23 Thomas, 1–2.
24 Carol Anderson, 'A "Hollow Mockery": African Americans, White Supremacy, and the Development of Human Rights in the United States', in Cynthia Soohoo, Catherine Albisa and Martha F. Davis, eds., *Bringing Human Rights Home: A History of Human Rights in the United States* (Westport, Connecticut and London: Praeger, 2008), 75–94 (90–1).
25 Penny M. Von Eschen, *Race Against Empire: Black Americans and Anticolonialism, 1937–1957* (Ithaca and London: Cornell University Press, 1997).
26 See, for example, Costas Douzinas, *The End of Human Rights: Critical Legal Thought at the Turn of the Century* (Oxford and Portland, Oregon: Hart Publishing, 2000).
27 See, for example, Paul Gilroy, *The Black Atlantic: Modernity and Double Consciousness* (London and New York: Verso, 1993).

13
American Foreign Policy and Women's Rights

Helen Laville

In the aftermath of the US-led invasion of Afghanistan, and, to a lesser extent, Iraq, feminist scholars have been quick to assess the increasing references and seeming importance of women's rights in US foreign policy. A substantial body of scholarship has emerged which has critiqued this linkage between women's rights and US foreign policy.[1] Emily Rosenberg has surveyed the efforts of the Bush administration and the US media to publicise the position of Afghanistan women in advance of the US invasion.[2] Jan Jindy Pettman has similarly argued that the use of women's rights in US justification of invasion in Afghanistan drew on a 'familiar romance, an international triangle, our men setting out to rescue their women from their men'.[3] More broadly, the association of the promotion of women's rights with a neo-conservative agenda of regime change in Afghanistan and Iraq is part of a recent association of women's rights with aggressive US military intervention. Journalist Virginia Heffernan adroitly identifies the position of 'Feminist Hawks', who make a specific link between the rights of women, particularly in Muslim countries, and a US project of regime change, advocating, 'the use of force to liberate Muslim Women from persecution and the burka'.[4] Phyllis Chesler, proud to be described as the 'godmother' of the Feminist Hawk ideology, has succinctly described her position, 'As a feminist, I have long dreamed of rescuing women who are trapped in domestic and sexual slavery against their will with no chance of escape.'[5] The 'Feminist Hawk' position promotes an unproblematic link between women's rights and regime change by putting the promotion of women's rights at the centre of a unilateral foreign policy which does not shirk from the use of military intervention to achieve its goals.

The focus of recent feminist scholarship on the War on Terror, the invasion of Afghanistan, and the rise of the 'Feminist Hawks' is unsurprising, following a concerted effort by the Bush administration to publicise and promote its prioritising of women's rights. Whilst before 9/11, women's rights were rarely mentioned as part of US foreign policy, after the event, and more specifically after the US invasions of Afghanistan and Iraq, women's rights became an oft-cited central tenet of that policy.[6] The Office of International Issues claimed, 'Promoting women's political and economic participation is an important element of U.S. foreign policy and a key component of transformational diplomacy. Global respect for women is a Bush administration foreign policy priority. The United States is in the forefront of advancing women's causes throughout the world.'[7]

Yet to focus exclusively on the recent manifestation of women's rights as part of the foreign policy agenda of a particular administration is to miss the wider picture of the US relationship to global women's rights since 1945. As Emily Rosenberg has argued, this relationship has had two 'historical imaginaries'.[8] One, which may be said to have reached its nadir in the Bush administration (and in the recent use of issues of Iranian women's rights by those in the US who favour a more aggressive approach to US-Iranian relations), represents the US as a unilateral force, promoting women's rights with what Rosenberg has characterised as 'claims of Western cultural superiority and masculine display'.[9] The second arena has been the development of an international legal structure which has supported and promoted women's rights through international law, treaties, and development policies.

This article will explore the engagement of the US with the development of an international framework of women's rights law since 1945. It will argue that the US, through a combination of ideological resistance to international women's rights (and, more broadly, international human rights) and structural factors which have restricted American participation in international treaties and conventions, has failed to become part of the transnational network of women's rights law that has emerged since 1945. After the mid-1980s the suitability of formal international law as a method of advancing women's rights and opportunity has been questioned and a new agenda on global women's rights has emerged, which has focused on how rights are articulated and promoted through women in development (WID) programmes. This article will explore the US Government's engagement with the WID agenda, exploring the importance of domestic ideological influences on US involvement in global women's rights through development. Finally, it will assess the relationship between US Government interaction with the international women's rights project and the place (or use) of women's rights within specific US foreign policies.

The US Government and international women's rights law

Before 1945 women's rights, as other human rights, were understood within the framework of the relationship between nation-states and their citizens. International law and governance, as they emerged in the League of Nations, were designed to mediate and negotiate relationships between nation-states, with no mandate to advance the rights of individuals or groups beyond those which were granted by those states. The League's role in protecting or advancing the rights of individuals was limited to those individuals, such as refugees, inhabitants of non-state territories and internationally-trafficked prostitutes, who were outside the relationship between the nation-state and its citizens. Women's rights were understood as a matter between national governments and their citizens. Historian Carol Miller explains, 'For most member states [of the League of Nations] the line between national and international jurisdictions was still firmly drawn when it came to legislating on women's rights.'[10] The language of the Covenant of the League was dominated by regulations governing disputes between nation-states. Women are mentioned only twice. Article 7 ruled that, within the machinery of the League, 'all positions... including the secretariat shall be open equally to men and women'. Article 23 dealt with women as they were vulnerable to international trade and economic networks, giving the League right to regulate for 'fair and humane conditions of labour' and to regulate traffic in women and children.[11] The Committee on the Legal Status of Women (often referred to as the 'Committee of Experts'), established by the League Assembly in 1938, was essentially a study-group which conducted a survey of women's status and was abruptly terminated by the onset of the Second World War. The Committee, beyond data collection, made no attempt to establish international standards or covenants on women's rights.

However, the aftermath of the Second World War, the emergence of the United Nations framework and a discourse on universal human rights saw a seismic shift in the relationship between human rights and international law. The language of the United Nations Declaration, in stark contrast to that of the Charter of the League of Nations, reflected this shift. Rather than limiting itself to the work of negotiation between nation-states, the UN established a framework of legal and institutional practices which facilitated their jurisdiction over international human rights issues. Nina Berkovitch explains, 'What used to fall under the sole jurisdiction of nation-states – the rights of their inhabitants – now became a concern for the international community.'[12] From the outset the rights of women were included in this shift in what Berkovitch has termed 'global polity', as an ideological context and institutional framework emerged within which the rights of women would be promoted as a global, rather than national issue. The Charter of the United Nations, signed in San Francisco in 1945, began with the affirmation of faith in 'fundamental human rights, in the dignity and worth of the human person, in the equal rights of men and women'.[13] With this pronouncement the Charter became the first international agreement to proclaim gender equality as a human right.

This acknowledgement of the 'equal rights of men and women', however, could be interpreted as a vague, inspirational rhetorical device which did not in itself constitute a plan of action or mandate a programme to secure these equal rights. Certainly Bertha Lutz, the Brazilian feminist activist interpreted it this way, writing to the American feminist Carrie Chapman Catt, 'The real truth, and to you I can tell it, is that the United Nations have written beautifully sounding words into the Charter, or are still writing them in, but have no intention of carrying them out.'[14] Determined to secure more decisive action, Lutz prompted the Brazilian delegation at San Francisco to take concrete steps, proposing that the Economic and Social Council should set up a Commission of women to study conditions and prepare reports on the political, civil and economic status and opportunity of women. The US Government's reaction to the proposal to set up specific bodies at the UN to monitor and promote human rights was unenthusiastic. Whilst the American delegation supported the inclusion of human rights in the UN's general statement of purpose, they steadfastly resisted proposals to include a Bill of Rights in the UN Charter or to establish special Commissions in areas such as health, education and human rights. Fearful of the ramifications of universal human rights on national sovereignty, both the Americans and the British approached the human rights language of the Charter with caution, insisting on the agreement, 'Nothing contained in the present Charter shall authorize the United Nations to intervene in matters which are essentially within the domestic jurisdiction of any state.'[15]

Initially the Americans were concerned not about women's rights *per se*, but the possibility that any human rights treaty or institution set up at the United Nations would challenge national sovereignty and their ability to rule over their own citizens. Whilst there were some groups within the US who were in favour of the emergence of this form of 'world government', there was also significant opposition in the US to the concept of universal human rights and fears about the ways that might infringe upon national sovereignty. This anxiety manifest itself in widespread opposition in US towards the work of the UN on the genocide convention, the Universal Declaration of Human Rights, and the work of the International Labour Organisations. The American Bar Association was particularly concerned about the implication of UN conventions on US law and worried that the UN Declaration of Human Rights, not the US Constitution, would become the highest authority in the US. US hostility to the establishment of an agency for assessing and promoting women's rights at the UN was part of this more general anxiety about sovereignty. The American delegation voted against the Brazilian proposal for the establishment of a sub-commission and attempted on two subsequent occasions to have the clause withdrawn or redrafted. Yet, despite the US opposition, it quickly became clear that the UN would go ahead with the establishment of a Commission on the Status of Women (CSW).[16] The State Department withdrew its objections, realising that it would be unfortunate if the US were perceived to be standing in the way of rights for women, particularly when the Soviet Union was making strenuous efforts to establish its own credentials as a world leader – in the promotion of women's rights. Whilst the US Government was reluctant to commit itself to a positive engagement with the development of a transnational women's rights agenda, it nonetheless was anxious to point out that the United States was, as a nation, fully committed to the ideals of women's rights and equality. The State Department frequently asserted that its lack of enthusiasm for the work of the CSW did not signify a lack of support for women's rights, but rather a profound unease with the internationalisation of human rights and the suitability of the treaty and law-making infrastructures of the United Nations to achieve advances in women's rights. At San Francisco the US delegation carefully explained:

> The position of the United States on the subject of equal opportunity for women is so well established and has been so often demonstrated in action that it does not need to be elaborated here. We expect women to play a constructive role in the development of the international community which the United Nations are today striving to organize.[17]

Whilst stressing this belief in the equality of women, the US Government nonetheless sought to oppose the establishment of the CSW as an activist agency. Secure in the knowledge that their allies in American women's voluntary organisations, cynical about the benefits of international legislation on women's rights, were working closely with the Women's Bureau of the Department of Labour – to limit the activism of the CSW, the US Government was content to delegate responsibility for dealing with the Commission to these women. They acceded to the suggestion of the Women's Bureau and its allies, and appointed Dorothy Kenyon, an officer of the League of Women Voters and a former member of the distinctly non-activist League of Nations Committee of Experts, as its delegate to the CSW.

However, as Kenyon was increasingly convinced that the US should take the lead in the work of the Commission and the promotion of global women's rights, she became an advocate of a more activist commission, supporting the move from sub-commission to full commission (a move she had initially blocked) and participating in the development of the convention on the Political Rights of Women.[18] The US Government, whilst recognising the publicity and propaganda value of women's rights, continued to refuse to cede any jurisdiction on issue of women's rights to the international arena. Kenyon concluded that the State Department were actively working against the CSW, confiding to her friend Kersten Hesselgren, 'There are people, even in our own State Department, who would rather see us fail than succeed!'[19] To fellow CSW member Bodil Begtrup, Kenyon went further, 'The real obstacle (in confidence) is some men in the US State Department who know that our Commission was a success this year and don't like it! We've had quite a battle with them.'[20]

Despite her troubled relationship with the State Department, and her growing conviction that the US Government was unwilling to engage with the development of a formal framework for the development of international standards and laws on women's rights Kenyon hoped to be reappointed to the CSW in 1949, when her term of office expired. Not only was Kenyon not reappointed, but, in an indication of the reluctance of the US Government to commit itself to the CSW as an activist agency, Kenyon's replacement was Lorna Hahn, a woman with no previous experience of (or demonstrable interest in) international women's organisations or the legal rights of women. Kenyon wrote to a colleague at the CSW, explaining:

> President Truman did what I expected and appointed someone else to the Commission… my successor is a nice woman, I am told, whose principle contribution is that she worked hard for the Democratic

Party. She isn't technically trained in anything, however, and so won't be able to contribute anything to our work on treaties and so on.[21]

The lack of legal expertise was particularly troubling to Kenyon, as the CSW was beginning work on developing what would become the first major international women's rights agreement, the Convention on the Political Rights of Women. In a somewhat forlorn recognition of the lack of status on women's rights within the US Government, Kenyon fretted, 'I am afraid that without me there to kick it into activity the State Department is going to lie down on the job and do nothing.'[22] Kenyon's fears were justified. The US Government, having appointed Kenyon to the CSW in the expectation that she would stand against the development of the CSW as an activist group, were unwilling to follow her lead and support the work of the CSW in promoting international law on women's rights.

In 1952 this conflicted approach to the development of international women's rights – characterised by vocal support for the principle together with a refusal to commit to legally binding means to the ends – was demonstrated by the US position on the Convention on Political Rights of Women, produced by the CSW and adopted by the Economic and Social Council. Despite their willingness to speak in support of the treaty at the UN, the US Government refused to sign the Convention, with Dean Acheson, the Secretary of State, explaining to the Senate Judiciary Committee on 6 April 1953, 'This administration does not intend to sign the convention on Political Rights of Women. This is not because we do not believe in the equal political status of men and women, or because we shall not seek to promote that equality. Rather it is because we do not believe that this goal can be achieved by treaty coercion or that it constitutes a proper field for exercise of the treaty-making powers.'[23] Annual letters from the Women's Party to the State Department complaining about the delay in signing the treaty were met with bland assurances that the US, whilst of course, in full favour of the equality of women, did not have time in a very busy schedule to debate the issue.

The leadership offered by the US Government in the early years of the CSW and the development of a women's rights agenda was, for the most part, lukewarm. This ambivalent approach was undeniably part of a wider pattern of the US approach to international human rights, reflecting an ideological position. The 'rights culture' critique has argued that Americans have traditionally believed that their *national* system of rights, expressed in constitutional documentation such as the Bill of Rights, is both superior to and more legitimate than any human rights negotiated and policed by international bodies. However, this influence of ideological factors must be understood in context with the strength of structural factors.[24] As Andrew Moravcsik has explained, the cumbersome nature of US political institutions made ratification of international treaties extremely complicated, ideological opposition to such ratification was particularly difficult to oppose or overcome. The US political system includes an exceptional number of 'veto players' who make the acceptance by the national government of international treaties and obligations difficult, and the US constitutional requirement for a two-thirds Senate majority to approve international treaties is, as Moravcsik notes, 'a threshold higher than that in nearly all other advanced industrial democracies, which generally ratify international treaties by legislative majority'.[25] Even where a particular administration might be in favour of a particular convention or treaty, it requires a Herculean effort to muster the 'supermajority' needed to secure its passage.[26]

The US failure to ratify the Convention to Eliminate all forms of Discrimination against Women (CEDAW) is an example of these structural hurdles. In 1980 President Carter signed CEDAW, which had been approved by the UN General Assembly in December 1979, after considerable involvement and support from US representatives. Under the Reagan administrations there was no attempt at ratification, and Ronald Reagan made clear his disapproval of the Convention. His successor, George H.W. Bush, was similarly unsympathetic to the Convention and made no efforts towards ratification. With a change of administration in 1993, however, the position changed. President Bill Clinton's Secretary of State, Warren Christopher, announced a change in attitude towards ratification of international treaties and involvement in international systems of law and governance. In 1994, Christopher announced that the Clinton administration was committed to ratifying the International Convention on the Elimination of All Forms of Racism, and, following that, securing ratification of all the other international treaties the US had signed but not yet ratified, including CEDAW. President Clinton repeated his commitment to the ratification of CEDAW in early 1994, and the US delegation to the Beijing World Conference on Women announced that ratification by 2000 was a priority for the US Government. Clinton's successor, President George W. Bush, also spoke in favour of CEDAW, writing to the Senate Foreign Relations Committee that it was 'generally desirable and should be ratified'. In addition to this presidential support, CEDAW received significant backing in Senate, including a 1994 bipartisan vote in the Senate Foreign Relations Committee, a move blocked by the significant opposition of Committee Chair Jesse Helms. Well-organised domestic opposition to the treaty, together with the institutional difficulties of the ratification process, have meant that the US remains one of the few countries in the world to have not ratified CEDAW. A combination of ideological resistance to international conventions and treaties and a structural political bias against ratification resulted in US failure to become an official part of the post-1945 system of international laws on women's rights. Structural factors have meant that the US Government's approach to international equality law has been largely consistent – beyond the different ideological approaches of different administrations, these factors have meant little or no legislative achievement in terms of ratification of international treaties or the application of international women's rights law within the US.

The US Government and WID

The US Government has had a far more significant impact on global women's rights through the WID agenda. Since development policies and US aid programmes are far less restricted by structural constraints, the government has been able to wield an immediate and dramatic influence on women's rights promotion through WID programmes. The UN Decade for Women (1975–1985) witnessed frequent, often heated debates between those who continued to believe in the need to develop international law to secure women's rights and those who argued that women's rights needed to be addressed by focusing on the impact of development policies. This debate was, to a significant extent, the result of the increasing level of activism by women's NGOs at an international level. These NGOs were often less convinced about the practical effectiveness of international law and more engaged with specific issues, such as health or educational opportunity, as a means of securing women's rights. They were fostered and encouraged through UN activities such as the women's conferences at Nairobi (1985) and the NGO International Women's Heath Conference in Cairo in 1994. These meetings and the networks of NGOs that grew out of them (such as the Women's Global Network for Reproductive Rights) served as important lobby groups within the United Nations, advocating that development programmes be used as a method of securing the promotion of women's rights.

The emergence of the WID agenda from the mid-1980s coincided with the Reagan administration and an ideological approach to WID, particularly reproductive rights, that stressed Christian, pro-life positions. International policy on reproductive issues between 1945 and the late 1950s had been largely focused on the relationship between family size and economic development. However, in the late 1970s and early 1980s the focus shifted away from a narrow approach to population control and towards a more holistic approach which encompassed women's sexual health and reproductive rights, including information about and access to contraception and abortion as part of women's human rights. While the US had been a strong supporter of population control policies since the 1950s, the Reagan administration sought to remove US international support from programmes which included access to abortion. The most notorious WID achievement of the Reagan administration was the Mexico City Policy, announced at the UN Population Conference in 1984. The Mexico City Policy, which was continued under the George Bush administration, meant that the US Government withheld funding to any NGOs that gave advice or information about abortion, or who lobbied foreign governments to provide abortion.[27]

During the presidency of Bill Clinton, a far more supportive position of the US Government for international action and promotion of women's rights through WID emerged. Clinton called for the State Department to include documentation of abuses of women's rights in their human rights reports. At the World Conference on Human Rights in June 1993 the US delegation assumed a leading role, with Secretary of State Warren Christopher declaring that 'guaranteeing women their human rights... was a moral imperative' and explaining that women's rights represented 'an investment in making whole nations stronger, fairer and better'. Christopher announced that the US would press for progress on formal legislation on international women's rights, explaining that the US would urge the appointment of a UN Special Rapporteur on violence against women and would encourage the UN to strengthen its focus upon and coordination of women's rights activities.[28] Clinton quickly nullified the Mexico City Policy, and at the second preparatory meeting for the International Conference on Population and Development (ICPD) in Cairo, the US delegate, Timothy Wirth announced US support for 'reproductive choice including access to safe abortion'.[29] Mindful of the strong anti-abortion sentiment in the US, and under pressure from the Vatican City delegate to the ICPD, the US delegate, Vice-President Al Gore felt the need to make a statement clarifying the US Government position, explaining, 'The United States has not sought, does not seek and will not seek to establish any international right to Abortion.'[30] However, whilst it would be misleading to say that the US Government *advocated* the access to abortion as part of its WID agenda, it would be fair to say that it was certainly not prepared to block discussion and advancement of women's rights and reproductive health over the issue. The Cairo Programme of Action (POA) of 1994 included the linkage of women's rights with reproductive rights, asserting, 'Advancing gender equality and equity and the empowerment of women, and the elimination of all kinds of violence against women, and ensuring women's ability to control their own fertility, are cornerstones of population and development-related programmes.'[31] Perhaps the most famous example of the Clinton administration's support of both international women's rights and women's rights through WID programmes was their participation in the Beijing Women's Conference in 1995. Hillary Clinton, heading the US delegation, brought an unprecedented degree of media attention to the conference, and her keynote address, which proclaimed, 'Women's Rights are Human Rights', symbolised the administrations high level of engagement with international women's rights.[32]

Whilst the US Government were providing support for the WID agenda, pressure groups with the US were profoundly unhappy with this promotion of international women's rights and the US Government's role in it. As Doris Buss and Didi Herman have demonstrated, the engagement of the US with the UN has been significantly influenced since 1994 by the Christian Right (CR).[33] The CR targeted the development of International Law through the United Nations for a number of reasons, including, for example, conservative premillennial Protestant belief, which linked the rise of 'one world government' to the Antichrist and the Second Coming.[34] The development of women's rights was a particular target, as it involved key CR concerns such as reproductive rights and family structure.[35] Buss and Herman date the campaigns for the American CR from two important conferences – the 1994 Cairo Conference on Population and Development and the 1995 Beijing Conference on Women. The successes of feminist groups at these conferences served as a 'wake-up' about the possible impact of international women rights law on reproductive rights and the 'natural family'. The framework of the UN-sponsored conferences such as Beijing gave non-state actors, predominantly NGOs, unprecedented access to the networks of international power and decision making. This proved a double-edged development: whilst feminists celebrated the importance of this process in encouraging and developing international networks amongst women's NGOs and allowing women access to decision-making processes, it also allowed NGOs who were hostile to the development of international women's rights law to influence and, in some instances, subvert that agenda.

With an ideologically sympathetic President in the White House, the Christian Right worked within the system to attempt to roll back, or at least prevent the advance of, international women's rights. One of President George W. Bush's first actions upon taking office was to reinstate the Mexico City Policy. Similar efforts to extend domestic positions on reproductive rights to the international stage resulted in the Bush administration withholding its contribution to the United Nation Population Fund (UNPF). Referring to the Kemp-Kasten Amendment of 1985, which banned the use of US aid to finance or support coercive abortion or forced sterilisation abroad, the administration accused the UNPF of supporting forced abortion and sterilisation in China – a charge vehemently denied by the agency and one that four separate investigations, including one by the US State Department, refuted. Other areas in which the US have been criticised for restricting women's rights through their access to adequate health care and information include AIDS/HIV programmes. President Bush's Emergency Plan for Aids Relief (PEPAR), for example, set aside 20 percent of its funds for prevention programmes. Of this restricted pot of funding, a third was set aside for programmes which promoted abstinence-until-marriage programmes. The influence of Christian Right, pro-life positions were also present at the United Nations and at UN-sponsored meetings. The US delegation to the 2002 UN Commission on the Status of Women meeting was led by Ellen Sauerbrey, the Maryland State Chairman of Bush's 2000 campaign.[36] Her companions on the delegation were drawn from the ranks of the Christian Right NGOs who had been targeting the CSW since 1995, such as Nancy Pfotenhauer of the Independent Women's Forum, Winsome Packer of the Heritage Foundation, and Kate O'Beirne, also of the Heritage Foundation and Washington editor of the *New Republic*. In an article for the *New Republic*, winsomely titled 'Our Girl at the UN', O'Beirne was explicit about the changing ideological approach to the CSW that this delegation represented:

> This year's delegation... clearly signalled that there had been a change in management at the State Department: We've come a long way from Beijing, baby. Hillary Clinton is no longer running the international sisterhood show. Over the years, conservative, pro-family non-governmental organizations (NGOs) have tirelessly patrolled the U.N., on guard against the establishment of 'international rights' to

engage in behaviours that most parents have nightmares over. They expect that the U.S. Delegations will now be composed of their allies.[37]

As with Kenyon in 1949, the issue of nominations of delegates was highly symbolic: experts on women's international law were dropped in favour of political appointments, with an emphasis on delegates from CR groups. Before the 2005 Beijing plus Ten meeting in New York, Congresswoman Carolyn Maloney lobbied the Bush White House to be appointed to the US delegation to the meeting. Maloney was well-qualified, having attended the initial Beijing Conference and made one of the opening speeches at the Beijing plus Five meeting in 2000. Maloney was excluded; instead the delegation appointed by Bush included Patricia Brister, State Chair of the Republican Party of Louisiana, Susan Hirschman, Tom DeLay's former chief of Staff, Mark Lagan, formerly of the American Enterprise Institute and, once again, Ellen Sauerbrey.

The delegation proceeded to challenge, and to try to roll back, the consensus on women's rights and WID which had emerged since the Beijing Conference. At the meeting, intended to review the progress governments had made towards implementing the Beijing platform on women's rights, the Commission on the Status of Women drafted an opening declaration to reaffirm the Beijing platform. The US delegation refused to support the declaration because of concerns that the platform legalised the right to abortion. It proposed an amendment which would allow the delegation to reaffirm Beijing only with the recognition that this 'did not create any new international rights and did not include the right to abortion'. The US delegation found it impossible to create international consensus for their amendment, with only Qatar and Egypt, prepared to support them, and was forced to withdraw it after announcing that the US did not consider their affirmation of the platform to be legally binding. The actions convinced many that the US was determined to block international women's rights in favour of a hard-line position on reproductive rights. Zonibel Woods, a senior advisor to the International Women's Health Coalition bitterly complained that the US 'claim[s] to defend women's rights, but they attack women's rights at every international meeting when they think no-one is looking'.[38]

The ideological commitment of any specific White House administration can thus be demonstrated to significantly influence on US engagement with international women's rights through WID policies. The playing out of domestic ideological preoccupations on the international stage is underscored by the fact that both Bush and Clinton chose to make their announcements about the Mexico City Policy on 22 January, the anniversary of the *Roe v. Wade* decision on abortion. President Obama, perhaps hoping to make the issue less ideologically divisive, chose to wait until 23 January to make his statement. At a time when international feminist groups have come to argue that the effective promotion of women's rights rests upon the understanding of the relationship between rights and development policy, the US insistence on playing out its domestic obsession with the ideological ramifications of reproductive rights on the international stage has been greeted with frustration by many activists. Amy Coen, President of Population Action International has asked, 'Why is it that the organizations that are making a difference in the lives of women and their families are being singled out again by the Bush administration in order to make its own political point? When the issue involves family planning, the White House will always look for new ways to satiate the voracious appetite of its right-wing political constituency. Political posturing should not endanger women's lives.'[39]

Conclusion

At its 46th session, the United Nations Commission on the Status of Women agreed to discuss the situation of women and girls in Afghanistan. A relatively simple declaration was put forward by the US delegate to demonstrate the Commission's support for women in Afghanistan. The declaration quickly grew, and became the subject of detailed debate. US delegate Kate O'Beirne explained, 'Our straightforward two-and-a-half-page draft, simply encouraging the Interim and Transitional Authorities to address the rights and needs of women and girls, grew to eight pages of specific prescriptive advice from our "negotiating partners.".' The sticking point of the declaration proved to be a seemingly straightforward recommendation that the transitional government in Afghanistan ratify CEDAW and commit itself to following its protocols and investigative requirements. The US delegation insisted that the Commission should not urge Afghanistan to ratify the treaty but rather that it should urge them to *consider* ratifying the treaty. O'Beirne explained, 'Our delegation made it clear that the resolution could not dictate that Afghanistan ratify the Convention on the Elimination of All Forms of Discrimination Against Women – which it, like the U.S., has signed but not ratified. Longstanding U.S. policy holds that it is inappropriate for the U.N. to pressure sovereign countries to join international conventions.'

O'Beirne fumed that the resistance of the CSW to the word 'consider' was directed less at Afghanistan and more at continued refusal of the US to ratify the treaty itself.[40] The Commission were not alone in arguing that there was a disparity between the US Government's stated support for women in Afghanistan and their reluctance to ratify CEDAW. US Congresswoman Carolyn Maloney, in her testimony to the US Senate Committee on Foreign Relations insisted, 'If we as a country are serious about helping women in Afghanistan, we will ratify the CEDAW treaty.'[41]

This linkage between US intervention in Afghanistan and their non-ratification of CEDAW represents an important connection between two different trajectories of women's rights and US foreign policy. Emily Rosenberg has argued:

> Drawing upon recent scholarship related to gender and foreign relations, it is possible to position calls for the assistance of women and children within two different historical imaginaries. One of these arises from a tradition marked by nationalism, maternalist assumptions, claims of Western cultural superiority, and masculine display... Another arises from a largely twentieth-century tradition of transnational networks, which emphasize both global issues and locally specific concerns related to human welfare and women's empowerment. Although these two imaginaries may blur together and seem allied in specific situations, they coexist uneasily and struggle toward different futures.[42]

The discussions at the 46th session and Maloney's testimony blur together the historical imaginaries of women's rights and US foreign policy, insisting that the US Government cannot claim that their foreign policy in Afghanistan and elsewhere is driven by the desire to promote the rights of women whilst at the same time it refuses to participate in the international systems, treaties, conventions, and infrastructure designed to promote women's rights around the globe. Maloney insisted, 'Ratification... would set the stage for U.S. leadership in ensuring women are fairly treated here and around the world.... It is time the United States resumed its rightful role as a leader in promoting full rights for women.'[43]

Feminist critics have argued that the unilateral promotion of women's rights, as manifested in the foreign policy of George W. Bush, or the position of Feminist Hawks towards Iran, is singularly lacking in sincerity. They have frequently argued that women's rights has served within the Bush administration as cover for an aggressive foreign policy and that the administration's claims to be seeking the rights of women have served as the *means* of justifying military intervention, rather than being the *ends* of invasion and nation-building. Alletta Brenner, for example, has argued, 'A strong case can be made that at least on some occasions, pro-women's rights language was used as a proxy measure for the furthering of other political agendas.'[44] Cynthia Enloe adds, 'It was only after George W. Bush declared "war on terrorists and those countries that harbour them" that the violation of Afghan women's human rights took center stage.' Enloe asks if Afghanistan women's well-being 'is worthy of our concern only because their lack of well-being justifies the US military occupation in Afghanistan?'[45] Jan Jindy Pettman, critiquing the Bush administration's appropriation of women's rights as 'rights of convenience', similarly argues, 'The worry about Afghan women has only become a battle cry of the West only after 9/11. Why not before? Why not now? Why not in other States hostile to women's rights, for example in Saudi Arabia?'[46] These critiques rightly resist the co-option of women's rights as a cover for the advance of US national strategic, military, or economic interests; as one liberal blogger succinctly requested, 'Note to Neocons: stop pimping the feminist arguments'.[47]

A second, perhaps more nuanced critique of the 'feminist hawk' position has questioned the pragmatic results of an association between women's rights and the unilateral foreign policy of the United States. Even if once accepted that the US was perfectly sincere in its desire to secure women's rights, several feminist critiques have questioned whether it is helpful for the cause of global women's rights for the US to loudly proclaim this as a foreign policy objective and have suggested it is problematic to associate women's rights with the foreign policy of any one nation-state. The critique continues that when women's rights become part of US foreign policy, it strengthens the case of those nations who seek to deny women their rights that these are part of a neo-colonial western imperialist project. To quote Katha Pollitt: 'US invasions have made the work of Muslim feminists much more difficult. The last thing they need is for women's rights to be branded as the tool of the invaders and occupiers and cultural imperialists'.[48]

It does not help that women's rights are perhaps the most photogenic 'quick hit' part of US invasion or occupation. As Naomi Klein has pointed out, 'Whenever [the head of the Coalition Provisional Authority in [Iraq] Paul Bremer needed a good news hit, he had his picture taken at a newly opened women's centre, handily equating feminism with the hated occupation.'[49] The articulation of the promotion of women's rights as part of US unilateral foreign policy hindered rather than helped the cause. Ann

Elizabeth Mayer suggests, 'Middle Eastern governments and ideologues may press the idea that, where women's rights are concerned, the human rights agenda is fundamentally a colonialist one, in which the West seeks to impose its standards on the Third World.'[50] Reserving the right to establish and abide by *national* rather than *international* law on women's rights has frequently served as a symbolic measure of the independence of the nation-state, and, in particular, its distance from former colonial authorities or western imperialist states.

The concrete impact of US ratification of CEDAW is contested. Some scholars have argued that the US practice of contributing to the development of formal legal international treaties but not ratifying them affects only American citizens, who do not have legal recourse to the provisions of these treaties. Others have argued that, in failing to make themselves subject to international human rights law, the United States Government singularly fails to offer itself as an example of the need for nation-states to accept international standards and the rule of international law. Amnesty International US, for example, contends, 'Lack of U.S. ratification serves as a disincentive for governments to uphold CEDAWs mandate and their obligations under it to end discrimination against women.'[51] Such an argument is difficult, probably impossible to prove. The significance of US ratification of CEDAW, insofar as the under-funded and relatively weak enforcement mechanisms of the convention allows, might well be underwhelming. However, ratification of CEDAW would serve as a powerful demonstration of a shift in the US position towards international women's rights.

The linkage between US support for women in Afghanistan and their place within a new era of international women's rights requires a broader understanding of the place of women's rights in US foreign policy since 1945 than that which can be gleaned from a study of the policy, actions, and pronouncements of any one administration. Fundamental to the 'historical imaginaries' described by Rosenberg is the relationship between the nation-state and women's rights. The development of an international framework of agreements and legal conventions on women's rights, together with the work of international NGOs and UN-sponsored development programmes have insisted on the need for international agreement, rather than unilateral will and power, as the best ways to promote the rights of women. The development of the post-1945 international system has moved inexorably, if haltingly towards an uncoupling of human rights from the nation-state. This shift has created a fundamentally different way of approaching women's rights than that which has traditionally tied the promotion of women's rights to either the democratic credentials or military superiority of any one nation. The US Government's relationship to this international agenda has been a troubled one, demonstrating both resistance to the concept and framework of formal international human rights, and a volatile engagement with WID issues which has seen domestic ideological struggles transposed to the international arena. Recent years have seen an increasing prominence for the promotion of women's rights within American foreign policy, either for cynical or sincere reasons, or a serendipitous mixture of the two. However, this chapter argues that it is the *detachment* of women's rights from the goals, language and pursuit of the foreign policy of any one state which is necessary in order to achieve global advances in women's rights. For the United States to promote women's rights in other nations, it is vital that it accepts and ratifies international jurisdiction over the rights of women within the United States itself. Ratification of CEDAW and full engagement with the international women's rights agenda, would, through the disassociation of women's rights with national expressions of power or assertions of superiority, do far more to promote global rights for women than can be achieved through unilateral US force.

Notes

1. See for example; I.M. Young, 'Feminist Reactions to the Contemporary Security Regime', *Hypatia*, 18 (2003), 223–31; C. Hirschkind and S. Mahmood, 'Feminism, the Taliban and the Policies of Counter-Insurgency', *Anthropological Quarterly*, 75 (2002), 339–54; Sonali Kolhatkar, 'Afghan Women: Enduring American Freedom', *Foreign Policy in Focus*, http://www.fpif.org/commentary/2002/0211afwomen_body.html, date accessed 19 September 2009; Sonali Kolhatkar, 'Saving Afghan Women', http://www.rawa.org/znet.htm, date accessed, 20 September 2009; Helen Laville 'American Women and Women's Rights in American Foreign Policy', in Andrew Johnstone and Helen Laville, eds., *The US Public and American Foreign Policy* (London and New York: Routledge, 2010), 87–104.
2. Emily Rosenberg, 'Rescuing Women and Children', *The Journal of American History*, 89 (2002), 456–65.
3. Jan Jindy Pettman, 'Feminist International Relations after 9/11', *Brown Journal of World Affairs* (2004), X, 85–96, 89.
4. Virginia Heffernan, 'The Feminist Hawks', *New York Times*, 23 August 2009, http://www.sisterfund.org/news/feminist-hawks%20, date accessed 5 March 2010.
5. Phyllis Chester, *The New Anti-Semitism: The Current Crisis and What We Must Do About It* (San Francisco: Jossey Bass, 2003), 198.
6. Alletta Brenner, 'Speaking of "Respect for Women": Gender and Politics in U.S. Foreign Policy Discourse', *Journal of Women's International Studies*, 10 (2009), 18–32.

7 US Department of State, Office of International Women's Issues, Homepage, http://2001 2009.state.gov/g/wi/c21438.htm, accessed 23 June 2010.
8 Emily Rosenberg, 'Rescuing Women and Children', *The Journal of American History*, 89 (2002), 456–65.
9 *Ibid.*
10 Carol Miller, 'Geneva: The Key to Equality: The Inter-War Feminists and the League of Nations', *Women's History Review*, 3 (1994), 219–45.
11 Covenant of the League of Nations, http://en.wikisource.org/wiki/Covenant_of_the_League_of_Nations#Article_7, accessed 25 January 2011.
12 Nina Berkovitch, *From Motherhood to Citizenship* (Baltimore: John Hopkins Press, 1999), 103.
13 Charter of the United Nations, http://www.un.org/en/documents/charter/index.shtml, accessed 25 January 2011.
14 *Ibid.*, 223.
15 *Ibid.*, 19.
16 See Helen Laville, 'A New Era in International Women's Rights? American Women's Associations and the Establishment of the UN Commission on the Status of Women', *Journal of Women's History*, 20 (2008), 34–56.
17 'The Response of the United States to the Brazilian Declaration Recommending Establishment of a Commission of Women in the United Nations Organization', 12 September 1945, file 'UN', Box 701, Records of the League of Women Voters, Library of Congress, Washington DC, hereafter LWV papers.
18 See, Helen Laville, 'Protecting Difference or Promoting Equality? US Government Approaches to Women's Rights and the UN Commission on the Status of Women 1945–1950', *Comparative American Studies*, 5 (2007), 266–91.
19 Kenyon to Hesselgren, 29 June 1948, Box 57, file 1, Kenyon papers, Sophia Smith Library, Smith College, Massachusetts.
20 Kenyon to Begtrup, 29 June 1948, Box 57, file 1 Kenyon papers.
21 Kenyon to Begtrup, 15 February 1950, Box 58, file 1, Kenyon papers.
22 Kenyon to Begtrup, 15 February 1950, Box 58, file 1, Kenyon papers.
23 Division of Public Services, Department of State, 'The 1953 Session of the UN Commission on the Status of Women and Subsequent Action on its Recommendations', November 1993. National Women's Party Papers, Series VII:195, reel 178.
24 For a more detailed discussion see Andrew Moravcsik, 'The Paradox of U.S. Human Rights Policy', and Paul W. Kahn, 'American Exceptionalism, Popular Sovereignty and the Rule of Law', in Michael Ignatieff, ed., *American Exceptionalism and Human Rights* (Princeton, Princeton: University Press, 2005).
25 Andrew Moravcsik, 'The Paradox of U. S. Human Rights Policy', 187.
26 See Louise Henkin, 'US Ratification of Human Rights Conventions: The Ghost of Senator Bricker', *The American Journal of International Law*, 89 (1995), 341–50.
27 Whilst the 'gag order' had many opponents amongst US pro-choice advocates, there were also anti-abortion campaigners who felt the order, by restricting access to abortion and information about abortion strictly as 'a method of birth control' did not go far enough, since it would still allow funding for information about access to abortion, as a result of rape or for medical reasons. For more details on the impact of the global gag order see Yussif Susskind, 'Ungagging Women's Human Rights', http://www.fpif.org/articles/ungagging_ womens_human_rights, accessed 23 May 2010.

28 Statement of Warren Christopher to World Convention on Human Rights, June 21, 1993, US Department of State Dispatch, http://findarticles.com/p/articles/mi_m1584/is_n25_v4/ai_14168099/?tag=content;coll, accesses 12 May 2010.
29 See Jutta M. Joachim, *Agenda Setting, The UN and NGOs: Gender Violence and Reproductive Rights* (Washington DC: Georgetown University Press, 2007), 153.
30 'Vatican Hits Gore on Abortion Rights', *Christian Century*, 7 September 1994.
31 Programme of Action of the International Conference on Population and Development, http://www.unfpa.org/public/cache/offonce/ sitemap/icpd/International-Conference-on-Population-and-Development/ICPD-Programme;jsessionid=D4326967E400DC60107D297C3C2803A8#ch7, accessed 20 June 2010.
32 Hillary Rodham Clinton, 'Women's Rights are Human Rights', Excerpts, 5th September 1995, *Women's Studies Quarterly*, 24 (1996), 98–101.
33 See Doris Buss and Didi Herman, *Globalizing Family Values: The Christian Right in International Politics* (Minneapolis: University of Minnesota Press, 2003).
34 *Ibid.*, 10–18.
35 Herman and Buss explore the irony of Christian Rights groups, who are fervently ideologically opposed to the very concept of the United Nations and its growing infrastructure and, at the same time, have launched successful campaigns to integrate themselves to that infrastructure and direct its agenda to their own aims. As they point out, 'Paradoxically, the CR UN [Christian Right at the United Nations], through its involvement in events such as UN conferences, has become a participant in the very international civil society it opposes.' Buss and Herman, 136.
36 Sauerbrey was later appointed by Bush as Head of the Department of State's Bureau of Population, Refugees and Migration, an area in which she had little expertise or background. Arguing that this represented a pattern of Bush appointments which favoured political loyalty and ideological position over expertise and experience, a New York Times Editorial on her nomination was titled, 'Inexpert Selection'. *New York Times*, 11 October 2005.
37 Kate O'Beirne, 'Our Girl at the U.N.', *New Republic*, 21 March 2002.
38 Don Monkerud, 'Religious Right Determines Foreign Policy', *Z Magazine*, http://www.thirdworldtraveler.com/Religion/ReligRight_ForPol.html, accessed 14 March 2010.
39 Population Action International, Press release, 27 June 2008, http://www.populationaction.org/Press_Room/Press_Releases/2008/06_27_UNFPA_Kemp-Kasten.shtml, accessed 13 May 2010.
40 Kate O'Beirne, 'Our Girl at the U.N.', *New Republic*, 21 March 2002.
41 Testimony of Representative Carolyn B. Maloney to the US Senate Committee on Foreign Relations, *Hearing on the Convention on the Elimination of All Forms of Discrimination Against Women (CEDAW) or the Treaty for the Rights of Women*, 13 June 2002, http://www.maloney.house.gov/index.php?Itemid=110&id=590&option=com_content&task=view (accessed 13 May 2010).
42 Emily Rosenberg, 'Rescuing Women and Children', *The Journal of American History*, 89 (2002), 20.

43 Testimony of Carolyn Maloney to the US Senate Committee on Foreign Relations, 13 June 2002, http://www.maloney.house.gov/index.php?Itemid=110&id=590&option=com_content&task=view, accessed 13 May 2010.
44 Alletta Brenner, 'Speaking of "Respect for Women": Gender and Politics in U.S. Foreign Policy Discourse', *Journal of Women's International Studies*, 10 (2009) 18–32, 30.
45 Cynthia Enloe, *The Curious Feminist* (California: University of California Press, 2004), 147.
46 Jan Jindy Pettman, 'Feminist International Relations after 9/11', *Brown Journal of World Affairs* (2004), X, 85–96, 89.
47 'Mad Melancholic Feminista', Post, 26 October 2006, http://melancholic-feminista.blogspot.com/2006_10_01_archive.html, accessed 22 June 2008.
48 Katha Pollitt, 'After Iraq and Afghanistan, Muslim Feminists are Leery of Seeming Close to the West', *The Nation*, 23 June 2007.
49 Naomi Klein, 'Brand US is in Trouble, So Take a Lesson from Big Mac', *The Guardian*, 14 March 2005.
50 Anne Elizabeth Mayer, '"Benign" Apartheid: How Gender Apartheid Has Been Rationalised', 5 *UCLA Journal of International Law and Foreign Affairs* (2000–2001), 273.
51 Amnesty International USA, http://www.amnestyusa.org/violence-against-women/ratify-the-treaty-for-the-rights-of-women-cedaw/page.do?id=1108216, accessed 13 May 2010.

Conclusion

Scott Lucas

Within weeks of the attacks of 11 September 2001, historian Paul Kennedy informed a general audience, inside and outside the United States: 'While the battle between the US and international terrorism and rogue states may indeed be asymmetrical, perhaps a far greater asymmetry may be emerging: namely, the one between the US and the rest of the powers.'[1]

Kennedy's declaration of American power, while serving as a statement of fact, was set amidst a US political discourse which sought to reassure a shaken and scared population, to warn adversaries, and to prepare the ground for future military action. President George W. Bush offered an impromptu response on 14 September at the World Trade Center's 'Ground Zero' – itself a semantic appropriation and conversion of an episode of US power 56 years earlier – to a rescue worker who shouted, 'I can't hear you': 'I can hear you! I can hear you! The rest of the world hears you! And the people – and the people who knocked these buildings down will hear all of us soon!'[2]

This assertion was re-deployed formally in sorrow, with Bush's statement at the National Cathedral hours after his Ground Zero appearance, 'This nation is peaceful, but fierce when stirred to anger. This conflict was begun on the timing and terms of others; it will end in a way and at an hour of our choosing.'[3] It was re-cast in the resolve of the President's address on 20 September to Congress, 'Our grief has turned to anger, and anger to resolution. Whether we bring our enemies to justice, or bring justice to our enemies, justice will be done',[4] and in the references of historical myth: 'I want justice. And there's an old poster out West that says, "Wanted: Dead or Alive".'[5]

At a time of national tragedy, the paradox was established: while the administration ostensibly was looking thousands of miles away to the terrorists and the countries who sheltered them, it was turning inward, casting the event and what was to come in distinctly American terms. The conflict would be framed though a US-centric conception, as it moved beyond Al Qa'eda and Afghanistan to other enemies and foreign theatres in a confrontation with an Axis of Evil: 'Steadfast in our purpose, we now press on. We have known freedom's price. We have shown freedom's power. And in this great conflict, my fellow Americans, we will see freedom's victory.'[6]

This inward turn might be expected – what other nations would not do the same? – but it came at a crucial moment in the shaping of America's place in the world in the twenty-first century. Once again, American power and American ideology was not just being mobilised for 'freedom' but also 'against' an enemy which was both concrete (Al Qa'eda, Taliban, Saddam Hussein) and abstract (the 'War on Terror'). Consequently, the Bush administration missed a pivotal opportunity. Failing to consider American power beyond unilateral capabilities and rhetorical invocations, the administration ultimately failed in its quest to convert that power from means into a long-term preponderance.

The invocation of US power is far from new, of course, but its twenty-first-century manifestation marked a shift in its conception, projection, and confirmation. Henry Luce's 'American Century', posited in 1941,[7] may have pointed towards an American dominance – political, economic, and cultural – but in the post-1945 terrains of the Cold War, that dominance was never established, if it was sought, around the globe. Whether because of the constraints of geopolitics, with entities like the Soviet Union and China posing challenges, of American political culture, with its widespread opposition to the 'empire' of others and silence on the prospect of its own, power as means was not universal in application.

The post-9/11 paradox was that the framing of the War on Terror in American terms, eliding the complexities of the local beyond the US, accompanied the unprecedented demonstration of American power. A brief glance outwards might have demonstrated the folly of such thinking, but administration officials had arguably embarked on their intellectual quest long before September 2001. Operating in a world where the Soviet Union had disappeared and China was perceived as a 'strategic competitor' which could be defeated through cultural and economic strength, officials in the administrations of both George W. Bush and George H.W. Bush, as well as allies in the media and 'think tanks' during and between those periods, had begun to promote the goal of a perpetual predominance. In the words of Charles Krauthammer, writing in 1990, 'The center of world power is the United States, attended by its Western allies.'⁸ The Bush Administration's Defense Planning Guidance set out two years later: 'Our first objective is to prevent the re-emergence of a new rival. This is a dominant consideration underlying the new regional defense strategy and requires that we endeavor to prevent any hostile power from dominating a region whose resources would, under consolidated control, be sufficient to generate global power. These regions include Western Europe, East Asia, the territory of the former Soviet Union, and Southwest Asia.'⁹

Several of the officials associated with the Defense Planning Guidance would return to the Executive Branch and the US diplomatic service a decade later: co-author Paul Wolfowitz took up the post of Deputy Secretary of Defense in 2001 while co-author Zalmay Khalilzad would become the US Ambassador to Afghanistan, the US Ambassador to Iraq, and the US Ambassador to the United Nations. Dick Cheney, Secretary of Defense in 1992, was now Vice President. Thus, when a reappraisal of US policy was carried out in 2001 – either as the pre-9/11 consideration of a US quest for preponderance, through enhanced capabilities and a demonstration case such as regime change in Iraq, or as a post-9/11 reassessment of US 'security' in a global context – this route was the path with least resistance.¹⁰

The vision of American predominance was not limited to administration officials, however. Academics, journalists, and political commentators were all swept up in projections – for better or worse – of a new US 'empire'. Krauthammer revisited his unipolar moment to pronounce, 'The new unilateralism argues explicitly and unashamedly for maintaining unipolarity, for sustaining America's unrivaled dominance for the foreseeable future. It could be a long future, assuming we successfully manage the single greatest threat, namely, weapons of mass destruction in the hands of rogue states.'¹¹

Nor was this only the construction of 'neo-conservative' commentators: Michael Ignatieff put forth a liberal consideration of 'Empire Lite': 'Being an imperial power... is more than being the most powerful nation or just the most hated one. It means enforcing such order as there is in the world and doing so in the American interest. It means laying down the rules America wants (on everything from markets to weapons of mass destruction) while exempting itself from other rules (the Kyoto Protocol on climate change and the International Criminal Court) that go against its interest.'¹² John Ikenberry, a leading analyst of US foreign policy, asserted, 'American power – and the American unipolar order – is different and less threatening to other states than that which is envisaged in theoretical and historical claims about the balance of power'; Michael

Cox wrote of 'The New Liberal Empire'.[13] Critical perspectives did not necessarily break down this projection: to the contrary, challenges from Noam Chomsky to Andrew Bacevich to Tom Engelhardt to Chalmers Johnson adopted the label and starting point of US dominance.[14]

Yet, within a few years, this conception was under pressure for a straightforward reason: the war in Iraq had not proven to be the demonstration case for the ascendancy of US power as an ends as well as a means. Instead, it had exposed the limits of that process. Within weeks of the fall of Saddam Hussein in April 2003, local groups in Iraq were protesting the presence of the American military; in locations like Fallujah, demonstrations turned to violent conflict after US troops fired on the population. By August, when insurgents killed one of Iran's leading Shi'a clerics, Ayatollah Mohammad-Baqar al-Hakim, and then blew up the United Nations complex in Baghdad, George W. Bush's declaration of 'Mission Accomplished' had become 'Mission Accomplished Against/For Whom?' A US diplomat reflected, 'The winter after the US occupation was solidified (if I can use that term), I wrote a posting stating that while I thought the US had about six months to try to reconstruct Iraq before they became occupiers instead of liberators, it took just a little over three months. It had lost any ability to influence Iraqi political reformation and that the only realistic option left open was to pick a reasonable date as possible to claim victory and leave.'[15] The gap between the narrow – one might posit 'exceptional' – American construction of politics and ideology and the complexity of perceptions and aspirations outside the US had been exposed, often violently, in and beyond Iraq.

On the surface, the difficulties in Iraq, interacting with other oppositions to US power, brought a re-consideration, if not a rejection, of the goal of American pre-eminence. The Bush administration re-presented the Iraq venture as part of a 'Freedom Agenda', supporting 'color revolutions' from the Ukraine to Georgia to the Lebanon. Commentators now fretted about an American eclipse, as in Thomas Friedman's 'We are a country in debt and in decline – not terminal, not irreversible, but in decline.' A report for the US National Intelligence Council, *Global Trends 2025*, was more measured but still pessimistic, 'Although the United States is likely to remain the single most powerful actor, the United States' relative strength – even in the military realm – will decline and US leverage will become more constrained.'[16]

The American political, economic, and intellectual elite supposedly embarked on the development of an alternative to the Bush administration's approach. 'Liberal intervention', a re-presentation of British Prime Minister Tony Blair's call during the 1999 Kosovo War[17] allied to the Clinton administration's identification of 'rogue states',[18] had served as a justification for the Iraq War, distinct from the Bushian rationale of a pre-emptive strike against weapons of mass destruction. Now it was put forth as a general approach to the world, both against and beyond the Bush Presidency, for example, in Peter Beinart's 2006 book *The Good Fight*.[19] At the same time, the Princeton Project on National Security, which drew from two years of meetings amongst hundreds of academics, activists, and former officials, intoned, 'Power cannot be wielded unilaterally, and in the pursuit of a narrowly drawn definition of the national interest, because such actions breed growing resentment, fear, and resistance.'[20] A commission for the Center of Strategic and International Studies, headed by Joseph Nye and former Undersecretary of State Richard Armitage, advanced on Nye's 'soft power' by declaring, 'The United States must become a smarter power by investing once again in the global good.'[21]

In key respects, however, the 'liberal intervention' approach was not a rejection of the preponderance of power sought by the 1992 Defense Planning Guidance and pursued by the Bush administration. It was merely another path towards that goal. As the Nye/Armitage report concluded, 'The goal of U.S. foreign policy should be to prolong and preserve American *preeminence* as an agent for good.'[22] The proponents of the new intervention might have alleged that the Bush administration had been misguided in the quest for the unipolar through the unilateral; however, these apparent requiems for Bush-era US power shared the assumption that America *should* be in a predominant position. Thus Charles Krauthammer, in his 2002 revisiting of the unipolar moment, set up a misleading straw-man: 'Liberal internationalism seeks through multilateralism to transcend power politics, narrow national interest and, ultimately, the nation-state itself';[23] in fact, the far more muscular conception of liberal intervention was being upheld to defend a wider national interest which, it claimed, was being betrayed by the mis-steps and misguided unilateralism of George W. Bush's advisors.

Andrew Johnstone, writing in this volume, puts the point concisely when he observes, beyond the unipolar v. liberal intervention positions (or the unilateral v. multilateral), 'the American desire to use its power to pursue its national interest through international organizations'. David Ryan establishes both the ideological rationalisation of power in the 'liberal' position and the inherent tensions that cannot be resolved, as he refers back to the 1990s.

The etymological tensions between these words rarely or explicitly rear their heads in the US culture in which they have appeared and constantly been reconstructed as a homogenous set of conditions, positing the United States as both the guarantor of certain negative liberties and simultaneously a power that is 'bound to lead' as, in Madeline Albright's words the 'indispensable nation'.

Of course, that desire is not exclusive to the US, but there is a distinctive in degree: 'America', with its global ambitions, has the *largest* national interest. So if all paths through the political, intellectual, and ideological maze merely return us to the centre of American primacy, how do we get out?

The critical position on US pre-eminence – be it expressed as 'empire', 'hegemony', or 'dominance' – does not necessarily give us an answer because 'America' still maintains its central location. Consideration of political, economic, or military power is not the issue here; rather it is the prevailing, if not exclusive, focus on *American* power. Consideration of the Bushian moment does not give us the solution for, only weeks before George W. Bush took office, his predecessor had proclaimed, 'America today has power and authority never seen before in the history of the world.' As Paul Bove has pondered, 'If America has had this structural intent to be identical to the world – for what else can it mean to be the world's only remaining superpower – then where can American people stand to get a view of all this?'[24]

The initial, essential step, in this interrogation of power, is to recognise that 'America' – whatever the structural or political intent – is not 'identical to the world'. Rather, American institutions interact with 'local' agencies and individuals who have aspirations and concerns that do not follow those from Washington, who pursue courses of action that may not necessarily revolve around the US. The essays in this volume illustrate, however, that this step is not necessarily an easy one in academic, intellectual, and political reality.

In Anna Hartnell's study of the response to and framing of Hurricane Katrina in 2005, the 'foreign' is brought in as a label to displace the populace who suffered in New Orleans, as they become residents of 'some devastated country' and 'refugees' from their own land. And then, in another shift, the 'foreign' becomes the terrain of American benevolence, brought in to illuminate the Federal Government's neglect of its citizens: 'The U.S. is the richest nation in the history of the world. Why cannot it restore electricity and water and help people rebuild their homes and neighbourhoods? If the U.S. can rebuild Afghanistan and Iraq, why not New Orleans?' Similarly, in Helen Laville's analysis, women's rights remains dormant, even stigmatised as a threat to American sovereignty, until they can be invoked as the exalted aim of a US diplomatic or military initiative.

Even if the 'foreign' is the physical terrain for US activity, it may remain as a cipher for American political or economic conceptions. The lessons of the American experience and negotiation of 'civil service', in Paul Kramer's, offer little for the Filipinos who were the nominal subject of administration, at least in comparison to the battles being waged over reform 'at home'. The 'local' may be subservient to the fixed viewpoints of American officials, as in Bevan Sewell's conclusion that 'the role of ideology stands out most clearly... as a conceptual framework by which US officials could situate the hugely complex issue of development into a much simpler understanding' of 'Latin America'. As Jason Parker notes, the framing of Washington was imposed upon the complexities to domestic politics in other countries – if indeed that domestic dimension was recognised – to produce a 'racialised' conception of the notions of neutralism and non-alignment. They are cases that cut against this grain – see Hugh Wilford's examination of the attempt by officials in the early years of the CIA to forge a working relationship and recognition of the emerging political groups in Middle Eastern countries – but even these fell away before Washington's demands for a straight-forward definition of allies and enemies. Entire populations were placed in the US geopolitical boxes or – as in George Kennan's definition in David Milne's essay – labelled as irresponsible and beyond moral order.

This is not to say that the flattening of the 'foreign' to a two-dimensional landscape is a work solely of American policymakers. As Parker writes, the projection of non-alignment and neutralism as a racial movement was furthered in part by African and Asian leaders and by African-American observers. Nor should it be assumed that, at all times and at all levels, the US Government imposed its political, economic, cultural, and ideological constructions upon the 'local'. In a brief glimpse beyond the standard Cold War framework, President Eisenhower pondered near the end of his administration, 'We were constantly hearing stories of Communist penetration and domination in countries all over the world. He wondered how many Communists had been won over to communism by bad living conditions and how many by the hope of power.'[25] Three months later he fretted, 'The US has been working since 1947 and very intensively since 1953 to achieve stability throughout the world but instead seems to have been faced with unrest and unhappiness.... Could we continue to support governments which would not carry out land reform and which would not lay out any constructive program for the betterment of the situation?'[26]

There were only glimpses, however, given the depiction of the 'local' as the terrain in a contest between the US and a Soviet adversary. Eisenhower's Secretary of State, John Foster Dulles, declared to British Prime Minister Harold Macmillan in 1957: 'These days may well be decisive for the next few centuries. For several hundred years the Christian West had dominated the world. Now it faced the question of whether that kind of society would be submerged for several centuries by ("Christian Socialism").'[27] The complications of foreign governments and societies were always placed in a contest beyond those borders, as a Presidential Committee reported in 1960, 'If... military or personal dictatorships collapse, the people, left without strong leadership, are highly vulnerable to the appeals, both economic and political, of Moscow and Peiping.'[28]

That conception in turn meant that the local had become a referent primarily, and arguably solely, for American capabilities and outcomes – political, economic, military, or ideological. The outcomes for the inhabitants of the local were secondary, if not peripheral. Walt Rostow, the head of the State Department's Policy Planning Staff, defined the terrain for President Lyndon Johnson in 1964:

> Unless we can find a way to make our enormous military and political power effective soon... the US will suffer a major defeat as a world power, we shall lose our leverage in the Western Pacific, the Indian subcontinent will become vulnerable..., the Communists will extend the technique of Wars of National Liberation into other continents, and these will be consequences, hard to define precisely, which will weaken our position in Western Europe.[29]

This was not just a historical occurrence, to be closed off with the collapse of the Soviet Union. A construction such as 'a racialized neutralism-nonalignment' did not necessarily 'assist American strategy by pulling neutralism out of practical play'.[30] Instead, that construction both distorted the local and wedged it into the conflict with Moscow and Beijing. Nasser's Egypt was considered not only in terms of its pan-Arabism or its relationship with Israel but as a potential client state of the Soviet Union. The Indonesia of Sukarno and then Suharto, as exemplified by the US response to the bloody events of 1965, was configured as potentially fertile territory for Communism. Henry Kissinger put the 'local' in its place in the case of Chile: 'I don't see why we need to stand by and watch a country go communist because of the irresponsibility of its own people.'[31]

This artifice did not resolve the specific political, economic, and military tensions; to the contrary, it fostered conflicts that, beyond the abstracted Cold War, were very real and would be present even as the Soviet demise was being marked with a supposed 'end of history'. Indeed, the distortion and even elision of the local would be compounded with a narrow, American-first invocation of past confrontations to justify or criticise current interventions, again paying scant attention to political, economic, and cultural dynamics outside a US-centric framework, the effects compounded because of the 'global' application of Washington's ideas. The protracted experience in Vietnam became a 'syndrome' either to warn against interventions or to be overcome by pursuing them. As Andrew Priest points out in this volume, the quarter-century of US involvement from military aid to the French to departure from Saigon was re-inscribed to sanction or oppose the 2003 Iraq War.

On the academic front, some scholars have proposed the remedying of this distortion/elision of the local through a history of US foreign policy which works with the trans-national, examining the dynamics of 'American debates paralleled – and... affected by debates in other nations'.[32] This approach, however, may reinforce rather than resolve the challenge because, in the case of the work from which this quote is taken, the 'other nations' brought into consideration are Britain and France. The area being considered by Washington, London, and Paris – Vietnam – remains a terrain to be acted upon, rather than a 'nation' whose debates are acknowledged, let alone put at the centre of the critique. Indeed, the author joins the process that he is analysing. He sets out a 'more literal notion of what it means for policymakers to have ("constructed") Vietnam... assembling an integrated, functioning whole out of disparate materials that might have been combined to created something different'. Thus, the author never considers that there might have been a Vietnam – 'constructed' by its own people – rather than 'disparate materials' in which there is no sign of human presence; instead, he narrates, and thus endorses, the policymakers' approach to an emptied terrain.[33]

This conception of the 'trans-national' is significant not just as a scholarly move in the 'historical' but as a reflection of contemporary American discourse and politics. Numerous stories of how US policymakers had a limited, if any conception of the Iraqi people they were 'liberating' emerged soon after the 2003 war, even as conflict between those people and American forces escalated. The State Department's volumes on 'The Future of Iraq', a months-long compilation of the political, economic, and cultural issues that the US would face after military success, was thrown out by the Pentagon. Prominent Iraqi expatriates, taken to the White House to meet the President, were taken aback to find that George W. Bush did not realise there were two major versions – Sunni and Shi'a – of Islam.[34] Later, Assistant Secretary of Defense Douglas Feith, asked 'if the Administration was too enamored of the idea that Iraqis would greet American troops with flowers', responded, 'They had flowers in their minds.'[35]

Just as 'liberal intervention' was a nominal response to the 'unilateral/unipolar' framework of the Bush era, so the Obama administration ostensibly offered 'engagement' as a counter to this political elision of the local. The President said in a major speech in Ankara in April 2009:

> No one nation can confront these challenges alone, and all nations have a stake in overcoming them. That is why we must listen to one another, and seek common ground. That is why we must build on our mutual interests, and rise above our differences. We are stronger when we act together....

We seek broad engagement based upon mutual interests and mutual respect. We will listen carefully, bridge misunderstanding, and seek common ground. We will be respectful, even when we do not agree.[36]

Both in the specific approach to Islamic communities and in the general message to the world beyond the US, Obama was offering a recognition based on acceptance of interests, perspectives, and cultures. Yet this position was complicated by an insistence on American primacy, highlighted in Obama's Inaugural Speech by his declaration 'that we are ready to lead once more'.[37] As Andrew Johnstone has observed this volume, 'If the US really is ready to lead once more, it "must learn to listen, as well as to preach".'

Even more importantly, the Obama administration faced – although it did not necessarily recognise – the inherent tension between engagement and liberal intervention. 'Engagement' could be based, even if it presumed or asserted American primacy, on recognition of the autonomy of the country, community, or individual being engaged. 'Liberal intervention', by its very nature, suspended that autonomy, as the US acted upon the country, community, or individual in question. And because that autonomy had been elided or removed, American values and ideology could be put forward or retracted at will. (For example, extending Helen Laville's essay in this volume, there has been little advance in 'women's rights' – nominally one of the reasons for the US military operations in Afghanistan since 2001 – during the American intervention.)

Instead of recognition of the local and its complexities, Washington returns to the projection of the abstracted threat, as in Obama's declaration of June 2009, 'We will... relentlessly confront violent extremists who pose a grave threat to our security.'[38] In repeated declarations from March 2009, justifying escalations of US troops, the President invoked 'the epicenter of violent extremism practiced by al Qaeda', even though American intelligence acknowledged there were less than 100 members of the organisation in Afghanistan.[39] Given such discourse from the top of the US Government, there is little chance to recover the local, as Josh Shahryar, who has covered Afghanistan for years, writes:

> Your average media-approved Afghan won't have a last name. There will be a quip informing you that, 'like most Afghans, he doesn't have a last name.' And there won't be any women. Forget about the opinion of Afghan women. They are veiled and will never speak to a foreigner – their voices censored by both the Taliban and the Western media. We work for less than a dollar day. Our names always include Allah or Mohammed. We have long beards and hopefully a turban around our heads. Did I mention the part where we can't read and write? Expectations fulfilled, your average foreign correspondent will ask this guy about Afghanistan and seriously expect a well-informed, well-balanced and to the point answer from an ordinary citizen. Then, they will publish this and inform you about a war that you've spent hundreds of billions of dollars on.[40]

In November 2008, less than seven years after he had set out the 'asymmetry... between the US and the rest of the powers', Paul Kennedy fretted about the American future:

> The sweeping election of Obama has generated extraordinary goodwill; who, apart from the most purblind, has not been excited? But such positivity must be tempered by the realisation that he comes into office during one of the most difficult and troubled periods in modern history; that he is to run a country far less dominant, relatively, than at the time of Wilson, Truman and Kennedy; and that,

while his international attractiveness is strong, great nations cannot survive on soft power alone.[41]

Kennedy's 2002 assertion of American 'hard power' had disappeared, leaving him to consider the prospect of a loss of US pre-eminence in the world. Yet at no point, in his jeremiad for 'soft power' – it 'cannot pay for foreign oil and gas, imported cars, electronic goods, kitchenware and children's toys'; it 'cannot handle the longer term secular shifts in the world's economic balances' – did he re-consider the relationship between the 'great nation' and the 'other'. Indeed, there was no recognition of the 'other' in his concern beyond sweeping invocation of 'an increasingly nationalistic Russia' and 'China and India's remarkable maritime expansion': 'To those folks, soft power doesn't count for much. To them, it is the old story of covenants without swords.'

Far from providing a resolution to the perceived crisis, Kennedy had merely exposed it further. His words came as others were hailing the US 'soft power'/'smart power' that would move the country beyond the foreign conflicts of the Bush years, but that concept was already entangled with the American presumption of dominance. Writing in 2004, John Lewis Gaddis maintained: 'Empire is an American as apple pie.... It seems to me on balance American imperial power in the 20th century has been a remarkable force for good, for democracy, for prosperity. What is striking is that great opposition has not arisen to the American empire.'[42] The issue with the statement – which, ironically, was made in an exchange with Kennedy – is whether America did or did not constitute an empire, the ostensible subject of the discussion. Instead, it was that an interpreter like Gaddis could so easily conflate values and power. He could blind himself to the 'opposition' which may have arisen in the twentieth and twenty-first centuries because, by putting that conflation under an 'American' umbrella, he had negated the values and power of others.

The response to Gaddis and to those who acclaim American primacy – through the unipolar or leadership of the multipolar, through pre-emption or liberal intervention, through hard or soft power – should not be based on the criticism of opposition. That merely replicates the conflations and elisions: 'American values/power are good'; 'American values/power are not'. Critique is limited, if it is indeed possible, because the US is still immutably at the centre of our frame of reference.

Instead, we should de-centre America. Non-Americans are far from an undifferentiated mass, either welcoming their US-delivered freedom or pursuing 'anti-Americanism'. Indeed, in their approach to political, economic, and cultural issues, they may not even wish to put 'America' at the forefront of their consideration.

In 1998 Janice Radway considered, 'What's in a Name?', in her Presidential address to the American Studies Association. The speech promised far more than nomenclature: Radway pointed to recent work in the field that challenged and moved beyond a contained American 'exceptionalism' to suggest 'territories and geographies need to be reconceived as spatially-situated and intricately intertwined networks of social relationships that tie specific locales to particular histories'. In the end, however, she fell back upon suggestions for a renamed association – International Association for the Study of the United States, Inter-American Studies Association, Society for Inter-Cultural Studies – and she retained 'placing the U.S. (conceived always in a global context) at the heart of the field's work while formally acknowledging that that work is carried out internationally'.[43]

Labels such as 'empire' and concepts such as 'liberal intervention' may play with the notion of American power, but they are primarily window-dressing for the retention of US pre-eminence as the starting point and the focal point of consideration. At the same time, however, that pre-eminence is challenged daily, not just in the grand narrative of a rising China or India presented by 'declinists' (usually to rationalise their own calls that the US must re-double its efforts to maintain a leading position) but in the actions of states, communities, and individuals who may or may not be receptive to American power, who may or may not include the US in their political, economic, and cultural spheres.

I find myself, at the conclusion of this volume and benefitting from the thoughts in all its essays, re-considering the statement Bevan Sewell and I set out in the Introduction. The approach may not be to 'avoid labels such as primacy, decline, and dominance' but to challenge them, break them down, and even set them aside through attention to and incorporation of the 'local'. The belief within the US in 'the power of American exceptionalism' may remain 'undiminished', but it does not follow that others embrace or even acquiesce to that power. The belief in exceptionalism may 'continue to guide the way that the US has presented itself to the rest of the world', but it does not follow that the world applauds or that it even sees 'America' at the centre of the stage.

Michael Hunt, quoted in this volume by David Ryan, suggests, 'Perhaps most challenging of all, thinking about decline involves accepting the importance of that insubstantial thing called legitimacy.' Absolutely: critiquing primacy and power as well as decline does turn upon legitimacy, assessing how it is constructed and how it is projected. Legitimacy does not consist, however, of a one-way claim such as 'America is bound to lead'; it has to be acknowledged, if not conferred, by others. It consists not only of political or diplomatic declarations; as the essays in the second half of this volume demonstrate, legitimacy also rests upon cultural negotiations of human rights, women's rights, local identities, and even the 'America' in American Studies.

Legitimacy cannot be claimed simply by proclaiming an 'empire' or 'power'; it cannot be dismissed merely by crying 'hegemony' or 'dominance'. Perhaps more importantly, this is not solely or centrally an issue of American legitimacy; in the US interactions in and with the world, the legitimacy of those beyond Washington is just as significant.

The issue is not 'What's in a Name?' but 'What is Beyond the Name?' It is in the space between the name of US 'pre-eminence' and the interactions beyond that asserted name – the space where legitimacy is negotiated, challenged, constructed – that, I suggest, we can operate as scholars rather than serve as an adjunct to it.

Notes

1 Paul Kennedy, 'The Greatest Superpower', *New Perspectives Quarterly*, Vol. 19, No. 1 (Spring 2002), http://www.digitalnpq.org/archive/2002_spring/kennedy.html
2 Bush speech in New York City, 14 September 2001, http://www.youtube.com/watch?v=MiSwqaQ4VbA
3 Bush remarks at the National Day of Prayer and Remembrance, 14 September 2001, reprinted at *American Rhetoric*, http://www.americanrhetoric.com/speeches/gwbush911prayer&memorialaddress.htm
4 Bush speech to Congress, 20 September 2001, reprinted in *The Guardian* (London), 21 September 2001, http://www.guardian.co.uk/world/2001/sep/21/september11.usa13
5 Toby Harnden, 'Bin Laden is Wanted: Dead or Alive, says Bush', *The Daily Telegraph* (London), 18 September 2001, http://www.telegraph.co.uk/news/worldnews/asia/afghanistan/1340895/Bin-Laden-is-wanted-dead-or-alive-says-Bush.html
6 Bush State of the Union address, 29 January 2002, reprinted at *CNN*, http://archives.cnn.com/2002/ALLPOLITICS/01/29/bush.speech.txt/
7 Henry Luce, 'The American Century', *Life*, 17 February 1941, reprinted at http://books.google.com/books?id=I0kEAAAAMBAJ&printsec=frontcover&source=gbs_atb#v=onepage&q&f=false
8 Charles Krauthammer, 'The Unipolar Moment', *Foreign Affairs*, Vol. 70, No. 1 (1990/91), reprinted at http://www.comunicazione.uniroma1.it/materiali/14.34.27_Charles%20Krauthammer%20The%20UnipolarMoment.pdf

9   Defense Planning Guidance, 18 February 1992, in 'Prevent the Reemergence of a New Rival: The Making of the Cheney Regional Defense Strategy', 26 February 2008, *The National Security Archive*, http://www.gwu.edu/~nsarchiv/nukevault/ebb245/index.htm
10 See Maria Ryan and Scott Lucas, 'Against Everyone and No-one: The Failure of the Unipolar in Iraq and Beyond', in David Ryan and Patrick Kiely, *America and Iraq: Policy-Making, Intervention, and Regional Politics* (Routledge, 2008).
11 Charles Krauthammer, 'The Unipolar Moment Revisited', *National Interest*, 70 (Winter 2002/03), reprinted at http://www.gwu.edu/~nsarchiv/nukevault/ebb245/index.htm
12 Michael Ignatieff, 'The Burden', *New York Times Magazine*, 5 January 2003, http://www.nytimes.com/2003/01/05/magazine/05EMPIRE.html
13 G. John Ikenberry, 'American Empire and the Empire of Capitalist Democracy', in Michael Cox, Tim Dunne and Ken Booth, eds., *Empires, Systems, and States: Great Transformations in International Politics* (Cambridge: Cambridge University Press, 2001), 191–212.
14 Noam Chomsky, *Hegemony or Survival: America's Quest for Global Dominance* (New York: Holt, 2004); Andrew Bacevich, *American Empire: The Realities and Consequences of US Foreign Policy* (Cambridge, MA: Harvard University Press, 2004); Tom Engelhardt, ed., *The World According to TomDispatch: America in the Age of Empire* (London, 2008); Chalmers Johnson, *Dismantling the Empire: America's Last Best Hope* (New York: Metropolitan Books, 2010).
15 Private correspondence with author, August 2010.
16 US Directorate of National Intelligence, National Intelligence Council, *Global Trends 2025: A Transformed World* (November 2008), http://www.dni.gov/nic/PDF_2025/2025_Global_Trends_Final_Report.pdf
17 Blair speech at Chicago Economic Club, 'Doctrine of the International Community', 24 April 1999, reprinted at http://keeptonyblairforpm.wordpress.com/blair-speech-transcripts-from-1997-2007/#chicago
18 Anthony Lake, 'Confronting Backlash States', *Foreign Affairs* (March/April 1994), 45–55, reprinted at http://people.reed.edu/~ahm/Courses/Reed-POL-358-2008-S1_SWP/Syllabus/EReadings/Lake1994Confronting.pdf
19 Peter Beinart, *The Good Fight: Why Liberals – and Only Liberals – Can Win the War on Terror and Make America Great Again* (New York: HarperCollins, 2006).
20 G. John Ikenberry and Anne-Marie Slaughter (Princeton Project on National Security), *Forging a World of Liberty Under Law: US National Security in the 21st Century*, 27 September 2006, http://www.princeton.edu/~ppns/report/FinalReport.pdf
21 Craig Cohen, Joseph S. Nye, and Richard Armitage, *A Smarter, More Secure America*, 6 November 2007, http://csis.org/files/media/csis/pubs/071106_csiss-martpowerreport.pdf
22 *Ibid.*
23 Krauthammer, 'The Unipolar Moment Revisited'.
24 Paul Bové, 'Can American Studies Be Area Studies?', in Masao Miyoshi and Harry Harootunian, eds., *Learning Places: The Afterlives of Area Studies* (Durham, N.C.: Duke University Press, 2002).
25 437th National Security Council meeting, 17 March 1960, *US Declassified Document Reference System (DDRS)* (Farmington Hill, MI: Gale, 1974–Present), 1991, 2044.

26 449th National Security Council meeting, 30 June 1960, *US DDRS*, 1991, 2029.
27 Dulles-Macmillan meeting, 23 October 1957, *US DDRS*, 1992, 458.
28 Conclusions and Recommendations of the President's Committee on Information Activities Abroad, December 1960, *US DDRS*, 1990, 2211.
29 Rostow to Johnson, 6 June 1964, *US DDRS*, 1989, 995.
30 See Jason Parker's chapter in this volume.
31 Henry Kissinger at a National Security meeting, 27 June 1970, quoted in Christopher Reilly, 'Justice for Chile: Will Kissinger Finally Pay?', *CounterPunch*, 4 April 2002, http://www.counterpunch.org/reillychile.html
32 Mark Attwood Lawrence, *Assuming the Burden: Europe and the American Commitment to Vietnam* (Berkeley, CA: University of California Press, 2005), 7.
33 My positing of the 'emptied terrain', both for policymakers and for those who write about them, is shaped by ideas in Giorgio Agamben, *State of Exception*, trans. by Kevin Attell (Chicago, IL: University of Chicago Press, 2005). See also Donald Pease, *The New American Exceptionalism* (Minneapolis: University of Minnesota Press, 2009). While Agamben and Pease both focus on the sovereign's application of the 'state of exception' to his/her domestic constituency, I believe the concept is just as powerful when mobilised in foreign policy.
34 George Packer, *The Assassins Gate: America in Iraq* (New York: Farrar, Straus, and Giroux, 2006), 101.
35 Quoted in Jeffrey Goldberg, 'A Little Learning', *The New Yorker*, 9 May 2005, http://www.newyorker.com/archive/2005/05/09/050509fa_fact?currentPage=all
36 Obama speech in Ankara, 6 April 2009, reprinted in *Enduring America*, http://enduringamerica.com/2009/04/06/video-obama-speech-in-turkey/
37 Obama inaugural speech, 20 January 2009, reprinted in *Enduring America*, http://enduringamerica.com/2009/01/20/the-prepared-script-of-barack-obamas-inaugural-speech/
38 Obama speech in Cairo, 4 June 2009, reprinted in *Enduring America*, http://enduringamerica.com/2009/06/04/video-and-transcript-president-obamas-speech-in-cairo-4-june/
39 Obama speech, 1 December 2009, reprinted in *Enduring America*, http://enduringamerica.com/2009/12/02/afghanistan-pakistan-video-transcript-of-obama-speech-1-december/; 'CIA Chief: Fewer than 100 Al Qaeda in Afghanistan: CIA Chief', *ABC News* (Australia), 28 June 2010, http://www.abc.net.au/news/stories/2010/06/28/2938358.htm
40 Josh Shahryar, 'Afghanistan: What Did Wikileaks Reveal? What I Wrote in Kabul in 2005', *Enduring America*, 28 July 2010, http://enduringamerica.com/2010/07/28/afghanistan-wikileaks-revelations-what-i-wrote-in-kabul-in-2005-shahryar/
41 Paul Kennedy, 'Soft Power is On the Up. But It Can Always Be Outmuscled', *The Guardian*, 18 November 2008, http://www.guardian.co.uk/commentisfree/2008/nov/18/usa-obama-economy-military
42 John Gaddis and Paul Kennedy, 'Kill the Empire! (Or Not)', *New York Times*, July 25, 2004, http://www.nytimes.com/2004/07/25/books/25GKEN.html
43 Janice Radway, 'What's in a Name?', *American Quarterly*, Vol. 51, No. 1 (March 1999), 1–32.

Index

Abrams, Elliott, 150–3
Acheson, Dean, 50, 58, 65, 199
Adams, John, 171
Adams, John Quincy, 188
Afghanistan, 1, 178, 184–5, 190–1, 198, 213–14, 226, 229–30, 234, 237–8, 253, 260–1, 273–6, 282–3, 291
Al Qa'eda (Al Qaeda), 193, 198, 230, 282
Albright, Madeleine, 187, 286
American Association for the United Nations, 207
American Bar Association, 264
American Friends of the Middle East (AFME), 99, 107
American Israel Public Affairs Committee (AIPAC), 108
American Studies, 9, 162–4, 167–71, 176, 178, 293–4
Amnesty International, 136, 276
Angola, 193, 199, 210
Arbenz, Jacobo, 118–19
Archer, Ernest, 44
Armitage, Richard, 285
Asian Relations Conference, 79

Bacevich, Andrew, 1, 227, 234, 236–7, 284
Baker, James, 194
Bandung Conference, 8, 76–7, 82–6, 88–90
Beard, Charles, 234
Beijing Women's Conference (1995), 270
Beinart, Peter, 285
Berlin, Isaiah, 185
Beveridge, Albert, 26
Bevin, Ernest, 37
Blair, Tony, 213, 284
Bohlen, Chip (Charles), 39, 46–9
Bolivia, 118
Bolton, John, 213, 217

Bonaparte, Charles, 20, 23, 27
Boot, Max, 1, 227, 230, 232
Bosnia-Herzegovina, 212, 228
Boston Globe, 228
Bourne, Edward, 19
Bowman, Isaiah, 167
Brazil, 118, 125, 263–4
Bzrezinski, Zbigniew, 192
Bremer, Paul, 275
Brioni Conference, 87
Britain (& British Empire), 81, 100–3, 110, 175, 289, 17–18, 24, 29, 42, 44, 58, 61–2, 64
Bryce, James, 18–19
Bullitt, William, 38
Burma, 80, 83
Bush Doctrine, 5, 187
Bush, George H.W., 189, 193, 212, 228, 282
Bush, George W., 1, 178, 185, 189–90, 195, 213, 226, 227, 229, 267, 271, 274, 281, 282, 284–6, 290
Buss, Doris, 270
Byrnes, James, 46, 49

Cambodia, 236
Canada, 163, 165, 169, 175
Caracas Conference, 119–20
Carter, Jimmy, 136–9, 144, 152–3, 192, 197, 211, 267
Carnegie Endowment for Peace, 211, 232
Carothers, Thomas, 217, 219
Castro, Fidel, 104, 125
Central Intelligence Agency (CIA), 8, 82, 99–104, 106–10
Cheney, Dick, 283
China, 63–5, 80–2, 84–5, 142, 177, 190, 198, 271, 282, 293
Chomsky, Noam, 1, 284
Christian Science Monitor, 235
Christopher, Warren, 267, 269

Churchill, Winston, 36, 42–3, 46, 50, 62
Civil Rights, 195, 246, 249, 252, 256, 75, 85
Clinton, Bill, 57, 63, 66–7, 212, 216, 228, 267, 269–70, 273, 285
Clinton, Hillary, 270–1
Coen, Amy, 273
Cohen, Eliot A., 227
Cohen, Warren, 213
Cold War, 2–8, 36, 41, 47, 48, 50–1, 57–8, 65–7, 68, 71–2, 75–80, 83, 85, 87, 89–91, 99–100, 104–6, 114–16, 129, 164, 166, 168–9, 185, 192, 195, 208–9, 212, 216, 218–20, 228–9, 232, 257, 282, 287, 289
Combined Action Program, 230
Community of Democracies, 216
Convention on the Political Rights of Women, 265–6
Convention to eliminate all forms of discrimination against women (CEDAW), 267
Copeland, Miles, 103–4, 110
Communism, 80–1, 84, 90, 141, 195, 228, 288
Containment, 71, 80, 227, 251
Council on Foreign Relations, 230
Cuba, 14, 19, 121, 125–6, 172, 174–5, 210

Dallek, Robert, 227, 231
Davies, Joe, 48–9
Deane, General John, 36–7, 41, 43–4, 47–8
Defense Planning Guidance (1992), 185–6, 283, 285
Department of State: Bureau of Human Rights and Humanitarian Affairs, 9, 137–8, 145, 152
Dillon, Douglas, 125
Dominican Republic, 118, 122, 126
Du Bois, W.E.B., 177, 255–7
Dukakis, Michael, 193
Dulles, Allen, 65, 82
Dulles, John Foster, 56, 63, 65–6, 82, 84, 108, 119, 122, 125, 127, 288
Durbrow, Elbridge, 39, 45, 49

East India Company, 17
East Timor, 210
Eaton, Dorman, 17–18, 22
Eddy, William, 102, 105, 109
Egypt, 25, 84, 103–4, 109–10, 272, 288
Eisenhower, Dwight, 84–5, 90, 108–9, 113–15, 117–21, 123, 125–9
Eisenhower, Milton, 117–18, 124
El Salvador, 118, 153
Ellsberg, Daniel, 227, 233–4
Engelhardt, Tom, 284
Enloe, Cynthia, 275
Ethnogeographic Board, 165–8, 178

Falk, Richard, 229
Feith, Douglas, 290
Ferguson, Niall, 1
Foreign Affairs, 235
Forrestal, James, 48, 50
Foulke, William Dudley, 20, 27–9
France, 81, 103, 173, 177, 218, 289
Franklin, Benjamin, 171
Friedman, Thomas, 284

Gaddis, John Lewis, 68, 292
Garrison Jr., William Lloyd, 22
Gates, Robert, 189
Germany, 57, 59–61, 70, 187
Ghana, 86
Goodrich, Carter, 167
Gore, Al, 67, 269
Graves, Mortimer, 167
Guatemala, 118–19, 128, 194
Gulbenkian Commission, 168

Haig, Alexander, 137–9, 145, 149, 152
Halberstam, David, 227, 235
Hall, Robert B., 167
Halle, Louis, 194
Harriman, W. Averell, 8, 36–7, 39, 41, 43–52
Hay, John, 174
Hayakawa, Samuel, 147
Heffernan, Virginia, 260
Helsinki Watch, 143–4, 150–2
Heritage Foundation, 211
Herring, George, 6, 227
Herter, Christian, 127

Hirschman, Susan, 272
Hitler, Adolf, 39–40, 188, 206
Hoar, George, 18, 20, 22
Holland, Henry, 122
Hopkins, Harry, 41
Howard, George Elliott, 24
Humphrey, George M., 116, 120
Hunt, Michael, 183, 189, 293
Hussein, Saddam, 193, 230, 282, 284

Ikenberry, G. John, 216, 283
Independent Women's Forum, 271
India, 17–18, 25, 77–81, 84–5, 101, 128, 198, 293
Indonesia, 80, 82–3, 128, 210, 253, 288
Inter-American Development Bank, 124, 126
International Conference on Population and development (ICPD), Cairo, 269–70
International Court of Justice (World Court), 211
International Labor Organisation (ILO), 211, 264
Iran, 103, 109, 190, 194, 199, 214, 261, 274, 284
Iraq, 1, 5, 9–10, 71, 101, 178, 183–5, 190–1, 194, 196–7, 212–15, 218, 221, 226–38, 245, 247, 249–50, 253, 260, 261, 276, 283–6, 289–90
Israel, 60, 63–4, 99–100, 107–11, 210, 214, 288

Japan, 39, 43, 61, 165, 189
Johnson, Lyndon B., 109, 126, 288
Jordan, David Starr, 19, 22, 26
Judt, Tony, 72

Kagan, Robert, 205–7, 214, 216–17
Karnow, Stanley, 227, 233, 235
Kassebaum, Nancy, 146
Kemp-Kasten Amendment, 271
Kennan, George, 8, 36, 39–40, 43, 49, 51–2, 56–72, 189, 193, 199, 287
Kennedy, John F., 66, 104, 109, 114, 124, 127–9, 199

Kennedy, Paul, 189, 193, 197, 281, 291–2
Kenyon, Dorothy, 265–6, 272
Kerrey, Bob, 229
Kerry, John, 232
Khalilzad, Zalmay, 283
Khmer Rouge, 211, 236
Kim (novel), 101, 106, 110
King, Martin Luther, 256
Kipling, Rudyard, 101, 106, 110
Kissinger, Henry, 57, 63, 189, 192–3, 197, 199, 288
Klein, Naomi, 251, 275
Kolko, Gabriel, 227
Kollontay, Alexandra, 40
Korean War, 71, 80–1, 189, 209
Kosovo, 228, 284
Krauthammer, Charles, 282–3, 285
Kubitschek, Juscelino, 125
Kutler, Stanley I., 231
Kyoto Protocol, 213, 283

Lagan, Mark, 272
Laird, Melvin, 227, 235
League of Nations, 205–7, 262–3, 265
  Committee on the Legal Status of Women (aka 'Committee of Experts'), 262
  League of Nations Association, 207
League to Enforce Peace, 207
Lefever, Ernest W., 9, 136–53
Liberal Intervention, 285, 290, 292–3
Lind, Michael, 235
Lippmann, Walter, 41, 46, 50
Lodge, Henry Cabot, 20
Los Angeles Times, 230
Luce, Henry, 188–9, 282
Luck, Edward, 215–16
Lukacs, John, 68–9
Lutz, Bertha, 263

McCain, John, 205, 216, 221, 229
McCarthy, Joseph, 56, 65
McKinley, William, 20, 27
McMaster, H.R., 235
Macmillan, Harold, 288
Maloney, Carolyn, 272, 274

Mann, Thomas, 126
Marcuse, Herbert, 164
Marshall, George, 48
Marshall Plan (1947), 186
Martin, Jose de San, 171
May, Ernest R., 225
Mayer, Ann Elizabeth, 276
Meiklejohn, Robert, 36, 38, 50
Meisler, Stanley, 212
Mexican War, 174
Mexico, 174
Mexico City Policy, 269, 271, 273
Molotov, Vyacheslav, 37, 40–2, 46–9
Monroe Doctrine, 169, 174
Moravcsik, Andrew, 267
Moyar, Mark, 227, 235
Moynihan, Daniel Patrick, 150, 210–11, 213
Murphy, Craig, 220

Nagl, John, 235
NAM (Non-Aligned Movement), 8, 75, 87, 91, 218
Nasser, Gamal Abdel, 84, 86–8, 97, 103–4, 108–10, 112
Nation magazine, 229
National Security Council (NSC), 82, 115, 126, 185
National Security Strategy (2002), 185–6, 191
National Security Strategy (2010), 208, 220
National Civil Service Reform League, 20
Nehru, Jawaharlal, 78–87, 94
Neustadt, Richard E., 225
Nicaragua, 153, 195, 199, 211, 218, 221
Nitze, Paul, 65, 68, 199
Nixon, Richard, 121–6, 179, 187, 199, 228, 233
Nkrumah, Kwame, 86, 88–9, 97
North Atlantic Treaty Organisation (NATO), 66, 67, 187, 205, 209, 218, 220–3
NSC 68 (1950), 68
Nye, Joseph, 184, 217, 285
Nyerere, Julius, 88–9

O'Beirne, Kate, 271, 273, 274
Obama, Barack, 1, 11, 184–5, 189–91, 193, 197–9, 215, 219–20, 261, 288, 290–1
Office of International Issues, 261
Office of United Nations Affairs, 63
Operation Pan America, 125
Organization of American States (OAS), 113, 125, 127
Ostrower, Gary, 206, 211

Pakistan, 78, 80–1, 128
Palestine, 63–4, 218
Palmer, Bruce Jr, 228
Palmer, Stephen, 149–50, 156
Paraguay, 118
Pell, Claiborne, 142, 148, 151
Pentagon Papers, 233
Percy, Charles, 140, 142, 145–7, 151
Peru, 166
Pettigrew, Richard, 22
Pettman, Jan Jindy, 260, 275
Philippines, 7, 16, 19, 25, 27–9, 34, 68, 81–2, 153, 174, 233
Podhoretz, Norman, 227–8, 234, 236
Poland, 39, 42–4, 46–9, 51
Pollitt, Katha, 275
Powell, Adam Clayton, 83
Powell, Colin, 213
Powell Doctrine, 198
Prebisch, Raul, 120
Princeton Project on National Security, 216, 285
Project for the New American Century, 232
Puerto Rico, 16, 174–5

Radway, Janice, 293
Reagan, Ronald, 9, 136–9, 141, 145–6, 148–55, 157, 159, 185, 187, 189, 191, 193, 195, 199, 211–12, 228, 267–9
Rice, Condoleezza, 190, 201
Rio de Janeiro Economic Conference, 119, 123
Roberts, Frank, 36, 46, 49
Roe Vs Wade, 273
Roosevelt, Archibald, 103–5, 109–10
Roosevelt, Eleanor, 255

Roosevelt, Franklin, 36–7, 41–5, 47,
    48, 50–2, 101, 176
Roosevelt, Kermit 'Kim', 101–4, 106,
    109–11
Roosevelt, Theodore, 20, 25, 28
Rosenberg, Emily, 260–2, 276
Rossbach, Richard, 37
Rostow, Eugene, 58
Rostow, Walt, 68, 288
Rowe, Leo, 24
Rumsfeld, Donald, 235
Rwanda, 212, 228

Safire, William, 229
Sauerbrey, Ellen, 271–2, 279
Schlesinger Jr, Arthur, 56, 227
Schurz, Charles, 20, 22
SEATO (South East Asia Treaty
    Organization), 81, 222
Senate Foreign Relations Committee,
    140–2, 145, 151, 267–8
September 11 (9/11), 166, 172, 187,
    196, 213, 229, 230, 245–7
Sharpton, Al, 249–51, 257
Sherwood, Robert, 40
Shultz, George, 153, 161
Slaughter, Anne-Marie, 216
Somalia, 212, 228, 240
Sorley, Lewis, 235
South Africa, 141, 148
Soviet Economic Offensive, 133–4,
    137
Soviet Union, 37, 41–3, 45, 49–50,
    64–5, 68, 72, 85, 128, 144, 149,
    153, 155, 168, 194, 209, 255, 264,
    282–3, 288
Spain, 14, 20, 34, 172–4, 181–2
Spanish-American War, 4, 169, 174
Stalin, Josef, 37–9, 41–5, 48–52, 59
Stassen, Harold, 115
Steinglass, Matt, 235
Stimson, Henry, 48
Storey, Moorfield, 20
Strong, William Duncan, 166–7, 180
Summers, Harry G. Jr, 228, 235, 241
Sudan, 216
Suez Crisis, 86–7
Sukarno, 82–3, 86–7, 288
Sweden, 40

Taliban, 193, 199, 230, 282
Teller, Henry, 21
Thailand, 81, 253
Third World, 75–7, 83–5, 87, 88–92,
    98, 117, 121, 130, 157, 185, 228,
    248, 276
Thompson, Dorothy, 107–8
Thompson, John, 10–11
Thompson, Llewellyn, 38
Thorpe, Francis Newton, 19
Timerman, Jacobo, 143
Tito, Josip Broz, 60, 78–9, 87
Truman, Harry, 8, 37, 41, 45–52, 109,
    265, 291
Trujillo, Rafael, 122
Tsongas, Paul, 141, 145–6, 148
Turner, Frederick Jackson, 19

United Nations, 9, 64, 80, 88, 142,
    194, 205–21, 230, 244–5, 252–3,
    255–7, 262–4, 266, 268–71, 276
  Charter of the United Nations, 263
  Commission on the Status of
    Women, 264–6, 271–4
  Educational, Scientific and Cultural
    Organisation (UNESCO), 211
  Economic Commission for Latin
    America (ECLA), 120
  General Assembly, 87, 90, 209–10,
    215, 219, 267
    Resolution 3379 (1975), 210
  Uniting for Peace Resolution, 209
  Population Fund, 271
  Security Council, 198, 210
    Resolution 678 (1990), 212
    Resolution 1441 (2002), 213
United Nationals Population
    Conference (1984), 269
United States, 1–7, 9–10, 14, 16,
    18–20, 23, 25–6, 28–30, 41, 43,
    45–7, 52, 58, 60–3, 71–2, 78,
    81–2, 90, 99, 102–6, 108–9, 110,
    113–14, 116–19, 121–7, 129,
    137–9, 141, 144–7, 150, 152, 157,
    163–6, 168–9, 171–4, 177–8,
    183–8, 190–9, 201, 205–21,
    225–37, 245–8, 250–7, 261,
    263–70, 272–5, 277, 281–2,
    284–8, 290–3

Universal Declaration of Human
  Rights, 252
US National Intelligence Council,
  197, 284
US Senate Committee on Foreign
  Relations, 262

Venezuela, 118–19, 124, 126, 190,
  218
Veterans of Foreign Wars, 224
Viet Cong, 230
Vietnam, 5, 9–10, 39, 103, 106, 187,
  191, 193, 197, 199, 211, 218, 221,
  225–38, 251, 289
Vietnam War, 5, 70, 168, 185, 192,
  194–5, 210, 215, 225–38, 256

Wallerstein, Immanuel, 168, 184
Ward, Angus, 38
Warsaw Pact, 209
Washington, George, 205, 214
Watergate scandal, 233
Westmoreland, William C., 228
Welsh, Herbert, 18, 20
When the Levees Broke, 247–8
Whitman, Walt, 165, 171
Williams, Tonya, 249–50
Williams, William Appleman, 234

Wilson, Charles, 145
Wilson, Geoffrey, 38
Wilson, Woodrow, 10, 14–16, 25,
  188, 207, 291
Wilsonianism, 10, 62, 76, 207
Wisconsin, University of, 231
Wolfowitz, Paul, 149–50, 283
Women's Bureau, Department of
  Labor, 265
Women's Global Network for
  Reproductive Rights, 268
Woods, Zonibel, 272
World Conference on Human Rights
  (1993), 269
World War One, 101, 207
World War Two, 2, 5, 7, 57, 78, 103,
  105, 108, 162–4, 166, 169, 182,
  194, 198, 207–8, 221, 234, 255,
  262
Wright, Richard, 82–3, 86

Young, Marilyn B., 227, 231
Yugoslavia, 60, 66, 77–8, 83, 91,
  212

Zedong, Mao, 209
Zhou Enlai, 65, 84
Zinn, Howard, 227, 230–1